take the kids

London

JOSEPH FULLMAN

About the series

take the kids guides are written specifically for parents, grandparents and carers. Each guide not only draws on what is of particular interest to kids, but also takes into account the realities of childcare – from tired legs to low boredom thresholds – enabling both grown-ups and their charges to have a great day out or a fabulous holiday.

x

Cadogan Guides
Network House, 1 Ariel Way, London W12 7SL
cadoganguides@morrispub.co.uk
www.cadoganguides.com

The Globe Pequot Press
PO Box 480, Guilford,
Connecticut 06437–0480

Copyright © Joseph Fullman 2000, 2002
Maps © Cadogan Guides,
drawn by Kingston Presentation Graphics

Art direction: Sarah Rianhard-Gardner
Cover design: Kicca Tommasi
Series design: Andrew Barker
Layout: Tracey Ridgewell
Original Photography: Travel Pictures
www.travelpictures.co.uk
Cover Photos:© Travel Pictures except for: Hamley's © Nicholas Kane 2000; © Geffyre Museum, London; Regent's Park © Kicca Tommasi

Editorial Director: Vicki Ingle
Series Editor: Melanie Dakin
Series Assistant: Tori Perrot

Proofreading: Simon Kent
Indexing: Isobel McLean
Production: Book Production Services
Printed and bound in Italy by Printer Trento srl.
A catalogue record for this book is available
from the British Library
ISBN 1-86011-844-5

Additional Picture Credits: p.46, p.121 © Museum of London; p.30, p.34, p.48, p.53, p.61, p.66, p.99, p.123 © Kicca Tommasi; p.31–32 © Zoological Society of London; p.34 © Madame Tusssaud's; p.36 © Alex Robinson; p.37 © The Wallace Collection, London; p.41, p.49 © Nicholas Kane 2000; p.42, p.45 © The British Museum; p.44 © Nigel Young; pp.46–47, p.65, p.71 © Pollock's Toy Museum; p.50 © The British Museum Shop; p.52 © Yo! Sushi; p.55 © London Tourist Board, © National Portrait Gallery; p.58 © National Gallery; p.60, p.68 © London's Transport Museum; p.63 © Rainforest Café; p.73 © Peter Durant/ arcblue.com; p.76 © Maxwell's; p.90, p.101, p.108 © Imperial War Museum; p.92 © Shepherd's Restaurant; p.93. p.97 © Dali Universe; p.96 © London Aquarium; p.97 © London IMAX; p.104, 106 © London Dungeon; p.104, p.112 © Hay's Galleria, © Shakepeare's Globe Theatre; p.123 © Barbican Centre/ J.P. Stankowski; p.125–126, p.129 © Science Museum; p.128 © The Natural History Museum; p.130–131 © Victoria & Albert Museum; p.132 © HRP 2001; p.133 © Royal Albert Hall; p.136 © Chutney Mary.

The author and publishers have made every effort to ensure the accuracy of the information in this book at the time of going to press. However, they cannot accept any responsibility for any loss, injury or inconvenience resulting from the use of information contained in the guide.

Please help us to keep this guide up to date. We have done our best to ensure that information is correct at the time of printing, but places and facilities are constantly changing, and standards and prices fluctuate. We will be delighted to receive your comments concerning existing entries or omissions. Authors of the best letters or emails will receive a copy of the Cadogan Guide of their choice.

About the authors

Joseph Fullman

Joseph Fullman is a professional travel writer who has lived in London all his life and cherishes happy childhood memories of traipsing around the country with his determinedly enthusiastic mum and dad. He is the author of Cadogan's *take the kids* England, Navigator Guides, *Britain's Top Tourist Attractions* and co-author of *take the kids* Paris & Disneyland® Resort Paris, as well as guides to Britain's steam railways and London's markets. He has also contributed various articles to newspapers, websites and WAP guides.

Series consultant

Helen Truszkowski is series consultant of Cadogan's *take the kids* series, author of *take the kids* Travelling and author of *take the kids* Paris & Disneyland® Resort Paris. Helen is an established travel writer and photographer. Over the past decade her journeys have taken her around the globe, including six months working in South Africa. She contributes to a range of magazines worldwide, and is a former travel editor of *Executive Woman* magazine. Helen's seven-year-old son, George, has accompanied her on her travels since he was a few weeks old.

Series editor

Melanie Dakin is series editor of Cadogan's *take the kids* series, having previously acted as consultant editor on the Time Out *London for Children* guide and editor of *Kids Out* magazine. As a mother of two, Eve age seven and John Hunter age one, Melanie has spent a great deal of time navigating London with children, pushchairs, toys and luggage. To date only a couple of baby bottles and a small coolbag have been left behind.

Contents

④

NEED TO KNOW 159

There's more for kids to do in London than you probably think.

You may know that the Science Museum is one of the best interactive museums in the country, but do you also know that it organizes sleep-overs for children wanting to explore and experiment in the dead of night? And were you aware that Borders, the giant bookstore on Oxford Street, holds regular storytelling sessions? Or that at the Victoria and Albert Museum you can have a go at reconstructing the Crystal Palace built for the Great Exhibition of 1851? Or spend the night pretending to be pirates aboard the *Golden Hinde*, a replica 17th-century sailing ship? And did you realize that kids can ride horses in Hyde Park or be pulled in a llama and trap at London Zoo? Or that at the IMAX 3-D cinema in Waterloo, they can take a swim with dolphins and 007? Well, you do now.

London is one of the most accommodating cities on earth for young visitors. Almost every month some new attraction opens. The amphibious Frog Tours, the Handel Museum, British Museum Great Court, The British Airways London Eye and the Tate Gallery of Modern Art are among the most recent additions to the thriving London scene. Projects nearing completion also include The Spiral Extension at the Victoria & Albert Museum, the revamped Museum of the Moving Image and the new headquarters of the Mayor of London, the Greater London Assembly building, set to be the capital's most environmentally friendly location.

This guide aims to spring more than a few surprises of its own, bringing to your attention London's lesser-known sights and some tales of life in the capital, as well as giving you the low-down on all the main attractions – the parks, palaces, museums, cinemas, arcades and experiences that make London perfect for discerning families and fun-hungry kids.

Guide to the Guide

Finding your way around this guide is easy. It is divided into three manageable sections as follows:

Ideas Ideas is full of helpful hints and tips to help you get to know London including what you can do for free, a London calendar, some days out organized along themes and some stress-free tours of the city.

See it do it is the main sightseeing section – the heart of the book, divided into 11 child-size areas. In each we've identified the primary sights, and secondary sights nearby; the best local shopping and places to eat; and other worthwhile attractions around and about. For every attraction there is up-to-date information on how to get there, access, opening times and admission prices, as well as workshops and activities specifically organized for kids. Some indication of appropriate age ranges is also given, as well as how long you should allow for each attraction. Throughout, the text is sprinkled with questions and challenges designed to help you and your children get the most from your stay, plus stories to keep them occupied as you travel from A to B. Should you fancy a change of scenery, we've also provided details of day trips – to historic Windsor and the University towns of Cambridge and Oxford, or to Chessington and Thorpe Park for some roller-coaster thrills – all within around an hour's journey of the city.

Need to know makes up the third and final section of the guide, 'Kids in' details the capital's best indoor attractions and entertainment, including everything from theatre shows and cinema clubs to music workshops and backstage tours. 'Kids out', identifies the best outdoor ones from parks to farm trips. There's even a section devoted to finding the best places to watch and participate in a number of sports and activities. Then there are chapters covering all the practical information you need for living and travelling in London: essential details on trains, taxis, post offices, supermarkets, banks, policemen, nappies and so on, as well as a selection of the best child-friendly hotels, restaurants and shops.

Get ready, the adventure begins here.

IDEAS IDEAS

IDEAS IDEAS

The best of kids' London

This is our choice of the very best that London has to offer for younger visitors: all the best things to see, eat, visit, shop, ride and play with that England's capital city has to offer.

Best animal attraction
London Zoo, *see* p.32

Best annual jamboree
The **London Parade**, *see* p.22.

Best café
Food for Thought, for veggie delights in Covent Garden, *see* p.75.

Best Christmas experience
Going skating on the outdoor ice rink at Somerset House, *see* p.73.

Best church
For dead kings & queens: **Westminster Abbey**, *see* p.88.

Best cinema
The big, big screen: **Imax 3-D Cinema**, *see* p.97.

Best firework display
The best view in town: **Primrose Hill**, *see* p.38.

Best funfair
Quality and quantity **Alexandra Palace**, *see* p.179.

Best for gruesomeness
The **London Dungeon**'s grisly tableaux, *see* p.106, or the **Old Operating Theatre**), *see* p.109.

Best interactive fun
The innovative British Galleries at the **Victoria & Albert Museum**, *see* p.130.

Best market
For budding fashionistas: **The Stables** in **Camden Market**, *see* p.39.

Best museum
The **Natural History Museum**, for its animatronic dinosaurs and sheer number of beasts, *see* p.128.

Best park
Regent's Park, for the boats, playgrounds, wild-fowl, open air theatre and sports facilities, *see* p.36.

Best restaurant
Giraffe, where you can sip a fruity shake or tuck into a bowl of noodles while listening to world music, *see* p.40.

Best shop
Semmalina, *see* p.242, or **Niketown**, *see* p.244.

Best sightseeing tour
Sailing down to Greenwich on a *Royal River Cruise*, *see* p.20.

Best sports event
The racy to the downright wacky: the **Oxford-Cambridge Boat Race**, *see* p.23, or the superannuated vehicles in the **London to Brighton Vintage Car Run**, *see* p.26.

Best statue
Nelson on his column, *see* p.56.

Best view
From a capsule in the **London Eye**, *see* p.98, or one of the galleries in the **Tate Modern**, *see* p.107.

Tips for getting around

▶ London has one of the most extensive public transport systems of any city in the world. Some bus and tube services are extremely overcrowded and unreliable. Trying to get around in your own car is too painful (the traffic's awful, and you'll spend half your time trying to park), while using taxis soon gets expensive and, again, you'll often be stuck in traffic.

▶ Children aged from 5 to 11 travel for less than half the full fare, and under-5s travel for free provided they do not take up a seat, on nearly all local transport.

▶ Travelcards can be used for the tube (underground/subway) and city buses, and for the DLR and local rail system.

▶ **Don't** buy tickets every time you use the tube – if you're sightseeing you're bound to make at leas 10 trips on local transport in any visit of more tha a day, so buy at least a *carnet*, or block of 10 ticket This works out cheaper than single tickets, and yo won't have to queue to pay your fare every time you travel.

▶ London offers a wide range of **sightseeing tours**, which are some of the best and most enjoyable ways of getting an idea of the city – and, since they often involve just sitting and looking from a boat or bus, provide a breather from too much traipsing the streets. The classic boat trips on the Thames are among London's don't-miss attractions that you have to try once, but don't pass over less well-known rides like the open-top bus tours, canal trips, the madcap fun of the amphibious Frog Tours, or for the energetic, guided walks. For details, *see* p.98.

Getting more for less

London is one of the wealthiest cities in the world and much of what it has to offer does not come cheap. Even so, it is still possible to have a fun day out without breaking the bank.
See **Practicalities A-Z** p.205 for more information.

Churches

Admission to all the churches in London is free – except for St Paul's Cathedral and Westminster Abbey. Carol services take place at several times a year, most notably at Christmas and Easter.

City farms

Coram's Fields and Vauxhall City Farm allow families to pet and stroke their animals and engage in a range of country crafts free of charge. *See* p.182.

Entertainment

Free foyer concerts are often given at the Royal National Theatre, Royal Festival Hall and the Barbican in the early evening. Covent Garden plays host to some of the country's top buskers and street performers on a daily basis (*see* p.65). The Covent Garden Festival of Street Theatre takes place every September.

Events & festivals

Various free events take place in London each year. *See* p.22 for more details of the London year.

Daily events

Changing of the Guard
Outside Buckingham Palace.

Ceremony of the Keys
The Tower of London.

Hyde Park Gun Salutes
By the Royal Horse Artillery; these take place on 6 February (Accession Day), 21 April (Queen's birthday), 2 June (Coronation Day), 10 June (Prince Philip's birthday) and 4 August (Queen Mother's birthday).

Museums & galleries

The number of museums and galleries that don't charge for admission is, believe it or not, actually increasing with some of the capital's most presti-gious collections, including the Natural History Museum, Science Museum, Museum of London, National Maritime Museum and the Imperial War Museum, having recently taken the decision to waive their entrance fees.

Apsley House *see* p.82
Bethnal Green Museum of Childhood *see* p.166
British Library *see* p.48
British Museum *see* p.44
Bank of England Museum *see* p.122
Geffrye Museum *see* p.166
Guards' Museum *see* p.91
Horniman Museum *see* p.167
Houses of Parliament *see* p.89
Imperial War Museum *see* p.101
Kenwood House *see* p.167
National Gallery *see* p.57
National Maritime Museum *see* p.140
National Portrait Gallery *see* p.59
Natural History Museum, *see* p.128
Prince Henry's Room *see* p.124

Museum trails

Several museums and galleries produce free leaflets and trails that children can use to make their visit more enjoyable. Ask at the foyer on entry if there are any audio guides, backpacks or free leaflets for kids to use.
London's Transport Museum (*see* p.68) produces a Family Learning Pack full of activities based around the museum. It's available from the museum shop price £2.50 .

Museums free for children

Parks & views

From elegantly manicured royal gardens to great swathes of ancient woodland, London's parks are all free. Wherever you're staying in London there will be a park, usually with a children's playground, not too far away. *See* **Kids out p.177** for more information. For stunning views try Hampstead Heath, The Mall, Oxo Tower, Westminster Bridge or the London Eye.

On foot

London comes in two different sizes: Greater London, which is huge – 28 miles north to south, 35 miles east to west; and Central London, where the majority of the capital's tourist attractions are located, which isn't very big at all. Touring on foot is the best way to get to know the smaller version; you can explore all the hidden nooks and crannies you would miss if you relied exclusively on public transport. A few words of warning, however.

▶ Vehicles travel on the left on Britain's roads, so when crossing remember to look right, then left, and not vice versa.

▶ Never cross the road except at a designated crossing zone such as a set of traffic lights, a pelican crossing (a green man will light up to let you know when it's safe to cross) or a zebra crossing – a black and white striped crossing point with an orange flashing beacon on either side. In theory, traffic should stop as soon as you put your foot on a zebra. Do, however, make sure that it has done so before you start to cross.

Travel discounts

If you're travelling after 9.30am on a weekday or at anytime on a weekend, your best bet is to get a One-Day Travelcard which lets you make unlimited journeys on London's tubes, buses (except night buses) and trains until 3am the following morning. At the time of writing, a Travelcard covering Zones 1 and 2 costs adult £4, child £2; a Travelcard covering all six zones is adult £4.90, child £2. London Transport offers a special family deal on Travelcards which, if purchased together, can be bought for adult £2.60, child 80p for a pass covering Zones 1–2 and adult £3.20, child 80p for a pass covering all 6 zones. You can also buy weekly and monthly travelcards which provide even greater savings but these are only really worthwhile if you plan to use public transport all through the week. You will need to provide a passport-sized photograph of yourself for the accompanying photocard.

One-Day Travelcards are available from tube and train station ticket windows and machines and from many newsagents. Weekly and monthly passes can also be purchased from newsagents.

If you travel beyond the limits of your ticket, you will be liable for an on-the-spot penalty fare. This is £10 on tubes and trains and £5 on the buses.

There are also a number of tourist buses plying their trade in the capital. The best is probably the Big Bus Company, **t** (020) 8944 7810. Adult £15, child £6 – for 24-hours unlimited travel on BBC buses.

London Pass

Recently introduced, this pass gives you free entry to museums, river cruises, historic houses, zoos, cinemas, galleries, and other attractions, plus special offers at restaurants, theatres, and shops. Participating sites include London Aquarium, St Paul's Cathedral, Thames Barrier and the Tower of London. Prices range from: 1 day adult £19, child £14; 2 days adult £29, child £22; 3 days adult £34, child £25; 6 days adult £47, child £30, tickets including transport range from 1 day adult £24, child £16 to 6 days adult £89, child £45. Available in person from the British Visitor Centre or by logging on at **www.**londonpass.com

London Rail and River Tour

Gives an overview of the best that the capital has to offer both old and new, from historical sights and attractions to the latest shopping and restaurant outlets around Canary Wharf and Docklands. The

---

Useful London websites

Contact your local borough council for details of local and seasonal events (firework nights in particular), plus free festivals. Council websites are as follows: **www**.....nameofborough....gov.uk
eg: **www**.barnet.gov.uk
www.londontown.com
The official tourist board site with various attractions, hotel details etc.
www.thisislondon.co.uk
The *Evening Standard*'s website. The kids' section is full of jolly ideas and up-to-the-minute events
www.timeout.com/london
Time Out magazine's website, the kids' section is selective and has some interesting features
www.londonnet.co.uk
This site doesn't have a huge kids' section but its savvy attitude is appealing
www.logon4london.co.uk
The best of the bunch. This site has an impressive kids section, a great, easy-to-use design, plus details of child-friendly events and workshops

Rail and River Rover Ticket is valid for one day and allows unlimited travel on both the Docklands Light Railway and City Cruises River Boats which run between Westminster, Tower Hill and Greenwich.

Fares Adult £7.80, child £3.90, family £20.50 (2 adults and up to 3 children) **www**.citycruises.com (020 7740 0400) **www**.dlr.co.uk (020 7363 9700)

Fun & games

Just in case the kids have time to be bored which we very much doubt, here are a few ways to keep them occupied.

Pub cricket

Pubs in London have names like the Dog & Duck and The Red Lion. You can play a game called pub cricket in which you score runs according to the number of legs a pub has, i.e The Dog & Duck scores six runs (a dog having four legs and a duck two). Just as in cricket, the object of the game is to score as many runs as possible. If you spot a pub with no legs, such as The Crown, then you lose a wicket. Ten wickets and you're out and it is someone else's turn to score a few runs. The game can get a little more complicated with a pub such as the Horse & Hounds – decide for yourself just how many hounds are to be counted.

What am I?

A London version of the guessing game What Animal Am I?
Q. What London landmark am I?
eg
I am quite tall
I have a pointed roof
I make a noise every hour
I have numbers on my face
A. Big Ben

Quick draw

You will need:
pocket-sized pad of plain paper
a pen that glides easily across the page
This really is the simplest game imaginable, rest the pad on your knee and lightly poise the pen over it. As the vehicle you are in moves around the pen will jump leaving a crazy pattern on the paper. Kids can either take turns making the patterns or trying to figure out what the drawings looks like, they could even spend time colouring in the shapes should you experience a long delay to your journey.

THEMES

Sometimes children can get madly interested in a particular subject, such as football, animals, film or the theatre. When this occurs, everything else becomes dull and uninspiring and just a little bit pointless. With this in mind, here are a number of suggested days out for excitable kids with abiding passions.

Stagestruck kids

Itinerary 1

Morning Take the tube to Covent Garden for the Theatre Museum, where you can explore the history of the performing arts and kids get to dress up in theatrical costumes. See p.69.

Lunch At the Covent Garden Market Café watching the performers on the Piazza.

Afternoon Take the tube to Waterloo for a tour of the Royal National Theatre. See p.99.

Theatre Museum
Russell Street, WC2
t (020) 7836 7891
www.theatremuseum.org
Open Tues–Sat 10am–6pm
Adm Adults £4.50, children & concs £2.50, under-5s **free**

Royal National Theatre
South Bank, SE1
t (020) 7452 3400
www.nt-online.org
Tour Mon–Sat 10.15, 12.45 & 5.30
Adm Adult £3.50, child £3

Itinerary 2

Morning Take the tube or train to London Bridge for a tour around the reconstructed Globe Theatre to see how plays were performed in Shakespeare's day. See p.109.

Lunch In the Globe Café or the nearby Anchor Inn. See p.113-4.

Afternoon Take a gentle walk along the riverfront past the South Bank (where a free performance may be taking place on Theatre Square outside the Royal National Theatre) to Waterloo. From Waterloo you can take the train to Wimbledon to catch an afternoon performance at the Polka

Theatre, the only purpose-built children's theatre in the country. See p.175.

Shakespeare's Globe Theatre
Bear Gardens, Bankside, New Globe Wall, Southwark, SE1
t (020) 7401 9919
www.shakespeares-globe.org
Open 10–5 daily, for performance times call in advance
Museum **adm** Adult £7.50, child £5 (under-5s **free**), concs £6, family ticket (2+3) £23

Anchor Inn
34 Park Street, Bankside, Southwark, SE1
t (020) 7902 1400
Open Mon–Sat 11am–11pm, Sun 12 noon–10.30pm
⊖/ ≷ London Bridge

Globe Café
Bear Gardens, Bankside, New Globe Wall, Southwark, SE1
t (020) 7902 1576
Open May–Sep 10am–11pm, Oct–April 10am–5pm

Polka Theatre
240 The Broadway, SW19
t (020) 8543 4888
www.polkatheatre.com
Open Tues–Fri 9.30–4.30, Sat 11–5.30
Adm Tickets for performances range from £4.50–£10.50; a one-day workshop is £25

Toy-mad kids

Itinerary 1

Morning Take the tube to Goodge Street for a trip to the wonderful Pollock's Toy Museum, a delightful collection of Victorian toys and trinkets. See p.47.

Lunch At Pizza Express on the adjacent Charlotte Street or, if you feel up to it, take the tube to Oxford Circus for the Metropolis Café in the basement of Hamleys on Regent Street where you can tuck into your burgers surrounded by bleeping video machines.

Afternoon Browse through Hamleys' six toy-stuffed floors (see p.49).

Pollock's Toy Museum
41 Whitfield Street, W1
t (020) 7636 3452
www.tao2000.net/pollocks
Open Mon–Sat 10am–5pm; last entry 4.30pm
Adm Adult £3, child (under 18) £1.50

Pizza Express
7 Charlotte Street, W1
t (020) 7580 1110
www.pizzaexpress.co.uk
⊖ Goodge Street
Open 12 noon–11.30pm daily

Hamleys
188 Regent Street, W1
t (020) 7734 3161
www.hamleys.com
Open Mon–Wed & Fri 10–7, Thurs 10–8, Sat 9.30–7, Sun 12 noon–6pm

Life at sea

Morning Take a riverboat cruise from Charing Cross Pier to Greenwich with Catamaran Cruises, to visit the Cutty Sark and National Maritime Museum with its vast collection of nautical equipment. *See* p.140.
Lunch In the Trafalgar Tavern, Park Row, overlooking the river.
Afternoon Take the train from Greenwich to London Bridge for HMS *Belfast*, a Second World War destroyer moored permanently on the riverfront. *See* p.110.

Catamaran Cruisers
t (020) 7925 2215
www.bateauxlondon.com
Fares Adult return £6.70 (rising to £7 July–Aug), child return £4.70 (rising to £5 July–Aug), family £20 (rising to £21 July–Aug)
Greenwich pass: adults £20, children £7 (includes entry to National Maritime Museum, Royal Observatory, and *Cutty Sark*).

The Trafalgar Tavern
Park Row, SE10
t (020) 8858 2437
Open Mon–Sat 11.30–11.00, Sun 12 noon–10.30

National Maritime Museum
Romney Road, Greenwich, SE10
t (020) 8 858 4422
Infoline **t** (020) 8312 6565
www.nmm.ac.uk
➤ Greenwich, **DLR** Greenwich, Cutty Sark
Open 10–5 daily, last admission 4.30pm
Adm Adult £7.50, child **free**, concs £6; combined ticket with Old Royal Observatory: adult £10.50, child **free**, concs £8.40

HMS *Belfast*
Morgan's Lane, off Tooley Street, SE1
t (020) 7940 6328
www.hmsbelfast.org.uk
Open Mar–Oct 10–6 daily, Nov–Feb 10–5 daily
Adm Adult £5, child **free**, concs £3.90

Gory kids

Morning Take a tube or train to London Bridge for the London Dungeon, the capital's premier gorefest. *See* p108.
Lunch At Pizza Hut in the London Dungeon.
Afternoon If you still feel like grossing out head either to the Old Operating Theatre, where surgeons gaily butchered people in the early 19th century. *See* p.109, or the Clink Museum (*see* p.111), built on the site of a former prison, which holds a collection of medieval torture instruments.

London Dungeon
Tooley Street, SE1
t (020) 7403 7221
www.thedungeons.com
Open Mon–Wed 10.30–9, Thur–Sun 10.30–6.30 (last entry 4.30pm)
Adm Adult £10.95, child (under 14) £6.95, concs £9.50

St Thomas' Old Operating Theatre
9a St Thomas Street, SE1
t (020) 7955 4791
www.thegarret.org.uk
Open 10–4 daily
Adm Adult £3.50, child £1.75 (under-8s **free**), concs £2.50, family ticket (2+2) £8

Clink Museum

1 Clink Street, SE1
t (020) 7403 6515
www.clink.co.uk
Open 10–6 daily
Adm Adult & child £4, concs £3, family £9

Animal-mad kids

London Zoo is still one of the best places for kids to come and learn about animals. See p.32.

11.30 Discovering Reptiles – question and answer session in the Reptile House.

12.30 Lunch at the zoo's self-service café.

1pm: Wonders of the Web – a look at biodiversity in the new Web of Life building.

1.30 Feed the pigs at the Children's Zoo.

2pm Animals in Action in the Amphitheatre – leaping lemurs and flying parrots demonstrate their skills.

2.30 Feeding Time – for the penguins in the Penguin Pool, the fish in the Aquarium and (Fridays) the snakes in the Reptile House.

3.15 A talk on sloths, bears and monkeys on Bear Mountain.

4.30 Flying display by predatory birds on the Display Lawn.

5pm Watch the giraffes being put to bed at the Giraffe House. (Note, that this takes place at 3.15pm in winter when some of the other events may not take place).

London Zoo

Regent's Park, NW1
t (020) 7722 3333
www.zsl.org
Open Mar–Oct 10–5.30 daily; Nov–April 10–4 daily
Adm Adult £10, child (under 14) £7, under-3s **free**, concs £8.50, family £30

Movie-mad kids

There's absolutely no way you can mention film anymore without reference to the Harry Potter phenomenon, London, of course, features in both the Potter books and on-screen, plus a number of other movies besides.

Itinerary 1

Morning London Zoo. Linger around the reptile house and see if your kids can communicate with the serpents as well as young Harry does. See p.32.

Lunch Pop over to Regent's Park for a picnic and see if you can spot any of Dodie Smith's One Hundred and One Dalmatians or head further north to Primrose Hill to re-enact the twilight bark. See p.36 and p.38.

Afternoon Hop on the Bakerloo Line down to Waterloo and catch a state-of-the-art film show at the 3-D Imax cinema, where Disney's Beauty and The Beast is the latest feature to get the big, big screen treatment. See p.97.

London Zoo

Regent's Park, NW1
t (020) 7722 3333
www.zsl.org
Open Mar–Oct 10–5.30 daily; Nov–April 10–4 daily
Adm Adult £10, child (under 14) £7, under-3s **free**, concs £8.50, family £30

IMAX 3-D Cinema

1 Cahrlie Chaplin Walk, SE1
t (020) 7902 1234
www.bfi.org.uk/imax
⊖/ ⇌ Waterloo
Bus 12, 53, 76, 77, 109, 211, 507, D1, P11
Open Mon-Thu 12.30-8, Fri 12.30-9.15, Sat 11.45-9.15, Sun 12 noon-8.
Adm For one film: adult £6.95, child (5-16) £4.95, under-5s **free**, concs £5.95

Itinerary 2

Morning Though not exactly the most desirable spot for hanging around with the kids, King's Cross station is a must for all Potter-ites, but do try to restrain them from throwing themselves at the barrier in an attempt to locate Platform 9³/4. Instead move swiftly along to the Piccadilly Line and head to Leicester Square – the heart of London's movie-going scene to watch the latest blockbuster or gaze at the handprints of famous stars set into the pavement around the square. See p.61.

Lunch On a fine day you can grab a picnic and sit in Leicester Square, alternatively catch a Northern Line train to Waterloo or Embankment and have a snack in the NFT café underneath Waterloo Bridge See p.99 and p.102.

Afternoon Stay in the NFT for an afternoon screening of an old b&w classic or a special kids film. On Saturdays kids can take part in a film-related workshop too.

Leicester Square Cinemas
Empire
t (0990) 888 990
www.uci-cinemas.co.uk
Odeon Leicester Square & Odeon West End
t (0870) 505 0007
www.odeon.co.uk
Warner Village West End
t (020) 7437 4343
www.warnervillage.co.uk

National Film Theatre
t (020) 7928 3232
www.nft.org.uk
Junior NFT **Adm** Child £1, accompanying adult £5

Arty kids

Self-expression is vital to a child's creative development and thankfully London has plenty of galleries where children can not only go for inspiration, but also have a go at making a masterpiece themselves.

Itinerary 1

Morning Take a trip to the vast Tate Modern for inspiration, with or without the tailor-made kids' audio guides. Weekend activities for children include art trails and creative workshops. *See* p.107.
Lunch The Tate Modern café can get very busy so opt for an early lunch. The brasserie-style food is a bit pricey but it's worth it just for the spectacular view of the river Thames.
Afternoon Head north on the Northern Line or walk over the Bridge to Charing Cross and Trafalgar Square. If it's fine you can always picnic in the square before stopping off at the National Gallery for a gawp at the famous paintings. The gallery hosts a variety of family events including storytelling sessions and drawing days under the tutelage of a professional artist. *See* p.57.

Tate Modern
Bankside, SE1
t (020) 7887 8000

www.tate.org.uk
⊖/ ⇌ London Bridge, Blackfriars
Bus 17, 21, 22a, 35, 40, 43, 47, 48, 133, 214, 344, 501, 505, 521, D1, D11, P3, P11
Open Sun–Thurs 10–6, Fri and Sat 10–10 (closed 24–26 Dec; open 1 Jan)
Free

National Gallery
Trafalgar Square, WC2
t (020) 7747 2885
www.nationalgallery.org.uk
⊖ Charing Cross, Leicester Square, Embankment
Bus 3, 6, 9, 11, 12, 13, 15, 23, 24, 29, 53, 88, 91, 109, 139, 159, 176, 184, 196
Open Mon–Sat 10–6, Sun 2–6pm
Adm Free, charges apply for some temporary exhibitions

Itinerary 2

Morning Art 4 Fun. Let your children's imaginations run riot painting plates or designing their own pots at these popular, creative workshops. There are five locations in London including Notting Hill and West Hampstead. *See* p.172.
Lunch The ICA has a good café and a shop selling jewellery, gadgets and prints made by local artists. *See* p.82.
Afternoon Tate Britain. Families could easily spend a whole day wandering around the galleries here, but it's also good for interactive fun. On Sundays and daily in the school holidays look out for the art trolley, doing its rounds, packed full of arty materials for kids to try. *See* p.90.

Art 4 Fun
Branches in Chiswick, Notting Hill, Muswell Hill, Mill Hill and West Hampstead
t (020) 8994 4800
www.art4fun.com
Open Sat, Sun & after school
Adm £20 half-day, £30 full

ICA Gallery
The Mall, SW1
t (020) 7930 3647
www.ica.org.uk
⊖ Picadilly Circus, Charing Cross
Bus 2, 8, 9, 14, 16, 19, 22, 36, 38, 52, 73, 82
Open Galleries 12 noon-7.30
Adm Membership Mon-Fri Adult £1.50, concs £1, Sat, Sun Adult £2.50, concs £1.50

Tate Britain

Millbank, SW1
t (020) 7887 8008
www.tate.org.uk
⊖ Pimlico, Vauxhall ⇌ Vauxhall
Bus 2, 3, 36, 77A, 88, 159, 185, 507, C10
Open 10–5.50 daily
Free, charges apply for some temporary exhibitions

Mini-monarchists

Of course, there are any number of royal exhibits in London – the following is our pick of the bunch.
Morning The Buckingham Palace tour (summer only). The tour has been criticised for including just 18 of a possible 600 rooms and giving little sense of what it's like to live there, but young royalists won't be happy without it. *See p.80.*
11.27 If you time things well, you could watch the Changing of the Guard after your 45-minute tour of the palace. Allow yourself time to get the children out and find a place to stand.
Lunch Unless her Majesty has invited you to lunch, it's not so easy to find a royal-themed eaterie. You could, however, encounter the royalty of rock (including The Artist Formerly Known as Prince and, of course, Queen) at the nearby Hard Rock Café. *See p.83.*
Afternoon Princess Diana's palace in Kensington Gardens has guided tours through the plush historic apartments and an excellent exhibition of royal clothes. Get there by 2.30 as it closes early: it might be easier (and less exhausting) to skip the Changing of the Guards today. After you've seen the Palace, the gardens provide a refreshing break from pomp and ceremony. *See p.133.*

Buckingham Palace

St James's Park, SW1
t (020) 7839 1377; booking line (020) 7799 2331
www.royal.gov.uk
Open Aug–Sep 9.30–5.30 daily (last admission 4.15pm)
Adm Adult £11, child (under 17) £5.50, under-5s **free**, concs £9
Tour Lasts 45-minutes

Changing of the Guard

t (020) 7930 4832
www.royal.gov.uk
Free
Suitable for all ages
The ceremony lasts over an hour
The ceremony takes place every morning between April and August at 11.27 sharp and on alternate days between September and March at the same time.

Hard Rock Café

150 Old Park Lane, W1
t (020) 7629 0382
⊖ Hyde Park Corner
Open Mon–Thurs 11.30am–12.30pm, Fri & Sat 11.30am–1am

Kensington Palace

The State Apartments, Kensington Gardens, W8
t (020) 7937 9561
www.hrp.org.uk
⊖ High Street Kensington, Bayswater, Queensway
Bus 9, 10, 12, 52, 73, 94
Open May–Sept 9.45–3.30
Adm Adult £8.50, child £6.10, concs £6.70, family £26.10

SEE IT DO IT

SEEING LONDON

So you're ready to hit the town, but what to do first? Do you rush headlong at the nearest attraction and proceed in haphazard fashion? Not if you want to preserve a little sanity to go home with at the end of the day. Here are a few enjoyable ways of getting a snapshot of the city before you take the plunge. Then be sure to move on to our sightseeing chapters in earnest.

Walks

It may seem an arduous task with kids in tow but pushchair bound kids need to limber and stretch. On a clear day there's really nothing nicer than a leisurely stroll along the river and on a misty morning where better to take a trip than through London's murky past?

The Original London Walks

PO Box 1708
London NW6 4LW
t (020) 7624 3978
www.london.walks.com

The original and best – there are several companies offering walking tours of London but this one (London's oldest) is easily the pick of the bunch and certainly the most child-friendly. As well as organizing tours around several specific areas of London, including the City, Greenwich, Westminster and Kensington, London Walks offer various themed treks including 'Shakespeare's London', 'Ghosts of the West End', the 'England of Winnie the Pooh' and 'Princess Diana's London'. The tours are led by knowledgeable, entertaining guides.

Globe Walkshop

Find out more about the decadent history of Southwark on a Globe Walkshop; a guided tour taking in the prisons, inns and theatres which used to make up the bulk of the area's buildings, (10–12 noon every Saturday; **adm** £6, concs £5, student £4; **t** (020) 7902 1433). *See p.109.*

London Silver Jubilee Walkway

A 10-mile walk is not every child's idea of a great day out. This walkway is generally more for strong thighed, big lunged adults than children but it's still worth considering for a family trip. The route is actually split into seven sections – which run from Leicester Square through Westminster across the river to the South Bank and then back through The City to Covent Garden – each topped and tailed by a tube stop, so you can walk as much or as little as you like. The route is marked by discs set in the pavement (there are 400 in total); kids love being the first one to 'find' the marker. The walk was created in 1977 to commemorate the Queen's Silver Jubilee, hence the name. For more information, visit the London Tourist Information Office at Victoria.

Millennium Mile

London's latest walkway, the Thameside path between Westminster Bridge and Tower Bridge, has recently been spruced up and rechristened the Millennium Mile. As a result, what was once one of the city's more tatty districts is now much smarter and one of the best places to come to for a family walk. The route is dotted with some of the capital's best attractions, including the London Aquarium, London Eye, the National Theatre, the Oxo Tower, the Tate Modern, the Globe Theatre, HMS Belfast and Tower Bridge. You can find out more by contacting Southwark Information Centre, 6 Tooley Street, SE1, **t** (020) 7403 8299, **Open**: April–Oct Mon–Sat 10–6, Sun 10.30–5.30.

The Thames Path

For a more ad hoc walking experience, you might like to try a portion of the Thames Path, a designated nature trail along the banks of the Thames. You might have a job finishing the route, however, as it stretches the entire length of the river, all 180 miles of it. For more information contact the Thames Barrier Visitor Centre, **t** (020) 8854 1373.

Blue Plaque Tours

Have you ever noticed that some London houses have blue plaques adorning their walls? These were erected by English Heritage to indicate that a famous person used to live there.

It can be quite good fun using these blue plaque as the basis for a walking route around the city as it enables you to explore streets and areas not normally covered on official sightseeing itineraries *See box p18.*

Pub Signs

As you walk around the city, look out for the painted signs hanging up outside pubs, particularly old pubs. The names displayed are often very distinctive, not to say occasionally rather peculiar

Blue plaque tours

If visiting the British Museum, try finding the following, all within a 10 minute's walk :

7 Fitzroy Square: Home of **George Bernard Shaw**, author of *Pygmalion* (which was subsequently used as the basis for the musical *My Fair Lady*), and the modernist writer Virginia Woolf.

110 Gower Street: Home of **Charles Darwin**, one of the world's greatest ever scientists and the man who, in his book *Origins of Species*, published in 1859, first put foward the now widely accepted Theory of Evolution which states that every living creature on the earth has come about as a result of natural selection over millions of years rather than divine creation.

At **48 Doughty Street**, you'll find the former home of **Charles Dickens**, Victorian Britain's most famous and celebrated novelist whose works, which include *Oliver Twist*, *Nicholas Nickleby*, *David Copperfield* and *Great Expectations*, are still widely read today and have been filmed on numerous occasions. His house is open to the public and is filled with period furniture and memorabilia relating to his life. See p.46.

If shopping on Oxford Street, look out for the following:

15 Poland Street: Home of the romantic poet **Percy Byshe Shelley**.

28 Dean Street: Home of **Karl Marx**, founder of communism.

23 Brook Street (it's just off New Bond Street): Home of the legendary rock guitarist **Jimi Hendrix**.

24 Brook Street, (next door to the above): Home of the 18th-century composer **George Handel** whose most famous work is the choral classic *The Messiah*.

If shopping on the King's Road, try and spot the following:

18 St Leonard's Terrace: Home of **Bram Stoker**, author of the vampire novel *Dracula*.

23 Tedworth Squre: Home of **Mark Twain**, the American author of children's favourites *Tom Sawyer* and *Huckleberry Finn*.

56 Oakley Street: Home of **Captain Scott**, the famous polar explorer who died in the early 20th century on the return journey following his unsuccesful attempt to become the first man to reach the South Pole.

13 Mallord Street: Home of **AA Milne**, creator of the Winnie the Pooh stories and one of the most popular children's authors of all time.

Lamb and Flag, Hoop and Grapes, Black Friar, Old Cheshire Cheese, Bleeding Heart Tavern, Red Lion, White Swan, Coach and Horses etc. These were chosen specially so as to be easy to represent as a picture on the pub sign. Remember, back in the 17th and 18th centuries, a large proportion of London's population couldn't read or write and would have had to rely on such pictures to make sure they found the right pub.

Look out, in particular, for pubs bearing the name 'The Royal Oak'. If you look closely at the tree depicted in the sign, you should after a while be able to pick out the image of a man hiding in its branches. This is the young Stuart prince Charles (later Charles II) who, after his Cavalier army was defeated by the Roundheads at the end of the Civil War in 1652, was forced to hide in an oak tree for a whole day to avoid being captured. He later escaped to France.

Boat trips

The following companies offer sightseeing boat trips along stretches of the Thames. The frequency depends on the time of year. For more details call (020) 7345 5122, or pick up the London Tourist Board booklet, 'Discover the Thames'.

Catamaran Cruisers

t (020) 7925 2215
www.bateauxlondon.com
Fares Adult return £6.70 (rising to £7 July–Aug), child return £4.70 (rising to £5 July–Aug), family £20 (rising to £21 July–Aug)
Greenwich pass: adults £20, children £7 (includes entry to National Maritime Museum, Royal Observatory, and *Cutty Sark*).
Tower Pass: adults £15.50, children £10 (includes entry to Tower of London).
River pass: adults £10, children £5 (unlimited one-day use of all cruisers)

These 50-minute cruises downriver have recorded commentary from Charing Cross Pier to the Tower of London, Greenwich and the Thames Barrier.

City Cruises

t (020) 7740 0400

www.citycruises.co.uk

Fares Westminster–Tower Pier: adult single £5, return £6; child single £2.50, return £3

Runs between Westminster Pier and Tower Pier (and offers a service between the South Bank and Greenwich). The boats are easily recognized by their bright red livery. City Cruises also runs a hop-on, hop-off ferry service around the Pool of London stopping at Tower Pier, St Katherine's Pier, London Bridge Pier and Butler's Wharf.

Royal River Thames Cruises

t (020) 7930 4097

Fares Adult £6.50, child £3.40 single

All the charms of the East End where aspects of Shakespeare's Globe theatre and St Paul's Cathedral merge with converted warehouses, wharves and smoking chimneys. The Thames Barrier itself is a sight to behold with light gleaming off its magnificent gleaming carapaces. See below.

Westminster Passenger Service

t (020) 7930 4721

www.wpsa.co.uk

Fares Adult £10 return, child £4 single

Head upriver with some spicy commentary about the occupants of a few well-appointed flats in Chelsea and titbits from the history of London. From Hammersmith onwards the journey becomes more serene and pastoral as you glide towards Kew Gardens, Richmond and Hampton Court.

Canal trips

Several companies make a leisurely journey along Regent's Canal between Little Venice and Camden Town, passing through London Zoo on the way:

Jason's Trip

60 Bloomfield Road, Little Venice, W9

t (020) 7286 3428

Warwick Avenue

Tours Every two hours, 10.30–4.30 in summer and 10.30–2.30pm in winter

Fares Adult single £4.95, return £5.95; child single £3.75, return £4.50, under-4s **free**, family ticket (2+3) £17.50

Also runs trips to the Canal Museum.

London Waterbus Company

Camden Lock, Camden Town, NW1

t (020) 7482 2550

Camden Town

Tours April–Oct daily service, boats run hourly; Nov–Mar weekends only

Fares Adult single £3.90, return £5.40, child single £2.50, return £3.20, under-4s **free**; combined canal trip and zoo visit: adult £9.90, child £7, under 4s **free**

Trips aboard traditional, painted narrow boats, stopping off at London Zoo – you get a reduction on the price of admission.

Sightseeing buses

Various companies offer services but the Big Bus Company – recognizable by its distinctive maroon and cream livery – is perhaps the best. It operates three colour-coded routes: Green, the West End and Bloomsbury; Blue, Knightsbridge and Mayfair, and Red; from Victoria to the Tower of London. Main departure points are Marble Arch, Green Park, Baker Street and Victoria, although you can board at any stop along the route.

The Big Bus Company

35/37 Grosvenor Gardens, SW1

t (020) 8944 7810

www.bigbus.co.uk

Fares Adult £15, child £6

Ticket allows 24-hours unlimited travel on BBC buses

Visitor centres

Heathrow Airport

Uxbridge, Middlesex

t (020) 8759 4321

Hatton Cross

Feltham

Bus 43, 105, 111, 140, 285

Open 10am–5pm daily

Free (£3 for 2 hours parking)

Suitable for ages 10 and over

Allow at least an hour

Heathrow Airport isn't every grown-up's idea of great day out but children, on the other hand, tend to love the place, as it is busy, noisy and brash with plenty to do and see. At the Visitor Centre they can find out the history of the world's largest and busiest airport. The Centre is big on interactivity. Kids can look inside a replica cockpit, sit in replica aircraft seats, walk through a metal detector, take rubbings of special plane brasses, read about undercover operations against smugglers and, of course, watch the planes landing and taking off. If you're very lucky, Concorde, the supersonic passenger jet, might even have a flight scheduled. Quizzes and eye-spys are available from the reception desk.

Thames Barrier

1 Unity Way, Woolwich, London, SE18
t (020) 8305 4188
⊖ New Cross, New Cross Gate
⇌ Charlton
River Cruise Regular service from Westminster Pier, call **t** (020) 8305 0300
Open Mon–Fri 10–5, Sat & Sun 10.30–5.30
Adm Adult £3.40, child & concs £2, family (3+2) £7.50

Suitable for ages 8 and over
Allow at least an hour

One of the marvels of modern London, the Thames Barrier is an astounding piece of engineering. Spanning the river's 1700ft width, these ten huge steel gates (each the size of a 5-storey house) are often all that stands between a dry London and one under 10 feet of water. The gates, which lie on 10,000 tonne concrete sills on the riverbed, can be raised into position in an astonishing 10 minutes flat in the event of a flood.

The barrier's construction was prompted by a flood in 1953 which killed 300 people. You can find out more about London's battle with its ever rising river as well as the history of the construction of the formidable barrier at the excellent multimedia Visitor Centre.

LONDON'S YEAR

Whatever time of the year you visit London, there's always something going on. From festivals and parades to major sporting events and exhibitions, hardly a week goes by without a noteworthy event. London is always busy, always fun, always buzzing and if you grow tired of the capital you must be, as Dr Johnson famously said, tired of life.

Daily events

Ceremony of the Keys
Tower of London, EC3
t (020) 7709 0765
www.tower-of-london.com
⊖ Tower Hill
Bus 15, 25, 42, 78, 100, D1
Adm Free. Every day at 9.53pm
The ceremony lasts approximately 20 mins
The nightly locking of the Tower of London is one of the oldest military ceremonies in the world. For free tickets apply at least four weeks in advance to The Resident Governor, Queen's House, The Tower of London, EC3.

Changing of the Guard
Buckingham Palace, SW1
t (020) 7930 4832
www.royal.gov.uk/**www.**royalresidences.com
Infoline **t** (020 7799 2331)
⊖ St James's Park, Green Park, Victoria
Bus 1, 16, 24, 52, 73
Free
An hour of pomp and pageantry outside Buckingham Palace beginning at 11.27am sharp everyday April–Aug and on alternate days Sep–Mar *see p.80 for further details.*

Annual events

January
London Parade
New Year's Day
Parliament Square to Piccadilly by way of Whitehall and Trafalgar Square
t (020) 8566 8586
www.londonparade.co.uk

⊖ Westminster, Embankment, Green Park, Piccadilly Circus
Adm Free along route. Seats in Piccadilly Circus Grandstand cost adult £12–15, child £8–10
The estimated 10,000 performers and over a million spectators make this one of the the biggest New Year's Day parties in Europe.

Chinese New Year Festival
Late January or early February
Gerrard Street, Lisle Street & Newport Place, WC1
⊖ Leicester Square
Bus 6, 7, 8, 10, 12, 13, 14, 15, 19, 23, 25, 38, 53, 55, 73, 88, 94, 98, 139, 159, 176, X53
Free
Chinatown celebrates its annual rebirth with firecrackers, paper lanterns and papier-mâché dragons that dance down the street.

February
Accession Day Gun Salute
Accession Day, 6 February, 12 noon
Hyde Park
⊖ Hyde Park Corner, Knightsbridge, South Kensington, Lancaster Gate, Queensway
Bus 2, 9, 10, 12, 14, 16, 19, 22, 36, 52, 70, 73, 74, 82, 94, 137
Free
This is the first gun salute of London's year. The Royal Horse Artillery gallop furiously into Hyde Park and unleash an extremely noisy 41-gun salute. The practice is repeated several times: on the Queen's birthday (21 April), Coronation Day (2 June), Prince Philip's birthday (10 June) and the Queen Mother's birthday (4 August).

Soho Pancake Race Day
Shrove Tuesday
Carnaby Street, W1
t (020) 7289 0907
⊖ Oxford Circus
Bus 7, 8, 10, 25, 55, 73, 98, 176
Free
On Shrove Tuesday competing teams run down Carnaby Street tossing pancakes as they go. A similar event takes place at Spitalfields Market, ca
t (020) 7372 0441.

March
Ideal Home Exhibition
Mid- to late-March
Earl's Court Exhibition Centre, Warwick Road, SW5

t (0870) 606 6080
www.idealhomeshow.co.uk
⊖ Earl's Court
Bus 31, 74, C1, C3
Adm Adult Mon–Fri £10, Sat & Sun £12, child Mon–Fri £5, Sat & Sun £6, under-5s **free**

At Europe's largest consumer show you'll find masses of designer bathrooms, bedrooms and other house interiors as well as all the latest labour-saving gizmos – juicers that cut as they peel and boil an egg etc.

Easter
Oxford–Cambridge Boat Race
www.theboatrace.org
Saturday before Easter or Easter Saturday
The Thames between Putney Bridge and Mortlake
For start ⊖ Putney Bridge; for finish
⇌ Mortlake
Bus For start 22, 265; for end 209, 485, R69
Free

The two teams have been battling it out over the 4$^{1/2}$-mile Thames course for over a hundred years now. The best viewing points (and the places with the best atmosphere) are Putney Bridge and Chiswick Bridge.

Easter Parade
Easter Sunday
Battersea Park, SW11
⇌ Battersea Park, Queenstown Road
⊖ Sloane Square
Bus 44, 137, 319, 344, 345
Open Dawn till dusk
Free

Easter Sunday carnival with a fairground, parade and special children's village featuring a bouncy castle, playground, clowns and puppet shows. Special events, such as displays by freefall parachute teams, are often laid on.

April
London Marathon
www.london-marathon.co.uk
Sunday in late April. Race starts at 9am
26 miles 385 yards between Blackheath and Westminster Bridge by way of the Isle of Dogs, Victoria Embankment and St James's Park.

Over 30,000 people put mind and body to the test each year over the 26-mile course between Blackheath and Westminster Bridge. There's a mini-Marathon for stretching little legs as well.

May
Covent Garden Festival
www.cgf.co.uk
Covent Garden, WC2
t (020) 7379 0870
⊖ Covent Garden, Leicester Square
Bus 9, 11, 13, 15, 23, 77a, 91, 176
Free

The home of impromptu theatrical and musical performance plays host to a unique celebration of the singing voice. The festival features a mix of concerts by seasoned performers and emerging talent.

Museums Month
t (020) 7233 9796
www.may2002.org
In participating museums throughout the capital

This annual celebration of the nation's collections and treasure troves is the largest museums promotion anywhere in the world. Over 850 museums participate, organizing a range of hands-on activities and events, many of which are free and family-friendly. Check out the above website which provides a year-round selection of games, science packs and activities for kids to download free of charge.

May Fayre and Punch & Judy Festival
Nearest Sunday to 9 May
St Paul's Church, Covent Garden
t (020) 7375 0441
⊖ Covent Garden, Leicester Square
Bus 9, 11, 13, 15, 23, 77a, 91, 176
Free

An annual celebration of puppet marital disharmony in the grounds of St Paul's Church.

June

Trooping the Colour
Second Saturday in June, starts at 10.45am
Buckingham Palace to Horse Guards Parade
t (020) 7414 2271
www.royal.gov.uk
Θ Charing Cross, St James's Park
Free along route

Tickets for this top piece of British pageantry are awarded by ballot – you must apply by the end of February. Write to the Brigade Major (Trooping the Colour), Household Division, Horse Guards Parade, SW1, enclosing a stamped addressed envelope. There is a maximum of two tickets per application. The ceremony, which marks the official birthday of the Queen, takes place at Horse Guards Parade and is preceded by a Royal Air Force jet display.

Biggin Hill International Air Fair
Mid-June weekend, starts at 8am
Biggin Hill Airfield, Biggin Hill, Kent
t (01959) 578101
www.airdisplaysint.co.uk
≋ Biggin Hill
Bus 246, 320, 4664, R2
Adm Adult £8.50, child £3, family £19

Every summer, plane enthusiasts from all over the country gather in order to get up close and personal with the truly high-flying machines of the aviation world. Second World War Spitfires and Hurricanes are the biggest draw but there are lots of other planes to see both on the ground and in the sky. A host of displays, fly-pasts and skydives take place over the two days and there's also a funfair and exhibition stands.

Henley Royal Regatta
Wed–Sat late June (sometimes early July)
The Thames at Henley
t (01491) 572 153
www.hrr.co.uk
≋ Henley
Free

This grand society occasion provides an elegant backdrop for a Thames-side picnic.

Wimbledon
Last two weeks in June
All England Lawn Tennis and Croquet Club, Church Road, Wimbledon, SW19
t (020) 8946 2244
www.wimbledon.org
Θ Southfields, Wimbledon Park
≋ Wimbledon
Bus 39, 93
Adm Centre Court and No.1 Court tickets are around £55 each, ground tickets are £20

The world's most prestigious tennis tournament. Tickets for Centre and No.1 courts are obtainable only by ballot, which must be entered the previous September. You can queue up during the tournament for a ground pass which will give you access to all the courts apart from Centre and No.1. Obviously, the atmosphere on these courts isn't as good as on the show courts but, owing to the sheer number of matches that must take place, you should be able to see a few famous faces and, from 2pm onwards, you can queue up to buy resale show court tickets.

City of London Festival
Late-June–mid-July
t (020) 7377 0540
www.colf.org

Musical kids can hit the high notes at this three-week festival of sound held in the magnificent churches and halls of the City. Free lunchtime recitals featuring everything from classical to jazz take place daily.

July

Coin Street Festival
Mid-July–mid-September
The South Bank at the Oxo Tower Wharf, Gabriel's Wharf and the Bernie Spain Gardens
t (020) 7401 2255
www.coinstreetfestival.org
Θ Waterloo, Westminster, Blackfriars
Bus 4, 68, 76, 77, 149, 168, 171, 176, 188, 211, P11, 501, 505, 507, 521, D1, P11
Free

There's plenty to please the kids at this three-month free arts festival on London's South Bank organized by the Coin Street Community Builders. Highlights include the splendid Latin-flavoured Gran Gran Fiesta, which features a children's fancy dress parade, and the popular 'Arts Desire' creative workshops.

Blitz
Three weeks from late July
Royal Festival Hall, South Bank, SE1
t (020) 7960 4242
Θ Waterloo, Westminster, Blackfriars

Bus 4, 68, 76, 77, 149, 168, 171, 176, 188, 211, P11, 501, 505, 507, 521, D1, P11
Free

The country's biggest free dance festival which takes place over three weeks at the Royal Festival Hall on the South Bank. Hundreds of performances and classes for beginners through to experts.

Greenwich & Docklands Festival

Ten days in mid-July
Various venues in Greenwich
t (020) 8305 1818
www.festival.org
⊖ North Greenwich
DLR Island Gardens
≋ Greenwich
Bus 177, 180, 188, 199, 286, 386
Free

This popular arts festival combines concerts and theatre as well as children's events and starts with a bang with an opening night firework display.

Kenwood House Lakeside Concerts

July–August
Hampstead Lane, NW3
t (020) 7413 1443 (English Heritage Box Office); info
t (020) 8233 7435
www.english-heritage.org
⊖ Hampstead, Archway, Highgate, Golders Green
Bus 210
Adm Adult £16.50–30, child £2–4, under-5s **free**

Families flock to this series of popular classical concerts and firework displays in the grounds of this grand old house. (*see* p.167).

August

Notting Hill Carnival

August Bank Holiday Sunday and Monday
Notting Hill and surrounding streets
t (020) 8964 0544
⊖ Westbourne Park, Ladbroke Grove (due to crowds avoid Notting Hill Gate)
Free

The largest carnival in the world after Rio. Steel bands, floats, costumed dancers, fancy dress, jugglers, face-painting, exotic food: this is one of the year's most intense experiences. In fact, it can be a little hairy for very young children. Older kids, however, will have a great time. There is a special children's parade on the Sunday.

August Bank Holiday Funfairs

Funfairs set up for business during the summer's premier bank holiday weekend at many of London's parks including Alexandra Palace Park and Hampstead Heath.

September

CBBC Proms in the Park

Hyde Park
t (020) 7765 3021
www.bbc.co.uk/proms
⊖ Hyde Park Corner

The BBC Philharmonic club together with the latest pop sensations to bring an afternoon of easy on the ear classical tunes and tweeny bop hits.

Covent Garden Festival of Street Theatre

Early September
Covent Garden
t (020) 7240 2255
www.coventgarden.org.uk
⊖ Covent Garden, Leicester Square
Bus 9, 11, 13, 15, 23, 77A, 91, 176
Free

Fire-eaters, escapologists, stilt-walkers, unicyclists and comedians put on a week of performances in Covent Garden's Piazza.

Regent Street Festival

Early September
Regent Street, W1
t (020) 7491 4429
⊖ Oxford Circus, Piccadilly Circus
Bus 3, 12, 15, 23, 139, 159
Free

This annual street fest began in 2000 and is going from strength to strength. For one Sunday only, the section of Regent Street between Oxford and Piccadilly Circus is closed to traffic and families are free to wander round the stalls and enjoy a series of staged events throughout the day. Many of the shops stay open for the occasion like Hamleys and The Disney Store and some offer discounts too. There's also a funfair, plus children's activity areas and play tents.

Thames Festival

Mid September
Various points on the Thames between Waterloo and Blackfriars Bridge
t (020) 7928 8998
www.thamesfestival.org

SEE-IT DO IT

⊖ Embankment, Charing Cross
Bus 11, 15, 23, 188
Free
Old Man Thames really comes to life with a whole host of events along the banks from firework displays to lantern processions. There's a food village, artworks and installations, a river race, stalls, music and funfair rides. Lantern-making workshops take place during the day.

October
Costermongers' Pearly Kings and Queens Harvest Festival
First Sunday in October, starts at 3pm
St Martin-in-the-Fields, Trafalgar Square, WC2
t (020) 7766 1100
www.pearlies.co.uk
⊖ Charing Cross, Leicester Square
Bus 9, 24, 109
Free
  A Harvest Festival with added sequins – London's community of Pearly Kings and Queens descends on St Martin-in-the Fields on the first Sunday of the month for an old fashioned knees-up.

November
London to Brighton Vintage Car Run
First Sunday in November, starts 7.30am
Hyde Park to Brighton
t (01753) 651 736
⊖ Hyde Park Corner, Marble Arch
Bus 2, 8, 9, 10, 14, 16, 19, 22, 36, 73, 82, 137
Free
  Entry to the race is free to all so long as you're in possession of a car built before 1905. This parade of clunking, clanking contraptions is one of London's great annual spectacles, attracting hordes of well-wishers to see them off at the start.

Bonfire Night
5 November
In parks and recreation grounds across London, see www.londontouristboard.co.uk for more details.
  Remember, remember the fifth of November... Parks all over London hold fireworks displays on this date to celebrate the capture and execution of Guy Fawkes and his failure to blow up James I and the Houses of Parliament. Some of the best displays take place at Blackheath, Primrose Hill and Alexandra Palace Park.

Lord Mayor's Show
Second Saturday in November, starts at 11am
Mansion House to the Old Bailey
t (020) 7606 3030
⊖ Mansion House, Blackfriars
Free
  The ceremonial parade to mark the beginning of the Mayor of London's year in office starts at Mansion House and wends its way to the Old Bailey. With over 5,000 participants and 70 floats, this is one of the largest street parades of the year. The Mayor himself rides at its head in the Lord Mayor's Coach which, for the rest of the year, is on display in the Museum of London.

The Christmas Lights
Mid-November
Oxford Street, Regent Street and Bond Street
  The elaborate street illuminations are turned on in mid-November by a celebrity du jour– usually a soap star or pop singer.

December
Carol Service
December–early January
Trafalgar Square, WC1
⊖ Charing Cross, Leicester Square
Bus 9, 24, 109
Free
  Carol singing takes place around the huge Trafalgar Square Christmas tree every evening from early December to early January. The tree itself is lit from dusk till midnight until the twelfth day of Christmas (6 January).

Pantomime Season
Mid-November to mid-February
All over the capital

Come December a motley collection of retired sportsmen, soap stars and TV magicians will join forces with a host of actors to produce a very British institution. For details of performances check out the listings section of the *Evening Standard* or *Time Out*.

Royal Institution Christmas Lectures for Young People

Between Christmas and New Year
21 Albemarle Street, W1
t (020) 7409 2992
www.ri.ac.uk/christmas
⊖ Green Park
Bus 8, 9, 14, 19, 22, 38
Adm Adult £14, child £6

A series of lectures aimed at school children on a variety of scientific subjects.

New Year's Eve in Trafalgar Square

The traditional venue for London's end of year bash, Trafalgar Square is within easy listening distance of Big Ben's bongs. The celebrations can get a little boisterous and it isn't recommended for young children.

CENTRAL LONDON

01 Regent's Park to Baker Street
02 British Museum to Oxford Street
03 Trafalgar Square & Piccadilly
04 Covent Garden
05 Buckingham Palace
06 Westminster
07 The South Bank
08 Southwark
09 The City
10 Museumland
11 Greenwich

2 miles
3 kms

HACKNEY

WHITE CHAPEL ROAD
WHITE CHAPEL
COMMERCIAL ROAD
WAPPING

BETHNAL GREEN

KINGSLAND RD

SHOREDITCH

CITY ROAD

ISLINGTON

CLERKENWELL

CALEDONIAN ROAD

King's Cross
St Pancras
Euston
EUSTON RD
BLOOMSBURY
British Museum
King's Cross

Liverpool Street
Museum of London
THE CITY
St Paul's Cathedral
Cannon Street
Fenchurch Street
Tower of London
Tower Bridge
TOWER BRIDGE ROAD

London Dungeon
London Bridge
Globe Theatre
Tate Modern
SOUTHWARK
Elephant & Castle

GREENWICH
National Maritime Museum
Greenwich Park
Royal Observatory

COVENT GARDEN
Theatre Museum
London Transport Museum
Covent Garden

Royal National Theatre
Royal Festival Hall
Waterloo
LAMBETH
The Oval
KENNINGTON

CAMDEN
Primrose Hill
London Zoo
Regent's Park
ALBANY ST
MARYLEBONE RD
Madame Tussaud's/ London Planetarium

ST JOHN'S WOOD
AVENUE RD

CAMDEN ROAD

OXFORD STREET
SOHO
Piccadilly Circus
PICCADILLY
National Gallery
National Portrait Gallery
Trafalgar Square
Charing Cross
County Hall/ London Aquarium
Big Ben
Houses of Parliament
Westminster Abbey
WESTMINSTER
Tate Britain
VAUXHALL BRIDGE RD
PIMLICO

MAYFAIR
Green Park
St James's Park
Buckingham Palace
Victoria

Paddington
PADDINGTON
BAYSWATER ROAD

Hyde Park
KNIGHTSBRIDGE
Kensington Gardens
KENSINGTON
Science Museum
Victoria & Albert Museum
Natural History Museum
SOUTH KENSINGTON
FULHAM ROAD

CHELSEA
CHELSEA EMBANKMENT
Battersea

Regent's Park to Baker Street

Some of the capital's best-loved attractions are grouped around Regent's Park. To the north are the birds and beasts of London Zoo, while to the south, on Marylebone Road, is Madame Tussaud's, London's most popular fee-paying attraction (with the great, green-domed Planetarium right next door). And you don't need to be a super-sleuth to find the little Sherlock Holmes Museum on Baker Street or the Wallace Collection's imposing frontage in Manchester Square. Then, of course, there's the park itself, where the whole family could easily idle away an entire day boating on the lake, running through the grass, playing ball, making friends in the playground, or watching a summer performance at the Open Air Theatre.

Highlights

The Wallace Collection's wheelie cart

Watching a show aboard the Puppet Theatre Barge

Slurping smoothies in Giraffe

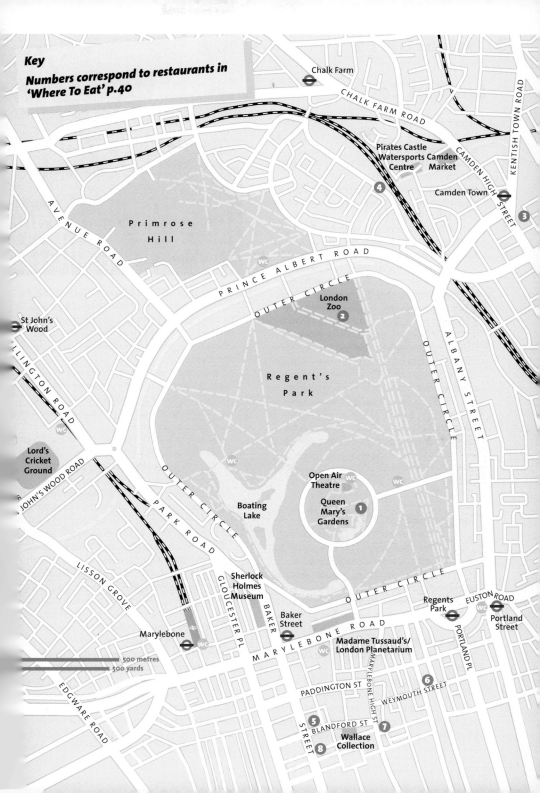

Key

Numbers correspond to restaurants in 'Where To Eat' p.40

Chalk Farm

CHALK FARM ROAD

KENTISH TOWN ROAD

Pirates Castle
Watersports Camden
Centre Market

4

Camden Town

3

CAMDEN HIGH STREET

AVENUE ROAD

Primrose
Hill

PRINCE ALBERT ROAD

OUTER CIRCLE

WC

London
Zoo

2

St John's
Wood

Regent's
Park

ALBANY STREET

OUTER CIRCLE

ILLINGTON ROAD

WC

Lord's
Cricket
Ground

ST. JOHN'S WOOD ROAD

OUTER CIRCLE

PARK ROAD

WC

Boating
Lake

WC

Open Air
Theatre

WC

WC

Queen
Mary's
Gardens

1

LISSON GROVE

GLOUCESTER PL.

Sherlock
Holmes
Museum

BAKER STREET

OUTER CIRCLE

Regents
Park

EUSTON ROAD

PORTLAND PL.

Portland
Street

Marylebone

Baker
Street

MARYLEBONE ROAD

Madame Tussaud's/
London Planetarium

WC

500 metres
500 yards

PADDINGTON ST

WEYMOUTH STREET

MARYLEBONE HIGH ST

6

EDGWARE ROAD

5

BLANDFORD ST

STREET

7

8

Wallace
Collection

THE SIGHTS

London Zoo

Regent's Park, NW1
t (020) 7722 3333
www.londonzoo.co.uk
⊖ Camden Town or Baker Street, then 274 bus
Bus 274
Open Mar–Oct 10–5.30 daily; Nov–April 10–4 daily
Adm Adult £10, child (under 15) £7, under-3s **free**,
concs £8.50, family £30
Some wheelchair access, adapted toilets
First-aid post in the centre of the zoo
Suitable for all ages
Allow a morning or afternoon or even a whole day

London Zoo is home to thousands and thousands of animals – lions, tigers, gorillas, chimps, giraffes, rhinos, snakes, penguins, camels...the list goes on – and has been a mainstay of school trips and family outings for years. Whatever you may think about the rights and wrongs of big city zoos, there's no doubt that London's famous menagerie does its best to justify its existence in the modern world. These days, its watchwords are conservation and education – simply gawping at animals is no longer the done thing. All the animals are here for a reason whether, as in the case of the Arabian Oryx, it's because they're now extinct in the wild or, as with the Sumatran tiger, because they soon could be. The zoo runs a very successful captive breeding programme and has played an important part in reintroducing many endangered species

back into the wild. This doesn't mean that the zoo has become dry and scientific. It takes its role as an educator very seriously and, as with all good teachers, understands that the best way to get children interested in something is by entertaining and involving them.

Every day the zoo organizes talks and sessions to 'meet the animals'. Turn up at feeding time and you can watch pelicans and penguins gobbling their way through buckets of fish or a snake slowly swallowing a rat – whole.

Spectacular animal shows are held in two special demonstration areas: you can see lemurs and parrots leaping, climbing and flying during the Animals in Action presentations in the Amphitheatre while, on the display lawn, there are regular exhibitions of aerobatic skill by the zoo's birds of prey – keepers will throw pieces of meat into the air for them to swoop down and catch.

It's all very impressive but your children will no doubt be itching to get involved in a more hands-on way, so take them to the Children's Zoo where, in the Touch Paddock, they can stroke and pet the resident sheep, goats and wallabies and help feed the pigs. To really get into the swing of things, kids can even have their faces painted to look like a lizard, a butterfly or (easily the most popular choice) a tiger. Be sure to pay a visit to the tiger enclosure in the main zoo. Stand at the round window when they're on the prowl and you may find yourself just a few inches away from these fearsome beasts.

Even on rainy days, the zoo is still worth visiting. While the animals in the outdoor enclosures take cover, you can do the same at the Aquarium, the

Can you spot?

London Zoo is part of the Zoological Society of London a charity committed to conservation and education. It has a very succesful captive breeding programme helping to build up stocks of rare and endangered animals – the upshot of which is that there are always lot of cute young animals running around its enclosures. See if you can find the following recent arrivals to the zoo:
▶ Ursula, the little sloth bear (she can be seen on the restyled Bear Moutain, formerly the Mappin Terraces)
▶ Noodles, the baby Bongo (a type of large, chestnut coloured African antelope)
Sol and Lua, the baby giant anteater twins
▶ The four baby bactrian camels (who, between them, have no less than eight humps)

Small Mammal Enclosure or the Web of Life Building. Opened in 2000 as part of the zoo's millennium project, this is the site's undoubted highlight. It's a hugely imaginative exhibition which tries not only to show animals in as natural a setting as possible, but to demonstrate how various animals and organisms combine to form ecosystems. You can see examples of different habitats from around the world – a mangrove swamp, a seashore, a coral reef, an underground burrow, a dung heap – and see how the resident animals have adapted themselves to their surroundings; how butterflies camouflage themselves against tree bark, how naked mole rats have developed enormous front teeth which allow them to chew their way through the earth, how robber crabs set up home in the shells of other creatures and how dung beetles use the material other animals reject – watch them carefully rolling their precious balls of dung. Even the tanks housing the exhibits are interesting. Several have magnifying lenses built into the glass to allow you to look at tiny organisms in greater detail while others are shaped like helmets enabling you to immerse yourself in the animals' environment. The centre is beautifully laid out with lots of interactive computer screens and kids are specially catered for at the Activity Den where they can take part in a broad range of crafts including brass rubbing and badge making.

The zoo has a central relaxation area with a café, gift shop, fountain and a small children's carousel. There are also several playgrounds dotted about with slides and climbing frames. In summer there's usually a bouncy castle.

All in all, London Zoo is a great place for a kids' day out. Here they can get up close to strange and exotic creatures, learn more about the environment and run about to their heart's content. Furthermore, the zoo organises a variety of family events including Easter Egg Hunts, Hallowe'en Parties (with prizes for the scariest costumes), Christmas 'Experiences' (meet Santa and his elves and and tuck into mince pies and fizzy drinks) and Animal House Evenings (summer and early autumn) when members of the public are invited on behind-the-scenes tours of the various parts of the zoo. In the Easter and summer holidays, the zoo also plays host to a series of five day Zoo Camps run under the auspices of AKA Rampage, a professional playscheme registered with Camden Council, when children aged 5 and over can, between 10am-4pm each day, take part in range of activities including games and sports in Regent's Park, arts and crafts, animal encounters and zoo tours. The camps must be booked in advance (they fill up very quickly) and cost £140 for a full week or £29 per day session.

Can you spot?

Many of the animals in the zoo have managed to adapt themselves to their surroundings. Just as chameleon will subtly change the colour of its skin, so other creatures have learned to blend in with the environment around them. Can you find any examples at the zoo?

Regent's Canal Trip

Perhaps the most novel way to arrive at London Zoo is aboard a canal boat. The London Waterbus Company runs a service from Little Venice along Regent's Canal to Camden Lock, stopping off at the Zoo on the way. You get a reduction on the price of admission with your ticket.

London Waterbus Company

50 Camden Lock Place
t (020) 7482 2550
⊖ Camden Town, Chalk Farm
Bus 6, 46
April–Oct daily service, boats run hourly from 10am–5pm; Nov–Mar weekends only
Fares Adult single £3.90, return £5.40, child single £2.50, return £3.20, under-4s **free**; combined canal trip and zoo visit: adult £9.90, child £7, under-4s free

There are a couple of other firms offering trips up Regent's canal.

The Floating Boater

Waterside, Litle Venice, Warwick Crescent, W2
t (020) 7266 1066
www.floatingboater.co.uk
⊖ Warwick Avenue

Jason's Canal Trips

60 Bloomfield Road, Little Venice, W9
t (020) 7286 3428
www.jasons.co.uk
⊖ Warwick Avenue

Madame Tussaud's

Marylebone Road, NW1
t (020) 08700 400 3000
www.madame-tussauds.com
⊖ Baker Street
Bus 13, 18, 27, 30, 74, 82, 113, 159, 274
Open 9–5.30 daily
Adm Adult £12, child (under-16) £8.50, under-5s **free**, concs £9.50, family ticket £39 (fast track timed entry only, free guide book)
Combined ticket with Planetarium: adult £14.45, child £10, under-5s **free**, concs £11.30. Under-16s must be accompanied by an adult.
No buggies or pushchairs allowed; baby carriers are provided. Wheelchair access
Suitable for all ages, apart from Chamber of Horrors which is only suitable for older children (over 8)
Allow at least an hour

It's odd to think that this collection of waxen dopplegangers is now London's third most popular tourist attraction. Only the British Museum and National Gallery welcome more tourists per

Did you know?
Madame Tussaud's always has huge queues. If you buy a joint Planetarium ticket you can, after the Planetary Quest Show, nip into the waxworks via the interior entrance between the two attractions and avoid the wait. You can also get a fast-track combination ticket for Mme Tussaud's and the London Eye at www.ba-londoneye.com

year and you can visit those, unlike Madame Tussaud's, free of charge.

Madame Tussaud's is world famous, the first thing on many people's lists of must-see-sights with queues that regularly stretch right round the block and yet, as a sane adult, you can't help thinking that it's all a little bit stupid – it's just a load of mannequins, after all, dolled up to look like famous people. It doesn't pay to be too snooty about Madame Tussaud's, however. Whatever its unfathomable attractions may be, your kids understand them and will undoubtedly have a whale of a time, running around pointing at all the famous faces and demanding to have their picture taken with the Spice Girls, Madonna or the Queen.

To their credit, the organizers have done their best to invest proceedings with a little excitement. The highlight is probably the Spirit of London Ride where you are carried in a mock-up 'Time Taxi' through representations of London history from Elizabethan times to the present day. Your kids' favourite section, on the other hand, will inevitably be the Chamber of Horrors with its collection of grizzly exhibits (for some reason yet to be explained, all children are fixated with blood, gore and mayhem).

London Planetarium

Marylebone Road, NW1
t (020) 08700 400 3000
www.london-planetarium.com
⊖ Baker Street
Bus 13, 18, 27, 30, 74, 82, 113, 159, 274
Open 9–5 daily
Adm Adult £7, child (under 16) £4.85, under-5s **free**, concs £5.60. Combined ticket with Madame Tussaud's: adult £14.45, child (under 16) £10, under-5s **free**, concs £11.30
Wheelchair access, induction loop for hard of hearing. Suitable for all ages
Allow at least 30-mins. Show in auditorium lasts 20 mins approx

There really is no better place to find out about the mysteries of the universe

Question 1
Can you name the nine planets that orbit our sun, starting with the nearest?
answer on p.249

Tell me a story: Max wax

Madame Marie Tussaud was born in France in 1761. When just six years old she was taken by her uncle to Paris where he instructed her in the art of modelling anatomical figures. By her early twenties, Marie had become so accomplished that she was hired to give art lessons to Louis XVI's children at Versailles; something which, in any other era, would have set her up for life. Unfortunately, in 1789, France underwent the Revolution – the monarchy was abolished, the King was executed and Marie, suspected of having Royalist sympathies, was thrown in jail and only released on condition that she attend public executions and sculpt the death masks of the Revolution's more celebrated victims.

In 1802, following a failed marriage, she emigrated to England taking her two children and 35 of her models with her. To make ends meet, she was forced to tour her waxwork gallery of heroes, rogues, victims and confidence tricksters around the country until, in 1835, a permanent home was found for them in London's Baker Street. By 1850, the year Madame died, 'Tussaud's' was sufficiently well known for the Duke of Wellington to have become a regular visitor. He was especially taken with the Chamber of Horrors and left instructions that he should be informed whenever a new figure was added to its gruesome ranks.

By 1884 the exhibition (now managed by Madame's sons) had grown to over 400 models forcing it to move to new premises in Marylebone Road, where it has stayed ever since. Madame's last work, a rather eerie self-portrait, is still on display in the Grand Hall.

than beneath Baker Street's famous green dome (which turns red every two years on Comic Relief or 'Red Nose' Day). The Planetarium is split into two parts, a museum and an auditorium. In the former, known as the 'Planet Zone', you can see waxworks of Neil Armstrong and Buzz Aldrin, the first men on the moon, watch live satellite weather transmissions from space telescopes, and step on to a special set of scales which tells you what your weight would be on the moon (where, happily, everyone is much lighter). Interesting though this section is, however, it's really just an appetizer to the celestial main course, the 'Planetary Quest' show in the main auditorium. Using computer-generated images projected on to the ceiling of the dome, the show takes you on a guided tour through our solar system, passing comets, planets and moons on the way. It must be admitted that some of the animation, particularly of man-made objects, looks rather dated, but the images of the celestial bodies themselves, based on data received from the Hubble Space Telescope and the Voyager space probe, are very impressive and it's an undeniably exhilarating experience. Children absolutely love it. And, what's more, it's informative as well as exciting – teaching your kids (and you) a good deal about our planetary neighbours.

Regent's Park

t (020) 7486 7905
www.open.gov.uk/rp
⊖ Baker Street, Great Portland Street, Regent's Park, Camden Town and then 274 bus
Bus 13, 18, 27, 30, 74, 82, 113, 159, 274, C2
Open 5am to dusk daily
Free
Suitable for all ages

One of London's great parks, Regent's Park has masses going on. There's the boating lake, home to a mass of wildfowl including ducks, moorhens and black swans, where you can also hire a rowing boat and take to the water yourself. There are four playgrounds (open daily from 10.30am), complete with toilets solely for the use of children (facilities for parents are separate, usually grouped around a

refreshment kiosk or café), sand pits, swings and play equipment. Sporty types, meanwhile, can make use of the tennis courts and several cricket and football pitches. In the centre are the neatly manicured Queen Mary's Gardens, best visited in summer when you'll find bed upon bed of wonderful, colourful roses. The gardens also house the renowned Open Air Theatre (one of the most enlivening places to introduce your children to the works of Shakespeare), an ornamental lake, a sunken garden and a fountain depicting a man blowing water out of a conch shell.

Open Air Theatre

Regent's Park, NW1
t (020) 7486 2431
www.open-air-theatre.org.uk
Adm tickets for daytime performances start at £8.50 (rising to £23) while evening tickets cost a flatrate £5, family tickets £12

This respected theatre company usually puts on some sort of child-friendly show during the summer holidays (in 2001 it was 'Pinocchio in the Park') as well as a selection from Shakespeare and a quality musical. A couple of years ago, it premiered a specially commissioned children's play entitled *The Last Fattybottypuss in the World*. Although the play began at the theatre, during each performance the actors and the audience got up and walked over to London Zoo where the play's final scene was set.

Sherlock Holmes Museum

221b Baker Street, NW1
t (020) 7935 8866
www.sherlock-holmes.co.uk
⊖ Baker Street
Bus 13, 18, 27, 30, 74, 82, 113, 159, 274
Open 9.30–6 daily
Adm Adult £6, child £4
No disabled facilities. Suitable for all ages although older children will get the most out of it
Allow at least half an hour

It all depends whether your children know who Sherlock Holmes is. The older ones (ten and over) may do and if, by chance, they are actually fans of Conan Doyle's classic detective, they will be completely bowled over by this little museum. It is a fictional address, of course, No:221 is actually the Abbey National Building Society, where a secretary is employed purely to tackle the thousands of letters sent to the great detective each year.

On entering the museum you are met by a 19th-century bobby and shown round the house by a Victorian maid. The rooms have been faithfully recreated (or should that be created) according to the descriptions in the book. Afterwards you can have a cream tea at Mrs Hudson's Old English Restaurant next door (Mrs Hudson was Holmes' housekeeper in the books). Opposite the museum is a memorabilia shop.

Wallace Collection

Hertford House, Manchester Square, W1
t (020) 7935 0687
www.the-wallace-collection.org.uk
⊖ Bond Street, Marble Arch
Bus 2, 13, 30, 74, 82, 113, 139, 159, 189, 274
Open Mon–Sat 10–5, Sun 2–5, Wallace Wheely Cart on Sunday afternoons and school holidays only.
Adm Free, Wallace Wheely Cart £1
Call ahead **t** (020) 7815 1350 for disabled access
Suitable for children over five, under-8s must be accompanied at all times. Allow at least an hour

Hertford House, the former home of the Wallace family – 19th-century art collectors extraordinaire – is probably not the first place that springs to mind when trying to think of somewhere to take the family. After all, examining one of the country's most important collections of French 18th-century paintings is not every child's idea of a great day

out. However, you'd be surprised. The conservators have made a real effort to involve children in the gallery. While parents examine the Sèvres porcelain, priceless furniture and suits of armour, kids can pick an activity from the Wallace Wheely Cart such as mobile-hanging, collage-making or Christmas card design. The gallery also organizes various themed special events where kids can try on historical costumes and handle some of the gallery's extensive collection of weapons.

In 2000, the museum underwent a centennial refurbishment resulting in four new galleries, a new education centre, a new restaurant, Café Bagatelle and, its most stunning feature, a new glass roof spanning its central courtyard which has been turned into an all weather sculpture garden and looks a bit like a miniature version of the British Museum's Great Court.

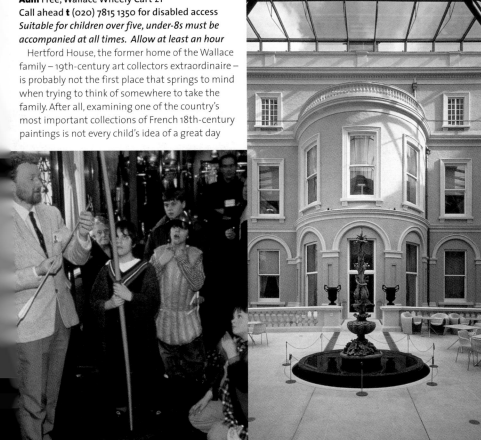

AROUND AND ABOUT

London Canal Museum

12–13 New Wharf Road, N1
t (020) 7713 0836
www.canalmuseum.org.uk
⊖ King's Cross
Bus 10, 17, 91, 259, 274
Free mooring is available outside the museum for canal boats
Open Tues–Sun 10–4.30, open Bank Holiday Mondays
Adm Adult £2.50, child £1.25 (under-8s **free**)
No disabled facilities. Suitable for children aged six and over. Allow at least an hour

That rare thing, a museum that makes children appreciate their parents. Back in the 19th century, 'canal kids' were expected to put in 18-hour days leading barge horses along tow paths, opening locks and keeping the boats clean. At the end of the day they would sleep, for just a few hours, on rough wooden benches. This museum tells their story and the story of all the people who tried to make a living ferrying cargo up and down London's industrial canals. It provides a wonderful evocation of a time when childhood was regarded as something less special than it is today.

Housed in a former ice warehouse by the side of Regent's Canal, the museum also has an exhibition on the history of ice cream.

Lord's Cricket Ground

St John's Wood Road, NW8
t (020) 7432 1033
www.lords.org
⊖ St John's Wood then bus
Bus 13, 46, 82, 113, 139, 189, 274
Tour 10am, 12 noon and 2pm daily. No tours during Test Matches or Cup Finals
Adm tickets from £7
Some disabled access, call above number. Suitable for all ages. The tour lasts one and a half hours

If your children like cricket, they'll enjoy taking a tour around Lord's (or the Marylebone Cricket Club to give it its offical title) the summer game's official headquarters, where they can take a walk through the famous longroom, find out about the great W.G. Grace and look at the Ashes Urn, the Holy Grail of cricket. You can also visit the Real Tennis Court.

Question 2
What are the Ashes?
answer on p.249

Puppet Theatre Barge

78 Middleton Road, E8
t (020) 7249 6876
www.puppetbarge.com
⊖ Warwick Avenue
Bus 6, 46
Open Varies, phone ahead
Some disabled access by arrangement. Suitable for all ages

A small puppet theatre on an old Thames barge. You can catch a show at Little Venice, to the south of Regent's Park, between October and May. During the summer it sails up and down the Thames putting on performances.

Primrose Hill

If you didn't manage to get your fill of green spaces down in Regent's Park, walk up the hill for some fantastic views over the city. The summit was the setting for the twilight bark in Dodie Smith's *One Hundred and One Dalmatians*, and the area is very popular with families, both canine and human. Regent's Park Road runs adjacent and is good for browsing in book and gift shops.

WHERE TO SHOP

Camden Market

⊖ Camden Town, Chalk Farm
Bus 24, 27, 29, 134, 135, 168, 214, 253, 274, C2

Older, more fashion-conscious children will enjoy a visit to Camden's bustling weekend markets: the Stables is the grooviest and grungiest, a casbah-like warren of clothes and fashion stalls; the Lock is craft-based and, as such, a touch more upmarket while Camden Market itself is probably the least interesting – it sells an assorted mixture of clothes, jewellery and general what-nots. Come early before the crowds arrive, unless you are willing to let your children mingle with the broadest cross-section of society imaginable spilling out around Camden Town tube station.

The Stables

Off Chalk Farm Road, opposite junction with Hartland Road, NW1
t (020) 7485 5511
www.camdenlock.net/stables
Open Sat, Sun 8–6

Sells secondhand and designer clothes, jewellery, antiques, books, crafts, furniture, candles, souvenirs, games, memorabilia and old toys. It pays to have a good old gawp for within this extremely popular mish mash of stalls are ones dedicated to musical instruments and some that specialize in street fashions and accessories.

Camden Lock

Camden Lock Place, off Chalk Farm Road, NW1
t (020) 7284 2084
www.camdenlock.net
Open Sat, Sun 10–6; a few stalls open throughout the week

Situated on the river bank this collection of yards sells craft goods, books, designer clothes, jewellery, food, mirrors, furniture, musical instruments, hand-made soaps, didgeridoos, hand-woven hammocks and sculptures. Thursdays and Fridays see an influx of bric-a-brac and there's fresh farm produce in abundance on Fridays too.

Camden Market

Camden High Street, at junction with Buck Street, NW1
t (020) 7938 4343
Open Thur–Sun 9–5.30

The seventies revivalist's dream – the markets stalls are brimming with secondhand clothes particularly from the days of disco and the perpetually resurfacing gothic phase, plus jewellery, leather belts, handbags and CDs, fruit and veg, as well as a good selection of leather and suede jackets.

For a quick pit-stop, try the **1 Queen Mary's Gardens Café** in Regent's Park, near the Open Air Theatre, or, if you're visiting London Zoo, remember there's a large central refreshment area with a good self-service **2 café. The Stables** in Camden Market also houses food stalls offering takeaway Thai, Chinese and Indian food.

For a quick bite and a drink, there's the **Primrose Patisserie**, 136 Regent's Park Road, NW1, **t** (020) 7722 7848, ⊖ **Camden Town**, serving up delicious fruit pastries and hot beverages; or for a swift pint try **The Queen**, 49 Regent's Park Road, NW1, **t** (020) 7586 0408, ⊖ **Camden Town**, which has a terrace for the kids to run around on overlooking the park.

Otherwise, you could tuck into a tasty thin–crust Italian–style pizza at **Pizza Express** – two branches at 133 Baker Street, **t** (020) 7486 0888 and, 85–87 Parkway, **t** (020) 7267 2600, ⊖ **Baker Street**; a bowl of pasta at **Café Uno** (100 Baker Street, **t** (020) 7486 8606; steak and chips at **Café Rouge**, 18 Chalk Farm Road, **t** (020) 7428 0998, ⊖ **Chalk Farm**; a plate of noodles at **Wagamama**, 11 Jamestown Road, **t** (020) 7487 4688, ⊖ **Chalk Farm**; or, if you fancy something really different, a wild boar sandwich at **Belgo**, 72 Chalk Farm Road, **t** (020) 7267 0718 ⊖ **Chalk Farm**, a trendy Belgian restaurant that offers a special menu for kids. See Eat p.223 for more details on the above restaurant chains.

3 Daphne

83 Bayham Street, NW1
t (020) 7267 7322
Open Mon-Sat 12 noon–2.30 & 6–11.30
⊖ Camden Town

Warm, welcoming and very popular Greek restaurant with a lovely sunny roof terrace. Children's portions and high chairs available.

4 The Engineer

65 Gloucester Avenue, NW1
t (020) 7722 0950

Gastropubs are all the rage with the parenting set, mainly because of their more relaxed café-bar atmosphere, where it's okay to linger over a coke and a newspaper, as well as enjoy the quality of the food. Often they stock a more discerning array of drinks, including decent wines, teas and coffee. The Primrose Hill area is very popular with families, so several of its pubs are family-friendly, but this one throws a special kids' menu and some crayons into the mix. Bar snacks, dining room upstairs, yard at the back.

5 Giraffe

6–8 Blandford Street, W1
t (020) 7935 2333
Open 8am–11.30pm daily
⊖ Baker Street

With its bright, colourful decor and piped world music, Giraffe has a rather groovy, youthful ambience. Both adults and children are well catered for – adults with a selection of inventive breakfast, lunch and dinner menus; children with a Kids' Pack filled with games and puzzles and a children's menu (just £2.25) of simple dishes (sausages, burgers and veggie noodles) and large fruity shakes which they can stir with a giraffe shaped cocktail stirrer.

6 Love Café

62-64 Weymouth Street, NW1
t (020) 7487 5683

Situated in the Aveda natural cosmetics store where most of the products smell good enough to eat. Kids are happy to linger around the tropical fish tank while you stock up on pampering treats.

7 Patisserie Valerie

105 Marylebone High Street, W1
t (020) 7935 6240
www.patisserievalerie.co.uk
Open Mon-Fri 7.30am-7pm, Sat 8am-7pm, Sun 9-6
⊖ Baker Street, Bond Street

First established in the 1920s by Belgian-born baker Madame Valerie, each branch of this patisserie-cum-café chain has a pleasant continental-style ambience and stocks a wonderful array of sticky treats as well as savoury snacks and salads.

8 Royal China

40 Baker Street, W1
t (020) 7487 4688
Open Mon-Sat 12 noon-11, Sun 11am-10pm
⊖ Baker Street

One of the capital's best chinese restaurants outside of Chinatown itself. Children are warmly welcomed and the Dim Sum is superb. Children's menu and high chairs available.

British Museum to Oxford Street

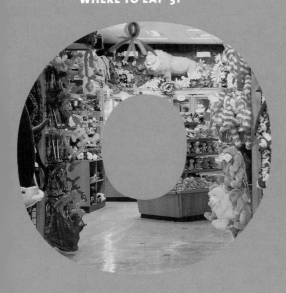

There's quite a lot to see here. To the east is the revamped and revitalised British Museum, one of the world's truly great museums, while, to the west lies London's mainstream shopping hub – Oxford Street, Regent Street and Bond Street – one of the best retail districts in Europe. Nonetheless, it's important to time your trip carefully. This whole district is fiercely popular and on summer weekends or at Christmastime, the streets can become choked with people. Thankfully there are a few well-placed small museums to nip into if you need to escape the throng. All in all, there really are few better places to come for an informative day out or a frenzied shopping spree.

Highlights

Having a sit down in the British Museum's Great Court

Handel House Museum's workshops

Watching the new toy demonstrations in Hamleys

Carnaby

CARNABY STREET

Key

Numbers correspond to restaurants in 'Where To Eat' p.51

OUTER CIRCLE
ALBANY STREET
HAMPSTEAD ROAD
CHESTER ROAD
Euston
British Library
King's Cross
St Pancras
GRAY'S INN ROAD
EUSTON ROAD
JUDD STREET
Euston Square
Petrie Museum
Russell Square
Coram's Fields
Dicken's House
GUILFORD STREET
Regent's Park
Portland Street
Warren Street
RUSSELL SQUARE
SOUTHAMPTON ROW
MARYLEBONE HIGH STREET
PORTLAND PLACE
GREAT PORTLAND STREET
Telecom Tower
GOWER STREET
TOTTENHAM COURT ROAD
Pollock's Toy Museum
Goodge Street
BEDFORD SQUARE
British Museum
WEYMOUTH STREET
NEW CAVENDISH STREET
LANGHAM PLACE
GREAT RUSSELL STREET
Holborn
Wallace Collection
MANCHESTER SQUARE
CAVENDISH SQUARE
REGENT STREET
OXFORD STREET
Tottenham Court Road
Dominion Theatre
WIGMORE STREET
Oxford Circus

500 metres
500 yards

British Museum

Great Russell Street, WC1
t (020) 7636 1555
Infoline **t** (020) 7580 1788
Infoline for disabled visitors **t** (020) 7637 7384
www.british-museum.ac.uk
⊖ Tottenham Court Road, Russell Square, Holborn
Bus 1, 7, 8, 10, 19, 24, 25, 29, 38, 55, 73, 98, 134, 242
Open Mon–Sat 10–5 (until 9pm on the first
Tuesday of each month),Sun 12 noon–6
Adm Free (a £2 donation is recommended), £5 for
evening opening on first Tuesday of the month
Suitable for all ages, but particularly older children,
museum shop (see p.50)
Allow at least a couple of hours

The British Museum has never looked so good.
Its central courtyard (known as the Great Court)
which has been closed to the public for nearly 150
years, recently reopened following a spectacular
architectural transformation. The circular reading
room at its centre, which used to house the British
Library, now holds a public reference library and
exhibition galleries. The huge domed interior looks
like a vast cathedral of books, while the
surrounding 2 acres of courtyard have been landscaped and rebuilt to contain an ethnographic
gallery, a new Clore Education centre as well as a
lecture theatre, a cinema, seminar rooms and a
young visitor centre offering a huge range of activities for children. The most stunning development,
however, is the new 6,000 square metre glass roof
that arches over the courtyard. Comprised of 3,312
unique triangular panels and weighing some 1,000
tonnes, it makes the courtyard the largest covered
public square in Europe. There's so much to look at
in the museum that you couldn't hope to do it all

Did you know?
The British Museum is now over 250 years old. It
was the first museum in the country ever to open
its doors to members of the general public.

in one, or even two, trips. In fact, once you've had
your fill of the awe-inspiring roof, it's probably best
to plan your route around a few must-see exhibits.
From the Great Court, you can choose from a
number of routes into the main galleries: head
west for the Egyptian Sculpture, east for the
impossibly huge King's Library and north for the
new Wellcome Wing of Ethnography. Inside the
courtyard, two massive staircases lead up to the
restaurant from where a bridge takes you into the
museum's upper galleries.

Whatever route you chose, however, you won't go
far wrong if you take your children to the ever
popular Ancient Egyptian galleries (rooms 62–66)
on the first floor. Here, they'll immediately be capti-
vated by the huge gold sarcophagi, the brightly
coloured frescoes and, of course, the mummies.
These 2,000-year-old dead bodies hold a strange
fascination for kids. The Egyptians, it seems, had a
bit of a thing about mummification. As well as
people, you'll find mummified cats, fish and cattle.

Elsewhere, look out for the enormous 11m high
early 19th-century totem pole that stands by the

Did you know?
In the early years of the ancient Egyptian
kingdom, only the rich could afford to be
mummified but, in later times almost everyone
was able to afford it. So many mummies were
dug up in Egypt in the 1800s that people started
using the bodies as fuel and the bandages to
make paper.

North Stairs; Lindow Man, the perfectly preserved leathery remains of a 2,000-year-old Briton (room 35), and the great fat, smiling ceramic Buddhas in the Oriental gallery (room 33).

The British Museum's other famous exhibits include the controversial Elgin Marbles (room 8), the frieze reliefs from the Parthenon in Athens which, depending on who you believe, were either rescued or stolen by Lord Elgin, British Ambassador to the Ottoman Empire, in 1802; the Rosetta Stone (room 25) an ancient tablet with the same decree inscribed upon it in three languages which allowed Egyptian hieroglyphics to be deciphered for the first time and the Sutton Hoo Treasure (room 41), a jewel-encrusted collection of Viking swords, helmets, bowls and buckles.

The British Museum is so vast that there's always the danger it will turn into a huge blurry mass for many children, especially the younger ones. Remember to reserve some time for quiet contemplation in the courtyard.

How to make a mummy

The ancient Egyptians believed that every human being was made up of a ka (spirit) and a ba (body). When a person died they would only be able to enter the afterlife if their body was prevented from decaying – hence the fascination with preservation through mummification.

The key to a successful mummification is to dry out the body as quickly and as thoroughly as possible. Remember, the body is 75 percent water and, in a hot climate such as Egypt's, anything wet or damp rots very quickly. Embalmers used natron, a chemical that occurs naturally in Egypt, to suck the moisture out of the body. The eyes and most of the internal organs, including the brain, kidneys and liver, were taken out. The brain was removed through a nostril, a chisel having first been wiggled around inside the skull cavity to mash it into small pieces. The brain would then be thrown away (for some reason the Egyptians didn't think it would be particularly useful in the afterlife). All the other organs, however, were stored safely inside jars and buried with the body ready for the post-life

Tell me a story: I want my mummy

The British Museum contains many artefacts with tales to tell, but none so colourful as the tale of the 'unlucky mummy'. The legend actually refers to a mummy board, or inner coffin lid, found at Thebes and dated between 950-900 BC. It was acquired by a group of four young holidaymakers in Egypt in around 1860-1870 and brought back to England shortly afterwards whereupon stange things began to take place. Before long, three of the men were dead (one shot, two of poverty) while the fourth had been seriously maimed in a shooting incident. The board was passed on to one of the men's sisters but so unnerved her that she donated it to the museum in 1889. Unfortunately, the carrier who transported it there died within a week. Once at the museum, the board reportedly began emitting strange sounds at night prompting the staff to take it off display and store it in the basement. An exact replica was then made and shown in its place allowing the original to be sold to an American who shipped it on the maiden voyage of the Titanic – which, of course, sank. Amazingly, the board survived the disaster and continued to wreak havoc in America until its distraught owner decided to send it back to England. The story finally came to and end when the ship carrying it, the Empress of Ireland, went down in the St Lawrence River. A leaflet on the 'unlucky mummy' is available from the information desk.

Make friends

The Museum's youth club meets every Sunday and organizes a variety of holiday events including behind-the-scenes visits, craft workshops and sleepovers. Membership is available to children aged 8–15 and costs £15 a year.

journey. The skull and body cavity were filled with a mixture of natron and plaster and the eyes replaced with small stones (or, in the case of the unlucky Rameses IV, with two small onions) in order to stop them from becoming sunken. Only the heart was left inside the body; this would have to be weighed in the afterlife against the 'Feather of Truth'. If the feather proved heavier, the heart would be eaten by a monster known as the 'Devourer' and the victim would be prevented from completing their journey.

Once the body was dry, it was wrapped in bandages. Sometimes over 300 yards of bandages were used, with charms written on pieces of papyrus slipped between the folds. The mummy would then be put into its coffin or sarcophagus and entombed; but not before its mouth had been opened to make sure it could breathe and talk in the afterlife – although, without a brain, conversation was presumably limited.

Dickens' House

48 Doughty Street
t (020) 7405 2127
www.dickensmuseum.com
⊖ Chancery Lane, Russel Square
Bus 8, 188
Open Mon-Sat 10–5, closed Bank Holidays
Adm Adult £3, child (5-15) £2, £9 family, under-5s free

Despite Dickens being a bit of a gadabout – much of the south coast lays more or less spurious claim to a pub where he once supped or scribbled, – he did manage to write a fair bit within the walls of this house, now a museum to his literary life. Although only his home for the first two years of his marriage, it was here that Dickens finished *The Pickwick Papers*, and went on to write *Oliver Twist*, *Nicholas Nickleby*, *The Old Curiosity Shop* and *Barnaby Rudge*. As the sole survivor of Dickens' London residences, the museum is chock-full of memorabilia and paintings and the drawing room has been restored to its mid-1800s state. On Wednesdays, from April-July, the 'Sparkler of Albion' a one-man show recreating scenes from Dickens' novels visits the house. Tours can be arranged by phoning in advance.

Handel House Museum

25 Brook Street, W1
t. (020 7495 1685)
www.handelhouse.org
⊖ Bond Street, Oxford Circus
Adm Adult £4.50, child £2, concs £3.50
Audio guide, shop

This was the home of the composer from 1723 until his death in 1759. He used the house as a recital room and a ticket office, besides writing the Messiah and many operas on the premises. The house contains artworks relating to the composer's life and times and has been refurbished with items of furniture based on an inventory of his posses-sions. A handling collection, a children's activity pack (ages 6-12) and a costumed actor (some week-ends, call for details) are all on hand to bring Handel's world to life and give young visitors a taste of 18th-century living. Workshops for children take place once a month on Saturday mornings and cover a range of themes from musical fun to craft sessions. Look out for additional special events for children in the school holidays.

Petrie Museum of Egyptian Archaeology

Malet Place, WC1
t (020) 7679 2884
www.petrie.ucl.ac.uk
⊖ Goodge Street
Bus 10, 73, 29, 134
Open Tue-Fri 1–5, Sat 10-1
Free

Part of University College London, this hidden gem may well inspire your children to get digging out in the back garden. The assembled artefacts were bequeathed to the University by Sir Flinders Petrie in 1933 following his excavations in Egypt. Among them are assorted pieces of jewellery and the oldest piece of cloth in the world (c2,800 BC). Mummy enthusiasts will love the 4,500 year old pot burial and the Egyptian version of a Barbie makeover mannequin – complete with real eyebrows, lashes and a big hairdo. In summer, fami-lies can pick up a backpack and follow the trail back in time to the ancient Valley of the Kings.

Pollock's Toy Museum

41 Whitfield Street, W1
t (020) 7636 3452
www.tao2000.net/pollocks
⊖ Goodge Street
Bus 10, 24, 29, 73, 134
Open Mon–Sat 10am–5pm; last entry 4.30pm
Adm Adult £3, child (under 18) £1.50
No disabled facilities. Suitable for all ages
Allow at least an hour

This captivating collection of Victorian toys and trinkets is housed in two interlinked 18th-century houses. It's named after Benjamin Pollock, one of Victorian London's leading toy-makers, and is stuffed full of wonderfully crafted playthings: hand-made paper and card miniature stage sets (Pollock's speciality), tin toys, board games, puppets and dolls' houses; as well as folk toys from Russia, Poland and the Balkans. The museum shop is a good source of stocking-fillers – pick up one of the theatre kits based on Pollock's original designs and bring your own version of Cinderella or Aladdin to life. *See* **Covent Garden** p.65 for an additional shop.

AROUND AND ABOUT

British Library

96 Euston Road, NW1
t (020) 7412 7000/7332
www.bl.uk
♍/↿ King's Cross, Euston
Bus 10, 30, 73, 91
Open Mon, Wed-Fri 9.30–6, Tues 9.30–8, Sat 9.30–5, Sun 11–5
Free

Wheelchair access and adapted toilets. Suitable for older children (over-8s). Allow at least an hour

It was completed ten years behind schedule and cost a mere £511 million (or £350 million more than it was meant to), but it's still been hailed as a great success. The new British Library looks rather ordinary (almost supermarket-like) from the outside, but inside it's quite magical with huge, bright reading rooms. Although many of the public displays are confined to the (rather dingy) basement, the library it still well worth a visit. It holds many of the country's most precious manuscripts including the Lindisfarne Gospels, the Magna Carta and Shakespeare's First Folio. Children are catered for in the Pearson Gallery of Living Words, where there is a display on children's literature (look out for Lewis Carroll's notebook version of *Alice's Adventures in Wonderland*, complete with hand-drawn illustrations), and the Workshop of Words, Sounds and Images which has an interactive display on the craft of book creation – from binding to desktop publishing. The library organizes children's activities during the summer holidays.

Camley Street Natural Park

12 Camley Street, NW1
t (020) 7833 2311
♍/↿ King's Cross
Bus 10, 30, 73, 91
Open Summer Mon-Thu 9–5, Sat & Sun 11-5, closed Fri, winter 10-4
Free

Do not let the sight of King's Cross waste transfer station's steely towers put you off. This hidden two-acre site has been teeming with flora and fauna since it became a nature reserve at the hands of the London Wildlife Trust in 1983. A host of supervised activities take place throughout the year, from pond-dipping to mask-making.

Coram's Fields

93 Guilford Street, WC1
t (020) 7837 6138
♍ Russell Square
Bus 17, 45, 46
Open Summer 9–8 daily, winter 9–dusk
Free

A city farm (home to goats, sheep, pigs, chickens, geese, rabbits and guinea pigs), aviary and park in the heart of Bloomsbury. Adults can visit only if accompanied by a child. There's also a playground, paddling pool and children's nursery.

Dominion Theatre

269 Tottenham Court Road, W1
t (0990) 405 040
♍ Tottenham Court Road
Bus 7, 8, 10, 25, 55, 73, 98, 176
Prices £10–£37.50

A great place to introduce children to the joys of the stage in true technicolour musical fashion. Its productions are nearly always child-friendly and have in recent years included *The Phantom of the Opera* and *Notre Dame de Paris*.

WHERE TO SHOP

Oxford Street, Regent Street and Bond Street together make up one of the busiest shopping districts in the country. You'll find lots of clothes and book shops, all with sections for kids, as well as some well-stocked department stores. There are also a number of shops, like Hamleys and the new Niketown, which will call to your children like sirens from a rock.

If you're keen on browsing for something to read, Borders on Oxford Street, a massive book, CD and magazine shop, will appeal equally to adults and children, who can both happily spend the best part of an afternoon browsing through its three floors. It's one of the capital's newest bookshops and also one of its most innovative, organizing storytellings for children on Saturday mornings – with a roster of costumed characters on hand to enliven proceedings.

Otherwise, head to Charing Cross Road, London's unofficial book centre, and particularly Foyle's, one of the largest bookstores in London. This huge, charming, sprawling shop has a superb collection of children's books. It also has a completely unfath-omable layout, but then looking is half the fun. The nearby branch of Waterstone's at Piccadilly is the largest bookshop in Europe.

If your kids are comic fans try Gosh! on Great Russell Street where you can pick up all your Marvel and DC favourites such as *Superman* and *The Incredible Hulk* (as well as compilations of newspaper strip cartoons like *Peanuts* and *The Far Side*) or Forbidden Planet on New Oxford Street, full of sci-fi comics, books and models. *See* **Shop** p.235 for more details.

Hamleys

188 Regent Street, W1
t (020) 7734 3161
www.hamleys.com
Open Mon–Wed & Fri 10–7, Thurs 10–8, Sat 9.30–7, Sun 12 noon–6pm

Toy heaven; Hamleys is one of the largest and certainly the most famous toy shop in the world. You can find absolutely every toy imaginable on its six jam-packed floors. In fact, if Hamleys don't stock it, it probably doesn't exist.

Briefly, this is what you can expect to find: The basement has been turned into an arcade with hundreds of video games – racing games, shooting games, fighting games – and there's also a small and rather noisy café. On the ground floor you'll find thousands of soft toys including one humungous fluffy tiger (in fact, it's not that much smaller than the real thing). The first floor is where to go for building block toys like Lego and K'nex as well as Scalextrix and traditional tin soldiers. On the second floor are pre-school toys, model cars and remote controlled vehicles while the third floor is dedicated to dolls: rag dolls, porcelain dolls and, of course, Barbie. The fourth floor, on the other hand, is packed with more cerebral games: jigsaw puzzles, board games and computer programmes. The fifth and final floor holds sporting goods and has a branch of the Manchester United Club shop. On each floor, you'll find shop assistants skillfully demonstrating the latest stocking filler – soft boomerangs, bubble machines, magic tricks and the like.

Question 3
Which London Premier League football club has a claret and blue home strip?
answer on p.249

Niketown

Oxford Circus, W1
t (020) 7612 0800
www.nike.com
Open Mon–Sat 10–6.30, Thurs till 8pm,
Sun 12 noon–6pm

The biggest sports name in town, the £50 million Niketown is more than just a sports shop. It's a theme store, a mini-museum, an 'experience' – or so the hype would have us believe. It's certainly a fascinating place. The reverance the shop shows for sports is practically religious. Each dedicated section – football, golf, tennis, running etc – has a distinctly sacred feel, with video images and memorabilia taking the place of rituals and relics. The centre of the store is dominated by an enormous chandelier covered in thousands of sporting pictures. Every now and then the lights will dim for a 'service' when a video of a classic sporting moment will be shown on the store's numerous giant screens to the accompaniment of rousing music – very strange but undeniably affecting. Check out the enormous tennis racket suspended from the shop ceiling and the mini-basketball court. There's even a golf pro on hand to analyse your swing.

Disney Store

104 Regent Street, W1
t (020) 7287 6558
www.disneystores.com
Open Mon–Sat 9.30–8, Sun 12 noon–6pm

Videos, play figures, mugs, costumes: the store holds a vast array of merchandise relating to Disney's enormous roster of cartoon characters. The video screen belting out singalong classics never fails to attract a gaggle of painfully warbling children. A selection of toddler's merchandise is in the basement.

Did you know?
Watch out! Every time you kick a football, your poor foot has to endure 110kg of pressure!

Warner Brothers Studio Store

178–82 Regent Street, W1
t (020) 7434 3334
Open Mon–Wed & Fri 10–7, Thurs & Sat 10–8, Sun 12 noon–6pm

You can pick up everything from key rings to tea towels. The highlight is an interactive paint station where kids can colour in a series of animated scenes on computer screens.

British Museum Shops

22 Bloomsbury Street London WC1
t (020) 7637 9449
Open Mon–Sat 9.30-6, Sun 12 noon-6

Almost a mini-museum in itself, the shop stocks unusual and innovative products from around the world. Here you can pick up such essential items as a Rosetta Stone pencil sharpener (99p), an origami kit (£12.99), or a bronze replica of a Roman bust (yours for just £2,000). They also stock a variety of books and activity sets about Viking, Romans and Egyptians. Younger children will probably be drawn to the animal masks and colouring-in sets, whilst older children can build their very own Egyptian tomb complete with resident mummy.

WHERE TO EAT

There's a good mix in this area. Obviously most people come to Oxford and Regent Street in order to shop, so you'll find lots of snack bars, sandwich shops, fast–food outlets and chain restaurants where you can grab a quick mouthful before heading back into the dizzying world of retail. You'll find half a dozen branches of the family-friendly **Pizza Express** chain: 21–22 Barrett Street, **t** (020) 7629 1001, ⊖ Bond Street; 7 Charlotte Street, **t** (020) 7580 1110; ⊖ Goodge Street 30 Coptic Street, **t** (020) 4636 3232, ⊖ Tottenham Court Road; 10 Dean Street, **t** (020) 7439 8722, ⊖ Tottenham Court Road; 13–14 Thayer Street, **t** (020) 7935 2167, ⊖ Oxford Circus, as well as one of its principal rival, **Ask Pizza**, 48 Grafton Way, **t** (020) 7388 8108, ⊖ Warren Street, both of these chains serve thin-crust Italian pizzas and offer children's portions and high chairs.

Continental–style cafés are also thick on the ground. Look out for **Café Flo**, 13 Thayer Street, **t** (020) 7935 5023, ⊖ Bond Street, a pleasant bistro chain based very much on the Café Rouge template; **Café Med**, 22–25 Dean Street, **t** (020) 7287 9007, ⊖ Tottenham Court Road, which serves a mediterranean-based menu (there's a kids' version for £5 comprising two courses and a drink) and **Caffè Uno**, 5 Argyll Street, **t** (020) 7437 2503, ⊖ Oxford Circus, a very reasonably priced Italian chain where kids get a – 'Secret Squirrel' menu offering a choice of main meal (penne bolognese, sausage and fries or mini pizza) ,two scoops of ice cream and a free drink – all for £3.95 – as well as games and balloons.

Burger fans, meanwhile, can choose between the rather upmarket delights of **Tootsies**, 35 James Street, **t** (020) 7486 1611, ⊖ Bond Street, a brightly–coloured trendy burger bar, and the simpler pleasures of the Happy Meal – there are branches of **McDonald's** at 8–10 Oxford Street, 120 Oxford Street, 185 Oxford Street, 291b Oxford Street, 40 New Oxford Street, 310–312 Regent Street and 134 Tottenham Court Road.

See **Eat** p.223 for more details on the above restaurant chains.

Coffee Gallery

23 Museum Street, WC1
t (020) 7436 0455
Open Mon–Fri 8–5.30, Sat 12–5.30,
Sun 12 noon–5.30
⊖ Tottenham Court Road

With its bright, cheerful interior, the Coffee Gallery makes the perfect setting for a light snack and provides a welcome retreat from the bustling West End crowds. It serves a wide range of sandwiches including filled foccacias.

2 RK Stanley's

6 Little Portland Street, W1
t (020) 7462 0099
Open Mon–Sat 12 noon–11
www.rkstanleys.co.uk
⊖ Oxford Circus

Its old-style fifties décor and sausage-heavy menu makes this a good, fun choice. Kids eat for free on Saturdays; otherwise the children's menu is £4.50. Baby-changing facilities and high chairs available.

3 La Rueda

102 Wigmore Street, W1
t (020) 7486 1718
Open Mon–Fri 12 noon–3 & 6.30–11.30,
Sat 12 noon–11.30, Sun 12 noon–10.30
⊖ Bond Street

Tired of pizzas and burgers? Then try your kids on the mini-portions of paella and patatas bravas served at this lively Tapas chain. There's live music and dancing on Friday and Saturday evenings. High chairs available.

4 Townhouse Brasserie

24 Coptic Street, WC1
t (020) 7636 2731
Open Mon–Fri 12 noon–11, Sat 3–11, Sun 10–6
⊖ Tottenham Court Road

Can you spot?

The Telecom Tower? One of London's most distinctive landmarks, the great cylindrical tower (it looks a bit like a huge spark plug) is clearly visible from the north side of Oxford Street. Standing some 580ft high, this was the tallest building in London when it opened in 1964 – it needed to be so tall in order to broadcast clear radio and TV signals over the city's rooftops. The views from the top are reportedly fantastic. Sadly, members of the public have been barred from climbing to the top of the tower since the closure of the revolving restaurant (yes, a revolving restaurant) in the seventies.

Question 4
How many of the individually-shaped glass panels were used to make up the roof of the British Museum's Great Court? Find the answer on p.44 or see p.249.

A good place to come for a hearty meal after a morning spent tramping around the nearby British Museum. The menu is an eclectic mish-mash of European, British, Chinese and Caribbean dishes and they extend a warm welcome to families. The ice cream is particularly recommended.

5/6 Wagamama

4a Streatham Street, WC1
t (020) 7323 9223
⊖ Tottenham Court Road
And, 101 Wigmore Street, W1
t (020) 7409 0111
⊖ Oxford Circus
www.wagamama.com
Open Mon–Sat 12 noon–11, Sun 12.30–10

Though rather canteen-like with its long refectory tables, this fast-growing noodle house chain is surprisingly family-friendly, although the (inevitable) hustle and bustle may appeal more to older children. High chairs available.

7 Yo! Sushi

52 Poland Street
t (020) 7287 0443
www.yosushi.co.uk
Open 12 noon–12 midnight daily
⊖ Oxford Circus, Tottenham Court Road

A dining experience unlike any other – you pick your dishes from an enormous conveyor belt whilst your drinks are prepared by a special drinks-mixing robot. Kids get a games bag and their own menu which offers such authentic Japanese delicacies as fish fingers and chicken nuggets and comes with a pair of special child-friendly chopsticks. During the week under-12s eat for free. High chairs and clip-on baby seats available.

8 Mildred's

58 Greek Street, W1
t (020) 7494 1634
Open Mon–Sat 12 noon–11
⊖ Leicester Square, Tottenham Court Road

A Soho institution, this vegetarian restarant offers tasty stir fries, bean burgers and falafels in pitta bread with salad at reasonable prices. Limited

Trafalgar Square and Piccadilly

In many ways Trafalgar Square is the perfect symbol of the city itself. Though noisy and congested it has great charm and contains many wonders – ranging from one of the world's greatest art collections to the country's smallest police station. Towering above these is Nelson's Column, that great monument to British pluck, guarded by four magnificent (albeit rather friendly-looking) iron lions. Nearby is Leicester Square, London's cinematic heart, and the neon-lit Piccadilly Circus, site of the Trocadero centre where many a teenage adventurer has strayed to sample the rides and play on the arcade machines.

Highlights

Trafalgar Square's cooling fountains

The latest arcade thrills at the Trocadero

Eating with chopsticks in Chinatown

300 metres
300 yards

REGENT STREET

WARDOUR STREET

SHAFTESBURY AVENUE

CHARING CROSS ROAD

LONG ACRE

Covent Garden

LISLE STREET

10 9
12
11

Leicester Square

ST MARTIN'S LANE

5

Trocadero

4

COVENTRY

WHITCOMB STREET

Leicester Square

8

1

Piccadilly Circus

7

National Portrait Gallery

ST MARTIN'S PL

2

St Martin-in-the-Fields

STRAND

Royal Academy

Piccadilly Circus

HAYMARKET

National Gallery

Charing Cross

LD BOND STREET

PICCADILLY

3

REGENT STREET

Trafalgar Square

Charing Cross

6

ST JAMES'S ST

PALL MALL

THE MALL

NORTHUMBERLAND AVENUE

WHITEHALL

Green Park

Key
*Numbers correspond to restaurants in
'Where To Eat' p.62*

⊖ Charing Cross, Leicester Square, Embankment
Bus 3, 6, 9, 11, 12, 13, 15, 23, 24, 29, 53, 88, 91, 109, 139, 159, 176, 184, 196

Did you know?
Just before the 40ft statue of Nelson was erected in Trafalgar Square, 14 stonemasons had a celebratory dinner perched on top of the column – 145ft in the air. Did you also know that the statue of Charles I (on the south side of the square) is the precise point from where all distances from London are measured?

The first thing you notice is Nelson's Column, all 185ft of it, a great granite finger pointing at the sky. Kids will instinctively roll their heads back in an attempt to catch a glimpse of the one-eyed, one-armed British hero perched on its summit. Lord Horatio Nelson (for it is he) was Britain's greatest naval commander. The square and column were built in the early 19th century to commemorate his victory over the combined Franco-Spanish fleet at the Battle of Trafalgar back in 1805. Unfortunately, Nelson was fatally wounded during the course of the battle and his body was brought home to Britain to a hero's funeral, perfectly preserved having been pickled in a barrel of brandy.

The lions at the base were sculpted by Edwin Landseer, and were unveiled in 1870, some 25 years after the construction of the column. Children always fall madly in love with them and will expend remarkable amounts of energy trying to clamber aboard the beasts' great shiny backs. A photo of your kids sitting between a pair of giant protective forepaws is one of the classic snapshots of London. Alternatively, you could pose them in front of one of the square's great gushing, gurgling fountains which spring into life at 10 o'clock each morning. At the northern end of the square sits the National Gallery, one of the world's finest collections of paintings and, next door, the National Portrait Gallery, the nation's scrapbook.

Until recently, one of the great joys of visiting the square (for children, at least) came from feeding the resident pigeons. With a small plastic cup of birdseed in hand, kids would happily spend the best part of an afternoon chasing the birds around the square and letting them settle on their arms and heads. It was always a strange tradition (after all, in most city centres pigeons are regarded as something of a nuisance) and in 2001, it finally came to an end when Ken Livingstone, London's first mayor and no pigeon lover ('rats with wings' was one of his more generous epithets) revoked the licence of the square's last remaining seed seller thus forcing the birds to search for their food elsewhere (although a fair proportion still remain, obviously hoping for a change of heart).

Christmas and New Year

Trafalgar Square is particularly popular in winter. Every year the Norwegian government donates an enormous Christmas tree to Britain as a thank you for Britain's help during the Second World War. The tree is erected in the square next to Nelson's Column watched by a suitably festive crowd. Carol singing takes place around the tree every evening from early December to Christmas Eve. Every 31 December (New Year's Eve) thousands of people cram into Trafalgar Square to celebrate the New Year – waiting for the 12 o'clock chimes of Britain's most famous clock, Big Ben, to ring out.

Can you spot?
Trafalgar Square is home to the world's smallest police station. See if you can find it. Hidden in a lamp post, in the southeast corner of the square, it has room for just one police officer.

National Gallery

Trafalgar Square, WC2
t (020) 7747 2885
www.nationalgallery.org.uk
⊖ Charing Cross, Leicester Square, Embankment
Bus 3, 6, 9, 11, 12, 13, 15, 23, 24, 29, 53, 88, 91, 109, 139, 159, 176, 184, 196
Open Mon–Sat 10–6, Sun 2–6pm
Adm Free, charges apply for some temporary exhibitions
Wheelchair access, adapted toilets, loop system for hard of hearing. Suitable for children aged 8 and over. Allow at least two hours

Lots and lots of pictures. Rooms and rooms of paintings. Over 2,300 canvases covering the last eight centuries of European art – and you don't have to pay a penny to see them (although a donation is always appreciated).

All the great artists are here: Cézanne, Constable, Leonardo da Vinci, Picasso, Turner, Van Gogh...think of a famous painter and it can be pretty much guaranteed that you'll find an example of their work here. The sheer size and scope of the gallery can make the prospect of a visit seem daunting for adults, let alone children.

Did you know?
The gallery's collection was begun in 1824 when the government bought 38 pictures from a wealthy merchant, John Julius Angerstein, for £57,000.

To get the best out of the gallery, it's often a good idea to pick perhaps a dozen or so pictures in advance and then plan your tour accordingly. That way you can turn the experience into a sort of treasure hunt. Fortunately, the wonderful resources of the National allow you to plan your trip in exactly this fashion. Your first port of call should be the Micro Gallery in the Sainsbury Wing at the west end of the Gallery. Here you can explore the gallery's entire collection on touch-screen computer terminals and print out your own personalized tour.

Alternatively, you could try the gallery's own 'Tell Me a Picture' audio guide, designed for ages 7-11, which comes with a map illustrated by Quentin Blake. For very young children, however, it's probably best just to let them wander and point, rather than structuring your trip too rigorously – you'll be surprised at what catches their eye.

The collection is divided into four colour-coded wings: the Sainsbury Wing (blue) shows paintings

Tell me a story: Nelson v Napoleon

By 1805, Napoleon, the Emperor of France, had conquered Spain and Italy and was making plans to invade Britain. To this end, he had assembled a fighting fleet of some 33 fearsomely armoured Spanish and French ships which he stationed at Cadiz Harbour under the command of Admiral Pierre de Villeneuve. In September, Villeneuve was ordered to sail the fleet to Italy to prepare for the invasion. The British, however, had different ideas and instructed the Royal Navy's premiere commander, Admiral Horatio Nelson, to lead his own fleet of 27 warships in an ambush against Napoleons ships. Nelson intercepted the enemy at Cape Trafalgar off the Spanish coast, whereupon he gave orders, using a system of flag signals, for his fleet to divide itself into two squadrons, each of which was to attack half the Franco-Spanish fleet. Nelson, meanwhile, would lead the fighting from aboard his flagship, the *Victory*.

At 11.50am, Nelson signalled his now legendary message: 'England expects that every man will do

his duty', and then ordered the fighting to commence. It soon became clear that the British forces would win the day as they quickly smashed through the enemy lines, their heavy cannon causing widespread devastation. A brief counter attack by the Frenco-Spanish forces had little effect and, by 5pm, the battle was over. Twenty enemy ships had been sunk and 7,000 men, including Villeneuve himself, taken prisoner.

It would have have been a time of great rejoicing among the British ranks had it not been for the fact that, at 4.30pm, Nelson, whilst commanding operations from the deck, had been mortally wounded by an enemy sniper. He died, at least, knowing that victory was assured. His final words, spoken to his second in command, Hardy, were supposedly either 'kismet' (which means fate) or 'kiss me' (which means something else entirely).

Nelson's legacy proved to be a lasting one. Not only did his final naval victory thwart Napoleon's plans but it assured Britain's naval supremacy in Europe for the next hundred years.

from 1260 to 1510; the West Wing (green) paintings from 1510 to 1600; the North Wing (yellow) paintings from 1600 to 1700 and the East Wing (red) paintings from 1700 to 1900.

There's a decent self-service café and a more expensive brasserie, but you're probably best off having lunch just around the corner in the Café in the Crypt (*see* p.62) or bringing your own picnic which can be eaten in the Education Centre's Sandwich Rooms. The Gallery shop is excellent and well worth a visit. In fact, kids often get as much enjoyment (if not more) from the shop as they do from the gallery itself. In particular, they love the scale model of Trafalgar Square that sits just outside the shop. Inside there are lots of good introductory art books as well as a variety of art products including pens, drawing pads, Monet mouse mats, Van Gogh pop-up books, CD-ROMs, videos, slides and a pair of 15th-century shoes based on those lying on the floor in Van Eyck's Arnolfini portrait (*see* above).

The gallery hosts a variety of family events including storytelling sessions and Second Sunday drawing days (when kids aged 4-11 get to take part in a range of artistic endeavours under the tutelage of a professional artist).

The pictures

There are certain pictures in the National that will especially appeal to children. The colour and vibrancy of many of the Renaissance canvases (to be found in the Sainsbury and West Wings) often touch a nerve with kids, and the subjects – St George killing the Dragon, St Sebastian shot full of

arrows, John the Baptist's head on a silver platter – are usually gory enough to impress. Paintings that employ overt forms of visual trickery also often grab children's attention. Here are five paintings they may enjoy.

Hans Holbein

The Ambassadors (West Wing)

Recently restored, this is a wonderfully bright and colourful picture of two very grand 16th-century courtiers. Everything seems quite normal apart from a strange stretched shape at the bottom of the picture. Get your kids to go as close to the wall on the right hand side of the picture as possible and then look back at the picture. By changing the point of view in this fashion, the stretched shape should now have transformed itself into the picture of a skull.

Van Eyck

The Arnolfini portrait (West Wing)

This 15th-century Dutch picture of a couple holding hands seems quite unremarkable on first glance. But if you look closely at the mirror hanging on the wall behind the couple you should be able to see the reflection of the back of the couple

Can you spot?
Hidden among the fruit and flowers of Jan van Os' picture are the following creatures and objects. How many can you find? There are two butterflies; three flies, a snail, a dormouse, a dragonfly, and a bird's nest.

stretching out their hands towards a visitor. The visitor is Van Eyck himself, come to paint the couple's portrait. Van Eyck seems to have been very keen for the viewer to know who painted the picture. The words 'Van Eyck fuit hic, 1434' appear on the wall above the mirror. Roughly translated they mean 'Van Eyck made this, 1434'.

Andrea Mantegna

The Introduction of the Cult of Cybele at Rome (West Wing)

A 15th-century painting designed to look like a sculpture. Mantegna painted this in such a way that, from a distance, it looks like it has been carved out of stone.

Samuel van Hoogstraten

Peepshow (North Wing)

Created in the 17th century, this isn't a conventional painting at all but a wooden box mounted on a plinth. In the side of the box is a peephole. If you look through the hole you'll see what looks like a miniature house filled with what appears to be 3-D furniture. It is, in fact a 2-D painting which cleverly uses perspective to make you think you are seeing things which aren't really there.

Jan van Os

Fruit, Flowers in a Terracotta Vase (East Wing)

This picture, from the late 18th century, is so realistic that it almost looks like a photograph. The trick is in the composition rather than the representation. Although the fruit and flowers in the picture appear quite fresh, in fact they couldn't possibly have all appeared together at the same time as they all ripen at different times of year. The painting was therefore painted over the course of a year, each new fruit and flower being added as it came into season.

National Portrait Gallery

St Martin's Place, WC2
t (020) 7306 0055
www.npg.org.uk
✪ Charing Cross, Leicester Square, Embankment
Bus 3, 6, 9, 11, 12, 13, 15, 23, 24, 29, 53, 88, 91, 109, 139, 159, 176, 184, 196
Open Mon–Sat 10–6, Sun 2–6pm
Adm Free, charges apply for some temporary exhibitions
Wheelchair access and adapted toilets. Suitable for older children (8 and over). Allow at least an hour

> **Can you spot?**
> Young visitors to the National Portrait Gallery will probably be less concerned with artistic merit than with spotting some famous faces.
> See if they can find portraits of the following: Princess Diana, Kate Winslet, David Beckham and assorted Spice Girls.

If history is, as Sir Thomas Carlyle once claimed, merely the 'biographies of great men', then the National Portrait Gallery is its picture album. Over 2,000 portraits of the greatest figures from the last 700 years of British history are on display here. It's best to start at the top in the new Ondaatje wing with the Tudors (look out for the clever picture of Edward VI by William Scrots which requires you to look at it from an acute angle in order to see the perspective) before making your way slowly down via the new Balcony Gallery to the 20th-century works on the ground floor. On the way children will find themselves putting faces to names they had previously only read about in textbooks or heard in history lessons: kings, queens, soldiers, statesmen, scientists, politicians, artists and sculptors, they're all here. Children might enjoy tracking down the picture of Edwin Landseer, portrayed carving the lions that would eventually go on display just outside the gallery on Trafalgar Square. The Gallery has also introduced a Rucksack Tour of the first floor; children are given a rucksack containing activity sheets and puzzles relating to the displays.

Most of the older paintings have been painted in a very traditional, formal style. The more modern works, however, are rendered in a great mish mash of different styles. The pictures have been chosen on the basis of identity rather than ability so the quality of the work varies enormously. The gallery

does house some great pictures by great artists – David Hockney, Lucien Freud and Francis Bacon among them – but it also holds a fair amount of awful ones.

Elsewhere on Trafalgar Square

On the northeast edge of Trafalgar Square stands the church of St Martin-in-the-Fields. Built in 1722, it's the square's oldest building. Today, its church-yard plays host to a rather touristy bric-à-brac market. Inside the church proper, free classical concerts are given every Tuesday lunchtime. Down in the creepy crypt you'll find the London Brass Rubbing Centre – with a selection of over 100 brasses including knights, dragons, griffins and elephants – and an appealingly dungeonesque eaterie, the Café in the Crypt.

London Brass Rubbing Centre

St Martin-in-the-Fields, Trafalgar Square, WC2
t (020) 7930 9306
⊖ Charing Cross, Leicester Square, Embankment
Bus 3, 6, 9, 11, 12, 13, 15, 23, 24, 29, 53, 88, 91, 109, 139, 159, 176, 184, 196
Open Mon–Sat 10–6, Sun 1212 noon–6pm
Adm Anything from £2.50 to £15 depending on how many rubbings you do
No disabled facilities

Royal Academy

Burlington House, Piccadilly, W1
t (020) 7439 7438
www.royalacademy.org.uk
⊖ Green Park, Piccadilly Circus
Bus 9, 14, 19, 22, 38
Open 10–6 daily, Fri till 8.30pm
Adm Depends on the exhibition
Wheelchair access to all areas, wheelchair hire avail-able in advance. Suitable for older children (10 and over). Younger kids may enjoy it but only for short bursts. Allow at least an hour

The most high-brow entertainment the Piccadilly area has to offer. It's not to everyone's taste but children with an artistic bent may well appreciate a visit to the summer exhibition (held every year since 1769) when the Academy displays more than 1500 works of art submitted by members of the public. Perhaps the best thing about the Royal Academy is the variety of its exhibitions. Because it specializes in temporary shows, you are guaran-teed to see something new almost every time you make a visit.

Can you spot?

Eros, London's most popular statue, which stands in the middle of Piccadilly Circus firing 'arrows of love' down the Haymarket. Although everyone calls it Eros, the man who designed it, Sir Alfred Gilbert, insisted that it was in fact meant to be an Angel of Christian Charity and not the God of Love at all. The trouble is, everyone ignored him. Poor old Alfred, he didn't much enjoy making this statue. When he cast it in 1893, he imagined it sitting on top of a cascading fountain. The people who were paying for it, however, refused to cough up causing Alfred to fly into a rage and boycott the opening ceremony.

Piccadilly

Bigheaded Baker

Piccadilly's first inhabitant was a wealthy tailor called Robert Baker who built a mansion on fields here in 1612. Baker's friends thought his wealth and fame had gone to his head and so christened his new house 'Piccadill' meaning 'shirt-cuff' in order to remind him of his humble origins. Today the area is London's neon heart, full of bright lights, traffic and enough video games to last a lifetime.

Trocadero

Piccadilly Circus, WC1
t (0906) 888 1100
www.troc.co.uk
⊖ Piccadilly Circus, Leicester Square
Bus 3, 12, 14, 19, 22, 38
Open Sun–Thu 10am–12 midnight, Fri–Sat 10am–1am
Free
Some wheelchair access. Suitable for ages 9–15. Allow at least two hours

Originally a plush hotel, the Trocadero has been revamped in recent years into a large and very noisy arcade-cum-electronic entertainment centre filled with souvenir shops and fast-food restaurants, not to mention a 7-screen cinema and, its biggest draw, Funland, six floors of the latest computer games.

Funland

t (020) 7439 1914
www.
Open Daily 10am–midnight, Fri and Sat till 1am
Free
Fast food restaurants

It may advertise itself as a giant indoor theme park, but Funland is essentially just a giant amusement arcade with six floors of flashing, beeping video games to explore – shoot-'em-ups, fighting

Can you spot?
The Alpine Clock on top of the Swiss Tourist Office. It springs into life at 6pm everyday when various clockwork figures come out to parade and dance to the accompaniment of bells and chimes.

Question 5
Other than being next to each other, what do Piccadilly Circus, Coventry Street and Leicester Square have in Common?
answer on p.249

games, flight simulators and racing games – interspersed with various 3-D simulator rides as well as a few more traditional attractions such pool tables, putting, dodgems, etc.

Don't be fooled by the free entry signs. Each video game costs at least £1 and each of the seven 3-D rides, £2-3 (there are small savings to be made by buying a combined ticket to several rides).
***Tip** The noise and flashing lights may make it a little overwhelming for very young children. Older children (over-9s and teenagers in particular), however, will love it.*

Leicester Square

Flanked by four giant cinemas, Leicester Square is *the* place in London to catch a film. This is where all the major film premieres are staged and where all the biggest releases get their first runs. Once a

Can you spot?

Engraved on a series of brass plaques in the garden's central cobbled area are the distances in miles from London to all the Commonwealth countries. See who's the quickest to find the distance to the following:

▶ Ottawa in Canada – 3,332 miles
▶ Jamaica – 4,684 miles
▶ Kenya – 4,237 miles

fashionable 19th-century meeting place with a Turkish bath, music and dance halls, the square is today (if we're honest) a bit tacky with its souvenir shops, chain restaurants, portrait painters and buskers. Still, the central garden offers some shade on a hot sunny day and you can buy half price tickets for West End shows at the TKTs booth.

Leicester Square Cinemas

Empire
t (0990) 888 990
www.uci-cinemas.co.uk
Odeon Leicester Square & Odeon West End
t (0870) 505 0007
www.odeon.co.uk
Warner Village West End
t (020) 7437 4343
www.warnervillage.co.uk

WHERE TO EAT

In Leicester Square, it's all sandwich houses and coffee bars – try **Café Fiori** on the corner of Leicester Square and Charing Cross Road – while Piccadilly Circus has little to offer except fast food and an **Aberdeen Steak House**, **t** (020) 7839 1059. There are branches of **McDonald's** at 5 Swiss Court, Leicester Square, 57–60 Haymarket, 69–73 Shaftesbury Avenue and 34–35 The Strand (next to Charing Cross Station). You'll find branches of the bistro chains **Café Flo** – 2 branches at 103 Wardour Street, **t** (020) 7734 0581, ⊖ Piccadilly Circus, and 11 Haymarket, **t** (020) 7734 0581, ⊖ Piccadilly Circus, Charing Cross; **Café Rouge** 15 Frith Street, **t** (020) 7437 4307, ⊖ Leicester Square, Tottenham Court Road; and the Italian pasta houses **Café Pasta** – 2 branches at 182–184 Shaftesbury Avenue, **t** (020) 7379 0198, ⊖ Leicester Square and 15 Greek Street, **t** (020) 7434 2545, ⊖ Leicester Square, Tottenham Court Road; plus **Caffè Uno** 24 Charing Cross Road, **t** (020) 7240 2524, ⊖ Charing Cross, Leicester Square; as well as several branches of **Pizza Express** – 3 branches – at 20 Greek Street, **t** (020) 7734 7430, ⊖ Leicester Square; 6 Upper James Street, Golden Square, **t** (020) 7437 4550, ⊖ Piccadilly Circus, 450 The Strand, **t** 020 7930 8205, ⊖ Charing Cross. *See* **Eat** p.223 for more details on the above restaurant chains.

1 Benihana

37–43 Sackville Street, W1
t (020) 7494 2525
www.benihana.co.uk
Open Wed–Fri 12 noon–3, Mon–Fri 6–11, Sat & Sun 12 noon–11
⊖ Piccadilly Circus, Green Park

Fun, Japanese Teppanyaki restaurant chain for families looking to experiment. Several dishes are specifically designed for children's tastes and kids, for their part, enjoy watching the skilful chefs preparing the food at their tables – Ninja style. High chairs available.

2 Café in the Crypt

St Martin-in-the-Fields, WC2
t (020) 7839 4342
Open Mon–Sat 10–8, Sun 12 noon–8 (hot food 12 noon–3.15 & 5–7.30)
⊖ Charing Cross

Atmospheric subterranean café whose semi-dungeonesque appearance should greatly appeal to youngsters. With a wide selection of hot dishes, snacks and vegetarian choices available, this is a good place to come and warm up with a bowl of hot soup after a hard morning's sightseeing. Half portions are (rather logically) half-price.

3 Fortnum & Mason Fountain Room

181 Piccadilly, W1
t (020) 7734 8040
www.fortnumandmason.co.uk
Open Mon–Sat 7.30–11
Piccadilly Circus

A wonderfully elegant tea room set in the basement of the Queen's grocers. They sell a wide and delicious range of specially made ice creams, sorbets, sundaes and sodas. It's a haven of old-fashioned style and charm, suitable for older children. Once you've finished your ice cream, pop outside to watch the workings of the famous Fortnum & Mason clock.

4 Planet Hollywood

13 Coventry Street, W1
t (020) 7734 6220
www.planet-hollywood.demon.co.uk
Open 11.30–1.30 daily except Sun 11.30–12.30
Leicester Square, Piccadilly Circus

Somewhat beleaguered, this once mighty chain is still hanging in there. Always filled with tourists and noisy beyond measure, it's nonetheless worth a look if you're in the area. Kids like the garish posters and cabinets full of memorabilia (highlights include the cyborg from *Terminator II*, Harrison Ford's whip from *Indiana Jones and the Last Crusade* and Charlie Chaplin's trademark hat and cane). The food is expensive but perfectly reasonable (burgers, ribs etc) and there is a 75-seat preview theatre.

Rainforest Café

20 Shaftesbury Avenue, W1
t (020) 7434 3111
www.therainforestcafé.co.uk
Piccadilly Circus, Leicester Square
Bus 3, 12, 14, 19, 22, 38
Open 12 noon–11 daily, Fri & Sat 12 noon– 12 midnight
Wheelchair access and adapted toilet. Suitable for all ages

A wonderful theme restaurant, particularly popular with young children. As the name suggests, the tables and chairs have been placed in among the trees and foliage of an artificial rainforest. Inhabiting the dense undergrowth are various mechanical animals, including chimps, monkeys, birds and snakes, who come alive every 15 minutes to whoop and chatter following an artificial thunderstorm. Games and face-painting are laid on at weekends. The American-style 'Wild Bunch' menu is straigtforward but tasty, if a little expensive (£7.95).

6 Richoux

172 Piccadilly, W1
t (020) 7493 2204
Open 8.30–5.30
Green Park

Old-fashioned upmarket French coffee shop/tearoom/patisserie serving a variety of cakes, snacks and sandwiches.

7 TGI Friday's

29 Coventry Street, W1
t (020) 7379 6262
www.tgifridays.co.uk
Open 12 noon–12 midnight daily
Piccadilly Circus

An ever-popular choice, this lively Tex-Mex diner can offer high chairs, booster seats, a special kids' menu, free balloons, colouring books and pointy

red and white hats – which children wear with an absurd level of pride.

8 Veeraswamy

99–101 Regent Street, W1
t (020) 7734 1401
www.veeraswamy.com
Open Mon–Sat 12 noon–2.30 & 5.30–11.30, Sun 12.30–3
⊖ Piccadilly Circus

A great child-friendly Indian restaurant (it claims to be the UK's oldest) where you can sit and watch the world go by while your kids demolish mountains of popadoms. Sunday is the restaurant's designated family day when they offer a special children's menu for £7 (made up of lightly spiced Indian dishes plus a few bland children's favourites – fish fingers, burgers, chips etc), and there are crayons, colouring books and goodie bags for the kids to enjoy while they wait for their food. High chairs available.

Chinatown

The pedestrianised Gerrard Street, just north of Leicester Square, along with the adjacent Lisle Street, makes up London's Chinatown district.

It's a fascinating place to go for a meal or just to explore with its decorative lamps and phone boxes made up to look like oriental pagodas. Every Chinese New Year (late January or early February) paper dragons dance down the street as part of a week of traditional celebrations.

9 China, China

3 Gerrard Street, W1
t (020) 7439 7502
⊖ Leicester Square

A good place to grab a quick bowl of noodles in between bouts of sightseeing.

10 Chuen Cheng Ku

17 Wardour Street, W1
t 020 7437 1398
⊖ Leicester Square

Has the longest menu in Chinatown, which can prove a little daunting – just ask for the day's specials, you're unlikely to be disappointed. If you're hoping to impress the waiters with your grasp of Cantonese, try asking for the following: Tsun Guen (mini spring rolls), Pai Gwat (steamed tiny spare ribs) or Har Gau (rice dumplings stuffed with shrimps). It's extremely child-friendly with booster

seats, high chairs and baskets of goodies for good little kiddies.

11 Mr Kong

21 Lisle Street, WC2
t (020) 7437 7341
⊖ Leicester Square

Good, solid Cantonese fare at a price that will not break the budget.

12 New World

1 Gerrard Place, W1
t (020) 7734 0396
⊖ Leicester Square

One of the best places to introduce your children to the joys of Chinese food. On Sundays it's packed with families tucking into bowls of dim sum – (Chinese dumplings, the restaurant's speciality). Try the special child-size mini dim sum.

Covent Garden

Covent Garden is lively and entertaining, but also rather cultured and sophisticated. In other words, children will enjoy themselves and parents won't feel guilty about letting them.

There's lots for kids to do here; they can clamber aboard a vintage bus at the London Transport Museum, dress up at the Theatre Museum or enjoy the ad hoc entertainment provided by the buskers outside in the Piazza. Spend a Saturday morning here and you're bound to encounter at least one impromtu performance from the army of mime artists, fire-eaters, comedians and opera singers that frequent the area. There are also two small markets to rummage around in and various toy and gift shops designed to attract the fancy of children as well as the wallets of their indulgent parents.

Highlights

Somerset House's fountains/ice rink

Alfresco dining in Neal's Yard

Messing around on the buses at London's Transport Museum

Key

Numbers correspond to restaurants in 'Where To Eat' p.75

CHANCERY LANE

HIGH HOLBORN

Holborn

Sir John Soane's Museum

LINCOLN'S INN

WC

FIELDS

GT QUEEN STREET

KINGSWAY

Oasis Sports Centre

SHAFTESBURY AVENUE

ENDELL STREET

DRURY LANE

❽

MONMOUTH STREET

❺

❷

SHELTON STREET

BOW STREET

RUSSELL STREET

ALDWYCH

LONG ACRE

Covent Garden

❻

FLORAL STREET

Covent Garden

WELLINGTON STREET

STRAND

❼

Theatre Museum

GARRICK ST

KING STREET

London's Transport Museum

Temple

❹

St Paul's Church

Somerset House

ST MARTIN'S LANE

WC

BEDFORD ST

MAIDEN LANE

EMBANKMENT

❸

❿

❾

❶

STRAND

The Savoy

VICTORIA

WATERLOO BRIDGE

WC

EMBANKMENT

Cleopatra's Needle

Charing Cross

National Theatre

Embankment

NORTHUMBERLAND AVENUE

WC

300 metres
300 yards

London's Transport Museum

Covent Garden, WC2
t (020) 7379 6344
www.ltmuseum.co.uk
⊖ Covent Garden/Leicester Square
Bus 6, 9, 11, 13, 15, 23, 77A, 91, 176
Open 10–6 daily, except Fri when it opens at 11am
Adm Adults £5.95, children **free**, concs £3.95
Wheelchair access and adapted toilets
Suitable for all ages
Allow at least two hours

This is a great child-friendly museum which neatly combines education (tracing the history of public transport from 1829 to the present day) with activity – there are buttons to push, levers to pull

Did you know? Transport Facts

▶ That in 1900 there were 50,000 horses working on the London Transport network. Everyday, they helped to transport more than 2,000,000 passengers and left behind over 1000 tonnes of dung on London's streets.

▶ That since 1910 over 15 billion passengers have travelled on London's buses. That's 3 times the population of the world.

▶ That Victoria is one of Britain's busiest train stations playing host to over 86,000,000 passengers a year.

▶ That when London's first underground line (the Metropolitan) opened in 1863, the carriages were pulled by steam trains and the passengers rode in open topped wagons. By the end of the journey, the passengers' faces were usually covered in soot and smoke.

▶ That in the late 19th century all motorists were expected to employ someone to walk in front of their car waving a red flag so as to prevent anyone from being run over. The practise was ended in 1896 when the speed limit was raised from 4mph to 20mph – travelling at that speed, the first person the car would run over would presumably be whoever was brave or foolish enough to hold the flag.

and exhibits to clamber over. Housed in a huge iron and glass structure (a flower market from the 1870s to 1974), the museum possesses a wonderful colourful collection of horse-drawn and motorized trams, buses and trolley cars.

There are 15 hands-on Kids' Zones where children can find out about the history of transport on touch screens, take the wheel on a tube or bus simulator or hop aboard the Fun Bus (specifically designed for the under-5s) which sports a see-through engine and soft play area. A roster of costumed actors, playing a variety of transport

Question 6
How many bus stops are there in London?
a) 1,000?
b) 7,000?
c) 17,000?
answer on p.249

characters including a First World War bus cleaner, a Second World War bus conductor and a thirties tram driver, are on hand to offer information and advice. The museum organizes school holiday activities including Easter Egg Hunts, collage workshops and storytelling sessions.

The Impossible Microworld Museum

33–34 Covent Garden **t** (020) 7240 2120
www.theimpossiblemicroworld.com
⊖ Covent Garden/Leicester Square
Open Daily 10–6 (last adm 5.30)
Adm Adults £3.95, children £2.95, under 6s **free**, family £11.95, concs £3.45
Suitable for all ages
Allow at least an hour

Covent Garden's latest attraction and a fitting replacement to the much missed Cabaret Mechanical Theatre, is this collection of impossibly-tiny hand-crafted statues, guaranteed to get the whole family going 'Aah!'. And by tiny, we really mean tiny, the statue's titles should give some idea of the scale involved: *The Tower of London on a Grain of Rice*, *Adam and Eve in the Lead of a Pencil*, *A Polar Bear on a Granule of Sugar*, *Posh 'n' Becks in a Cocktail Stick*, *A Boxing match on a Pin-head*, *Samson inside a Human Hair*, *A Camel in the Eye of Needle*, *Birds Tending a Nest on an Eyelash*, each displayed under a powerful magnifying glass allowing you to pick out the extraordinary miniature detail. These amazing examples of craftsmanship are all the work of Willard Wigan, a native of Birmingham, who suffered from learning disabilities as a child and began his career carving mini cartoons of his teachers as a sort of revenge 'because they made me feel so small'. The carving process, as Mr Wigan describes it, sounds frighteningly intense. He has trained himself to hold his breath for up to three minutes, during which time he stands completely immobile, apart from the hand holding the scalpel. The slightest movement or tremor could cause a wayward cut which is why, during the most crucial moments, he claims to work between heartbeats. Whatever the process, the results are truly astonishing.

Question 7
What were decency boards and where would you find them?
answer on p.249

Theatre Museum

Russell Street, WC2
t (020) 7943 4700
www.theatremuseum.org
⊖ Covent Garden/Leicester Square
Bus 6, 9, 11, 13, 15, 23, 77A, 91, 176
Open Tues–Sat 10–6
Adm Adult £4.50, child & concs £2.50, under-5s **free**
Wheelchair access and adapted toilets
Suitable for all ages
Allow at least an hour

The name of the museum is a little misleading. It's dedicated to all aspects of the performing arts, not just the theatre; so there are displays on ballet, circus, opera, pop music and magic. Its more notable exhibits include John Lennon's black Beatles suit, some of Elton John's outrageous stage costumes and, in the Magic exhibition, the wheelbarrow that legendary tightrope walker Charles Blondin wheeled across Niagara Falls in 1859.

The museum is big on interaction and the price of the ticket includes a make-up demonstration (where your children have the choice of ending up with the face of a tiger or a huge gaping fake scar), a costume workshop and a wonderfully overwrought guided tour by a professional actor.

Tell me a story: Covent Garden

Covent Garden was once part of a great estate owned by the Earls of Beford. Formerly a convent garden (hence the name, the 'n' ceased to be pronounced over time), it came under the ownership of the first Earl during the dissolution of the monasteries in 1552 and was turned into the city's very first square in 1630 by the fourth Earl who instructed his architect, Inigo Jones, to follow the design of the classical Italian piazza.

Initially inhabited by high society, it became home, for much of its existence, to the capital's great wholesale 'fruit 'n' veg' and flower markets. In 1974, however, the markets relocated to Vauxhall and the square underwent a genteel facelift. The market buildings were transformed into al fresco cafés, chic boutiques and stylish museums, while the square's pedestrianized confines were reborn as a sort of semi-bohemian crafts centre. Today, these gently cobbled streets and shopping arcades are perhaps London's closest approximation of European café culture.

Street performers

Some of the capital's most talented and exuberant street performers strut their stuff at Covent Garden. The approach to the tube station is usually occupied by a spray-painted mime artist or two, while on the lower levels of the shopping area, you will often encounter highly skilled classical and jazz musicians belting out tunes with merry abandon. The proximity to the newly refurbished Royal Opera House means you'll also occasionally find a plain-clothes Carmen or two warbling powerfully. Children who've never heard opera in the raw before will be impressed by the sheer volume of noise produced by these sturdy divas.

The main performing space, however, is the Piazza, in front of St Paul's Church where some of London's great physical comedians come to ply their trade. You may even spot a star of the future

wobbling on their unicycle or juggling with fire. This was where comedian Eddie Izzard made his living before he became famous.

On weekends large crowds gather to watch a steady stream of jugglers, mime artists, fire-eaters, unicyclists and escapologists. All the children stream to the front, eager to help out by throwing a juggling club, secure some handcuffs or take part in a seemingly death-defying stunt. The masses on the balcony of the Punch and Judy pub overlooking the Piazza offer constant encouragement (and criticism). Remember, these people are not paid to perform and depend on the generosity of the audience. A £1 coin (around $1.50) is usually considered an appropriate donation.

St Paul's Church

Open Mon 9.30–2.30, Tues–Fri 9.30–4.30 and for services on Sun the entrance is around the corner through the rose garden

Bordering the Covent Garden Piazza, this is one of the few major buildings in London to survive the Great Fire of London in 1666. Its proximity to the theatres of the West End has gained it the nickname of the 'Actors Church'. If you've seen the film *My Fair Lady*, take a look at the front of St Paul's Church, the place where the film's two principal characters, Professor Henry Higgins and the Covent Garden flower-seller Eliza Doolittle, are meant to have first met.

Can you spot?

The French-born Claude Duval was one of 17th-century London's most successful and famous highwaymen, holding up hundreds of stagecoaches during his career. He was particularly renowned for the daring nature of his robberies and the gallantry and charm he displayed toward his female victims – many of whom were said to have fallen in love with him. He was hanged in 1670. See if you can find the floor stone in St Paul's on which is written a four-line poem dedicated to this dandy highwayman. It reads:

*Here lies Du Vall: Reader, if male thou art,
Look to thy purse, if female to thy heart...
Old Tyburn's glory, England's
illustrious thief,
Du Vall, the ladies' joy, Du Vall
the ladies' grief...*

WHERE TO SHOP

Its museums and street performers aside, Covent Garden is known principally for its shopping. It boasts a number of places that will appeal to families including a branch of Hamleys, Peter Rabbit & Friends (a shop dedicated to Beatrix Potter's furry favourites), Bumpsadaisy (a maternity wear shop), a Disney Store, the Covent Garden Candle Shop, The Gadget Shop and Thornton's chocolate makers. Also look out for the London Dolls House Company, on the lower level of the market building, contains an amazing and expensive, collection of miniature houses, each a perfect recreation of period style – from Georgian and Victorian to Art Nouveau and Modern – with stacks of furniture and accessories for the discerning small house buyer.

Benjamin Pollock's Toy Shop

44 Covent Garden Market, WC2
t (020) 7379 7866
www.tao2000.net/pollocks
⊖ Covent Garden/Leicester Square
Bus 6, 9, 11, 13, 15, 23, 77a, 91, 176
Open Mon–Sat 10.30–6, Sun 12 noon–6

This lovely little shop (the sibling of Pollock's Toy Museum, see p.47), full of olde worlde toys and games, is a great place to take the kids in order to show them that not all toys need batteries and joysticks. Here you'll find hand-painted puppets, carved yo-yos, butterfly kites, dragon mobiles, intri-cate paper planes and flying machines powered by ingenious rubber band technology. There are also kaleidoscopes, die-cast soldiers and musical boxes. Pride of place, however, goes to some exquisite replica paper theatre sets, complete with scale scenery and actors. You can buy home assembly kits – suitable for older, more dextrous children.

Apple Market

Open 9–5 daily

This cheerful weekday market occupies part of the old central market building. You'll find a wide variety of craft produce including hand-painted jewellery, knitwear and candles. In particular, look out for Sarah Jane Browne's stall selling some colourful children's clothes.

Jubilee Market

Jubilee Hall
Open 9.30–6 daily

Rebuilt in the 1980s on the site of the old foreign flower market, this deals mainly in tourist fare – Union Jack tea towels and the like. It is, however, a good place to hunt for cheap versions of the latest must-have toys.

Neal Street & Neal's Yard

North of the square towards the tube station and Long Acre lies the real heart of Covent Garden's shopping district. The Kite Store, at 48

Neal Street, sells just about every shape and colour kite imaginable, from super-speedy stunt numbers to novelty kites. Serious comic fanatics should head for Comic Showcase, also on Neal Street (no.76), and, just a couple of roads away, at 34 Floral Street, the Tintin shop, dedicated to the comic adventures of the Belgian boy detective. Dorling Kindersley, who publish a wide range of high-quality children's books, have a dedicated shop on King Street.

For clothes – there's a branch of Baby Gap/Kids Gap on Long Acre or, if you fancy splashing out, you could pick up an item or two of mini-high fashion at Paul Smith for Children on Floral Street. And for that little extra adornment try the Bead Shop at 21a Tower Street (behind Cambridge Circus), full of coloured baubles and necklaces.

You might also like to pay a visit Neal's Yard, a little alternative-lifestyle Utopia between Long Acre and Floral Street, filled with vegetarian restaurants, health food shops, alternative therapy outlets, herbal treatment stores and world music stockists. *See* **Shop** p.235 for more details.

Hamleys
3 The Market, Covent Garden, WC2
t (020) 7240 4646
www.hamleys.com
Open Mon–Wed Fri & Sat 10–7, Thurs 10–8, Sun 12 noon–6pm

Peter Rabbit & Friends
42 The Market, Covent Garden, WC2
t (020) 7497 1777
Open Mon–Sat 10–6

The London Dolls House Company
29 The Market, Covent Garden, WC2
t (020) 7240 8681
www.london-dolls-house.sagenet.co.uk
Open Mon–Sat 10–7, Sun 12 noon–5

The Tintin Shop
34 Floral Street, WC2
t (020) 7836 1131
Open Mon–Sat 10–6, Sun 12 noon–5

AROUND AND ABOUT

Drury Lane & Bow Street

You could pay a visit to the Drury Lane Gardens, a small enclosed open space for the under-5s with various climbing frames and soft rubbery floors. There are several benches where parents can sit and watch their charges – recommended on sunny days. Built in 1877, this was one of London's first public gardens and was constructed, on the recommendation of the public health reformer Edwin Chadwick, on a former burial ground. Bow Street, one of London's most famous streets, is just east of Covent Garden, while nearby is the architectural oddity of Sir John Soane's Museum, home to a bizarre collection of art and curiosities. After a heavy day's sightseeing you could cool off with a dip in the Oasis Sports Centre Pool, at 32 Endell Street, just to the north of Covent Garden, **t** (020) 7831 1804.

Sir John Soane's Museum
12–14 Lincoln's Inn Fields, WC2
t (020) 405 2107
⊖ Holborn
Open Tues–Sat 10–5, until 9pm on first Tues of each month
Free

Situated on Lincoln's Inn Fields, this wonderful museum is made up of three interlinked houses containing some weird architectural features – false walls, catacombs, distorting mirrors etc. The museum received a fresh burst of fame in 2001 as the subject of Turner Prize nominee Isaac Julien's film *Vagabondia 2000* which flaunted the collection's curios and unusual perspectives to full effect It also contains a collection of lively Hogarth cartoons – follow the 'Rake's Progress' from wealthy young ne'er-do-well to the madhouse.

The Strand & Embankment
⊖ Embankment, Charing Cross
Bus 6, 9, 11, 13, 15, 23, 77a, 91, 176

The Strand, one of London's most famous thoroughfares, runs east from Trafalgar Square just to the south of Covent Garden. Here you'll find the world-famous Savoy Hotel with its elegant tea room, the newly restored Somerset House and the Stanley Gibbons stamp emporium – a must for young stamp collectors everywhere. Determined

Did you know?
The world's first postage stamp, the Penny Black, was introduced in 1840. Previously, the cost of sending a letter was born by the recepient rather than the sender. You can see an example of a Penny Black in the well-stocked Stanley Gibbons stamp emporium.

accumulators should also consider paying a visit to the Charing Cross Collectors' Fair, which is held every Saturday morning in the basement of the PriceWaterhouseCoopers car park on Villiers Street behind Charing Cross Station. Here, as well as stamps and first day covers, you'll find hordes of ancient Roman and British coins for sale. Call **t** (01483) 281771 for details.

Until 1860, the great mansions on the Strand's southern side faced on to the Thames. The constant threat of flooding and disease, however (in 1849, over 2,000 people a week were dying of cholera), forced the authorities to construct the Victoria Embankment as a buffer. Today, the Embankment is flanked by a four-lane carriageway and is, in truth, rather gloomy. The area is principally worth visiting in order to take a look at Cleopatra's Needle, a 50ft tall, 1500-year-old Egyptian monument erected here in 1879. There is also an embarkation point for a sightseeing catamaran that will take you east along the river as far as Greenwich.

Somerset House

The Strand, WC2
t (020) 7845 4600
www.somerset-house.org.uk
⊖ Temple, Charing Cross, Embankment, Covent Garden
Open Mon–Sat 10–6, 12 noon–6
Adm Courtauld Gallery: adult £4, child free, concs £2; Gilbert Collection: adult £4, child free, concs £2; joint ticket adult £7; Hermitage Rooms adult £6, child £4
Wheelchair access and adapted toilets

Rather overlooked during the Millennium year, what with all the hoopla surrounding the Dome, the Eye and the Millennium Bridge, the re-opening of Somerset House has, in its way, been more impressive than any of them, particularly for familes. Closed to the public for nearly a century, it is now once again possible to explore one of London's great riverside palaces. The building you see today is in fact an 18th-century construction erected on the site of the original Tudor palace built for the Duke of Somerset and has, over the course of its history, served a variety of functions. It was home to the Navy Board and Inland Revenue and, most famously of all, was for a long time occupied by the Register of Births, Marriages and Deaths. Following a multi-million pound refurbishment, however, its grand wings now provide venues for three outstanding artistic attractions: the Courtauld Gallery, which has a large collection

of Impressionist and post-Impressionist paintings (including Van Gogh's *Bandaged Ear*); the Hermitage Rooms, where Russian imperial treasures from the State Hermitage Museum in St Petersburg are displayed; and the Gilbert Collection of jewellery, silverware and other assorted treasures donated by the late American collector and philanthropist, Arthur Gilbert. Interesting though these are, it's the building itself which is the real attraction with its wonderful river views (particularly from the River Terrace which is linked by a walkway to Waterloo Bridge) and glorious courtyard set with dozens of water jets that have been specially programmed to put on choreographed displays. The New York-style ice rink installed here each Christmas is particularly nice touch.

Refreshment is available at the very grand Admiralty restaurant, the much more relaxed River Terrace Café Bar or the takeaway delicatessen next to the Seaman's Hall. The Courtauld Institute organises various weekend workshops when kids can take part in a range of activities such as 'making a silver goblet' and 'animal safaris'. You can also meet strolling players in the courtyard, take part in tours or simply pick up a free family trail guide at the main desk.

Cleopatra's Needle

Cleopatra's Needle, a 50ft tall, 1500-year-old Egyptian obelisk, is one of London's odder monuments. When first you see it, plonked somewhat haphazardly in the gloomy surrounds of the Victoria Embankment, your immediate thought is 'why couldn't they have found somewhere nicer to put it?'. But, truth be told, it's a wonder they got it here at all. Bequeathed to Britain in 1819, by Mohammad Ali, the Turkish Viceroy of Egypt, it took over 59 years to get to its present site. At first, no one could work out how to move it and then, when an engineer did devise a means of transport using an iron cylindrical pontoon, it very nearly sank. The intended site for the obelisk, near the Houses of Parliament, turned out to be unsuitable because of subsidence forcing the Board of Works, whose responsibility the needle had become, to hurriedly find a new spot for it at the Victoria Embankment. To top it all, the sphinxes sitting at the needle's base are facing the wrong way

Buried beneath the Needle are two time capsules. They contain a picture of Queen Victoria, several newspapers, four Bibles, a railway guide and photographs of the 12 prettiest girls in Britain at the time.

Stanley Gibbons

399 The Strand, WC2
t (020) 7836 8444
www.stanleygibbons.com
Open Mon–Fri 8.30–6, Sat 9.30–5.30

Boat trips
Catamaran Cruisers

Embankment Pier, Victoria Embankment
t (020) 7987 1185
Times April–Oct cruises depart every half hour between 10.30–4, Nov–Mar cruises depart every 45 minutes between 10.30–3

WHERE TO EAT

There are few more pleasant places in London to sit watching the world go by than Covent Garden, and if you can do it while tucking into a tasty snack, all the better. Try the **Bar Creperie**, 21 South Row, or the **Market Café**, which can offer ringside seats for the daily entertainment on the piazza. For something a little more substantial, however, you'll have to head into the surrounding streets.

On Saturday and Sunday lunchtimes, you could do worse than **Pizza Express** at 9–12 Bow Street, WC2, **t** (020) 7240 3443 ⊖ Covent Garden or at 80–81 St Martins Lane, WC2 **t** (020) 7836 800 ⊖ Covent Garden. From the same stable is **Café Pasta**, 2 Garrick Street, WC2, **t** (020) 7497 2779. ⊖ Leicester Square, Covent Garden. Other staples in the area include **Café Rouge**, 34 Wellington Street, WC2, **t** (020) 7836 0998 ⊖ Covent Garden; **Caffè Uno**, 37 St Martin's Lane, WC2, **t** (020) 7836 5837 ⊖ Leicester Square. There's also a branch of **McDonald's** at 68–69 St Martin's Lane. *See* **Eat** p.223 for more details on the above restaurant chains.

1 Smollensky's

105 The Strand, **t** (020) 7497 2101
www.smollenskys.co.uk

This is the restaurant that started the whole craze for putting on children's entertainment at weekends – kids can have their faces painted, watch a Punch and Judy show, take part in magic tricks and eat something from the American-style kids' menu. Parents meanwhile will appreciate the tinkling piano music and succulent grill steaks and fish specials. Open 12 noon–12 midnight daily, children's entertainment on Sat & Sun afternoons.

2 Belgo Centraal

50 Earlham Street, WC2
t (020) 7813 2233
www.belgo-restaurants.com
Open Mon–Thu 12 noon–11.30, Fri–Sat 12 noon–12 midnight, Sun 12 noon–10.30
⊖ Covent Garden

Kids eat for free, funky unisex toilets

While adults try some Belgian specialities such as Moules Marinières (mussels with celery and onion) and Wild Boar sandwiches (they'll put hairs on your chest) kids can tuck into the restaurant's more kiddy-friendly fare (fish fingers, chicken nuggets etc) from the colour-in 'Mini-Belgo' menu. Be warned, the restaurant is very trendy and, as a result can get pretty busy, especially at weekends.

3 Brown's

82–84 St Martin's Lane, WC2
t (020) 7497 5050
Open 12 noon–12 midnight daily
⊖ Leicester Square, Covent Garden

Large branch of this well-to-do (but eternally family-friendly) brasserie chain. Children get their own menu and crayons can be requested. The restaurant occasionaly runs deals whereby under 12s get to eat for free if accompanied by an adult. Be warned, at other times it can be a bit pricey.

4 Calabash

Africa Centre, 8 King Street, WC2
t (020) 7836 1936
Open Mon–Fri 12.30–3 & 6–11
⊖ Covent Garden

Situated in the Africa Centre's basement, this provides a welcome alternative to the seemingly ubiquitous American-style menu. It specialises, as you might expect, in African dishes such as cous cous, groundnut stew and Yassa (grilled chicken cooked in a lemon sauce). If your kids are at all adventurous (and some, I'm told, are) they'll love this. You can get reduced price children's portions.

5 Food For Thought

31 Neal Street, WC2 **t** (020) 7836 0239
⊖ Covent Garden
Open Mon–Sat noon–8.30, Sun noon–5

Cheap and friendly vegetarian café serving quiches, salads, soups etc. It can get a little crowded so turn up for an early lunch to be sure of a seat.

6 Maxwell's

8/9 James Street, WC2
t (020) 7836 0303
Open Mon–Sat 10am–12 midnight, Sun 10am–11.30pm
⊖ Covent Garden

The children's menu is full of games and puzzles; there are join-the-dots, pictures to colour in and word searches. Each week a prize is given for the menu that's been completed in the most imaginative way. It serves lots of kids' favourites including waffles, burgers and hot dogs, as well as a few tasty surprises of its own – Mega Chocolate Madness Cake and deep-fried ice cream. The pavement seating outside provides good views of the musicians and 'robot' men who busk this patch. Do be aware that the restaurant is rather less family-friendly during the evening when it fills up with groups of young revellers.

7 Rez's

17–21 Tavistock Street, WC2
t (020) 7379 9991
⊖ Covent Garden
Open Daily 12 noon–4 and 5–11.45 (till 10.45 Sun)

Fantastic pizza and pasta dishes. Under-10s eat for free if accompanied by an adult (1 adult per child). You can sit outside in the summer.

8 Rock and Sole Plaice

47 Endell Street, WC2
t (020) 7836 3785
Open 11.30am–10.30pm daily
⊖ Covent Garden

The oldest fish and chip shop in the capital (it opened way back in 1871) and still one of the best serving large portions of battered fish and big fat chunky chips.

9 TGI Friday's

6 Bedford Street, WC2
t (020) 7379 0585
www.tgifridays.co.uk
Open 12 noon–12 midnight daily
⊖ Covent Garden, Leicester Square

An ever-popular choice, this lively Tex-Mex diner can offer high chairs, booster seats, a special kids' menu, free balloons, colouring books and pointy red and white hats – which children wear with an absurd level of pride.

10 Marquis of Granby

51 Chandos Place
t (020) 7836 7657
⊖ Covent Garden, Embankment, Leicester Square, Charing Cross
Open Mon-Sat 11-11, Sun 12 noon-10.30

This appealing slice of Victoriana features an upstairs dining room where kids can tuck into half-portions of wholesome cottage pie, fishcakes or even a traditional Sunday roast. Food from 12 noon-5pm daily. Kids welcome to 7pm.

Buckingham Palace

This is picture postcard London at its finest – an elegant tree-lined boulevard leading down to the magnificent regal architecture of Buckingham Palace where, as every schoolchild knows, the Queen lives and where you can take a guided tour in summer. Afterwards, why not have a picnic and run around in one of the two great parks flanking the palace before heading down to Horse Guards to see the Queen's soldiers parading up and down, kitted out in their chocolate-box uniform of red tunic, breastplate and sword.

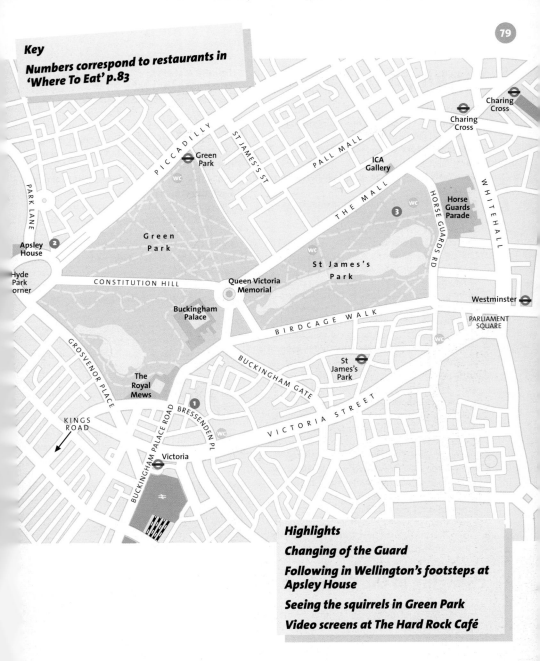

Key

Numbers correspond to restaurants in 'Where To Eat' p.83

Charing Cross

Charing Cross

PICCADILLY

Green Park

ST JAMES'S ST

PALL MALL

ICA Gallery

WHITEHALL

PARK LANE

Green Park

THE MALL

Horse Guards Parade

HORSE GUARDS RD

Apsley House

WC

WC

St James's Park

Hyde Park Corner

CONSTITUTION HILL

Queen Victoria Memorial

Westminster

PARLIAMENT SQUARE

Buckingham Palace

BIRDCAGE WALK

WC

GROSVENOR PLACE

The Royal Mews

BUCKINGHAM GATE

St James's Park

KINGS ROAD

BUCKINGHAM PALACE ROAD

BRESSENDEN PL

VICTORIA STREET

WC

Victoria

Highlights

Changing of the Guard

Following in Wellington's footsteps at Apsley House

Seeing the squirrels in Green Park

Video screens at The Hard Rock Café

Buckingham Palace

St James's Park, SW1
t (020) 7930 4832; booking line (020) 7799 2331
www.royal.gov.uk
St James's Park, Green Park, Victoria
Bus 1, 16, 24, 52, 73
Open Early Aug–Sep 9.30–5.30 daily (last admission 4.15pm)
Adm Adult £11, child (under 17) £5.50, under-5s **free**,
Wheelchair access
Suitable for older children (10 and over)
The tour lasts 45-mins

It's all change at the palace. Previously, the very private London residence of the Royal Family, the great 19th-century palace has, since 1993, been opening its doors to the public for two months each summer. Or, at least, some of its doors; in fact the official guided tour takes in just 18 of a possible 600 rooms (plus a small section of the gardens). These include the Grand Hall, the Throne Room, the State Dining Room, the Music Room, the Royal Picture gallery and the Silk Tapestry Room. All are quite splendid in a formal, rather haughty sort of way, although the Throne Room is a bit of a disappointment as it doesn't even contain a throne, just two pink and yellow chairs marked EIIR (Elizabeth Regina) and P (Philip). To be honest, the palace will proabably prove a little dull for most children. Many of the more interesting areas are (frustratingly) roped off and the rarefied 'don't touch' atmosphere is a little restricting, not to say annoying. If it's just a little pomp and ceremony you're after, you would be better off watching the Changing of the Guard from the railings outside.

Remember, if the Union Flag is raised the Queen is at home; if it's lowered, she's out.

Changing of the Guard

t (020) 7930 4832
St James's Park, Green Park, Victoria
Bus 1, 16, 24, 52, 73
Times The ceremony takes place every morning between April and August at 11.27 sharp and on alternate days between September and March at the same time
Free
Suitable for all ages
The ceremony lasts over an hour

This daily costume drama has become a veritable symbol of Britishness attracting hundreds of tourists every day and yet, it has to be said, it's just a teensy bit dull. To begin with it'll probably capture your interest – the rows of bearskinned, red-coated soldiers, the barked orders, the military band, the complex, regulated marching patterns but, after an hour of the stuff, you could be forgiven for wishing that they'd get to the point (which, in case you're wondering, is to replace the 40 men guarding Buckingham Palace with another contin-

gent from Wellington Barracks). Nonetheless, it's extremely popular and the views from outside Buckingham Palace can quickly become obscured. Even perched on your shoulders, kids may have trouble seeing. Your best bet for a glimpse of the marching soldiers is to take up one of the alternative vantage points at St James's or Birdcage Walk.

Horse Guards

London's own toy soldiers, the Horse Guards, are perhaps the most photographed military personel in the world. Sitting astride their horses in full dress uniform of red tunic, breastplate and sword, it's an image that has graced a million postcards. The stillness of the soldiers – both horse and man are trained not to move and to look straight ahead – fascinates children, who will try hard to pull the funniest face and break the soliders' concentration. At 11am every summer morning you can see them move as they march to Buckingham Palace for the changing of the Guard. They also take part in a great military show in front of the Queen in early June known as the Trooping the Colour. *See* **London's year** p.22.

The Royal Mews

Buckingham Palace Road, SW1
t (020) 7839 1377, recorded info t (020) 7733 2331
www.royal.gov.uk
⊖ St James's Park, Green Park, Victoria
Bus 1, 16, 24, 52, 73

> ### Can you spot?
> A famous London monument. It's fairly hard to miss. It's 124ft tall and supports a statue of George III's son Frederick, the Commander-in-Chief of the British forces during the Napoleonic wars or, as he's more famously known, the Grand Old Duke of York – yes, that Grand Old Duke of York.

Open Aug–Sep Mon–Thurs 10–4.30 (last admission 4pm), Oct–July Tues–Thurs 12 noon–4pm (last admission 3.30pm)
Adm Adult £4, child (under 18) £2, concs £3
Call in advance for disabled access. Suitable for ages seven and up. Allow at least an hour

These are the stables where the horses that work for the Royal Family are kept. As you would expect, the stalls themselves are rather magnificent, with tiled walls and gleaming horse brasses. You can touch and pet the horses and admire the beautiful gold coach used for coronations – it's so heavy, it takes eight horses to pull it!

The Mall

The capital's most majestic avenue was built in the early 20th century as a memorial to Queen Victoria. It runs from Trafalgar Square to Buckingham Palace. Note the Victoria memorial in front of the Palace gates. The views from Admiralty Arch at the Trafalgar end, down along the beautiful tree-lined sweep, are particularly impressive.

Question 8
How did Birdcage Walk, which borders St James's Park to the south, get its name?
answer on p.249

Double indemnity

In 1842, as Queen Victoria rode through crowds lining the Mall with her husband, Prince Albert, by her side, a man stepped forward out of the crowd and attempted to fire a shot at the Queen. Luckily for Victoria, the gun misfired. The police were unable to catch the culprit so the incident was dropped. The very next day, however, the same thing happened again, except this time the gun did go off... Luckily for Victoria the bullet was a blank and caused no damage. The gunman, a John Francis, was arrested and sentenced to death, but was then granted a reprieve before execution.

ICA Gallery

The Mall, SW1
t (020) 7930 3647
www.ica.org.uk
⊖ Picadilly Circus, Charing Cross
Bus 2, 8, 9, 14, 16, 19, 22, 36, 38, 52, 73, 82
Open Galleries 12 noon-7.30
Adm Membership Mon-Fri Adult £1.50, concs £1, Sat, Sun Adult £2.50, concs £1.50

The Institute for Contemporary Arts is generally more concerned with presenting arthouse films than entertaining families, but come summer there's plenty for 11-16 year olds to do. The ICA's Summer University offers fortnightly courses in web design, movie-making and computer game creation. Half-term workshops in drawing and sculpture are also organised and there's a series of primary school activities covering dance, animation and art history in the pipeline. The shop is good for arty bits and bobs, including original jewellery designs and gifts made by local artists.

Apsley House: The Wellington Museum

Hyde Park Corner, Piccadilly, W1
t (020) 7499 5676
www.apsleyhouse.org.uk
⊖ Hyde Park Corner
Bus 2, 8. 9, 10, 14, 16, 19, 22, 36, 38. 52, 73, 74, 82, 137
Open Tue-Sun 11–5 , closed Mon
Adm Adult £4.50, under-18s **free**
Free entry on Waterloo Day (18th June). Sound guides, access via steps to house and lift.

Home of the first Duke of Wellington, and still the family's London residence, Apsley House or No.1 London, was built by Robert Adam between 1771-78.

Ten rooms have been lovingly restored under the auspices of the Victoria and Albert Museum. The collection, assembled by the Duke following his triumphant return from the Battle of Waterloo, includes paintings by Goya, Velaquez, Van Dyck, Landseer and Rubens, as well as medals and

memorabilia. Specific sound guides and trails for children are available throughout the year and there are special family-friendly activities organized for Museums and Galleries Month in May, on Waterloo Day in June and at Christmas.

Green Park

Piccadilly W1 & The Mall, SW1
t (020) 7930 1793
www.open.gov.uk/rp
⊖ Green Park
Bus 2, 8, 9, 14, 16, 19, 22, 36, 38, 52, 73, 82
Open Dawn till dusk, daily
Free

The most basic of London's Royal parks. The name says it all – this is a green park, with lots of lush grass and trees, but not much else: no pond, no playground, not even any statues. Nonetheless, it's a lovely serene place and very popular with London's children. Every spring, for a few weeks, it becomes a Yellow and Green Park when hordes of daffodils pop up.

St James's Park

The Mall, SW1
t (020) 7930 1793
www.open.gov.uk/rp
⊖ St James's Park
Bus 3, 11, 12, 24, 53, 77A, 88, 109, 211
Open Dawn till dusk, daily
Free

A must for all bird-lovers. In the 17th century, the park held several aviaries (hence the name of the road that runs alongside the park, Birdcage Walk) and today is home to one of London's finest wildfowl ponds, a great stretch of water where you can find more than 20 species of bird including ducks, geese and even pelicans (housed in a special enclosure). There's also a playground with a sandpit and a teashop. If your kids have seen the film *One Hundred and One Dalmatians* (the live action version, not the cartoon), they may recognize certain parts of the park – it was the scene of the bicycle chase where poor old Pongo gets thrown into the lake. See if you can spot the black swans who nest on the pond's central island?

There are branches of **McDonald's** at 155 Victoria Street and in the Victoria Place Shopping Centre in Victoria station. There's also a branch of **Ask Pizza** 160–162 Victoria Street, SW1, t (020) 7630 8228 ⊖ Victoria, or **Pizza Express** at 154 Victoria Street, SW1, t (020) 7828 1477 ⊖ Victoria and at 152 King's Road, t 020 7351 5031, ⊖ Sloane Square; 352a King's Road, t 020 9352 9790, ⊖ Sloane Square. Plus there's a **Café Rouge** at 390 King's Road, t (020) 7352 2226, ⊖ Sloane Square. See **Eat** p.223 for more details on the above restaurant chains.

1 Marché Mövenpick

Portland House, Bressenden Place, SW1
t (020) 7630 1733
Open Mon–Fri 7.30am–11pm, Sat 9am–11pm, Sun 9am–9pm
⊖/≩ Victoria

Health-conscious fast-food from Switzerland. The decor is guaranteed to wow the youngsters with a bar in the shape of a sailing ship and sharks' heads peering out of the walls. They will probably also revel in the interactive nature of the restaurant. You are given a card when you enter which you must get stamped as you collect the various parts of your meal. High chairs and kids' menu available.

2 Hard Rock Café

150 Old Park Lane, W1 t (020) 7629 0382
www.hardrock.com
⊖ Hyde Park Corner
Open Daily 11.30am-12.30am

Younger kids can enjoy the colour-in Lil' rocker menu featuring macaroni cheese or fried chicken, as well as the staple burger and chips. Their older siblings will love the videos and spotting the jackets of surprisingly diminutive rock stars. Pop across the road to the shop afterwards and be sure to go downstairs to the **Vault** for an impromptu tour of the curious bits and bobs left behind on the road to eternal stardom. Bo Diddley's home-made guitar, John Lennon's military jacket and Buddy Holly's trademark specs are among the highlights.

3 Cake House Café

St James's Park, SW1
t (020) 7930 1793
www.open.gov.uk/rp
⊖ St James's Park
Bus 3, 11, 12, 24, 53, 77A, 88, 109, 211

Currently being refurbished, but hot snacks are available. There also a refreshment kiosk near the children's playground.

Around and about

Benihana
77 King's Road, SW3
t (020) 7376 7799,
www.benihana.co.uk
open 12 noon–2.30 & 6–10 (till 11pm Fri–Sat, till 9.30pm Sun)
⊖ Sloane Square;

Fun Japanese restaurant for families looking to experiment. Several dishes are specifically designed for children's tastes and kids, for their part, enjoy watching the skilful chefs cook the food at the table – Ninja style. High chairs available.

Big Easy
332–4 King's Road, SW3
t (020) 7352 4071
⊖ Sloane Square
Open Mon–Sat 12 noon–11.30pm, Sun 12 noon–11

If your kids like seafood, then you've come to the right place. This excellent Louisiana-style diner specializes in huge plates of prawns, crabs and lobster (they also do burgers and ribs). Children under eight can eat for free if accompanied by an adult (1 adult per child; second child £3.95). Crayons and high chairs available on request.

Chelsea Kitchen
98 King's Road, SW3
t (020) 7589 1330
Open Mon–Sat 8am–11.30pm, Sun 9am–11.30pm
⊖ Sloane Square

Good for a quick pit-stop to pick up some of this old-fashioned café's wide range of sandwiches, salads and pasta dishes.

Ed's Easy Diner
362 King's Road, SW3
t (020) 732 1956
Open Sun–Thu 11.30am–12 midnight, Fri–Sat 11.30am–1am
⊖ Sloane Square

It's a bit noisy and in your face but the burgers and chips in this mock 1950s' diner are good and they have a very reasonably priced kids' menu. High chairs available.

The Jam (Buona Siena)
289a King's Road, SW3
t (020) 7352 8827
Open Tues–Fri 12 noon–3pm & 6–11, Sat & Sun 12 noon–1pm
⊖ Sloane Square

A restaurant that also doubles as a climbing frame. The tables are tiered like bunkbeds and the top level can only be reached by use of a ladder. Kids love climbing up to their table and will find any excuse to climb down and clamber back up again. Children's portions available but there are no high chairs.

Cadogan Arms
298 King's Road (020 7352 1645)
⊖ Sloane Square
Open Food from 11am-11pm Mon-Sat, 12 noon-10.30pm Sun. Kids welcome to 8pm.
Bus 11,19, 22

How could we fail to recommend this namesake establishment? Sadly we can claim no link with this traditional King's Road local complete with roaring fires and cosy nooks, but we can at least vouch for its child-friendly atmosphere and affordable child-sized portions of burgers, chicken or sausage and chips.

Westminster

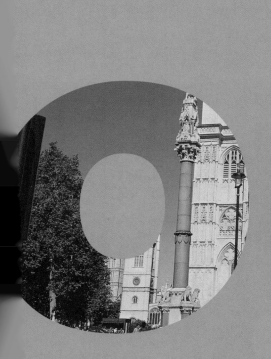
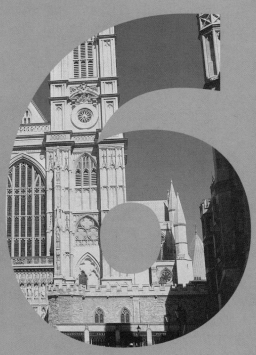

Westminster, the nation's political heartland, is likely to be of most interest to older children, those with some knowledge and understanding of history, rather than youngsters and toddlers who, once they've finished pointing excitedly at the big clock, will quickly grow bored. Remember, a tour of this area can easily be combined with a trip to Trafalgar Square, or across the river to the South Bank.

You could describe Westminster as the very epicentre of Englishness, home of Big Ben, the world's most famous big clock, whose bongs are relaid around the country at midnight every New Year's Eve. Adjoining it are the Houses of Parliament where the great and good of the country come to thrash out the issues of the day while, across Parliament Square, is the 900-year-old Westminster Abbey where the coronation of all British monarchs takes place.

Take a quick walk along Parliament Street and you'll find Downing Street, where the Prime Minister lives, the Cenotaph, the country's most important war memorial, and the Cabinet War Rooms, where Britain's Second World War campaign was formulated. It's all very serious stuff and yet, at the same time, also quite touristy. Should you decide to pay the area a visit, you'll no doubt be accompanied on your travels by hordes of camera-wielding tourists furiously clicking at everything in sight.

Remember, the newly revamped Tate Britain, one of the nation's pre-eminent art galleries and home of the Turner Prize, is just a short walk south along the river.

Highlights

Clock-watching with Big Ben

Getting arty at the Tate Britain

Having a dead good time amongst the tombs in Westminster Abbey

Key

Numbers correspond to restaurants in 'Where To Eat' p.92

THE SIGHTS

Westminster Abbey

Broad Sanctuary, SW1
t (020) 7222 5152, tours **t** (020) 7222 7110
www.westminster-abbey.org
⊖ Westminster, St James's Park
Bus 3, 11, 12, 24, 53, 88, 109, 159, X53, 211
Open Mon–Fri 9–4.45, Sat 9–2.45
Adm Adult £6, child £3, concs £3
Wheelchair access, audio guides are available
Suitable for ages six and up
Allow at least an hour

Kids are not always interested in churches, even ones as famous and important as this, and you may feel disinclined to subject them to the Abbey, whatever its history or however lovely the stained glass. But, then, it all depends on how you approach it. Left to their own devices your kids will probably have seen enough here in three minutes flat, but point out the fact that the stones they are touching and, often as not, walking over conceal dead bodies, regale them with a few choice stories of how an assortment of the assembled met their end (see below) and they'll find the whole experience much more interesting.

The Abbey could be described, if you were feeling a little disrespectful, as a great indoor graveyard filled with the remains, relics and reminders of the last thousand years of British history. You enter through Statesmen's Aisle, which features memorials to three of the country's most famous past

prime ministers, Gladstone, Disraeli and Palmerston. Continue on your travels around the Abbey and you'll find the tombs of Elizabeth I and Mary, Queen of Scots whom she beheaded, and what is thought to be the last resting place of the two young princes, Edward V and his brother Richard, who were supposedly murdered by their uncle (later Richard III) in the Tower of London in 1483. Explore still further and you'll find the centre-piece of the Abbey – the shrine of St Edward. Or, at least, you will if you can come to terms with the Abbey's rather higgledy-piggledy layout. The clutter, however, just makes it more interesting for kids who happily wend their way through, under and around the assorted statues, stones, memorials and shrines. See if they can find Poets' Corner where Geoffrey Chaucer was buried in 1400. Ever since, some of the country's most famous poets and writers have ended up here including Dryden, Samuel Johnson, Sheridan, Browning and Tennyson. Others, such as Shakespeare, Shelley and Keats, are memorialized without actually being interred here.

The Abbey is a very beautiful place with great vaulted ceilings and richly coloured stained glass windows, but the best thing about it is that it manages both to engage the macabre interest of children while, at the same time, offering a more serene, reflective air which adults will appreciate. In recent decades, views of the Abbey have been beamed around the world at times of great national significance. Two of the most watched TV

Tell me a story: Emperors' new clothes

Supertunica and Imperial Mantle may sound like good titles for a couple of glam-rock songs but actually they are the names given to the Royal Coronation Robes and, when worn together, the outfit weighs in at a hefty 23lbs. The Imperial Mantle was made for the coronation of George IV, whose overall ensemble was so heavy -including a specially-made crown bearing 12, 314 diamonds and 204 pearls - that he very nearly fainted and had to be revived with smelling salts. Throughout the five-hour ceremony his estranged wife Queen Caroline hammered angrily on the doors of the Abbey in an attempt to gain admittance. She was refused, however, much to the displeasure of the crowd assembled outside, most of whom despised the flashy 'show-off' George.

Can you spot?
See if you can find statues in Parliament Square of three of Britain's most famous Prime Ministers: Palmerston, Disraeli and Winston Churchill. How is Churchill's statue different to the others? It is, how shall we put it, cleaner than the other statues. This is because it's heated from the inside to stop pigeon droppings from sticking.

This is where the British government goes about its daily business, where the ruling party of the day debates policy with the opposition and where the lords and ladies of the land have, for centuries, come to comment on legislation. As you stand on Westminster Bridge or Parliament Square looking up at the beautiful neo-Gothic building, you'll probably find yourself wondering what it's like inside, supposing, rightly, that it's blessed with an equally fabulous interior. If you want to watch a debate in the House of Commons, you'll have to queue up (probably for several hours) at the St Stephen's entrance and will be seated on a first come, first served basis. The most popular day is Wednesday when Prime Minister's Question Time takes place and the place is full. Visitors from other countries are often amazed at just how uncivilized these debates can be. Despite a weird level of formality requiring that politicians refer to each other as the 'honourable member' or 'friend' rather than use their actual names, the debates themselves often descend into bun fights with both sides hurling thinly veiled insults at one another. These can be great fun to watch for older children. Pick the wrong day, however, and they can also be interminably dull.

Big Ben

The most famous part of the Houses of Parliament is Big Ben, the great clock tower, which was completed in 1859. The clock was named after a Mr Benjamin Hill, the rather portly commissioner of works at the time. Big Ben is actually the name of the bell rather than the tower – its distinctive sound is due to a crack that appeared during its installation.

Cabinet War Rooms

King Charles Street, SW1
t (020) 7930 6961
www.iwm.org.uk
⊖ Westminster, St James's Park

events in history, the coronation of Elizabeth II and the funeral of Princess Diana, took place here, when the wonderful interior became the image of England for the whole world. There's a café and a souvenir shop in the cloisters, the area where the monks who resided in the Abbey until the middle of the 16th century lived and worked.

Houses of Parliament

Parliament Square, SW1
t (020) 7219 4272
⊖ Westminster
Bus 3, 11, 12, 24, 53, 88, 109, 159, X53, 211
Open To watch a debate from the House of Commons Visitors' Gallery, you must queue from 2.30pm onwards Mon-Wed, from 11.30am Thu and from 9.30am Fri. Guided tours of the building itself can only be taken during the summer recess from July-Sep and must be booked in advance.
Adm Free, tours £3.50, under-2s **free**
Wheelchair access
Suitable for ages 12 and up

Its official name is the Palace of Westminster. Politicians refer to it simply as 'the House'. Whatever you call it, it is one of the unmistakable sights of London. Most of the huge building (it covers an eight-acre site and contains two miles of corridors) dates from the 1830s, the original medieval building having burned down in a fire in 1834, although parts of the interior, including Westminster Hall, were built at the end of the 11th century.

wonderfully evocative, their very smallness (Churchill's office was a converted broom cupboard) giving some sense of the desperate pressure which must have been felt by the men and women who worked here. Each individual detail, so ordinary in itself, becomes, in this context, charged with significance: coloured drawing pins still stuck into faded maps of Europe, papers laid out in the Cabinet Room as if for an imminent briefing and the desk in Churchill's bedroom from where he made his legendary radio broadcasts. For the full effect, make use of the free self-paced audio guides on which you can hear several of Churchill's rousing speeches accompanied by period music.

Tate Britain

Millbank, SW1
t (020) 7887 8008
www.tate.org.uk
⊖ Pimlico, Vauxhall ⇌ Vauxhall
Bus 2, 3, 36, 77A, 88, 159, 185, 507, C10
Open 10–5.50 daily
Free, charges apply for some temporary exhibitions
Lift, wheelchair access via the new entrance in Atterbury Street, disabled parking spaces in the Clore car park can be booked on **t** *(020) 7887 8813/4*
Suitable for ages six and over
Allow at least an hour

The Tate was originally intended as a showcase for British art when it opened in 1897. Unfortunately, over the next century, it built up such a large collection of international works that the amount of space being given over to British art was continually being reduced and, indeed, much of the Tate's collection sat permanently locked away in dark vaults. Something needed to be done. That something took the shape of a disused power station on Bankside which was opened in 2000 as Tate Modern (*see* p.107). The old Tate, meanwhile, was reborn as Tate Britain (*see* p.90), a gallery, once again, devoted solely to British art.

As with its younger sibling, Tate Britain now organizes its collection according to themes rather than chronologically, so you'll find sections named 'Literature and Fantasy' with works by William Blake, Sir John Everett Millais and John William Waterhouse (including his famous *Lady of Shallot* 'Public and Private', which seeks to explore visions of the city; 'Home and Abroad' with works by war

Bus 3, 11, 12, 24, 53, 88, 109, 159, X53, 211
Open April–Sep 9.30–6, Oct–Mar 10–6
Adm Adult £5.40, child **free**, concs £3.90, half-price entry for disabled visitors
Free audio guide available, wheelchair access, lift to museum ground floor, adapted toilets
Suitable for ages six and over
Allow at least an hour

This is a great place to take children provided they at least have some knowledge of the Second World War. These 21 cramped, low-ceilinged rooms 17ft underground were, for the last few years of the conflict, the nerve centre of the British war effort, the headquarters where Winston Churchill and his ministers made decisions which changed the course of history. To visit these rooms today is to take a step back into the past; they have remained untouched since the final days of the war. They are

Can you spot?
The big beige office building with green windows opposite the Tate on the other side of the river. This is the HQ of MI6, Britain's secret service. Until recently, the British government denied that this service existed, which meant that, officially, the building also didn't exist – and neither did the people who worked in it.

artists such as Paul Nash and John Singer Sargent
and 'Artists and Models' which focuses on self-
portraits and nudes with an entire room given over
to the colourful work of David Hockney.

Just as before, there are still plenty of things for
children to do at the Tate. The curators have long
understood that children can quickly grow bored
staring at painting after painting, and so provide
plenty of activities to keep them amused. The ever-
popular Art Trolley is wheeled out on Sundays
between 12 noon-5 and every day during the holidays from 2-5. There's no need to book. Designed
for adults and children to work on together, all you
have to do is turn up to choose from a range of
games and activities related to the many artworks
on display. Then, suitably armed with crayons, pens,
pencils and what-not, you can head off into the
museum – budding Picassos will love it.
Alternatively, pick up one of the new Tate Trails
from the information desk. These offer a number of
imaginative drawing and looking activities which
provide kids with a fun way to navigate the
museum on their own.

Look out for the transparent collection box just
inside the main entrance. Although it wasn't
created by an artist, it has become an attraction in
its own right crammed with colurful notes of
varying denominations from different nations. You
may even be tempted to add to it.

AROUND AND ABOUT

Banqueting House
Whitehall, SW1
t (020) 7930 4179
www.hrp.org.uk
⊖ Westminster, Charing Cross
Bus 3, 6, 9, 11, 12, 13, 15, 23, 24, 29, 53, 88, 91, 109, 139,
159, 176, 184, 196
Open Mon–Sat 10–5
Adm Adult £3.80, child £2.30, concs £3
Suitable for ages 10 and up
Allow at least half an hour

Next to Horse Guards, this grand old building will be
of more interest to parents than children with its
magnificent ceiling paintings by Rubens. It does,
however, hide one particular secret which may get
the young ones pricking up their ears. Charles II was
beheaded here, just outside the great dining hall
in 1649 following his army's defeat by the forces
of parliament.

Downing Street
You can catch a glimpse of No.10, the house
where the Prime Minister lives, through a pair of
great black iron railings at the end of the road.
Unfortunately, you are no longer allowed to go and
have a close-up look. Britain's official centre of
power is certainly not as grand as the White House
in Washington or the Elysée Palace in Paris. But
then, the man who built it, George Downing, never
meant it to be anything other than a simple residential house. When Robert Walpole moved here in
the mid-18th century (once the preceding tenant, a
Mr Chicken, had moved out) he had no idea that all
the Prime Ministers would follow in his footsteps
and to this day, no one really knows why they have.

Near the junction of Downing Street and
Whitehall stands the Cenotaph, the nation's chief
memorial to the dead of the two world wars. An
official ceremony of remembrance takes place
here every year on Armistice Day, 11 November,
when wreaths of poppies are laid at the base of
the memorial.

Guards' Museum
Wellington Barracks, Birdcage Walk, SW1
t (020) 7414 3271
⊖ St James's Park
Bus 3, 11, 12, 24, 159
Open 10-4, daily
Free

WHERE TO EAT

The museum traces the history of British troops from Cromwell's New Model Army and Charles II's five regiments (who still make up the infantry forces) to the present day with plenty of battle memorabilia on display. There's also an excellent toy soldier shop. You can compare the mini uniforms here with the real ones at the Changing of the Guard ceremony (*see* p.22).

Westminster Cathedral

Victoria Street, SW1
t (020) 7798 9055, tours (020) 7798 9064
www.westminstercathedral.org.uk
⊖ St James's Park, Victoria
Open Mon-Fri 7am–8pm, Sat 8am-7pm.
Adm Free, *Campanile* Adult £2, child £1, family £5
Pushchair/stroller access, café, audio guide (£2.50, £1.50 concs) worksheets, tours by arrangement
Suitable for ages 8 and up
Allow at least half an hour

Principally worth visiting for the fantastic views from the platform at the top of St Edward's Tower, some 280ft up – you can see right into the gardens of Buckingham Palace. Built in 1903, Westminster is London's main Roman Catholic Cathedral and has the widest nave in Britain, its green pillars were hewn from the same stone as the 6th century Basilica of St Sophia in Istanbul. It took over two years to transport them all the way to London.

You're not exactly spoiled for choice, but there are one or two places worth considering in this area. Head down Victoria Street, past Westminster Cathedral, where you'll find various old favourites including a branch of the country's top pizza house, **PizzaExpress** No.85, **t** (020) 7222 5270 and the current contender for its title, **Ask Pizza** No.160, **t** (020) 7630 8228). There's also a branch of **McDonald's** at No.155. *See* **Eat** p.223 for more details on the above restaurant chains.

1 Kundun

3 Horseferry Road
t (020) 7834 3211
⊖ Pimlico, St James's Park
Open Mon–Sat 12 noon–3 & 7–11.30

Excellent Pakistani restaurant which will cook less spicy dishes for children on request.

2 Shepherd's

Marsham Court
t (020) 7834 9552
⊖ Pimlico, St James's Park
Open Mon–Fri 12 noon–3 & 6.30–11

Shepherd's serves traditional English fare (steak and kidney pie, roast rib of beef etc) at fairly stiff prices. Though not terribly family-friendly, it is nonetheless very interesting with its grand old–world stylings and Division Bell which rings to tell any MPs present that they must return to the House of Commons to vote. The owner of the restaurant is a well known eccentric and has decorated the dining room with regally dressed teddy bears. Should a party arrive numbering unlucky thirteen, an extra place will be set and the party will be expected to welcome one of theses teddies to dinner – thankfully teddies don't eat much. If you're visiting the Abbey, however, you might want to save your money and try the very good café there, set in arcaded cloisters.

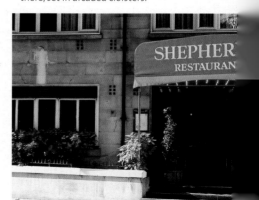

The South Bank

There are some tremendous attractions along the South Bank but the area itself is currently in a state of flux with the South Bank Arts Centre undergoing a much needed facelift. Sadly, this means that one of the centre's very best children's attractions, MOMI (the Museum of the Moving Image), has had to close until 2003. There's still plenty to draw in the crowds, however. Just west of the centre is County Hall, home to the London Aquarium with its thousands of sea creatures, and standing proudly on the riverfront, the London Eye, the biggest big wheel in the world, which takes passengers on a fantastic tour, high up above the London skyline. Back down on the ground there are river walks to enjoy, plus live music events and riverside festivals. Budding movie buffs are spoilt for choice with the National Film Theatre and the IMAX cinema right on the doorstep.

Highlights

Driving into the Thames on a Frog Tour

Eating up in the Oxo Tower

Watching dolphins in 3-D

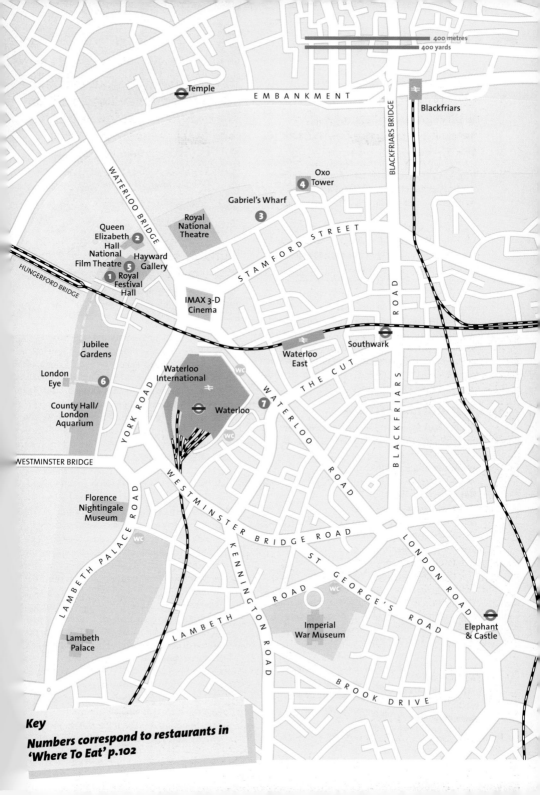

400 metres
400 yards

Temple

E M B A N K M E N T

Blackfriars

BLACKFRIARS BRIDGE

WATERLOO BRIDGE

Oxo
Tower **4**

Gabriel's Wharf
3

Royal
National
Theatre

S T A M F O R D   S T R E E T

Queen
Elizabeth
Hall **2**
National
Film Theatre **5**
Hayward
Gallery
1 Royal
Festival
Hall

HUNGERFORD BRIDGE

IMAX 3-D
Cinema

Waterloo
East

Southwark

THE CUT

Jubilee
Gardens

Waterloo
International

WC

London
Eye **6**

County Hall/
London
Aquarium

Waterloo

7

WATERLOO ROAD

BLACKFRIARS ROAD

YORK ROAD

WC

WESTMINSTER BRIDGE

Florence
Nightingale
Museum

WC

WESTMINSTER BRIDGE ROAD

KENNINGTON ROAD

ST GEORGE'S ROAD

LONDON ROAD

LAMBETH PALACE ROAD

WC

Imperial
War Museum

Elephant
& Castle

Lambeth
Palace

LAMBETH ROAD

B R O O K   D R I V E

Key

*Numbers correspond to restaurants in
'Where To Eat' p.102*

County Hall

⊖ Waterloo, Westminster ⇌ Waterloo
Bus 1, 4, 68, 76, 77, 149, 168, 171, 176, 188, 211, P11, 501, 505, 507, 521, D1, P11

For much of its existence County Hall, the beautiful Edwardian building that sits on the South Bank opposite the Houses of Parliament, was home to London's premier administrative body, the Greater London Council or GLC. Following the council's abolition in 1986, however, the building sat empty for many years with no one quite sure what to do with it – there was even talk of knocking it down. Thankfully, it has once again found a purpose. The political animals may have long gone, but there are still many weird and wonderful creatures to be found swimming around the vast tanks of the London Aquarium which now occupies the building's basement. Here, too, can be found Namco Station, a sort of giant video game arcade and Dali Universe, a museum dedicated to the great Spanish surrealist artist, as well as numerous restaurants and hotels.

London Aquarium

County Hall, Riverside Building, Westminster Bridge Road, SE1
t (020) 7967 8000
www.londonaquarium.co.uk
⊖/ ⇌ Waterloo
Bus 12, 53, 109, 211, X53
Open 10–6 daily
Adm Adult £8.75, child £5.25 (under-3s **free**), concs £6.50, wheelchair users **free**
Suitable for all ages
Allow at least an hour

In the half decade since it opened, the London Aquarium has become firmly established as one of the capital's premier animal attractions. Its vast tanks are home to thousands of sea creatures, from water-spitting archer fish and gruesome-looking

eels to multi coloured corals and translucent floating jellyfish. It's arranged according to habitat and region with displays on freshwater rivers, coral reefs, mangrove swamps and rainforests as well as the Indian, Pacific and Atlantic Oceans – the ocean tanks are particularly huge, holding millions of gallons of water and spanning several floors. The prime attractions, of course, are the sharks which swim in lazy circles around the Pacific tank. They're about 6–7ft long and quite startlingly ugly with big bulgy eyes and teeth that don't fit their mouths properly but stick out on all sides like mouthfuls of razor-sharp chips. Nonetheless, they hold a powerful attraction for both adults and children alike who can sit, goggle-eyed, watching the great sea killers for hours. Because they are kept well fed by the aquarium keepers, the sharks show little interest in attacking the groupers who share their tank (or even the staring faces on the other side of the glass).

More serene pleasures can be found at the touch pool where visitors are invited to stroke the resident rays who seem to get a dog-like satisfaction from the experience. Children, who usually need little encouragement to get their hands wet and start touching things, love this. Do make sure, however, that they treat the rays gently.

Dotted in among the tanks are a number of interactive terminals where more can be learnt about the aquarium's inhabitants. There are touch screen quizzes and short-play videos in which

Did you know?
The world's biggest fish is the whale shark which can grow to over 70ft in length. Unlike some other sharks, it is perfectly harmless, feeding only on plankton.

Question 10
What do lobsters and the Royal Family have in common?
answer on p.249

cartoon sea creatures explain themselves and their environment to children.

The aquarium has a strong environmental slant – there are exhibitions on the decline of the rainforest and the pollution of the oceans. Also, as you enter, you'll find a display on the history of the Thames from thriving salmon river in the Middle Ages to disease-ridden mess by the 19th century, and the subsequent attempts to clean it up.

Dali Universe

County Hall, Riverside Building, Belvedere Road, SE1
t (020) 79620 2720
www.daliuniverse.com
Open Daily 10–5.30
Adm Adults £8.50, children £5, under-5s **free**, family £22
Shop, wheelchair access

Dedicated to the great Spanish Surrealist, this is filled with bizarre sculptures and paintings. In particular, look out for the sofa designed to resemble an enormous pair of red lips (it was modelled on the Hollywood actress Mae West) Outside the building itself, there is a collection of weird and wonderful sculptures lining the riverfront walkway and a good bit of space for kids to run around in and let off steam. The Frog Tours stop is right outside here.

Namco Station

County Hall, Riverside Building, Westminster Bridge Road, SE1
t (020) 7967 1066
www.namcostation.co.uk
Open 10am–12midnight daily
Free, although each game costs between £1–2

Love it or hate it, this noisy arcade-ridden labyrinth is packed with hundreds of video games and simulators as well as a full-size car racing game, bowling, dodgems and pool tables. The downstairs section is for over-18s only.

IMAX 3-D Cinema

1 Cahrlie Chaplin Walk, SE1
t (020) 7902 1234
www.bfi.org.uk/imax
⊖/ ≷ Waterloo
Bus 12, 53, 76, 77, 109, 211, 507, D1, P11
Open Mon-Thu 12.30-8, Fri 12.30-9.15, Sat 11.45-9.15, Sun 12 noon-8.
Adm For one film: adult £6.95, child (5-16) £4.95, under-5s **free**, concs £5.95
Wheelchair access, lifts, adapted cinema seats and toilets
Suitable for all ages
Shows last approximately one hour each

Britain's largest cinema screen is housed in a seven-storey glass cylinder in the middle of the Waterloo bullring. The screen itself is the height of five double-decker buses, the sound system trans-

mits 11,000 watts and the films are recorded and projected using the most up-to-date 3-D format available – it's a pretty all-encompassing experience. The programme changes regularly but you can usually be confident of seeing some kind of outer space/wildlife-type spectacular. *See* p.129 for the IMAX cinema in the Science Museum.

British Airways London Eye

Next to County Hall, South Bank, SE1
General information and advance booking **t** 0870 500 0600, customer service (020) 7654 0828
www.ba-londoneye.com
Open Jan-Mar 10–7, Apr-June, Oct-Sept 10-8, Jul-Sept 9-10 daily
Adm Adult £8.50-£9, child (5-16) £5 (under-5s **free**), concs £7.50-£7. Tickets must be purchased in advance, online discounts available

One of the few Millennium projects that can claim to have been a truly successful venture, this 453ft rotating observation wheel perched the south bank of the Thames has provided both tourists and London residents alike, with a whole new way of looking at the capital. Despite a few teething problems which saw its maiden turn – originally set for New Year's Eve 1999 – having to be postponed, the wheel has attracted near universal acclaim, its wonderful views and sturdy architecture garnering the sort of reviews that the people behind the erstwhile Millennium Dome could only dream of. Night rides are spectacular, especially when the Christmas lights go on, although the best sightseeing opportunities are afforded during the day. Look out for Big Ben, the Houses of Parliament and the long phalanxes of Somerset House and Buckingham Palace which together look like parts of a model village, all overlooked by the novelty pencil of the BT Tower.

From the very top you can, on a clear day, see for over 25 miles in every direction and, even on an overcast one, you should still be able to make out many of London's most famous landmarks including Canary Wharf and St Paul's.

Officially the fourth highest structure in the capital, each of the Eye's 32 enclosed glass-sided capsules (they can hold up to 25 people each) takes around 30 minutes to complete its circumferential journey . Don't worry though, the movement is so slow and smooth that there's little chance of travel sickness and there's a central seating area for passengers in need of a sit down.

Frog Tours

County Hall, Belvedere Road, SE1
t (020) 7928 6162, booking line **t** (020) 7928 3132
www.frogtours.com
⊖/ ≊ Waterloo
Open Daily 10–dusk
Adm Adults £15, children £9, family £42, concs £12

A novel approach to sightseeing – Frog Tours have adapted a number of former Second World War amphibious vehicles into bright yellow sightseeing 'frogs' capable of tackling London by both road and river. Each frog begins its 80-minute tour on land at County Hall, before crossing Westminster Bridge and making its way through the streets of London to Vauxhall Bridge, taking in key sights such as Trafalgar Square, Hyde Park Corner and Buckingham Palace on the way. 'Splashdown' into the Thames occurs at Lacks Dock in Vauxhall, after which you are taken on a half-hour sightseeing cruise down the river to the starting-point opposite Dali Universe. Live commentary is provided by an onboard guide, aptly named Phileas Frogg. Kids can join in as well with a rousing chorus of 'Frogg Frogg - Ribbitt Ribbitt'. It's a different and fun way of navigating through London and the plunge into the drink is truly exciting. While the company claims you won't get too soggy on 'Splashdown', it may be advisable to wear a waterproof jacket just in case.

South Bank Arts Centre

Can you spot?
The country's one and only floating police station, just to the side of Waterloo Bridge?

the South Bank, SE1
General Information **t** (020) 7960 4242
www.sbc.org.uk
⊖ Waterloo, Embankment
≷ Waterloo
Bus 1, 4, 26, 68, 76, 77, 168, 171, 176, 188, 341, 501, 505, 521, D1, P11, X68

One of the world's great art complexes, the South Bank comprises, at present, the Royal Festival Hall, the Queen Elizabeth Hall, the National Film Theatre, the Hayward Gallery and the Royal National Theatre. The Museum of the Moving Image (MOMI), formerly one of the capital's best family attractions, is currently closed for renovation and not due to reopen until 2003 at the earliest. Until then, part of the collection will be on display at the Science Museum in London and National Museum of Photography Film and TV in Bradford and there will also be a UK wide-touring exhibition. Despite this, the centre is still well worth a visit with a range of events suitable for families put on throughout the year including Gamelan classes where beginners can learn the basic elements of a traditional Indonesian percussion ensemble, plus concerts by youth orchestras, ballet, theatre shows and poetry sessions. The centre is also the venue for the National Festival of Music for Youth, 'Blitz', a three-week free dance festival and 'Rhythm Sticks', a three-week festival of percussion with shows by international performers.

Royal Festival Hall

t (020) 7960 4242
Open 10am–10.30pm daily

Along with the adjacent Purcell Room and the Queen Elizabeth Hall, this is one of the top venues for classical music in the country. Look out, in particular, for the National Festival of Music for Youth which takes place every summer. It holds regular free concerts and exhibitions in its foyer.

National Film Theatre

t (020) 7928 3232
www.nft.org.uk
Junior NFT **Adm** Child £1, accompanying adult £5

The Junior NFT Film Club shows a variety of films for children throughout the year with pre-screening workshops for ages 6-12 on Saturday afternoons. The NFT is also the main venue for the London Film Festival, held each November.

Hayward Gallery

t (020) 7690 4242
www.hayward-gallery.org.uk
Open 10–6 daily, until 8pm on Wed & Thur
Adm Varies, depending on the exhibition

The Hayward has no permanent exhibition but puts on a series of temporary shows throughout the year with children's art trails and activities attached wherever possible. It often organizes art workshops for children in the holidays as well. The Hayward shop can be accessed via the foyer and stocks a large and impressive range of art and activity books for children from board books and bath books to project-based art boxes.

Royal National Theatre

t (020) 7452 3400
www.nationaltheatre.org.uk
Open 10am–11pm daily

Three theatres in one; in descending size these are the Olivier, the Lyttleton and the Cottesloe. All offer a year-round programme of drama. For a taster, pop along to Theatre Square, just outside, where free performances are staged throughout the year. Backstage tours are also offered call for details on **t** (020) 7452 3400, and there's an excellent bookshop.

Coin Street Community Builders

The Coin Street Community Builders is the name given to the non-profit organization which manages Gabriel's Wharf, the Bernie Spain Gardens, the Oxo Tower Wharf and organizes the three month free Coin Street Arts Festival every summer. From near dereliction in the early 1980s, the CSCB has transformed the area into a thriving arts centre. Contact **t** (020) 7401 2255.

Gabriel's Wharf

Just down from the South Bank is Gabriel's Wharf, a bohemian collection of shops, restaurants and snack places. Look out for the London Bicycle Tour Company, who will rent you bikes to ride around the capital or arrange a guided bike tour. There are plans to build a floating lido on the Thames in front of the Bernie Spain Gardens.

London Bicycle Tour Company

1A Gabriel's Wharf
t (020) 7928 6838
www.londonbicycle.com
Bike hire Adult £2 per hour, child £1.50 per hour

Oxo Tower

Bargehouse Street, SE1
t (020) 7401 2255
⊖ Blackfriars, Waterloo
Bus 455, 63, 149, 172, D1, P11
Open Studios Tues–Sun 11–6; bars & restaurants every day until late

Topped by its famous Art Deco tower (one of the capital's great landmarks) the Oxo Tower Wharf is now an artsy shopping arcade housing designer boutiques, art studios and fashionable eating places, most notably its celebrated rooftop restaurant which offers fantastic views out across the city – there's also a free viewing gallery next door. On the ground floor is an exhibition detailing the history of the building. In the 1930s, when the Oxo Tower was first commissioned by the famous stock cube company, it was their intention to have the company's name spelled out in lights on the top.

Unfortunately, the strict advertising laws of the time forbade this forcing the company to come up with an ingenious alternative. They instructed the

architect to incorporate the Oxo logo into the design of the tower's windows, thus enabling them to claim that is was an architectural feature rather than an advert.

The Coin Street Festival

t (020) 7401 2555
Three months each summer, usually June–Aug

For three months every summer, the Oxo Tower Wharf, Gabriel's Wharf and the Bernie Spain Gardens play host to a range of art, music and dance events from across the globe.

Fixtures include the Latin-flavoured Gran Gran Fiesta, which involves a children's fancy dress parade, and the 'Arts Desire' creative workshops, where the whole family can take part in a range of arts and crafts activities – the lantern-making sessions are particularly popular with the kids.

Tell me a story: **Evacuation**

When Britain declared war on Germany on 3 September 1939, Londoners began preparing for the worst. It would surely only be a matter of time, they reasoned, before the German air force began bombing raids on the city (it actually took over a year) and it was therefore crucial that the capital's children were quickly evacuated to safer parts of the country. Soon, London's train stations were bidding farewell to train after train packed with children heading out to new lives in the countryside, each carrying with them just their bare essentials packed in a bag or case, a gas mask and an attached label giving their name. Of course, finding places for all the children to stay (not to mention the blind and disabled people, teachers and helpers) proved to be no easy task. The sheer numbers involved meant that there was no way of guaranteeing which child went where with the result that many middle-class kids found themselves in labourer's cottages while slum children were billeted in stately homes. In this way, the evacuation process helped to foster a level of social integration that would have been impossible outside wartime. That's not to say that it was a popular policy, however. For some it proved to be a frightening and unhappy experience although others, with fresh food to eat and space to run around in, saw it more as a holiday.

AROUND AND ABOUT

Florence Nightingale Museum

2 Lambeth Palace Road, SE1
t (020) 7620 0374
www.florence-nightingale.co.uk
⊖/ ⇌ Waterloo
Bus 12, 53, 77, 109, 171, 171a, 507, C1
Open Mon-Fri 10-5, Sat, Sun 11.30-4.30, last admission one hour before closing
Adm Adult £4.80, child & concs £3.60 (5-18), under-5s **free**, family £10
Wheelchair access
Suitable for ages six and up
Allow at least an hour

A wonderful place to take any aspiring doctors or nurses. The museum tells the story of the founder of modern nursing via a mixture of videos, reconstructions and articles from the life of Florence Nightingale, including several of her letters. You walk through a recreated ward scene from the Crimean War where you can see 'the lady with the lamp' tending to the wounded soldiers. The museum is very much geared towards the interest of kids, so there are lots of interactive consoles and audio-visual displays including a 20-minute film on Florence's achievements in health care.

Imperial War Museum

Lambeth Road, SE1
t (020) 7416 5320
Infoline **t** 0891 600 140
www.iwm.org.uk
⊖ Lambeth North, Elephant & Castle
Bus 1, 3, 12, 45, 53, 63, 68, 159, 168, 171, 172, 176, 188, 344, C10
Open 10–6 daily
Free
Wheelchair access
Suitable for ages six and over
Allow at least an hour

Upon catching sight of the enormous 15" naval guns by the museum's entrance you could be forgiven for thinking that this is a place that glorifies war and treats it as some great gung-ho 'Boys Own' adventure. In fact, the museum is largely dedicated to exploring and demonstrating the human experience of war; the lives of the ordinary men and women charged with settling the arguments of nations on the battlefield. It's true, there are some fantastic machines to look at in the large central hall, including tanks, planes, one-man submarines and even a 30ft Polaris missile, but the museum never loses sight of the very real cost of conflict. For every piece of dazzling equipment, there's a more sobering exhibit – the Trench Experience, for instance, is an affecting recreation of the life of a foot-soldier on the Western Front during the First World War, while the Blitz Experience gives you the chance to see what conditions were like for Londoners during the Second World War, huddled in shelters under the streets as Hitler's bombs rained down overhead.

The museum's latest display, a two-floor exhibition on the Holocaust, is the most moving of all but is not recommended for children under 14. It charts the rise of Hitler and the Nazi party through to the horror of the Final Solution.

Alongside two galleries devoted to paintings from the First and Second World Wars, you'll find an exhibition on that perennial children's favourite, Meccano, and another, Secret War, dedicated to revealing the secrets of wartime spies. There's also an exhibition on code-breaking that's been specifically designed for younger visitors. Can you crack the enigma machine?

There's a good proportion of interactive exhibits – you can clamber around the cockpits of some of the fighter planes, assume the role of an RAF pilot on a secret mission in a flight simulator or watch some archive footage on one of the touch-screen TV terminals that dot the museum floor. The museum organizes children's quizzes (called 'Spy School Training Missions'), which take kids all over the museum in the hunt for clues, as well as activity workshops in the school holidays.

After a visit, it may come as something of a relief to take a walk to the Tibetan Peace Garden just outside: a small, sculptured, enclosure opened by His Holiness, The Dalai Lama in 1999.

WHERE TO EAT

The South Bank is one of the busiest places on the London arts scene and, as such, has lots of fast food outlets, cafés and restaurants. There's the informal **Foyer Café** in the Royal Festival Hall, open 12 noon–to just before interval, or the café in the Tate Modern which has great views of the river.

Gabriel's Wharf also has several snack places including **House of Crêpes** and **Sarnis**, which specializes in continental sandwiches made from panini, ciabatta, focaccia and baguettes.

County Hall, site of the London Aquarium and London Eye booking hall, also has numerous places to eat including a branch of **McDonald's**, a branch of **Fish!**, t (020) 7234 333; a small branch of **Yo! Sushi**, t (020) 7928 8871. *See* **Eat** p.223 for more details on the above restaurant chains.

If you're after a good local Chinese, try **Four Regions**, t (020) 7928 0988, open 12 noon–3 & 6–11.30, or for a warm, friendly Italian welcome, visit **Shino's** for good, reasonably priced pasta and pizzas, t (020) 7401 6514, **www**.shinos.com, open 11am–11.30pm.

1 51 Café and Coffee Bar

Royal Festival Hall, South Bank Centre, SE1
t (020) 7921 0946,
Open 9am–9pm
⊖/≈ Waterloo

Perhaps the most family-friendly of the South Bank's restaurants, serving up pastas, salads, sandwiches and drinks throughout the day.

2 NFT Café

t (020) 7928 3232
Under Waterloo Bridge

An excellent place to eat. Children can tuck into pizzas and jacket potatoes while their parents rummage through the stalls at the Riverside Book Market or listen to the musicians who often busk along this vibrant stretch of the river.

3 Gourmet Pizza Company

Gabriel's Wharf, 56 Upper Ground, SE1
t (020) 7928 3188
www.gourmetpizzacompany.co.uk
Open 12 noon–10.30pm
⊖/≈ Waterloo

Small, rather upmarket chain serving reliably excellent pizzas including a few rather unusual combinations – sauteed leak and pecorino cheese,

salami and artichoke. Thankfully, the kids menu is a little more conservative. High chairs available.

4 Oxo Tower Restaurant

Oxo Tower, Barge House Street, South Bank, SE1
t (020) 7803 3888
Open Mon–Sat 12 noon–3 & 6–11.30,
Sun 12 noon–3.30 &6.30–10.30
⊖/≈ Waterloo

Serves great food in a family-friendly atmosphere and can offer some of the most stunning river views to be found anywhere in the capital (it's particularly magical at night). They offer a special brasserie children's menu at weekends.

5 The People's Palace

Royal Festival Hall, South Bank Centre, SE1
t (020) 7928 9999
Open 12 noon–3 & 5.30–11
⊖/≈ Waterloo

A very grand eaterie offering superb river views and a refined contemporary European menu. Best suited for older, better behaved children.

6 Pizza Express

The White House, 9c Belvedere Road
t (020) 7928 4091.
Open 12 noon–12 midnight daily

This is a particularly well-to-do branch of the country's best pizza chain with soft lighting and a tinkling piano in the evening but still happy to accommodate families.

7 Fire Station

150 Waterloo Road
t (020) 7620 2226)
Open Food from 12 noon-11pm Sat, 12 noon-9.30pm Sun. Kids welcome weekends.
⊖/≈ Waterloo

Packed out Monday–Friday with commuters and office workers, this sprawling bar lying literally cheek by jowl with Waterloo Station is happy to accommodate families on weekends. High chairs are available and there's a kids' menu on Sundays consisting of pub grub staples like sausage and beans or chicken with chips, plus tasty pasta dishe for £4.95.

Southwark

There really isn't much that you can't do here. From London Bridge station it's a short walk to some of London's oldest and best loved attractions including the nautical treasures of *HMS Belfast* and *The Golden Hinde*, plus Tower Bridge, Southwalk Cathedral and the ghoulish London Dungeon. There's also a few hidden gems to discover like the Old Operating Theatre, The Design Museum and, if you fancy a spot of retail therapy, Hay's Galleria and the bijou shops around Butler's Wharf. Alternatively, if you really must be up-to-the-minute, head for the very latest blockbusters: Shakespeare's Globe and the Tate Gallery of Modern Art, formerly Bankside Power Station.

Highlights

Quoting Shakespeare at The Globe

Deli shopping in Butler's Wharf

Discovering that Tower Bridge Experience

Blackfriars

BLACKFRIARS BRIDGE

TOWER HILL

Cannon Street

BANKSIDE

3

SOUTHWARK BRIDGE

LONDON BRIDGE

Tower of London

2

St Katharine's Dock

Tate Modern

Globe Theatre

BRIDGE ROAD

Clink Museum

CLINK ST

Southwark Cathedral

1

Hay's Galleria

HMS Belfast Golden Hinde

Tower Bridge

SOUTHWARK STREET

London Dungeon

Old Operating Theatre

London Bridge

Britain at War Experience

SHAD THAMES

Butler's Wharf

Design Museum

UNION STREET

SOUTHWARK

ST THOMAS STREET

Bramah Tea & Coffee Museum

BOROUGH HIGH STREET

BERMONDSEY ST

TOWER BRIDGE ROAD

4

LONG LANE

GREAT DOVER STREET

5

300 metres
300 yards

Key
Numbers correspond to restaurants in 'Where To Eat' p.114

Tower Bridge Experience

t (020) 7378 1928
www.towerbridge.org.uk
⊖ Tower Hill, London Bridge
Bus 15, 42, 47, 78, 100
Open: April–Oct 10–6.30 (last admission 5.15pm),
Nov–Mar 9.30–6 (last admission 4.45pm)
The Experience tour lasts 1hr 15mins
Adm Adult £6.25, child & concs £4.25, under-5s
free, family ticket (2+2) £18.25`
Wheelchair access
Suitable for ages six and over
Allow at least an hour

With its fairytale turrets and huge decks which raise to let tall ships through, this is easily London's most recognizable and popular bridge. On the Tower Bridge Experience tour, you can see the steam-powered machinery which was used to raise the decks in Victorian times – these days the bridge relies on hydraulics and electricity – play with some interactive models and climb the 200 or so steps (or if you're sensible take the lift) to the covered walkway that runs along the top of the bridge, from where you can enjoy spectacular views up and down the river and out across London. Look out, in particular, for the new Greater London Authority building taking shape on the riverside next to the bridge which, when completed, will look a bit like an enormous glass paperweight. The bridge is still raised at least once a day; you can find out exactly when by calling **t** (020) 7378 7700.

London Dungeon

Tooley Street, SE1
t (020) 7403 7221
www.thedungeons.com
⊖/ ≈ London Bridge
Bus 10, 44, 48, 70, 133
Open Oct-Mar 10.30-6 , Sept, Oct, Apr-July 10-5.30,
Nov-Mar 10–5. Mid-July-early Sept 10-8 daily.
Adm Adult £10.95, child (under 14) £6.95, concs £9.50
Wheelchair access
Suitable for ages eight and up
No unaccompanied children allowed
Allow at least an hour

The concept behind the London Dungeon is rather odd but it's one that seems perfectly attuned to the interests of children, who often harbour a strange desire to be scared in a 'safe' way. In the dark, candlelit 'dungeon' (actually a series of railway arches next to London Bridge station), you'll find a series of gruesome waxwork tableaux depicting some of the more grisly episodes from British history: a human sacrifice by druids at Stonehenge, Boadicea stabbing a Roman soldier to death, Anne Boleyn being beheaded (in the middle of her farewell speech), as well as the blotchy, bloated victims of the great plague and the mana-cled maniacs of Newgate Prison. The highlight, however, is a recreation of the life and times of everyone's favourite serial killer, Jack the Ripper. You can walk the streets where his crimes took place and hear the muffled cries of his victims. You'll have to judge for yourselves whether you consider this sort of fare suitable for your children. It's probably not a good idea to take very young children to the London Dungeon (those under 8) or anyone (young or old) susceptible to nightmares.

Did you know?
▶ That each bridge deck weighs an astonishing 1,000 tonnes. That's as much as 200 elephants.
▶ That the 'proper' name for one of the bridge's decks is a 'bascule'.
▶ That in 1952 a double decker bus had to jump a three foot gap between the opening bridge decks when the traffic lights didn't turn red?

Tate Modern

Bankside, SE1
t (020) 7887 8000
www.tate.org.uk
⊖/ ⇌ London Bridge, Blackfriars
Bus 17, 21, 22a, 35, 40, 43, 47, 48, 133, 214, 344, 501, 505, 521, D1, D11, P3, P11
Open Sun–Thurs 10–6, Fri and Sat 10–10 (closed 24–26 Dec; open 1 Jan)
Free
Disabled facilties
Suitable for ages eight and up
Allow at least a couple of hours

Tate Modern was one of the unqualified success stories of the millennium year and has been packing them in ever since the day it opened. Housed in a former power station, the collection is arranged around a vast turbine hall which serves as both entrance and exhibition space and has to be seen to be believed. Make sure you come in by the main entrance for the full 'wow!' effect.

Inside, the museum has a mighty 100,000 square feet of display space dedicated to modern international works from the 19th century to the present

day. That's a lot of art, but don't be put off. There are actually only four galleries (albeit rather big ones) to explore. These are arranged thematically rather than chronologically with umbrella topics used to trace links and resonances between artists who might otherwise seem to have little in common. Much of the work on show, such as Marcel Duchamp's *Fountain* (actually a toilet) and Carl Andre's *Equivalent VIII* (a pile of bricks) are the kind of works of art that the British public love to hate, although there are also many famous works by more 'traditional' artists such as Bacon, Dali, Freud, Hockney, Matisse, Picasso, Pollock, Rothko, Spencer and Warhol. Children, however, will probably appreciate the more off the wall exhibits. Peter Fischli and David Weiss, for instance, have constructed what for all the world looks like an unfinished room, waiting for paintings to be hung. You might easily walk right past. Yet every object here has been hand-carved from polyurethane foam and painted by hand. Up on the fifth floor in History/Memory/Society, there's the chance to have a game of Fluxipingpong using impossible bats – one bat has a large hole, another a tin can attached to it which sends the ball zipping off in every direction but the one you intended.

To help get the most from your visit, audio guides can be picked up from a variety of information points (children's versions available) and cost only £1. Should your legs start to get tired, lightweight collapsible stools are on hand free of charge to take round. In addition, there are plenty of comfortable sofas, as well as two restaurants and a café. And before you leave, head up to the top floor where the café offers wonderful views of the river, the Millennium Bridge and St Paul's. On Sundays and some selected school holidays, the gallery organises a programme of art-related activities for children known as 'Start'.

Save time, too, for the gift shop on the ground floor where you can pick up, among other things, Tate T-shirts, mugs, umbrellas, and a stationery box in the shape of the Bankside building which includes a magnetic 'lightbeam' lid.

Tip *Tate Modern is one of the capital's newest and most popular attractions and by mid-afternoon is usually heaving with visitors. Indeed, the old Tate (now Tate Britain), just down the road in Pimlico, often seems practically empty by comparison. To avoid the crush, visit early in the morning or later on in the day.*

Britain at War Experience

Tooley Street, SE1
t (020) 7403 3171
www.britainatwar.co.uk
⊖/ ⇌ London Bridge
Bus 10, 44, 48, 70, 133
Open April–Sep 10–5.30 daily, Oct–Mar 10–4.30 daily
Adm Adult £5.95, child (under 15) £2.95 (under-3s **free**), concs £3.95, wheelchair users **free**
Wheelchair access
Suitable for ages six and up
Allow at least an hour

On Tooley Street, under the same set of arches as the London Dungeon, is perhaps the best place for kids to come and find out what life was like in this country during the Second World War. You start by taking a lift down to a replica underground shelter of the type used by Londoners hiding from the Blitz, when bombs rained down night after night

Tell me a story: The Blitz

The deliberate and systematic bombing of London by the German airforce, or 'Luftwaffe', began on the afternoon of Sunday 7 September 1940. Squadron after squadron hit the East End where the warehouses at Surrey Docks, filled with rubber, paint and rum, were soon ablaze. That night the Luftwaffe struck again and by the dawn of 8 September, 448 Londoners had lost their lives. The 'Blitz', as it came to be known, had begun and continued unabated for the next 76 days during which time vast swathes of the capital were flattened and thousands of lives lost. There were, however, some miraculous escapes along the way. Buckingham Palace was hit but escaped relatively undamaged while St Paul's Cathedral, despite the destruction around it, survived the bombing virtually intact and became a symbol of London's defiance. Night after night, Londoners took cover in steel shelters or on the platforms of the Underground stations as the German planes attempted to crush their morale in preparation for a land invasion. Much to the Nazis' chagrin, however, the bombing, if anything, served to stiffen British resolve to resist the enemy at all costs. Even so, London paid a heavy price for its brave resistance. Over the next four years 20,000 people were killed in the raids and a further 25,000 wounded.

on the city. In order to really get a sense of the times, children can dress up in period costume complete with gas masks, tin helmets and ARP (air-raid patrol) uniforms. A mixture of sounds, smells and visual effects are used along with archive footage, radio broadcasts and music to conjure up a period atmosphere. The overall effect is fun and exciting but also informative, successfully conveying a little of the reality of the time: the desperate fear that must have been felt by the people sheltering here and also the community spirit that helped them to get through. You finish the tour by walking through a replica bombed street as sirens wail and spotlights criss-cross over head. It's a great interactive museum where kids can get their hands dirty finding out about what war was like in the past.

Question 11
What is a groundling?
answer on p.249

Globe Theatre

Bear Gardens, Bankside, New Globe Wall,
Southwark, SE1
t (020) 7401 9919
www.shakespeares-globe.org
⊖/ ≋ London Bridge
Bus 17, 95, 149, 184
Open 10–5 daily, for performance times call in
advance
Museum adm Adult £7.50, child £5 (under-5s **free**),
concs £6, family ticket (2+3) £23
Saturday Child Workshops adm £8
Limited wheelchair access
Suitable for ages 8 and up
Allow at least an hour to see the museum
Performances can last a few hours

The Globe is a perfect modern recreation of the
Elizabethan theatre where Shakespeare premiered
many of his most famous plays, including *Othello*,
Macbeth and *Romeo and Juliet*. The original theatre
burnt down in 1613 during a performance of *Henry
VIII*, when an ember from a stage cannon set fire to
the thatched roof.

You can take a guided tour of the new Globe
(which, begun in the early eighties, was finally
completed in the mid-nineties), visit the multimedia museum which explains the history of the
Globe (old and new), or watch a performance of a
Shakespeare play almost as his contemporaries
would have done: seated on wooden benches or
standing in the open in front of the stage. This can
add to the atmosphere at performances but can
also serve to obscure children's views.

Children aged between eight and 11 can take part
in Saturday afternoon Shakespeare workshops at
the Globe's education centre, which involve storytelling, drama and art. The building of a smaller
theatre based on a rediscovered design by Inigo
Jones is currently underway next door.

Shakespearian theatre

Welcome to the bad side of town....In the 16th
century, when the first Globe theatre was built, this
was the area of town frequented by the city's
reprobates and ne'er do wells; where people came
to indulge in bawdy, rowdy entertainments like
drinking and gambling, bear and bull baiting, cock
and dog fighting (any sort of mayhem with
animals seems to have been particularly popular)
and, of course, going to the theatre. While, today,

Did you know?
The Globe's roof is the first thatched roof to top
a London building since the Great Fire of 1666. In
order to prevent another disaster, the thatch sits
on an insulating layer of fibreglass and is dotted
with sprinklers

we often regard theatre-going as something rather
refined and elegant, in Shakespeare's day it was
seen as a much more rough and ready form of
entertainment. Children can find out more about
the decadent history of Southwark on a Globe
Walkshop; a guided tour taking in the sites of the
prisons, inns, brothels and theatres which used to
make up the bulk of the area's buildings (10–12
noon every Saturday; **adm** £6, concs £5, student £4;
call **t** (020) 7902 1433).

Old Operating Theatre

9a St Thomas Street, SE1
t (020) 7955 4791
www.thegarret.org.uk
⊖/ ≋ London Bridge
Bus 17, 21, 22a, 35, 40, 43, 47, 48, 133, 214, 344, 501,
505, 521, D1, D11, P3, P11
Open 10–4 daily
Adm Adult £3.50, child £1.75 (under-8s **free**), concs
£2.50, family ticket (2+2) £8
No disabled access
Suitable for ages eight and up
Allow at least an hour

Just think what it would be like to have your
tonsils taken out here, in the country's only
surviving example of an early nineteenth century
operating theatre. These days, we tend to think of
surgery as a skilled job involving the delicate repa-
ration of internal organs by trained professionals.
That wasn't the case in the early 1800s when a
surgeon's main task was amputations – the
removal of damaged or diseased limbs with a fine-

Did you know?
In the early 19th century, surgeons were
regarded by the medical establishment as being
little better than butchers. Even today, when they
are among the most highly skilled of all medical
practitioners, they do not take the title 'Dr' but
remain a simple 'Mr'.

tooth saw. And, just to make it interesting, the patient wouldn't even have an anaesthetic (this wasn't wanton cruelty, it hadn't been invented yet). Surgeons relied instead on speed and the bravery of the patient (and six or seven able-bodied men to hold them down). Patients could actually watch while someone sawed off their leg – imagine what that must have felt (and looked) like. There was also no antiseptic and standards of hygiene were poor (surgeons often didn't bother to clean their instruments between operations). In fact a third of all amputees died from an infection caught during surgery – the museum cheerily explains that surgeons often performed operations 'stinking with pus and blood'.

It's a fantastic place, thick with atmosphere and a very real sense of horror. You can see all the grue-some medical equipment (almost indistinguishable from the tools of torture at the nearby Clink Museum), the operating table (actually a wooden board which held patients upright) and various pickled bits of unlucky patients in jars.

The theatre itself has had a fascinating history. It was housed in a medieval tower that formed part of the old St Thomas' hospital. When the hospital relocated to Lambeth in 1860, the old building was demolished and only the tower was left standing. The operating theatre within, however, was forgotten about for nearly a century until rediscovered and turned into a museum in 1956.

HMS Belfast

Morgan's Lane, off Tooley Street, SE1
t (020) 7940 6328
www.hmsbelfast.org.uk
⊖/ ⇌ London Bridge
Bus 47, P11
Open Mar–Oct 10–6 daily, Nov–Feb 10–5 daily
Adm Adult £5, child **free**, concs £3.90
Suitable for ages six and up
Allow at least an hour

This huge, heavily armed, heavily armoured cruiser was used during the D-Day landings, the 1944 invasion of Normandy that finally turned the Second World War in the Allies' favour. These days it is a kind of floating nautical museum moored permanently between London Bridge and Tower

Bridge. Children love running around the ship's clunking metal decks, looking down the barrels of the huge naval guns, manoeuvring the lighter anti-aircraft guns and exploring the seven floors of narrow winding corridors.

The Golden Hinde

St Mary Overie Dock, Cathedral Street, SE1
t (0870)011 8700
Infoline **t** 0541 505 041
www.goldenhinde.co.uk
⊖/ ⇌ London Bridge
Bus 17, 95, 149, 184
Open Call in advance
Adm Adult £2.50, child £1.75, concs £2.10 Guided tours: adult £3, child £2.25, concs £2.60. Pirate Birthday Parties: £155 for 15 children and food (£8 for each additional child). Overnight Living History Experiences: £30 per person plus £10 deposit. Daytime Experience £21 (ages 6-12 *only*)
No disabled access
Suitable for ages six and up

This full-size replica of the 16th-century ship on which Sir Francis Drake became the first Englishman to circumnavigate the globe sits in dry dock, just back from the river front. There are five levels to explore including Drake's cabin and a 14-cannon gun deck. As the children roam the ship, the crew, dressed in Tudor costume, will entertain them with tales of adventure and treachery on the high seas. Although a replica, this is a fully functioning vessel and has sailed the Atlantic several times since it was built in 1973. It's available for children's parties and families are invited to attend the ship's Overnight Living History Experiences which start at 4pm and last until 10am the next day. During this time the whole family is expected to assume the roles of a crew of Tudor sailors; performing shipboard tasks, eating Tudor food and sleeping in the cabins on the lower decks.

Clink Museum

1 Clink Street, SE1
t (020) 7403 6515
www.clink.co.uk
⊖/ ⇌ London Bridge
Bus 17, 95, 149, 184
Open 10–6 daily
Adm Adult & child £4, concs £3, family £9
No disabled access
Suitable for ages eight and up
Allow at least half an hour

If your kids aren't quite up to the big frights of the London Dungeon, try them on the smaller fun-size frights offered here. The museum has attempted to recreate many of the scenes and settings of the medieval Clink Museum which stood on this spot in the Middle Ages. Although the prison building was demolished in 1780 the name 'the Clink' has survived to this day as a nickname for all prisons. It clearly hasn't got the budget of other big-name horror attractions like the London Dungeon or the Chamber of Horrors and many of its supposedly gory effects are actually a bit ordinary. Even so, it boasts a historical authenticity which the other two attractions can't match and, despite its limitations, still manages to convey something of the eerie gruesomeness of these primitive and brutal forms of punishment.

It's divided into a number of cells, each inhabited by some rather unhappy-looking mannequins undergoing some of the various forms of torture popular during the Middle Ages. There's the Stocks, which is basically two wooden planks used to hold a prisoner's head and hands fast (many medieval village greens boasted stocks; the villagers would throw rotten fruit and vegetables at the poor people trapped within); the Fure, a hole in the

Did you know?
Medieval prisoners were expected to pay for the privilege of being manacled and tortured. They had to contribute towards their food, their cells and the wages of the men who kept them locked up. They even had to pay for their own ball and chain!

ground where trussed up prisoners were left to rot, and the Cage, a wire contraption fitted to the head of 'scolds and gossips'—in other words women who, in the eyes of their husbands, talked too much. In one particular cell you'll find a torture chair to which a victim would be strapped before being forced to confess by use of pincers (for tooth extractions), knives and foot crushers. The section detailing the history of the Stews (medieval brothels) is for over-18s only.

The prison closed soon after the Great Fire of London in 1666 when the local area began to go upmarket. City merchants and investors started moving in, putting the brothels, drinking houses and gambling dens that had provided the majority of the prison's clientele out of business. For a while the building continued to be used as warehouse before finally being knocked down in 1780.

The Millennium Bridge

Designed by Norman Foster, Anthony Caro and the engineering firm Arup, this elegant walkway linking Tate Modern with St Paul's on the other side of the river was definitely not one of the millennium year's success stories. As people walked across the bridge on its first day of opening, it started shaking from side to side in such an alarming (and potentially dangerous) manner that the authorities were forced to close it. It has remained closed ever since while the designers search for a (cheap) way of fixing it. Its proposed reopening day is, as yet, still unconfirmed.

AROUND AND ABOUT

The new Butler's Wharf complex is one of London's trendiest property developments and is made up of a collection of former dock buildings and warehouses (you can still see the elevated metal walkways running between the two). It is also home to the Bramah Tea & Coffee Museum and the Design Museum.

Bramah Tea & Coffee Museum

1 Maguire Street, Butler's Wharf, SE1
t (020) 7378 0222
www.bramahmuseum.co.uk
⊖ London Bridge, Tower Hill
Bus 15, 25, 42, 78, 100, D1
Open 10–6 daily
Adm Adult £4, child and concs £3, family ticket (2+4) £10
Suitable for ages eight and over
Allow at least half an hour

Discover the history of the country's two favourite non-alcoholic beverages at this little museum housed in a former spice warehouse. You can find out how the drinks were introduced to Britain in the 17th century, how public tastes have changed since then and how the ritual of drinking tea and coffee has become such a part of British life. Children will like the collection of teapots and coffee-makers. There are over 1000 in all shapes and sizes: dragons, monsters, lions, pillarboxes and even policemen. Perhaps the most interesting section is devoted to the way the drinks have been advertised during this century. If all this talk of tea and coffee gets you thirsty, you can always head for the tea room and sample one of the museum's own blends.

Design Museum

Butler's Wharf, Shad Thames, SE1
t (020) 7403 6933
www.designmuseum.org
⊖ London Bridge, Tower Hill
Bus 15, 25, 42, 78, 100, D1
Open 11.30am–6pm daily
Adm Adult £5.50, child & concs £4, under-5s **free**
Suitable for ages 10 and over
Allow at least an hour

This probably won't interest youngsters very much but older children may well get something out of it. The museum's purpose is to explain why various ordinary, everyday objects – such as telephones, vacuum cleaners, toothbrushes and cars – look the way they do, examining them from both a functional and an aesthetic perspective. There is a very good (albeit expensive) café, the Blueprint, more of a restaurant really, and a shop selling books as well as various modern design classics.

Just near the wharf's entrance is Potter's Park, a small expanse of greenery built on the site of a former pottery which, in centuries past, specialized in making pots for tea and coffee importers. It's also a nice place to have a picnic overlooking the river. A new glass office complex is currently being built here on the Jubilee Walkway. The new Mayor of London and the Greater London Authority are due to move in upon completion.

Hay's Galleria
London Bridge, Tooley Street, SE1
t (020) 7403 3583
Open 10–6 daily

A rather posh shopping arcade. Its main entrance is on Tooley Street, almost directly opposite the London Dungeon, and it can be used as a quick short cut to the Thames riverside path. Should you decide to linger you'll find lots of well-to-do shops and restaurants (look out for a branch of the child-friendly chain, Sweeney Todd's) while the kids' attention will no doubt be caught by the great statue-cum-fountain, *The Navigators*, which stands at the arcade's riverside end. Other notable landmarks in the area include Southwark Cathedral, the cathedral for the south of the city, and the Southwark Information Centre which stands on the corner of London Bridge and Tooley Street. It's easy to find – just look for the 16m-high pointy stone needle that stands outside.

Southwark Cathedral
t (020) 7407 3708
www.dswark.org
✆/ ≽ London Bridge
Bus 17, 21, 22a, 35, 40, 43, 47, 48, 133, 214, 344, 501, 505, 521, D1, D11, P3, P11
Open 8–6 daily
Free, although the Cathedral asks that you make a £2 donation
Wheelchair access, call in advance, restaurant, shop, lifts

The Cathedral's newly landscaped grounds are practically crying out for a picnic. There's also a small museum full of medieval, Roman and Victorian artefacts reflecting the periods of building and rebuilding in the life of the church.

Southwark Information Centre
6 Tooley Street, SE1
t (020) 7403 8299
✆/ ≽ London Bridge
Bus 17, 21, 22a, 35, 40, 43, 47, 48, 133, 214, 344, 501, 505, 521, D1, D11, P3, P11
Open April–Oct Mon–Sat 10–6, Sun 10.30–5.30; Nov–March Mon–Sat 10–4, Sun 11–4

WHERE TO EAT

There are plenty of chains. Try **Pizza Express** – 2 branches at Cardomom Building, Shad Thames, t (020) 7403 8484, ⊖ Tower Hill, London Bridge; and 4 Borough High Street, London Bridge, t (020) 7407 2995, ⊖ London Bridge, Borough); the large branch of the family-friendly French bistro chain **Café Rouge** in Hay's Galleria, t (020) 7378 0097, ⊖ London Bridge – it's just a stone's throw from the river and within a minute or two's walking distance from *HMS Belfast*, the London Dungeon and Britain at War Experience) or, if you think your stomach can stand it, the **Pizza Hut** in the London Dungeon. *See* **Eat** p.223 for more details on the above restaurant chains.

1 Anchor Inn

34 Park Street, Bankside, Southwark, SE1
t (020) 7902 1400
Open Mon–Sat 11am–11pm, Sun 12 noon–10.30pm
⊖/≷ London Bridge

One of the grand inns of old London town, this 18th century pub was built on the site of a 15th century predecessor and can count Dr Johnson among its former patrons (he supposedly wrote part of his dictionary here). It serves decent pub fare and has an outdoor terrace where you can sit watching life on the river pootling by. Inside is a small collection of Elizabethan artefacts found nearby. It's just a few dozen yards from Shakespeare's Globe.

2 Dickens Inn

St Katherine's Way
t (020) 7488 2208
Open Mon–Sat 12 noon–3 & 6.30–11
⊖ Tower Hill

Despite its name and antique appearance, this is actually a modern pub – albeit one housed in a converted 18th century spice warehouse. Indeed, almost everything about this place is fake – not only is the Dickens connection entirely spurious, but the building doesn't even occupy the same space as it did when first built but has been moved to its current position on wheels. It has three places to eat: the Copperfield Snack bar, a very reasonable pizza restaurant and a rather expensive main restaurant. High chairs available.

3 Globe Café and Restaurant

Bear Gardens, Bankside, New Globe Wall, Southwark, SE1
t (020) 7902 1576, restaurant t (020) 7928 9444

Open May–Sep 10am–11pm, Oct–April 10–
Restaurant open daily from 12 noon–2.30 &
6–10.30
⊖/≷ London Bridge

Overlooking the theatre piazza, this serves snacks and light lunches throughout the day. There's also a coffee shop in the main foyer open daily and a restaurant that should really be reserved for special occasions only. They are happy to welcome children – who are served half portions from the grill-based menu – but it is rather expensive, although the grand river views almost make it worth it.

4 La Lanterna

6–8 Mill Street, SE1
t (020) 7252 2420
Open 12 noon–11pm
⊖ Tower hill

Small, homey traditional Italian restaurant serving, good reasonably priced fare. Half portions and high chairs available. It can get quite crowded, especially in the evenings when live music is staged at the next door café (which is owned by the same people).

5 Manze's

87 Tower Bridge Road, SE1
t (020) 2407 2985
www.manze.co.uk
Open 10.30am–9pm daily
⊖ London Bridge, Tower Hill

Manze's is the oldest pie and mash shop in London (it first opened in 1862) and, despite the capital's many competing eateries, still one of the most popular with queues that regularly stretch right down the street at lunchtime. The food is traditional and determinedly unglamorous – minced beef pies, jellied eels and big dollops of mash all topped with bright green parsley sauce known as liquor – not to mention very cheap. Where else would you be able to feed a family of four for under £15?

The City

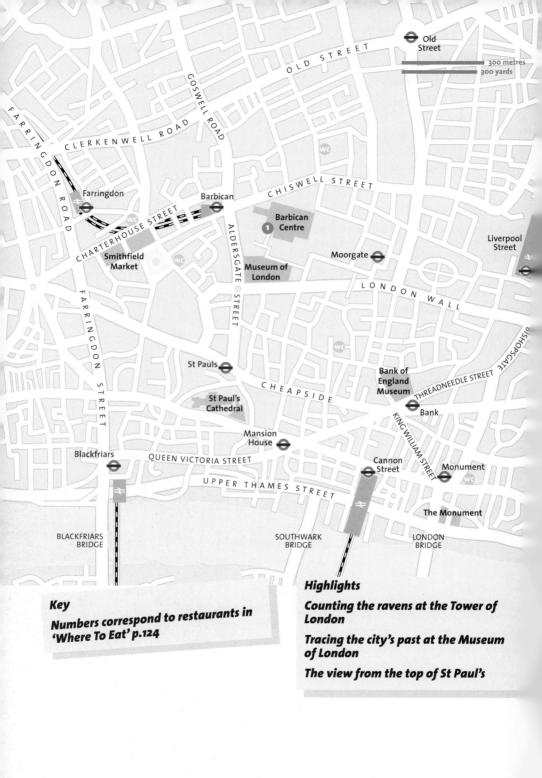

Old Street

300 metres
300 yards

OLD STREET

GOSWELL ROAD

CLERKENWELL ROAD

CHISWELL STREET

FARRINGDON ROAD

Farringdon

Barbican

Barbican Centre

Moorgate

Liverpool Street

CHARTERHOUSE STREET

ALDERSGATE STREET

Smithfield Market

Museum of London

LONDON WALL

FARRINGDON STREET

St Pauls

CHEAPSIDE

Bank of England Museum

THREADNEEDLE STREET

BISHOPSGATE

St Paul's Cathedral

Bank

KING WILLIAM STREET

Mansion House

Blackfriars

QUEEN VICTORIA STREET

Cannon Street

Monument

UPPER THAMES STREET

The Monument

BLACKFRIARS BRIDGE

SOUTHWARK BRIDGE

LONDON BRIDGE

Key

Numbers correspond to restaurants in 'Where To Eat' p.124

Highlights

Counting the ravens at the Tower of London

Tracing the city's past at the Museum of London

The view from the top of St Paul's

This is the wealthiest, non-residential, area of London, home of the Bank of England, the Stock Exchange and the Royal Mint as well as dozens of other seriously filthy rich institutions. Billions and billions of pounds change hands here every day at the blink of an eye.

It's always been the most commercial area of London and the least residential. In the Middle Ages, when the City *was* London, people would come here from miles around to sell their goods and livestock at market, as the surviving street names Bread Street, Wood Street and Poultry can testify.

As you would expect, it's an area thick with history (ably explored at the excellent Museum of London) and dotted with famous landmarks such as the richly historic 900-year-old Tower of London, the great domed St Paul's Cathedral and the Bank of England itself, perhaps the most famous bank in the world and a symbol for centuries of Britain's financial stability.

Tower of London

Tower Hill, EC3
t (020) 7709 0765
www.hrp.org.uk
⊖ Tower Hill
Bus 15, 25, 42, 78, 100, D1
Open Mar–Oct Mon–Sat 9–5, Sun 10–5; Nov–Feb Tue–Sat 9–4, Sun–Mon 10–4
Adm Adult £11.30, child £7.50, concs £8.50, family (2+2) £35
Very limited wheelchair access, call **t** *(020) 7403 1115 for access guide, tours, family trail guides*
Suitable for ages seven and up
Allow at least three hours

Murders, executions, assassinations, conspiracies and betrayals – the Tower of London has been the setting for them all. In order for kids to get the most out of their visit here, it's important that they know a little bit of the history. An old building is not particularly interesting in itself, but if your children are told that this is the building in which two princes were murdered and bricked up behind a wall by their wicked uncle so that he would become King instead of them, it suddenly becomes much more exciting. The famous Yeoman Warders or 'Beefeaters' come in very handy in this regard as they are generally more than willing to regale your children with tales of intrigue and murder.

At around 900 years old, the tower is one of London's oldest major landmarks and also one of the best-preserved medieval castles in the world. Its construction was ordered by William the Conqueror soon after his invasion of England in 1066 in order to shore up his position and provide a

stronghold against future rebellions. It was to prove a great success; its massive 15ft walls have never been breached. The tower has not always served a purely defensive role, however. In the 16th and 17th centuries it proved just as good at keeping people in as it had been at keeping them out. Lady Jane Grey, Anne Boleyn and Robert Devereux, Earl of Essex, all ate their final meals here. You can visit the spot on Tower Green where they met their grizzly ends.

The tower's fantastic security record led to it being entrusted with the safekeeping of the nation's most precious treasure – the Crown Jewels. You can see them in all their sparkly glory at the Jewel House, where you are carried past the priceless crowns, sceptres and orbs on a moving walkway. Be sure to look out for the Cullinans I and II, the largest top-quality cut diamonds in the world. Elsewhere in the tower you'll find Edward I's medieval palace, where guides dressed in period costume will demonstrate crafts such as calligraphy and quill-making; the White Tower, where

***Tell me a story:* A Bloody coup**
Today, the crown jewels are protected by an array of sophisticated security devices, but did you know that in 1671 the fantastically named Irish adventurer and Civil War veteran Colonel Thomas Blood almost succeeded in stealing them from the Tower? On the day in question, Blood disguised himself as a clergyman and, accompanied by his wife and nephew, went to the tower where his wife pretended to faint. When the Keeper of the Jewels came to her assistance, Blood hit him on the head with a mallet rendering hime unconscious. Blood then grabbed the crown, which he bent so it would fit under his cloak, while his nephew put the orb in his pocket. The nephew then tried to file the royal sceptre in half so he could hide it more easily under his coat. He took so long, however, that the keeper's son was able to raise the alarm and the two men were captured and thrown into a dungeon in the tower. It seemed that Blood's number was up. Yet, unbelievable as it may seem, Charles II was apparently so impressed by the daring shown by the Colonel that he not only granted him a pardon but gave him a pension of some £500 a year (a fortune in those days). Sometimes, it seems, crime does in fact pay.

Guy Fawkes confessed to having tried to blow up James I (he confessed, it must be said, only after his legs and arms were almost pulled off on the rack); and, of course, the shiny black ravens in the Tower Gardens. According to legend, if the ravens ever leave the tower, the country will topple.

The tower is one of the top-listed sites in London which means that, if you're visiting in summer, you're going to have to queue. It can also be quite hard on the legs, especially for young children, but it does provide a memorable day out. …Lady Jane Grey, Walter Raleigh and Anne Boleyn all ate their final meals here. You can visit the spot on Tower Green where they met their grizzly ends – and grizzly, in this instance, really means grizzly. The sword blow that killed Anne Boleyn, Henry VIII's second wife, was delivered with such speed that her lips continued to recite a prayer for several moments after her head had been separated from her body.

Question 12
What was the name of the king who supposedly had his nephews killed in the Tower of London?
answer on p.249

Tell me a story: **Watch the birdie**
It is not known when the ravens first came to the Tower of London, but their presence is protected by legend. Traditionally seen as birds of ill omen, it is their absence rather than their presence which is feared at the Tower for, according to the stories, if they ever leave a great disaster will befall the kingdom. To guard against misfortune, the tower authorities ensure that there are always at least six ravens in residence at any one time. A seventh is kept in reserve so as to accommodate any deaths or (believe it or not) dismissals for bad behaviour – of which there have been more than you might think. In 1986, Raven George was given his marching orders after he developed an unhealthy taste for TV aerials, while Ravens Hugine and Jackie were given the boot in 1996 when the Governor of the Tower issued the following statement: 'On Thursday, 4 May, having spent the past few months in close arrest… for conduct unbecoming Tower residents, Ravens Hugine and Jackie were removed from the Tower establishment. Services no longer required'.

Sometimes, however, the ravens are simply the victims of unfortunate circumstances. For instance, it is the custom, when the Queen visits the tower, for it to be searched in advance by police sniffer dogs. On one such occasion a sniffer dog called Charlie was searching near where the ravens reside when a particular raven, also called Charlie, took exception to this intrusion and pecked Charlie (the dog) on the head – whereupon Charlie (the dog) attacked Charlie (the raven), killing him with a single bite. The kingdom trembled momentarily but stood firm. Charlie (the raven) has since been replaced while Charlie (the dog) has retired from the force.

The ravens themselves are looked after by their 'ravenmaster' Tom Trent who, although never openly declaring a favourite, seems to have developed quite an attachment to Raven Thor, the 'speaking' raven who can repeat the ravens' bedtime call of 'come on then' (interpreted by most visitors as 'good morning') with remarkable accuracy and in a disturbingly similar voice to his keeper. Thor is a little bit naughty too. He tends to make a bit of a commotion about being put to bed and will only go in after all the others and then with some considerable difficulty.

St Paul's Cathedral

St Paul's Churchyard, EC4
t (020) 7236 4128
www.stpauls.co.uk
⊖ St Paul's, Mansion House
Bus 4, 8, 11, 15, 17, 23, 25, 26, 56, 76, 172, 242, 501, 521
Opening times Mon–Sat 8.30–4
Adm Cathedral only: adult £4, child £2, concs £3.50;
additional charge for Galleries adult £3.50, child
£1.50, concs £3
Wheelchair access to all areas except the galleries
Suitable for ages five and over
Allow at least an hour

St Paul's Cathedral is undoubtedly one of
London's most recognizable landmarks. Its great
plump dome, which seems to dominate the City's
skyline, will be familiar to many children from the
film of *Mary Poppins*. It's a great place for kids to
come and burn off some excess energy. The 521
steps up to the viewing gallery will calm even the
most hyperactive of temperaments. The climb,
though hard on the thighs, is well worth it. The
panoramic views from the top of the dome, some
365ft up are, quite simply, stupendous. You can see
more or less the whole of London stretched out
before you like a great 3-D tapestry. There's more to
St Paul's, however, than just a high vantage point.
Designed by Sir Christopher Wren, and built in the

Can you spot?

The following landmarks, visible from the top of
St Paul's. The Thames is due south.
► To the west: the British Telecom Tower
(formerly the Post Office Tower), a tall, thin,
round building that looks like an enormous spark
plug. Its sides are covered in transmitters and
satellite dishes.
► To the northwest: The Old Bailey (the collo-
quial name for the Central Criminal Courts),
which looks a bit like St Paul's but with a much
smaller dome. Perched on top is a golden statue
of a woman holding a sword in one hand and a
pair of scales (representing the balance of
justice) in the other.
► To the south, across the river: the Tate Gallery
of Modern Art – formerly a power station, this is
a huge square brick building with a tall central
square tower. Eventually, you will be able to
reach the gallery from St Paul's via the
Millennium Bridge.
► To the east: Canary Wharf, London's (and
indeed Britain's) tallest building (812ft), which
has a triangular top with a light that winks 40
times a minute to prevent low-flying aircraft
from hitting it.
► Tower Bridge, with its two great turrets and
raising decks.

late 17th century after the original, wooden cathedral burnt down in the Great Fire in 1666, this is arguably London's most beautiful church.

The fantastically decorated interior is almost as impressive as the view from the top of the cathedral, particularly the massive domed ceiling – your children will quickly send themselves dizzy staring up at it. About half way up the inside of the dome is the Whispering Gallery. You can put its name to the test by doing the following: stand on one side of the gallery while a friend goes over to the other. Now, providing it's quiet enough, you should be able to whisper something to the wall on your side and have your friend hear it quite clearly on the other, 107 feet away.

In the crypt (the largest in Europe) you'll find the tombs of many of Britain's greatest military leaders – Admiral Nelson (his coffin is made out of the main mast of a defeated French flagship) and the Duke of Wellington (the conqueror of Napoleon at Waterloo) among them – as well as a model of the cathedral made by Sir Christopher Wren himself (it is, in fact, an early draft model of the cathedral featuring a considerably thinner dome). There is in addition a shop and an excellent child-friendly restaurant down in the crypt.

Did you know?

▶ That the first St Paul's Cathedral was built by the Saxons way back in 604 AD

▶ That the present building took 35 years to build at a cost of £721,552 (over £50 million in today's money) and was paid for by a tax put on coal coming into the city.

▶ That the Cathedral clocktower 'Great Tom' houses Britain's heaviest bell (17 tonnes) and that the dome itself weighs a staggering 65,000 tonnes.

▶ That when the medieval cathedral caught fire in 1666, it generated such a tremendous amount of heat that the 250-year-old corpse of the former Mayor of London, Robert Braybrooke, was blasted out of his grave and thrown clear of the churchyard.

Museum of London

London Wall, EC2
t (020) 7600 3699
Infoline **t** (020) 7600 0807
Booking office **t** (020 7814 5777)
www.museumoflondon.org.uk
⊖ Barbican, Bank, St Paul's
Bus 8, 22b, 56
Open Tues–Sat 10–6, Sun 12 noon–6pm
Free
Wheelchair access. Suitable for all ages
Allow at least two hours

This fascinating museum tells the story of life in London from prehistoric camps to concrete tower blocks. It may not have the range of one of the great Kensington collections, but this is still a

Question 13
The Lord Mayor's gold coach resides in the museum for 364 days of the year. Where is it on the remaining day?
answer on p.249

lovely little museum with a charm and style all its own. Rather than simply displaying ancient fragmentary exhibits in glass cases, the museum has created some wonderful scale models which vividly illustrate the various stages of London's history: there's a prehistoric mammoth hunt, a Roman town, a Viking ship, Shakespeare's Rose Theatre, London Bridge c.1600 (with cramped wooden houses along its length), London burning during the Great Fire, even a modern terraced street. Each is rendered in perfect miniature detail. There are also a number of restored and reconstructed interiors which give visitors the chance to imagine themselves in a variety of historical settings: a Roman kitchen complete with floor mosaics and frescoes, a sumptuous, albeit rather gloomy, Stuart dining room, a cell from the infamous Newgate Prison, and a 1920s shop interior. Also on show, for 364 days of the year, is the fabulously ornate Lord Mayor's State Coach.

The museum tries hard to make history come alive for its younger visitors. In fact, the curators allow families to attend regular artefact handling sessions on weekends. During the school holidays the museum also organizes a number of workshops, demonstrations and performances for children on a range of subjects from metalwork to preparing Roman food.

Bank of England Museum

Threadneedle Street, EC2, entrance is on Bartholomew Lane
t (020) 7601 5545
www.bankofengland.co.uk
⊖ Bank, Cannon Street
Bus 9, 11, 22
Open Mon–Fri 10–5
Free
Wheelchair access
Suitable for children aged 10 and over
Allow at least an hour

Take a trek through the monetary world to see how financial transactions have developed from paper IOUs to whizzing numbers on a computer screen. The curators have obviously thought long and hard about how to make what is, after all, a rather dry subject interesting for children. So there are waxworks of 18th-century bankers, lots of interactive video screens where you can find out the history of the bank (topics include the development of banknotes, and foxing the forgers) and,

---

Tell me a story: **Filthy lucre**

Have you heard the one about the man who got into the bank of England's gold vaults by way of the sewers? It's no joke.

In around 1836 the Directors of the Bank are said to have received an anonymous letter stating that the writer had discovered an underground passage to the bullion. He offered to meet them there to prove his claim at any hour they chose. Although initially sceptical, the Directors were finally persuaded to assemble one night in the vault. At the appointed hour a noise was heard from beneath the floor and the mysterious correspondent suddenly appeared from below merely by displacing a few floorboards.

Apparently he was a sewerman who, during repair work to the tunnels, had discovered an old drain which ran immediately under the bullion vault. He might have carried away enormous sums but he resisted the urge and for his honesty the Bank is said to have rewarded him with a gift of £800, so he came up smelling of money after all.

Following the incident the Directors decided to take precautions against further unwanted intrusions, several letters were sent to George Bailey, the Curator of the Soane Museum*, asking that plans of the drains beneath the Bank Premises, which had been retained by Soane when he retired, should be returned to the Bank. There was evidently some anxiety that there might be other drains leading to the interior of the premises.

* Sir John Soane was the Bank of England's architect 1788-1833. *See* p.72 for more on his extraordinary house, now a museum.

---

the highlight, a large perspex pyramid filled to the brim with gold bars – the goggle-eyed kids seemingly glued permanently to its side are not part of the exhibit.

The museum also contains perhaps the most difficult interactive game on the planet. In it, you assume the role of a foreign exchange dealer buying and selling currencies on the international money markets. It might sound easy but it soon gets parents tearing their hair out with frustration. To kids, however, who have been brought up on this sort of fast-moving visual technology, it is second nature. The museum produces worksheets and quizzes for children which you can pick up from the front desk.

Question 14
The Bank of EnglandMuseum has a collection of British coins. However, the bank only issues notes. Who issues British coins?
answer on p.249

The Monument

Monument Street, EC3
t (020) 7626 2717
⊖ Monument
Bus 15, 22a, 35, 40, 48
Open April–Sep Mon–Fri 9–6, Sat & Sun 2–6, Oct–Mar Mon–Sat 9–4
Adm Adult £1.50, child 50p, under-5s **free**
No disabled access
Suitable for ages four and up
Allow at least half an hour

If the Monument were to fall over, its top would (provided it fell in the right direction) land on the very spot in Pudding Lane where the Fire of London began more than 300 years ago. It was designed by Sir Christopher Wren as a memorial for the victims of the Fire. At 202ft high, it was, when it was completed in 1677, the tallest free-standing column in the world. Of course, by modern standards, 202ft isn't very tall at all and today the monument is rather obscured by the medium-sized buildings surrounding it. You can climb the 311 steps to the top where you take a close-up look at the great bronze urn that sits on the monument's summit spouting shiny metallic flames. The views are good albeit not as good as those from the top of St Paul's, but your kids will enjoy sending themselves dizzy running down the spiral staircase.

The Barbican

Silk Street, The Barbican, EC1
t (020) 7368 8891
www.barbican.org.uk
⊖ Barbican, Bank, St Paul's
Bus 8, 22b, 56

Nobody could describe the Barbican as beautiful but it is one of the capital's major arts centres and, as such, always has a lot going on. These great concrete tower blocks and labyrinthine corridors are home to several of the country's most prestigious artistic bodies including the Royal Shakespeare Company, the London Symphony Orchestra and the English Chamber Orchestra, as well as three cinemas, an art gallery and a semitropical garden. Special children's events and performances are put on in the school holidays as part of the centre's 'Barbican Family' programme. These include the annual LSO Discovery Concert (*see* p.171), and Discovery Creative Music Workshops which offer informal instrument tuition for 7–2 year olds. There's also a Family Film Club which meets every Saturday morning. Call
t (020) 7382 7000 for details.

AROUND AND ABOUT

Smithfield Market, now the capital's largest meat market, was a popular site for jousting in the Middle Ages and also witnessed the bloody conclusion of the Peasants' Revolt (see below). Opposite the market, on the wall of St Bartholomew's Hospital, is a blue plaque marking the spot where another revolt came to an end when William Wallace (as featured in the film, *Braveheart*), the leader of the Scots, was hung, drawn and quartered by the English in the 13th century.

Further afield, on Fleet Street, is Prince Henry's Room, one of the few domestic houses to survive the Great Fire of London while, just off King Edward Street is Postman's Park, which has a memorial wall dedicated to ordinary people who have sacrificed their lives for others.

The peasants are revolting

In 1381 a band of commoners marched on London demanding the repeal of the newly imposed Poll Tax (which charged everyone the same amount, regardless of their ability to pay). Once in the city, they stormed the Debtors' Prison and slaughtered as many lawyers and tax collectors as they could find. The 14-year-old king, Richard II, met them at Smithfield to discuss their grievances. At first it seemed that the rebels would get their way with the king agreeing to a number of concessions including the repeal of the tax and the abolition of serfdom. However the Mayor of London became so incensed at the protesters' presumption that he stepped forward and stabbed the rebel leader Wat Tyler, fatally wounding him. Rather than continue their protest, the rebels decided to accept the word of the king and disband. Bad move – once they had turned for home, Richard's troops captured and killed as many of the protesters as they could find. A picture of the dagger used to stab Tyler was subsequently incorporated into the City of London's coat of arms.

Prince Henry's Room

17 Fleet Street, EC4
t (020) 7353 1190
⊖ Aldwych
Open 11am–2pm
Free

WHERE TO EAT

Situated next to Tower Bridge, St Katharine's Dock is a good place for cafés and restaurants. Elsewhere, the primary function of the City's food outlets is to assuage the lunchtime appetites of its thousands of day workers. Consequently, you'll find branches of **McDonald's** at 143 Cannon Street, 41–42 London Wall, 12 Tower Hill Terrace and 50 Liverpool Street. **Ask Pizza**, 103 St John Street, EC1, **t** (020) 7253 0323 ⊖ Farringdon. **Café Rouge**, Hillgate House, Limeburner Lane, EC4.**t** (020) 7329 1234 ⊖ Blackfriars. **Café Flo**, 38–40 Ludgate Hill, EC4 **t** (020) 7329 3900⊖ St Paul's. **PizzaExpress** has several branches in the area: 125 Alban Gate, London Wall, 26 Cowcross Street, 49 Curtain Road, and 2 Salisbury House, London Wall. *See* **Eat** p.223 for more details on the above restaurant chains.

1 Searcy's

Level I, Barbican Centre, EC2
t (020) 7588 3008
Open Mon–Fri 12 noon–2.30 & 6–10.30, Sat & Sun 12 noon–3pm, 5–6.30pm
⊖ Barbican

Recently refurbished, this bright, airy modern-looking diner overlooks the Barbican's central courtyard and fountains. It's a bit pricey and hi-falutin, but does its best to accommodate families.

2 Dickens Inn

St Katherine's Way
t (020) 7488 2208)
⊖ Tower Hill, Tower Gateway
DLR London Bridge

The best of both worlds, this Tower stalwart, houses a pizzeria to keep the kids happy and a pint or two for the adults. In summer, it's a great spot for dining alfresco by the river. Children's portions, high chairs and baby-changing available.

Museumland

There are few better places to come for a top day out than this. In the morning, start with a quick tour around one of the capital's great museums, and, if there's time, a workshop or themed-event in support of the current exhibitions. You can choose from the Natural History, the Science or the Victoria & Albert. All are within spitting distance of each other and all offer guaranteed entertainment, plus, most importantly, entry is now free for all visitors. From here it's a five minute walk to Hyde Park for a picnic and a quick jaunt in a rowboat on the Serpentine before finishing the day with some last-minute souvenir and gift shopping in the resplendent halls of Harrods.

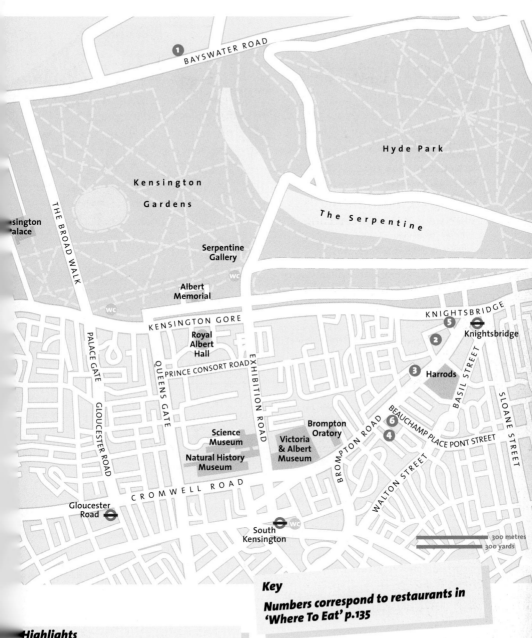

Hyde Park

Kensington Gardens

The Serpentine

Serpentine Gallery

Albert Memorial

KENSINGTON GORE

Royal Albert Hall

KNIGHTSBRIDGE

Knightsbridge

PALACE GATE

QUEENS GATE

PRINCE CONSORT ROAD

EXHIBITION ROAD

Harrods

BASIL STREET

SLOANE STREET

GLOUCESTER ROAD

Science Museum

Natural History Museum

Brompton Oratory

Victoria & Albert Museum

BROMPTON ROAD

BEAUCHAMP PLACE PONT STREET

WALTON STREET

CROMWELL ROAD

Gloucester Road

South Kensington

300 metres
300 yards

THE BROAD WALK

ensington alace

BAYSWATER ROAD

Key

Numbers correspond to restaurants in 'Where To Eat' p.135

Highlights

The new British Galleries at the Victoria & Albert Museum

Boating in Hyde Park

Encountering the dinosaurs at the Natural History Museum

THE SIGHTS

Natural History Museum

Cromwell Road, SW7
t (020) 7942 5000
www.nhm.ac.uk
⊖ South Kensington
Bus 14, 49, 70, 345, C1
Open Mon–Sat 10–5.50, Sun 11–5.50
Free

Wheelchair access, adapted toilets
Suitable for all ages
Allow a morning or afternoon

One of the must-see sights in London for both children and adults alike, the Natural History museum is, quite simply, a fabulous place. Huge monsters, replica volcanoes, earthquake simulators, creepy crawlies, precious stones, big things, small things, shiny things – there's so much to look at. This is the sort of museum where kids tend to rush off pointing at everything.

It's been revamped in recent years. All the old favourites are still here – the great fossil monsters, the impossibly huge blue whale suspended from the museum ceiling – but these have been augmented with new exhibits and more up-to-date technologies.

Whatever entrance you choose, there's an almost immediate 'Wow!' awaiting you. Walk through the main door and you'll be confronted by the great swooping head of a fossil diplodocus looming down above you. Nip around the side and you'll find yourself walking through a guard of honour made up of bizarre futuristic statues before riding up an escalator into a huge clunking, clanking metal globe. The two entrances mark the beginnings of the museum's two themed areas, the Life and Earth galleries.

Pride of place in the Life galleries goes to those perennial children's favourites, dinosaurs. There is

an illuminated walkway to take you past the various superstar fossils (T-Rex and the horned-faced Triceratops among them). Videos and interactive displays provide background information and there's an intriguing section looking at how these long-extinct beasts have become staples of popular culture – from *The Flintstones* to *Jurassic Park*. The piece de resistance, however, is the new 2/3 size animatronic Tyrannosaurus Rex— it growls, it slavers, it snaps its jaws, it really is rather excellent. It even smells, although not authentically. The stench of rotting meat which presumably would have pervaded from the dinosaur's mouth was considered a touch overpowering. Instead the dinosaur gives off a weaker, 'swampy' odour.

The Earth galleries play to their strengths. Detailed, in-depth geology has been ditched in favour of spectacular volcano and earthquake exhibitions: videos of exploding craters, models of lava flows, plastercasts of the Pompeii victims frozen in mute agony and, best of all, an earthquake simulator – every five minutes you can stand inside a mock-up Japanese supermarket as it undergoes a minor tremor.

In the Easter and Summer school holidays, the museum opens a special gallery devoted to children called the Discovery Room. Here, again, the emphasis is on interaction; most children's favourite exhibit is the 'feely' box into which they put their hands in order to see if they can guess what's inside by touch alone – not as easy as it sounds.

The museum also organizes a range of activities, talks and family events throughout the year.

Did you know?
The Natural History Museum is every collector's idea of paradise. It contains a staggering 68 million plants, animals, fossils, rocks and minerals from all regions of the world.

Question 15

The word 'dinosaur' itself means 'terrible lizard' in Latin. What do the following dinosaur names mean?

a) Triceratops
b) Deinocheirus
c) Baronyx

answer on p.249

Science Museum

Exhibition Road, London SW7
t (020) 7942 4455
www.nmsi.ac.uk
⊖ South Kensington
Bus 14, 49, 70, 345, C1
Open 10–6 daily
Free
An 'Access and Facilities Guide' is available
*Disabled Person's Enquiry Line **t** (020) 7938 9788*
Suitable for all ages
Allow a morning or afternoon

The Science Museum, perhaps more than any other museum, understands children. It understands that children like to be involved with the exhibits; they like to touch, to feel, to press and push as well as merely see. Nowhere is this better demonstrated that in the new £48 million Wellcome Wing, the opening of which in 2000 launched the Science Museum into the 21st century. Bathed in futuristic blue light, the new 4-storey wing offers state-of-the-art exhibits and lots of hands-on fun. There are three permanent

Short of time?

There's far too much in the museum to be covered in a single day and you may prefer to plan your tour around a few headline exhibits. Here are some suggestions:

▶ A 1903 Burnley mill engine. This is the show-piece of the Power Gallery on the ground floor, dedicated to the great machinery of the Industrial Revolution.

▶ The Black Arrow. Britain's first and only satellite launch rocket. The enormous craft is attached to the ceiling of the Space Gallery.

▶ The Apollo 10 Command Module. In 1969 it flew three astronauts into space as a rehearsal for the moon landing mission later in the year. Note the scorch marks on the craft, which were caused when it re-entered the earth's atmosphere at great speed.

▶ Foucault's Pendulum. A giant pendulum suspended from the ceiling of the ground floor, designed to demonstrate the rotation of the earth.

▶ One of the last working mechanical telephone exchanges in Britain. It can be found in the Telecommunications Gallery on the first floor.

▶ Charles Babbage's Difference Machine. This collection of cogs, gears and levers was the world's first ever computer. In Computing Then and Now on the second floor.

▶ On Air. Here, on the third floor, kids can learn how a radio station works.

▶ A model of a 16th-century medical teaching theatre and a life-size recreation of a modern operating theatre, in which waxwork doctors perform open-heart surgery. Both in Glimpses of Medical History on the fourth floor.

exhibitions: 'Who am I?' which looks at how science has helped us to understand what it means to be human (you can morph your features on a computer to make yourself look older or younger or even switch gender); 'Digitopolis', which explores today's digital landscape (you can digitally manipulate your voice to sound like Darth Vader or Micky Mouse) and 'In Future' which predicts how technology will develop over the next 20 years – play the In Future interactive game and decide for yourself which technologies you think will be most relevant in the decades to come. The wing also houses an IMAX film theatre showing science-related films on huge 4-storey-high screens.

Impressive though this wing is, you'll want to save some time for some of the museum's other exhibits, several of which are specifically designed for children. These include the Launch Pad in the basement where there are various games and pieces of equipment through which kids can learn a few basic scientific principles – they can create a giant bubble, touch a plasma ball and see electricity following their fingers, build a rubber bridge or perhaps try and tiptoe past the vibration detector. Staff are on hand to guide the youngsters through the apparatus. In the basement there are two further child-centric galleries – the Garden, aimed at 3–6 year olds, which gives children the chance to experiment with water using pumps, dams and buckets, and Things, aimed at slightly older children (7–11) which has a wide range of interactive video displays. Also try not to miss the Secret Life of the Home which takes a humorous look at domestic gizmos and gadgets from vacuum cleaners and washing machines to WCs, fridges and heaters.

Of course, there are plenty of other galleries which, while not specifically designed for children, will appeal nonetheless. The Flight gallery, for instance, will bring out the latent pilot in both parents and children. Here you can pedal a propeller to see how helicopters work, sit in the cockpit of a single-seater aircraft, watch as a water-powered rocket is fired across the gallery, or take a ride (for a small fee) in a state-of-the-art flight simulator (adults £2.50, children £1.50, height restriction 1.20m) and go on an intergalatic mission to 'save the world'.

Before leaving, make sure you check out the museum shop which is filled with 'sciencey' toys and games – junior astronomy kits, rainbow Slinkies, holograms, binoculars, models, kaleidoscopes and the like.

Science Nights

Kids will like the museum so much, they'll probably wish they could spend the night. Well, guess what? The museum has started running Science Nights when children aged between 8 and 11 (plus an accompanying parent) can come and camp overnight and will be treated to midnight tours of the museum, workshops and bedtime stories.

Victoria & Albert Museum

Cromwell Road, SW7
t (020) 7942 2000
www.vam.ac.uk
⊖ South Kensington
Bus 14, 49, 70, 345, C1
Open Mon 12–5.50, Tue–Sun 10–5.50, Wed late view 6.30–9.30 (seasonal)
Free
Wheelchair access. Use Exhibition Road entrance or call **t** *(020) 7938 8638 to book an escort in advance*
Suitable for ages 10 and up
Allow at least two hours

Dedicated to the decorative arts, the Victoria & Albert (or the V & A as it is known) has, over the course of its long history, gathered together a huge collection of treasures from all over the world: silverware from European royal palaces, ceramics from eastern temples, sculptures by African tribesmen and vast hoards of jewellery, furniture, textiles, tapestries and paintings – it's like an enormous magpie nest full of the world's most gaudy, glittery things. The dress gallery usually appeals to

Question 16
How many years did it take to build the V&A Museum's current home and in what year was it finished?

answer on p.249

clothes-conscious teens. It traces the evolution of fashion from the 17th century to the present day, from ruffs and crinolins to mini skirts and trainers.

For something to gasp at, head to the Cast Court where you'll find an exhibition of plastercasts of some of the world's greatest (and biggest) statues and monuments – Michelangelo's *David* and Trajan's column (in two, huge pieces) among them.

The British Galleries 1500-1900, are a welcome addition, with play areas where kids can try on Victorian clothes or attempt to rebuild the Crystal Palace using perspex blocks, as well as touch-screen information points, reconstructed room sets and banks of computer workstations.

There's not much to push or pull in the other galleries, though the museum more than compensates by organizing plenty of activities for kids to take part in. These are usually themed according to the gallery in which they are being held – so you might have origami in the Japanese Gallery, paper clothes-making in the Dress Gallery and jewellery-

Tell me a story: Tudor tales

The V&A is home to a number of rare and precious objects, among them are Charles Dickens' pen case and manuscript for *Oliver Twist*, as well as Joseph Paxton's first 'back-of-an envelope' sketch for the Crystal Palace, built for the Great Exhibition of 1851. Here are a selection of Tudor curios each with their own story to tell. Try and find them on your way round this eclectic museum.

▶ The Great Bed of Ware – said to be Britain's most famous bed; it is over 11 feet long and ten feet wide and is steeped in folklore. The bed is mentioned in Shakespeare's *Twelfth Night* and in a poem by Lord Byron. Charles Dickens is reputed to have tried to buy it. It was conceived as a Tudor marketing ploy, to attract visitors to The White Hart Inn at Ware in Hertfordshire. The bed is supposed to be haunted and in 1689, on the night before King William III was crowned, is recorded as having slept '26 butchers and their wives'.

▶ A rare 16th century Standing Salt or ceremonial salt cellar. In the Tudor period salt was a luxury commodity and was kept in a precious container called simply a 'salt'. The position of the salt on a banqueting table indicated the importance of the diners – distinguished guests sat 'above the salt' and had the choice of the best dishes.

▶ The beautiful hanging panels from Oxburgh Hall which were embroidered by amongst others, Mary Queen of Scots during her imprisonment between 1569-1585. Some of the emblems represent fortitude and courage in adversity.

▶ A fine 16th century Silver Tankard. These were introduced into England during the reign of Henry VIII and soon became fashionable gifts at court for men and women. They could be personalised, engraved with the individual's heraldry, and were used to hold warm beer for breakfast or ass's milk.

making in the Silver Gallery. Activity backpacks are available for kids on Saturday afternoons (1–4.30) which are full of jigsaws, stories, puzzles and construction games relating to the collections. There are six themed packs to choose from, designed for ages 5–11. On Sundays and in the school holidays a roving activity cart tours the museum's seven miles of corridors. Note, during the next few years some exhibitions may close temporarily to accommodate construction of the museum's controversial 'Spiral' extension.

Hyde Park

t (020) 7298 2100
www.open.gov.uk/rp
⊖ Hyde Park Corner, Knightsbridge, South Kensington, Lancaster Gate, Queensway
Bus 2, 9, 10, 12, 14, 16, 19, 22, 36, 49, 52, 70, 73, 74, 82, 94, 137
Free

Suitable for all ages, although only children aged five and over can go boating on the Serpentine

A wonderful expanse of greenery, Hyde Park provides a welcome oasis of calm in the hectic, bustling city. In fact, only the eastern side is officially called Hyde Park; the western side is known as Kensington Gardens, but there is no official border and it's really just one big park. In the middle is the Serpentine, as the name suggests, a great snake-shaped lake populated by swans, ducks, geese and other wildfowl. You can hire rowboats – a great way to spend a lazy summer afternoon (adults 30mins £3, one hour £4; children 30mins £1, one hour £2; rowing lessons £5).

Did you know?
Rotten Row is a corruption of the French 'route de roi' (king's way). It became the first road in London to have street lighting when William III hung 300 lanterns from the trees along its route to deter highwaymen.

Alternatively, if the kids would rather play on the grass, help yourself to one of the many green and white striped deckchairs that dot the park – an attendant will eventually find you and charge you the required £1. You can also swim in the Serpentine Lido, paddle in the children's pool (between May and September) and clamber aboard the climbing equipment in the new Princess Diana Adventure Playground which is located near the famous Elfin Oak (a tree decorated with dozens of tiny elf sculptures) and features a large adventure galleon (not a pirate ship, it was felt that such violent imagery might be inappropriate). The park's famous Peter Pan statue is also near here. Author J. M. Barrie lived at 100 Bayswater Road, not 500 yards from the park, and erected the statue secretly in the middle of the night.

Because of its location, Hyde Park is extremely popular but it is also, owing to its sheer size, serene and quiet. Furthermore, it's clean and largely free of dogs. The only real problem is the footpaths, which seem to be the favoured thoroughfares of London's roller-skating and jogging community, and if the weather's fine, you'd be better off walking on the grass.

Speaker's Corner

Some of London's more passionate (some would say barmy) citizens have, since 1872, been allowed to let off steam every Sunday at Speaker's Corner which is located at the northeastern end of the park. People can say whatever they want (about whoever they want) here and, standing on a

makeshift platform (traditionally a soapbox), attempt to rally passing pedestrians to their cause (be it Buddhism, Marxism or the uses and abuses of potting compost), providing they can make themselves heard above the traffic on Park Lane.

Kensington Palace

The State Apartments, Kensington Gardens, W8
t (020) 7937 9561
www.hrp.org.uk
⊖ High Street Kensington, Bayswater, Queensway
Bus 9, 10, 12, 52, 73, 94
Open May–Sept 9.45–3.30
Adm Adult £8.80, child £6.30, concs £6.90, family £26.10
Suitable for ages eight and over, audio-tour guides
Allow at least an hour

On the western edge of Kensington Gardens, this rather reserved-looking palace is where Princess Diana, the 'People's Princess', lived following her divorce from Prince Charles. The gardens outside were covered in 1.5 million bunches of flowers in the week following her untimely death in 1997. There are guided tours between 10am and 3.30pm, when you can wander through the plush historic apartments and see the excellent exhibition of royal clothes. Princess Diana's evening

Can you spot?
Can you find the Pet Cemetery by the Victoria Gates in Hyde Park's northwest corner?

gowns return from tour in Jan 2002 to take up permanent residence in the palace. From May 2002 they will be joined by royal wedding dresses.

The Albert Hall

A great red barrel of a building, it sits opposite the Albert Memorial on Kensington Gore. Despite its so-so acoustics and legendary echo, this 19th-century construction is one of London's most popular concert venues playing host in summer to 'the Proms' – a series of cheap classical concerts that have become a national institution. A special 'Children's Proms in the Park' concert takes place every year in Hyde Park. Call **t** (020) 7589 8212 for details of concert programmes.

The Albert Memorial
This huge gold statue set in an elaborate 175ft stone frame was built in the 1860s on the orders of Queen Victoria as a memorial to her late husband, Prince Albert. Around its carved stone sides are tributes to all the important men of letters, arts and sciences of the Victorian era. Women are somewhat few and far between. The statue itself was considered so bright that the gilding was removed during the war to stop it attracting the attention of enemy planes. It has recently been renovated to stunning effect. There are guided tours every Thurs, Fri, Sat & Sun at 2pm and 3pm, adults £3, concs £2.50, **t** (020) 7495 0916.

There's Knightsbridge of course, home to two of the world's most famous department stores: the ultra-chic Harvey Nichols and Harrods with its enormous toy department and magnificent food halls. If you've got the shopping bug, however, remember that you're just a tube stop or two away from two of London's best shopping areas: High Street Kensington and the King's Road (*see also* **Shop** p.235).

Harrods

Knightsbridge, SW1
t (020) 7730 1234
www.harrods.com
⊖ Knightsbridge
Bus 10, 19, 52, 74, 137
Open Mon, Tues & Sat 10–6, Wed–Fri 10–7

Harrods, which celebrated its 150th anniversary in 1999, is famous for its luxurious interiors. The food halls, in particular, are fabulously opulent – your children may well take a passing interest in the exotic fruit displays, fresh fish sculptures and straw-boatered shop assistants as they drag you towards the toys on the fourth floor. Here, you can find everything from limited edition Steiff teddies and one-third size Ferraris with full leather interior (a snip at £42,000) to the latest video games. Down a couple of floors is the pet store, full of talking parrots and cute kittens and dogs (plus rather sad-looking birds in cages). There are places

to eat on each of the four floors including a tapas bar, an oyster bar, a sushi bar and a rotisserie. Your kids will probably insist on dining at Planet Harrods, however, next to the toy department where cartoons play constantly on big screens. Harrods toy department organizes various events and activities for children including Teddy Bear days and Easter Egg hunts.

Harvey Nichols

109–125 Knightsbridge, SW1
t (020) 7235 5000
www.harveynichols.com
⊖ Knightsbridge
Bus 10, 19, 52, 74, 137
Open Mon–Fri 10–6, Sat 10–5

Though less child-friendly than Harrods, this can still provide a singular shopping experience. It's renowned as London's most fashionable department store and always stocks the latest high fashions for men, women and children. Its food halls on the fifth floor are, in their own way, just as impressive as those to be found at Harrods, and offer some great views of the Knightsbridge skyline, especially in the evening.

The Spy Catcher

25g Lowndes Square, SW1
t (020) 7245 9445
www.spycatcher.uk.com
⊖ Knightsbridge
Bus 10, 19, 52, 74, 137
Open Mon–Fri 10–6, Sat 10–5

Your mission, should you choose to accept it, is to get your children to leave this shop once they're inside. It's packed to the rafters with outlandish spy equipment. The staff will cheerfully explain what all the cunningly disguised bits and bobs are supposed to do. Intriguingly, this is actually supposed to be a serious grown-up shop, catering to a serious (if slightly suspicious) grown-up clientele, but it touches a nerve with children who revel in all this cloak and dagger stuff.

Please Mum

85 Knightsbridge, SW1 **t** (020) 7486 1380
⊖ Knightsbridge
Bus 10, 19, 52, 74, 137
Open Mon–Sat 10–6.30, Thurs till 7.30

The place to go for spectacular frocks and smart suits for special occasions.

WHERE TO EAT

All three Kensington museums have good cafés. The pick of the bunch is probably the **Science Museum Café** which can be found on the ground floor in the Power Gallery. There's also an **Eat-Drink** shop in the basement which sells confectionery, sandwiches and cold drinks and is very much geared towards children. Food may be consumed in any uncarpeted area of the museum and seating is provided at the Mega-Bite picnic area on the first floor. If shopping in Knightsbridge, be aware that the Brompton Road is lined with pavement cafés, delicatessens and sandwich bars. Though there isn't much in the immediate vicinity of Hyde Park, you can get excellent toasted sandwiches at the **Kensington Gardens Café** on the Broad Walk.

There are numerous chains to choose from including branches of the family-friendly French bistro, **Café Rouge** at 27–31 Basil Street, **t** (020) 7584 2345, ⊖ Knightsbridge, and the nation's favourite pizza chain, **Pizza Express** at 6–7 Beauchamp Place, **t** (020) 7589 2355, ⊖ Knightsbridge, as well as a branch of **McDonald's** at 177 Brompton Road. *See Eat* p.223 for more details on the above restaurant chains.

Hyde Park

The Swan
66 Bayswater Road
t (020) 7262 5204
⊖ Lancaster Gate

What sets this unassuming pub apart from the others is the fact that it has a children's licence, which means you can (and should) expect child-friendly service at all times and a variety of facilities for family use. In this popular tourist haunt, this translates to a heated terrace, a children's toilet and half-portions of staples like shepherds pie or sausage and mash.

Knightsbridge

Chicago Rib Shack
1 Raphael Street, SW7
t (020) 7581 5595
Open Mon–Sat 12 noon–12midnight, Sun 12 noon–11pm
⊖ Knightsbridge

On Sunday lunchtimes, kids can look forward to balloons, activity menus, colouring books, competitions and some delicious barbecue-style food. The portions (even on the kids' menu) are huge and kids are entitled to a free soft drink.

3 Gloriette Patisserie
128 Brompton Road, SW3
t (020) 7589 4750
Open Mon-Sat 7am–7pm, Sun 9am–6pm
⊖ Knightsbridge

This is a great place for anyone with a sweet tooth. Boasting a fantastic selection of tempting cakes, from creamy chocolate gateaux to glazed fruit tarts, it also sells a wide variety of snacks, ranging from salads to assorted tasty sandwiches.

4 Monza
6 Yeoman's Row, SW3
t (020) 7591 0210
Dinner Daily 7–11.30pm, lunch Tues–Sun 12 noon–2.30pm
⊖ South Kensington, Knightsbridge

A small, quaint Italian restaurant offering a range of pizza, pasta and risotto dishes to suit all tastes. Family-orientated with excellent service, its walls are decorated with motor-racing memorabilia (Monza being the venue for the Italian Formula 1 Grand Prix).

5 Pizza on the Park
11 Knightsbridge, SW3
t (020) 7255 5273
Open Mon–Fri 8.15am–12midnight, Sat–Sun 9.30am–12 midnight
⊖ Hyde Park Corner, Knightsbridge

This bright, cheery pizza restaurant is the perfect place to fill up after a morning spent in the park or nearby museums. Colouring books, crayons and balloons are handed out at weekends when you may also be able to hear live jazz being played. Children's portions and high chairs available.

6 Pizza Pomodoro
51 Beauchamp Place, SW3
t (020) 7589 1278
www.pomodoro.co.uk
Open 12 noon–1am daily
⊖ Knightsbridge

Overlooking the very swanky Beauchamp Place, this is only really family friendly at lunchtimes, (the evenings often being given over to live music) when it's fun to sit at a window table watching the great and the good of Knightsbridge parading up and down in their high fashions. The interior is decorated with pictures of the owner standing with famous patrons such as Clint Eastwood and

Sylvester Stallone. In case you're interested, 'Pomodoro' is the Italian for tomato.

King's Road
Chutney Mary
535 King's Road, SW10
t (020) 7351 3113
www.chutneymary.com
Open Mon–Sat 12 noon–2.30pm &
5.30pm–11.30pm, Sun 12.30–3pm
⊖ Fulham Broadway

The twin sister of the Veerswamy, this pleasant, modern indian restaurant is very popular with familes, particularly on Sundays when they offer a children's menu for £7 consisting of a mixture of mild curry dishes and reliable standbys for fussy eaters – fish fingers, burgers etc. There is a very pleasant conservatory. High chairs available.

La Rueda
642 King's Road, SW6
t (020) 7384 2684
Open Mon–Fri 12 noon–3pm & 6.30pm–11.30pm, Sat 12 noon–11.30pm, Sun 12 noon–10.30pm
⊖ Fulham Broadway

Tired of pizzas and burgers? Then try your kids on the mini-portions of paella and patatas bravas served at this lively tapas chain. There's live music and dancing here on Friday and Saturday evenings. High chairs available.

...

Greenwich

Greenwich is just a hop and a jump on the new DLR extension from central London, but has an entirely different ambience. It's as relaxed, cultured and stately as the city is brash, racy and commercial.

Of course, elegance and beauty don't always cut it with children. They want action, not elegantly crafted buildings and parks. Thankfully, Greenwich can also offer plenty of fun.

Despite its proximity to central London, Greenwich is one of the best places to come and learn about life on the ocean waves. There's the National Maritime Museum, stuffed full of ships and nautical equipment for kids to clamber over, the *Cutty Sark*, the fastest tea clipper of the 19th century, and the *Gypsy Moth*, in which Sir Francis Chichester sailed solo around the world in the mid-1960s.

Greenwich is also the home of time (Greenwich Mean Time has been used to set the watches and clocks of the world since 1884) and marks the point of the Prime Meridian which lead to it being chosen as the venue for the nation's millennium celebrations at the now empty Dome.

At the Royal Observatory you can stand above a line marked on the ground with one foot planted in the world's western hemisphere and one in the east.

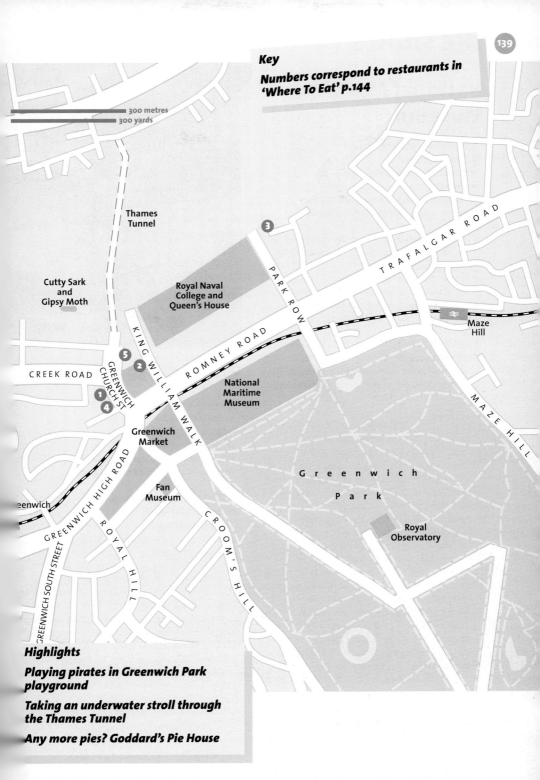

Key

Numbers correspond to restaurants in 'Where To Eat' p.144

300 metres
300 yards

Thames
Tunnel

Cutty Sark
and
Gipsy Moth

Royal Naval
College and
Queen's House

3

PARK ROW

TRAFALGAR ROAD

Maze
Hill

ROMNEY ROAD

KING WILLIAM WALK

5
2

CREEK ROAD

GREENWICH CHURCH ST

1
4

National
Maritime
Museum

MAZE HILL

Greenwich
Market

Greenwich

GREENWICH HIGH ROAD

ROYAL HILL

Fan
Museum

CROOM'S HILL

Greenwich
Park

Royal
Observatory

GREENWICH SOUTH STREET

Highlights

Playing pirates in Greenwich Park playground

Taking an underwater stroll through the Thames Tunnel

Any more pies? Goddard's Pie House

THE SIGHTS

National Maritime Museum

Romney Road, Greenwich, SE10
t (020) 8 858 4422
Infoline **t** (020) 8312 6565
www.nmm.ac.uk
≥ Greenwich, **DLR** Greenwich, Cutty Sark
Open 10–5 daily, last admission 4.30pm
Free
Bosun's Café with outdoor seating, souvenir shop
Wheelchair access to all floors – ramps and lifts
Suitable for all ages

The National Maritime Museum, one of the nation's favourite family museums, has always been good at sparking off controversy. For years, its exhibitions were criticized for being too triumphalist, glossing over the murkier episodes in British history. Now, following the creation of a British Empire Gallery, it is the turn of the museum's former supporters to be outraged. The exhibition, they argue, portrays the British Empire in an unremittingly hostile light, highlighting the murkier episodes to the exclusion of all else. Certainly, the exhibition tries to show the spread of Empire, not just from the point of view of the conquering British, but also from the vantage point of the conquered, who didn't always regard it as such a good thing. The museum's curators, for their part, argue that they have simply tried to achieve a proper sense of historical balance.

Besides the British Empire Gallery, there are plenty of great nautical exhibits to explore and study, including reconstructed engine rooms, boat decks and cabin interiors in which kids can run about, as well as various activities for them to take part in including 'pulling flags' and 'firing cannons'. For a little touch of gore, pop into the Nelson Gallery where you can see the bloodstained uniform worn by the famous Admiral during his final battle at Trafalgar. *See p.57 for more on this famous nautical encounter.* Every Saturday, the museum runs its 'Shipmates' sessions where children aged seven and over can learn more about the lives and skills of sailors through a series of interactive workshops.

Royal Observatory

Greenwich Park, SE10
t (020) 8858 4422
Infoline **t** (020) 8312 6565
www.rog.nmn.ack.uk
≥ Greenwich, **DLR** Greenwich, Cutty Sark
Open 10–5 daily, last admission 4.30pm
Free
Guided tours by prior arrangement
Baby changing room
Suitable for all ages

Just behind the Royal Naval College, the Royal Observatory stands on the Greenwich Meridian, the official dividing line between east and west, declared to be 0° degrees longitude. The line is marked out in the courtyard so you can stand with one foot in the western hemisphere and the other in the east. In 1884 the observatory was given the task of setting the time for the whole world, and Greenwich Mean Time (GMT) is still the standard against which all other times are measured. Every day at exactly 1pm, a red timeball on the Observatory roof drops to allow passing ships to set their clocks accurately.

The observatory, built in the late 17th century by Sir Christopher Wren, has long been at the forefront of astronomy. Today it houses the country's largest refracting telescope. It has become a compelling attraction for anyone interested in the cosmos. You can visit the apartments of the Astronomers Royal and find out how astronomy has developed, attend a 'space show' in the dome or try some astronomical experiments at the children's 'science station'.

The search for longitude

Until the late 18th century nobody knew how to measure longitude – the distance east or west around the earth. People could work out latitude (the distance north or south) using the position of the pole star, but no such system existed for longitude. In 1754, the government put up a reward of £20,000 for anyone who could come up with a solution. The strangest idea to emerge involved the sprinkling of several dogs with a 'powder of sympathy'. They would then be taken to a number of locations throughout the world. Once a magic incantation had been performed, the dogs would, so it was argued, bark simultaneously when a knife was stuck into the dog kept at home. Happily, the scheme was never tested. Instead, the reward was claimed, in 1772 by a clockmaker called John Harrison who constructed a clock which would measure time accurately at sea and so permit navigators to calculate a ship's east-west position to within 30 miles.

Royal Naval College

King William Walk, SE10
t (020) 8269 4747
www.greenwichfoundation.org.uk
≈ Greenwich, **DLR** Greenwich, Cutty Sark
Open Mon–Sat 10–4, Sun 12noon–4pm
Adm Mon–Tues free, Wed–Sun adult £5, child £2.50
Coffee shop, souvenir shop
No disabled facilities
Suitable for ages 10 and over

Can you spot?
The self-portrait of James Thornhill on the wall of the Painted Hall in the Royal Naval College? Despite being paid £1 per foot for decorating the walls and £3 per foot for the ceilings – which, in the early 18th century, was quite a lot of money – Thornhill still decided to paint himself with his hand outstretched as if asking for more cash.

Tell me a story: Mean time

A meridian is a north-south line made special by the fact that an astronomer has chosen it as the zero point for all his observations and measurements. By comparing thousands of observations taken from the same meridian it is possible to build an accurate map of the sky. Since the late 19th century, the Prime Meridian at Greenwich has served as the co-ordinate base for the calculation of Greenwich Mean Time. Before this time, almost every town in the world kept its own local time. There were no national or international conventions to set how time should be measured, or when the day would begin and end, or what the length of an hour might be. However, with the vast expansion of the railway and communications networks during the 1850s and 1860s, the worldwide need for an international time standard became imperative.

In 1884, the International Meridian Treaty established in law that 'every new day begins at mean midnight at the cross-hairs of the Airy Transit Circle telescope at the Royal Observatory'. Forty-one delegates from 25 nations met in Washington DC for the International Meridian Conference. By the end of the conference, Greenwich had won the prize of Longitude 0° by a vote of 22 in favour to 1 against (San Domingo), with 2 abstentions (France and Brazil). There were two main reasons for the victory. The first was the fact that the USA had already chosen Greenwich as the basis for its own national time zone system. The second was that in the late 19th century, 72 per cent of the world's commerce depended on sea-charts which used Greenwich as the Prime Meridian. The decision, essentially, was based on the argument that by naming Greenwich as Longitude 0°, it would inconvenience the least number of people.

With its grand classical façades overlooking the river, the Royal Naval College (now home to the University of Greenwich) provides a wonderfully elegant first sight of Greenwich to anyone arriving by boat.

The building is the work of three of Britain's most famous architects, Sir Christopher Wren, who was given the original commission by Queen Mary in the late 17th century, Nicholas Hamilton and Sir John Vanbrugh, and was originally used as a hospital for disabled sailors before being turned into a college in 1873.

Only the chapel and Painted Hall are open to the public. These fabulously painted interiors were designed by James Thornhill, who also decorated the dome of St Paul's.

Queen's House

Romney Road, SE10
t (020) 8312 6565
⇌ Greenwich, **DLR** Greenwich, Cutty Sark
Open 10–5 daily, last admission 4.30pm
Free

In between the Royal Naval College's façades stands the Queen's House, an earlier Italianate palace designed by Inigo Jones. The interiors are just as sumptuous as the college adorned with frescoes and paintings (including the 'Sea of Faces', a collection of portraits of sea captains), but it's a touch more child-friendly and organizes regular holiday activities and workshops for children.

Cutty Sark

King William Walk, SE10
t (020) 8858 3445
www.cuttysark.org.uk
⇌ Greenwich, **DLR** Greenwich, Cutty Sark
Open 10–5 daily, last admission 4.30pm
Adm Adult and child £3.50, concs £2.50, under-5s **free**, family £8.50
Souvenir shop
Wheelchair access to first floor only
Suitable for all ages

In her time, the *Cutty Sark* was the speediest sailboat in the world, completing the round-Africa journey from Shanghai to London in a record 107 days. Unfortunately the advent of steam-powered boats in the late 19th century, coupled with the opening of the Suez Canal which drastically cut down all voyage times to the east, put an end to her usefulness.

Such was her fame, however, that she was never dismantled and today is the only surviving example of a tea clipper in the world. As she stands in dry dock near the Greenwich riverfront, you can explore her decks and cabins and learn all about

the vessel's illustrious history through a display of pictures and models.

Gipsy Moth IV

King William Walk, SE10
Open Easter–Oct Mon–Sat 10–6, Sun 12noon–6pm, last admission 5.30pm
Adm Adult 50p, child 30p
Suitable for all ages

Near the very grand *Cutty Sark* stands the tiny 54ft yacht in which Sir Francis Chichester sailed single-handedly around the world in 1966–7. In honour of his achievement, Chichester was knighted with the very same sword with which Elizabeth I had knighted Sir Francis Drake (the first Englishman to circumnavigate the globe) some 300 years earlier. Children love to explore the tiny cramped cabins and to imagine how they would have coped alone on the high seas for 274 days.

Greenwich markets

Greenwich is home to three excellent weekend markets: a small antique market, where you can often pick up good old toys, a larger central market – including the two-storey Village Market and the South London Book Centre with its enormous collection of comics – and a rather well-to-do covered craft market.

Antiques market

Off Greenwich High Road, between junctions with Stockwell Street and Royal Hill, SE10
Open Weekends 9–5

Second-hand clothes, workman's tools, smoking paraphernalia, watches and silverware.

Central market

Stockwell Street, opposite the Hotel Ibis, SE10
t (020) 8766 6844
Open Weekends 9–5; organic food market Sat only;
Village Market open Fri, Sat 10–5, Sun 10–6
Second-hand clothes, furniture, books plus
vintage bottles and military uniforms.

Craft market

College Approach, with entrances on Turpin Lane
(off Greenwich Church Street) and Durnford Street
t (020) 7240 7405
Open Weekends 9–5
Jewellery, candlesticks, cushions, candles, prints,
sweets, ethnic sculptures.

Fan Museum

12 Croom's Hill, Greenwich, SE10
t (020) 8305 1441
www.fanmuseum.org
⇌ Greenwich, **DLR** Greenwich, Cutty Sark
Open Tues–Sat 11–5, Sun 12noon–4.30pm
Adm Adult £3.50, child £2.50, under-7s **free**
Shop, baby changing room
Wheelchair access and adapted toilet
Suitable for all ages
Housed in a beautiful 18th-century townhouse,
this is a delightful collection of over 2000 fans
from the 17th century to the present day. It holds
regular demonstrations of fan-making.

Question 17
How long did it take Sir Francis Chichester to
sail around the world?
answer on p.249

Thames Tunnel

Open 24 hours daily. Lift open 5–9
Wheelchair and pushchair access when lift open
It's a simple pleasure, standing in a tunnel
beneath the River Thames, but one which never
fails to enthrall children who marvel at the sheer
impossibility of being under so much water. The
glass-domed entrances to the tunnel are easy to
spot on the south side of the river by the *Cutty Sark*
and on the north in Island Gardens.

Greenwich Park

Charlton Way, SE3
t (020) 8858 2608
www.open.gov.uk/rp
Open Dawn till dusk daily
Free
Everything in Greenwich Park has been touched
by the brush of elegance, from the beautiful flower
gardens and stately avenues lined with chestnut
trees to the ornate Ranger's Mansion and landscaped heights offering stunning views over the
Thames. The park was created as a hunting ground
by Henry VI in 1433 – it still contains a small deer
enclosure on its southern side – and was landscaped in the 17th century by the great French
gardener André Le Nôtre.
For all its class and refinement, however, this is
still a park that will greatly appeal to children, with
a boating lake, well-equipped playground and
picnic tables.

Blackheath

Blackheath, SE3
t 020 8854 8888
⇌ Blackheath
Bus 53, 54, 108, 202, 89
Open 24 hours a day
Free
A great windswept piece of open common next
door to the neatly manicured Greenwich Park,
Blackheath is hugely popular with kite flyers and,
each year, holds one of London's best Guy Fawke's
night firework displays. It's also where 40,000 odd
runners begin the London Marathon's 26 miles of
annual hell.

Although somewhat more sparsely equipped than central London, Greenwich has more village-style eateries and countryside inns. There's a new branch of up-and-coming gastro-chain **Fish!** at 1 Lawn Terrace, Blackheath, **t** (020) 7234 3333 – an eternally family-friendly spot overlooking the park. Other staples include **Pizza Express** 4 Church Street, **t** (020) 8853 2770; and **Café Rouge**, Ibis Hotel, Stockwell Street, **t** (020) 8293 6660. See **Eat** p.223 for more details on the above restaurant chains.

1 Goddard's Pie House
45 Greenwich Church Street, SE10
t (020) 8293 9313
www.pieshop.co.uk
Open 10.30am–9pm daily

Traditional London food served up by the restaurant's fifth generation of Goddard's – minced beef, steak and kidney, eel or cheese and onion pie accompanied by a large potion of mash and topped with a bright green parsley sauce known as liquor. And if you've still got room after that, the restaurant does an excellent blackberry and apple pie, served with a generous helping of ice cream.

2 The Tea House
14 King William Walk, SE10
t (020) 8858 0803
Open Mon–Fri 10.30–6, Sat & Sun 10–6

Situated on the road leading from the *Cutty Sark* to Greenwich Park, this serves lovely cream teas and makes a welcome afternoon pit-stop.

3 The Trafalgar Tavern
Park Row, SE10
t (020) 8858 2437
Open Mon–Sat 11.30–11.00, Sun 12noon–10.30

Just east of the Royal Naval College, this friendly pub has been welcoming visitors since 1837. In the mid-19th century Liberal cabinet ministers used to gather here on the Sunday after Whitsun to feast on whitebait caught from the Thames. Unfortunately, the pollution of the river put an end to their revelries in 1868. Today, the refurbished pub provides an elegant setting for a riverside meal and was voted 'Pub of the Year' in 1996. Whitebait is even back on the menu, although it's no longer caught in the Thames.

Millennium Dome

One of the most visited tourist attractions in the whole of 2001, the Millennium Dome was, nonetheless, an unmitigated disaster. Though the building and displays were widely praised, the inept way in which the whole project was managed by the government, coupled with its enormous cost – in the end nearly a billion pounds of lottery money was spent on just 12 months worth of entertainment – has left a sour taste in the nation's mouth. Surely, people ask, there must surely have been a better, more lasting way to celebrate the millennium.

But now it's all over. The displays have been removed with all the haste with which they were assembled leaving behind an undeniably spectacular structure that no one, it seems, wants to buy. The biggest roof ever constructed now covers precisely nothing. It stands, huge and empty, on the Greenwich peninsula, a monument to government folly.

Still, it looks nice, especially at night, and the views from the Trafalgar Tavern and nearby Canary Wharf are particularly worth checking out.

4 The Spread Eagle
1–2 Stockwell Street, SE10
t (020) 8853 2333
www.spreadeagle.org
Lunch Served daily 12–3pm, dinner Mon–Sat 6.30–10.30pm

This rather grand restaurant is just one of several businesses – including a bookshop, an antiques shop and a junkshop – occupying this restored coaching inn complex. Specialising in modern french cuisine, this is really only suitable for older well-behaved children. High chairs and children's portions on request.

5 Time
7a College Approach, SE10
t (020) 8305 9767
Open Daily for lunch and dinner

An attractive setting with fantastic food, a good atmosphere and occasional live jazz – best to book in advance. A family-orientated restaurant; toys on request for the kids.

Days out

Brighton

Getting there By road: The A23 links Brighton directly with London. Alternatively, take the M23 part of the way, rejoin the A23, then follow the signs. The journey should take a little over an hour. By rail: A regular train service runs from London Victoria (30 departures a day), the journey takes around 50-mins. Trains also run from London Bridge, Clapham Junction and King's Cross. National Express coaches and Southdown bus services arrive at Pool Valley bus station on Old Steine, not very far from the seafront.

If your kids are aged 5 or over, it's a good idea to travel to Brighton by train. The seafront is an easy 10-minute downhill walk from the station (making the station a slightly harder 15-minute uphill walk from the seafront) giving your kids plenty of time to get excited about seeing the sea. It comes into view about halfway down.

Tourist office 10 Bartholomew Square **t** (01273) 292589/599 **www.**brighton.co.uk/tourist

Britain's seaside resorts tend to have largely similar characteristics. They are cheery and cosy and somewhat old-fashioned. Brighton, however, is different. It's brash and loud and determinedly modern and remains so all year round. The great thing about Brighton is that it manages to be both fashionable, with its clubs and designer stores, and yet extremely family-orientated with lots of child-friendly attractions. There's the pier, of course, with its funfair, arcades and inexhaustible supply of giant teddy bears; the Marina, with its arcades and bowling alleys; and, last but not least, the beach itself. Brighton boasts a mighty eight miles of seafront, made up of pebbles rather than sand, so bring your sturdiest pair of sandals. One word of warning, according several reliable sources, a suspicious line of brown scum has recently been spotted bobbing along in the sea. Swimming, therefore, is really not advised.

Booth Museum of Natural History

194 Dyke Road **t** (01273) 292777
Open Mon–Wed and Fri–Sat 10–5, Sun 2–5
Free
Gift shop, mother and baby room, guided tours, wheelchair access

Based on the collection of the Victorian naturalist and Brighton resident, Edward Thomas Booth, this holds a fascinating display of insects, butterflies, fossils and animal skeletons. Events for children are organized during the school holidays when kids can turn their hand to fossil collecting, butterfly mounting or even taxidermy.

Brighton Palace Pier

Off Madeira Drive **t** (01273) 609361
Open Summer 9am–2am, winter 10am–12 midnight
Adm Free, rides are individually charged
Three bars, various fast food outlets, wheelchair access, disabled toilets

After the beach, this should probably be your first port of call. Vaguely reminiscent of an ocean liner on stilts, this beautiful snow-white pier stretches a mighty 1,722ft out to sea and is lined with snack bars, stalls and child-friendly attractions. About halfway down you'll find an amusement arcade full of all the latest video games, a few fairground-style stalls plus a couple of old-fashioned and rather neglected one-arm bandits. Next door stands a 250-seat fish and chip restaurant while, beyond this, right at the end of the pier, is a funfair with several gentle carousel-type rides, a small go-kart track, a helter-skelter, a log flume and a rollercoaster 'The Crazy Mouse'.

Royal Pavilion

North Street **t** (01273) 290900
www.brighton.co.uk/tourist
Open Oct–May 10–5; June–Sept 10–6
Adm Adults £4.50, children £2.75
Queen Adelaide Tearoom, gift shop, children's quiz sheets, mother and baby room, guided tours, many disabled facilities

The Pavilion is, without a doubt, Britain's most over-the-top Royal Palace. Designed by John Nash in the 1810s on the orders of the Prince Regent, it's usually described as being 'in the Indian style with a Chinese interior'; in other words, it's a bit of a mishmash. Kids usually respond favourably to its fairytale-like exuberance. Forget notions of taste and style, just come and enjoy the excess: the vast crystal chandeliers, the lashings of gilt, the hand-knitted carpets and bizarre trompe l'oeil decor.

Vintage Penny Arcade

On the beach, 50 yards west of the Palace Pier
Open Easter–Oct weekends and school hols 12 noon–late

A collection of original Edwardian penny slot machines (strength testers, fortune-tellers, 'what the butler saw' gizmos, etc.) that will probably prove just as popular as the more modern whizz-bang stuff on offer at the pier. Buy a collection of old pennies at the entrance to feed into the slots.

Brighton Marina
Brighton **t** (01273) 693636
www.brighton-marina.co.uk
Open Daily 10–6

Quite a way east of the town centre, the Marina is still well worth a visit. It's a nice place to eat (try one of the various cafés and restaurants that line the water's edge) and there's a large entertainment complex with a cinema, an arcade, tenpin bowling and pool. Boat cruises around the harbour, to the pier and out to sea are also offered. The best way to reach the Marina is on the Volk's Railway, Britain's oldest electric railway, built in 1883.

Where to Eat

Alfresco
The Milkmaid Pavilion, King's Road Arches
t (01273) 206523
Open Daily 12 noon–10.30

Pleasant, friendly Italian restaurant overlooking the seafront with an outdoor seating area. Although it doesn't have a children's menu, it is popular with families, especially in summer when it can get very full. High chairs available.

Cactus Canteen
5 Bright Square **t** (01273) 725700
Open Mon–Sat 11.30–11, Sun 12 noon–10.30

Lively Tex-Mex diner offering a children's menu. High chairs available.

Devil's Dyke
Poynings **t** (01273) 857256
Open Daily 11.30–10

Family pub overlooking the hugely popular beauty spot of the same name. It offers a children's menu, high chairs, a mother and baby room and outdoor seating on sunny days.

English's
29–31 East Street **t** (01273) 327980
Open 12 noon–10.30pm, Sun 12.30–9.30pm

Seafood restaurant and oyster bar for kids with adventurous culinary tastes (apparently there are some) who wouldn't mind something other than cod and chips.

Harry Ramsden's
1–4 Marine Parade **t** (01275) 690691
Open 12 noon–9.30, till 10pm Fri and Sat, till 9pm Sun

For kids who do want the usual cod and chips, this branch of the famous northern fish and chip chain is situated opposite the entrance to the pier and Sea Life Centre and can seat over a hundred people. There are two special children's menus: a Postman Pat menu for £2.99 and a Cool Kids menu for £3.99. High chairs available. Eat in or takeaway.

The Regency Restaurant
131 King's Road **t** (01273) 325014
Open Daily 9am–11pm

Traditional seafront fish restaurant with white plastic chairs and tables on the pavement shaded by coloured umbrellas and a range of locally caught fresh fish and seafood dishes on the menu. Children's menu and high chairs available.

Cambridge

Getting there By air: Stansted airport is about 30 miles south of Cambridge and is linked to the city by a regular bus service (and the M11). By road: Cambridge is 55 miles north of London and can be reached by the M11 from the south and A14 from the north. Driving into Cambridge city centre, which is largely pedestrianized and ringed by an impenetrable mass of one-way streets, isn't really an option. You'll either have to come by train (the train station is a good mile and a half south of the centre; there's a regular bus service) or take advantage of the city's Park & Ride scheme. There are four car parks on the outskirts of Cambridge: Cowley Road on the A1309 to the north, Newmarket Road on the A1303 to the east, Babraham Road on the A1307 to the south and Madingley Road on the A1303 to the west. Parking is free and buses leave for the city centre every 10–15 mins between 7am and 8pm. For more details contact Stagecoach Cambus **t** (01223) 423554. By train: there are frequent rail services to London King's Cross (50-min) and London Liverpool Street (1hr 10min). By coach: an hourly coach service from London Victoria coach station is provided by National Express
Tourist office The Old Library, Wheeler Street **t** (01223) 322640 **www.**tourismcambridge.com. The

centre has a souvenir shop and can provide details of guided walking tours led from here by Blue Badge Guides throughout the year (dramatic tours with costumed characters take place in summer).

Cambridge, like its great rival Oxford, is principally famous for its university, one of the oldest and most respected in the world (although it's not quite as old as Oxford, as Oxford graduates are always at pains to point out). Also like Oxford, it's an exceedingly beautiful place with some of the country's prettiest architecture, several beautiful parks and, of course, the River Cam, a great sash of water flowing to the north and west of the city.

Being smaller and more condensed than Oxford, it's a great place for pottering, be it on foot, by bike or on the river. The centre of town, where you'll find most of the colleges and university buildings, is largely pedestrianized. The two main thoroughfares, Bridge Street (which turns into Sidney Street, St Andrew's Street and Regent Street) and St John's Street (which becomes Trinity Street, King's Parade and Trumpington Street) are lined with shops, tearooms and (for the students) bookstores.

Cambridge and County Folk Museum
2–3 Castle Street **t** (01223) 355159
Open Tues–Sat 10.30–5, Sun 2–5; also open Mon from April–Sept 10.30–5
Adm Adults £2, children 50p, under-5s **free**
Gift shop, guided tours

Housed in a 16th-century, half-timbered farmhouse, this looks at the non-academic side of life in Cambridge, with displays on the people who have lived and worked in this area for the last 400 years. Activity days for children aged 6–10 are organized on some Saturday afternoons and workshops for 7–11 year-olds are held during the school holidays.

Cambridge Museum of Technology
The Old Pumping Station, Cheddars Lane
t (01223) 368650 **www**.cam.net.uk/home/steam
Open Easter–Oct Sun 2–5; Nov–Easter first Sun of every month 2–5
Adm Steaming £4, non-steaming £2
Shop, disabled access

Housed in a preserved Victorian pumping station, this is filled with the noisy contraptions of the industrial age: boilers, engines and pumps, which are set in motion during the museum's occasional 'steam days'.

Fitzwilliam Museum
Trumpington Street **t** (01223) 332906
www.fitzmuseum.cam.ac.uk/
Open Tues–Sat 10–5, Sun 2.15–5
Free
Café, gift shop, guided tours, mother and baby facilities, limited wheelchair access
Not suitable for pushchairs although baby slings/harnesses available

The city's most respected museum, parts of which will be of interest to children, although you may want to skip all the endless cases full of European porcelain, Chinese vases and Korean ceramics (there's only so much fun to be had from old plates) and head straight to the mummies and painted coffins in the Antiquities gallery, or the room full of armour and weapons in the Applied Arts section. Family activity sheets are available.

Museum of Archaeology and Anthropology
Downing Street **t** (01223) 333516
www.cumaa.archanth.cam.ac.uk
Open Tues–Sat 2–4.30; phone to check extended summer hours June–Sept
Free

The ground floor 'Rise of Civilization' gallery, full of ancient pots and bits of flint, is only worth a cursory inspection. Instead, make a beeline for the ethnographic collection on the first floor, a wonderful array of treasures brought back by 18th- and 19th-century explorers: native American feathered headresses, Eskimo canoes and parkas (made from dried walrus hide), scary African tribal masks and suits of Japanese ceremonial armour, all arranged around a 50ft high totem pole.

Sedgwick Museum of Earth Sciences
Downing Street **t** (01223) 333456
www.esc.cam.ac.uk/SedgwickMuseum
Open Mon–Fri 9–1 and 2–5, Sat 10–1
Free (Discretionary donation encouraged)
Shop, some wheelchair access/assistance available

Houses the oldest geological collection in the world (although, in geological terms, this is a pretty slight claim) with various multi-million-year-old rocks and minerals displayed in antique walnut cases. It also has a large collection of fossil dinosaurs. Following a period of redevelopment, (due for completion in spring 2002), the museum will have even more space dedicated to the weird and wonderful world of nature; planned displays include exhibits on giant dragonflies, how volcanoes work, and whether there might be life on other planets.

University Botanic Garden

Cory Lodge, Bateman Street **t** (01223) 336265
www.plantsci.cam.ac.uk/Botgdn/index.htm
Open Jan, Nov, Dec 10–4; Feb and Oct 10–5; March–Sept 10–6
Adm (March–Oct, weekends and Bank Hols) adults £2, children £1.50, under-5s **free**
Café–restaurant (summer only), picnic areas, gift shop, mother and baby facilities, guided tours by arrangement, disabled access

The 40-acre University Botanic Garden, just south of the Cambridge's centre, was founded in 1762 and is the city's most beautiful open space with lots of trees and flowers, several glasshouses, a lake, a geographical rock garden and numerous rare plants laid out amid an elegant landscaped setting. It may prove a little formal for younger tastes, however. If you're after a spot where kids can enjoy more uninhibited play, try Jesus Green, to the north of the city centre near the river, a large, open grassy space with a children's play area and an open air swimming pool in summer. Otherwise, just to the west, you'll find Midsummer Common, a huge riverside meadow that plays host to fairs and circuses in summer and a large firework display on 5 November.

Punting

The archetypal Cambridge pursuit can be enjoyed every day between Easter and October. Punts can be hired from Magdalene Bridge, Mill Lane, Garret Hostel Lane, the Granta Pub on Newnham Road and the Rat and Parrot pub near Magdalene Bridge. A deposit of around £25 is usually required while the punts themselves will cost something in the region of £6–8 per hour. Chauffeured punt trips are also available.

You'll be shown how to use the pole before you set off although it will still take a lot of getting used to – and you should also prepare your children for disappointment as they will probably be unable to deal with the pole's considerable weight.

Do be aware that it can be a pretty wet and soggy experience, especially during the initial learning process, although the Backs do provide an idyllic space in which to dry off and have a quick picnic while you refine your technique. Remember to stick to the left.

Where to Eat

Cambridge Blue

85-87 Gwydir Street **t** (01223) 361382
Open Daily 11-11

Family-friendly pub which serves evening and lunchtime meals. Children are allowed in the conservatory and in the large garden which has a Wendy house and various toys. Children's menu available.

Cambridge Tea Room

1 Wheeler Street **t** (01223) 357503
Open Daily 10–6

Opposite the tourist information centre, this tearoom serves good cream teas, as well as baked potatoes and sandwiches.

Copper Kettle

King's Parade **t** (01223) 365068
Open Daily 8.30–6

A Cambridge institution where generations of undergraduates have come to discuss the meaning of life over coffee and a Chelsea bun. Overlooking the glorious vista of King's College, it is a good place for a 20-minute sandwich pit-stop. No credit cards accepted.

Don Pasquale

12 Market Hill **t** (01223) 367063
Open Mon–Thurs 8–6, Fri & Sat 8am–9.30pm, Sun 9–6

With seating on the market square and a plentiful supply of high chairs this is a fun place to come for a slice of pizza, if blood sugar is running low, and watch the world go by.

Oxford

Getting there By road: Oxford is about 48 miles from London and can be reached via the M40. By train: Services arrive frequently from London Paddington. By bus/coach: There are regular National Express coach services to Oxford from London Victoria

Tourist information The Old School, Gloucester Green **t** (01865) 726871 **www**.oxfordcity.co.uk

Oxford, of course, is more than just a pretty town for tourists (and it is pretty with its magnificent college architecture and parks), it's a world famous centre of culture and learning. Indeed, over the centuries, it has become symbolic of a quintessential sort of élitist, flannel-trousered, cloistered Englishness. It is home to one of the country's two most prestigious universities (the other is Cambridge) and, ever since its foundation in the 13th century, has been preparing the great and the good for roles in public life. Tony Blair, Bill Clinton, Margaret Thatcher and even Henry VIII all studied at the university, although the term 'university' is slightly misleading – Oxford actually contains several independently operated colleges which together form the university and define the shape of the city. Most of the colleges are open to the public although, to preserve the academic ambience, many operate restricted opening times and charge hefty admission fees.

With so much accumulated learning and history, you might expect Oxford to be rather dull for children and, approached in the wrong way, it probably would be. But, plan your itinerary carefully and you'll find lots to occupy your days. Oxford actually boasts a good many child-friendly attractions including parks, interactive museums, punts and lots of good spots providing panoramic views of the 'dreaming spires' and surrounding countryside.

Curioxity Science Gallery

The Old Fire Station, George Street
t (01865) 247004
Open Sat, Sun and school hols 10–4
Adm Adults £2.10, children £1.80, family £7.20

Hands-on science museum for children full of interactive games and experiments.

Museum of the History of Science

Old Ashmolean Building, Broad Street
t (01865) 277280 www.mhs.ox.ac.uk
Open Tues–Sat 12 noon–4
Free

Recently refurbished, the museum contains displays of scientific instruments dating back to the 16th century (look out for Einstein's blackboard) as well as an education room and library.

Pitt Rivers Museum

Parks Road **t** (01865) 270927
Open Mon–Sat 1–4.30, Sun 2–4.30
Free

This elegant Victorian building houses a large ethnographic collection featuring numerous artifacts brought back by Captain Cook from his 18th century journeys of discovery – a witch in a bottle, a puffer-fish lantern, shrunken heads, samurai swords and totem poles are just some of the gruesome horrors bound to attract the children.

University Museum of Natural History

Parks Road **t** (01865) 272950 www.oum.ox.ac.uk
Open Mon–Sat 12 noon–5
Free
Picnic area, some disabled access

Check out the dinosaur galleries and working beehive (summer only).

The Botanic Gardens

Rose Lane **t** (01865) 276920
Open Garden: 9–5; glasshouses: daily 10–4.30
Adm Adults £2, under-12s **free** (**free** to all in winter)

Created in 1621, this is the oldest botanic garden in Britain. You can wander through nine small glasshouses filled with tropical and sub-tropical plants, including palms, orchids, giant ferns, etc. From the gardens you can follow the course of the river, though the turnstiles at either end may prove challenging with a buggy. About half-way along the route and to the left, there's a wooden bridge that leads to the college boathouses. Each boathouse has its own distinctive style and team, if you're lucky you might encounter a training session or even a race.

Magdalen College Park

High Street **t** (01865) 276000
Open Daily 2pm–dusk
Free

The grounds of Magdalen (pronounced 'Maudlin') contain a deer park and river walks through water meadows.

Port Meadow

Access via Walton Well Road and Thames Towpath
Open Any reasonable time, it is common land
Free

This huge water meadow is the largest green space in Oxford. You can see horses, cows and geese roaming freely.

University Parks

Parks Road **t** (01865) 271585
Open Daily 8am–dusk
Free

Seventy acres of parkland on the west bank of the River Cherwell with gardens, trees, riverside walks and a duck pond.

River trips

Punting, the practice of pushing yourself along the river in a flat-bottomed boat using a long wooden pole is particularly associated with England's two great university towns. The image of young men in flannels and straw hats mucking about in boats on hot summer days is, for some, as typically English as tea shops and cricket on the village green. It's great fun, if more than a little tricky (young children probably won't be able to handle the heavy pole) but, once mastered, provides a good way of seeing the local country-side. Punts and (for the less adventurous) rowing boats for trips on the River Cherwell down past the Botanic Garden and Christchurch Meadow are available for hire from Magdalen Bridge, Folly Bridge and the Cherwell Boathouse. Sightseeing trips to Iffley, Sandford Lock and Abingdon are also offered from Folly Bridge by Salter Brothers **t** (01865) 243421. **www**.salterbros.co.uk

Where to Eat

Donnington Doorstep

Townsend Square **t** (01865) 727721
Open Mon–Sat 10–4

Good for a snack or a simple lunch, this drop-in centre has nappy-changing facilities, high chairs and toys for children.

Edgar's Café

Carfax Gardens **t** (01865) 790622
Open Mon–Sat 9–6

Once you've finished gazing at the views from the top of the Carfax Tower, you can enjoy a pleasant lunch at this small café at its foot.

Florence Park Family Centre

Rymers Lane **t** (01865) 777286
Open Mon, Thurs and Fri 10–3

Good for a snack or a simple lunch, this drop-in centre has nappy-changing facilities, high chairs and toys for children.

Gourmet Pizza

2 The Gallery, Gloucester Road **t** (01865) 793146
Open Sun–Thurs 11–10.30, Fri and Sat till 11

An excellent pizza chain, it can offer a full chil-dren's menu plus games and colouring books.

The Isis Tavern

On the towpath between Donnington Bridge and Iffley Lock **t** (01865) 247006
Open Daily 11–11 (children till 7)

Good pub food and a garden with swings.

Windsor

Getting there By road: Windsor is 20 miles west of London, off the M4 exit 6 and 50 miles northeast of Southampton, off the M3 exit 3. By train: Services run direct from London Waterloo to Windsor and Eton Riverside (every 30min Mon–Fri) and from London Paddington via Slough to Windsor Central (every 30min Mon–Sun). By bus/coach: Services leave London, Victoria coach station at regular intervals throughout day **t** 08705 808080 for details

Tourist office Royal Windsor Information Centre, 24 High Street **t** (01753) 743900 **www**.windsor.gov.uk. Above the information centre itself is a small exhi-bition on the history of the town.

Were its streets not seething with tourists, Windsor would be absolutely adorable. Indeed, with its picturesque Georgian houses and demure shops overlooked by the glorious 900-year-old castle, it's almost cartoonishly genteel. People, however, are an integral part of the Windsor expe-rience. Visit on a fine summer weekend and it can seem as if you're stuck in the midst of a travelling Tower of Babel as, hemmed in by visitors on all sides, you shuffle past the town's attractions. Should you manage to escape the crowds, however, there's no reason why you shouldn't have a very pleasant time. Although its narrow cobbled streets, full of twee souvenir shops and ye-olde tearooms, are fun to explore, Windsor is really a three-site town. First and foremost is the castle which will be upon you as soon as you leave the train station (either one). It doesn't so much domi-nate the town as define it, the roads flowing around the fortress walls. It's the official residence of the Queen and, although a little dry and dusty in places, it's still a castle and thus great fun to explore. Just to the north across the river is the adjoining town of Eton, home of the famous public school (and second on our list of must-see attrac-tions), first established in the 15th century, where countless government ministers and members of the Royal Family have been educated (including the princes William and Harry; Harry is still there). It is open to visitors throughout the year when you can take a tour of the grounds and see the oldest class-room in the world, its ancient desks scored with generations of schoolboy graffiti. If you come in term time you should be able to see the boys themselves walking around in their distinctive (not to say rather archaic) uniform of top hat and tail-coat. If you think they look adorable and would like to see your little boy dressed the same, you had better start saving – school fees cost around £14,000 a year. Nearby there are lots of grassy meadows for picnicking and watching the boats coming and going on the river. However, you're unlikely to linger long as your kids will no doubt keep reminding you of the *real* reason you're here, to visit the third most important site, Legoland (*see* p.158), the exuberant heart beneath the cultured exterior, one of the country's best theme parks, full of rides, games, models, activity centres, roller-coasters and, no matter when you visit, hordes of fun-seeking kids.

Windsor Castle

Windsor **t** (01753) 869898; infoline **t** (01753) 831118 www.royal.gov.uk
Open Mar–Oct 9.45–5.15 (last adm 4); Nov–Feb 9.45–4.15 (last adm 3)
Adm Adults £11, children £5.50, under-5s **free**, family £27.50
Souvenir shop, wheelchair access to most areas of castle; car parking available in town

This splendid concoction of towers, ramparts and pinnacles is, today, the official residence of the Queen and the largest inhabited castle in the world – and it is *big*, almost the size of a small town. In 1992, the State Apartments were ravaged by fire although, following £37 million worth of restoration work, you would be hard pressed to tell. They are today as opulent as they ever were, decorated with hundreds of priceless paintings from the royal collection, including Van Eycks and Rembrandts, as well as porcelain, armour and fine furniture. Children may find them a little dry, however, in which case you should make a beeline for the Queen Mary dolls' house which never fails to illicit a gasp of envy (particularly from the girls). If you've got the energy climb to the top of the 12th-century Round Tower where, on a clear day, you can see no fewer than 12 counties. The Changing of the Guard takes place outside the Palace on most days at 11 o'clock sharp.

Windsor Great Park

For something a little more sedate, head to Windsor Great Park, a vast 4,800-acre tree-filled green space stretching out to the south of the town. It contains a 35-acre formal botanic garden, the Swiss Garden, and a huge lake, Virginia Water, with a 100ft totem pole standing on its banks. The paths are well marked, so it is pushchair-friendly.

According to legend, the ghost of Herne the Hunter is supposed to haunt the park on moonlit evenings, when he can be seen, dressed in his stag antler headdress riding a black stallion, at the head of a pack of black hounds, which he leads in a midnight chase across the park.

Where to Eat

Crooked House Tea Rooms

51 High Street **t** (01753) 857534
Open Daily 10–6
Tearoom housed in the oldest free-standing building in Windsor.

Cyber Café

36 St Leonard's Road **t** (01753) 793164
Open Mon–Fri 9–5, Sat and Sun 10–4
Surf the net while you munch your sandwiches.

Good Measures

Boots Passage 18a Thames Street **t** (01753) 860720
Open Mon–Sat 12–2.30 and 6–10.30, Sun 12–3.30
Quality bistro with an outdoor patio – accompanied children eat for free.

Haagen Dazs ice-cream emporium

22 Thames Street **t** (01753) 832973
Open Daily 10–10
Wide variety of delicious ice-cream, for a kid's (and adult's) treat.

New College Inn

55 High Street, Eton **t** (01753) 865516
Food served 12–2.30 and 6–9
For a traditional English cream tea try this inn near the bridge in Eton.

Royal Oak

Datchet Road (opp Windsor and Eton Riverside Station) **t** (01753) 865179
Open 11–11
This attractive pub is festooned with flowers in summer, and has a children's menu and high chairs.

Sally Lunn's

11 Peascod Street **t** (01753) 862627
Friendly branch of the original tearoom in Bath.

Bricks and mortar

Hampton Court

Getting there Hampton Court is just southwest of London near Kingston-upon-Thames, off the A3 and A309 (J12 from the M25). Trains run regularly from London (Waterloo) to Hampton Court Station or you can take a cruise up the Thames with the Westminster Passenger Service from Westminster Pier.

Open Oct–Mar Mon 10.15– 4.30, Tues–Sun 9.30– 4.30; Mar–Oct Mon 10.15–6, Tues–Sun 9.30–6

Adm Adults £10.50, children £7, under-5s **free**, concs £8, family £31.40

Café, restaurant, souvenir shops (look out for the Tudor Kitchen shop which sells a range of Tudor cooking implements and medieval herbs), guided tours, disabled facilities, on-site parking

Suitable for all ages

One of the best loved of all royal palaces, Hampton Court provides a fabulous day out for children. This grand old building is stuffed full of 500 years' worth of treasures including Henry VIII's sumptuous state apartments, a real tennis court and a Renaissance picture gallery containing works by Brueghel and Mantegna. Your children's favourite area, however, will be the huge Tudor kitchens where every day a Tudor banquet, complete with spit roast, is prepared by cooks in full period dress. It's like stepping into a time-warp where you can see the sights, hear the sounds, smell the smells and even taste the tastes of days gone by. The guided tours are highly recommended, given by costumed characters who will enchant your children with tales of marriage and murder – this was where Henry VIII lived, remember.

During his reign Henry spent a staggering £62,000 on Hampton court (that's around £18 million in today's money) turning it into the most modern, sophisticated palace in England. Only part of the structure we see today, however, dates from this time. Sir Christopher Wren undertook a further £131,000 worth of rebuilding work (today £9.5 million) in the late 17th century, the most important element of which was the planting of new landscaped gardens. These beautiful gardens have always been as big a draw as the palace itself. The main attraction, of course, is the maze, the most famous in the world. It was planted in 1690 for William III and lures in around 300,000 people a year (and lets roughly the same number out again, give or take a few).

Castles

Bodiam Castle

Bodiam, Robertsbridge **t** (01580) 830436

Getting there Bodiam is 10 miles north of Hastings off the B2244. In summer there are river cruises to Bodiam from Newenden. The Kent and East Sussex Steam Railway also makes trips from Bodiam to the nearby town of Tenterden

Open Mid Feb–Oct daily 10–6; Nov–mid Feb Tues–Sun 10–4

Adm Adults £3.50, children £1.75, family £8.75

Café–restaurant, gift shop, picnic areas, mother and baby facilities, some disabled access, on-site parking

When children try to draw a castle, they nearly always come up with something that looks like Bodiam. Bodiam is a proper storybook castle with round turrets on each corner, crinkly battlements, arrow-slit windows, and a portcullis, and is surrounded by a deep moat. The inside of the castle, most of which is covered in grass, makes a perfect spot for a picnic and there are family events throughout the year, including treasure hunts, donkey rides and open air theatre performances. In summer there are boat trips from Bodiam up and down the river to Newenden and back (it's a 90-minute round-trip) and you can also take a ride aboard The East Sussex Steam Railway which runs between here and the nearby town of Tenterden.

Hever Castle

Hever, near Edenbridge **t** (01732) 865224

www.hevercastle.co.uk

Getting there Hever is about 8 miles west of Tonbridge off the B2027

Open Mar–Nov daily 11–6

Adm Adults £7.80, children £4.20, under-5s **free**, family £19.80

Café, gift shop, guided tours, mother and baby facilities, disabled access, on-site parking

It may look similar, with its turrets, battlements and moat, but Hever is very much the antithesis of the rough and ready Bodiam; its interior sumptuously decorated with antiques, fine tapestries and suits of armour – although many of the more interesting areas are (frustratingly) roped off. There are, however, a few nooks and crannies worth exploring, as well as costumed waxworks of Henry VIII and his six wives (this was where Anne Boleyn, his second wife, lived as a child), a display of dolls houses and the castle's picnic-perfect grounds contain a yew maze, a lake and an Italian garden with a lakeside theatre where a renowned season of plays, musicals and opera performances takes place each summer. There's also a water maze (from April to October), lined with water jets that spray visitors every time they take a wrong turning.

Leeds Castle

Maidstone **t** 0870 6008880
www.leeds-castle.co.uk
Getting there Leeds Castle is 40 miles southeast of London near Maidstone off the M20 and B2163. There are direct services from London Victoria to Bearsted, the nearest train station, from where there's a regular shuttle bus to the castle. Eurostar services from London Waterloo stop at Ashford International, 20 minutes away
Open Castle: Mar–Oct 11–5.30; Nov–Feb 10.15–3.30; park and gardens: Mar–Oct 10–5; Nov–Feb 10–3
Adm Adults £9.30, children £6, under-5s **free**, family £25
Gift shops, restaurant, guided tours, some wheelchair access

Leeds Castle looks like a castle should look; dramatic, romantic and mysterious. Set on two islands in the middle of a lake in 500 acres of beautifully sculpted Kent countryside, this was the famously hard to please Henry VIII's favourite castle. He spent a fortune on it during his lifetime, much of it on the fabulously opulent Banqueting Hall with its ebony wood floors and carved oak ceiling. The interior is stuffed full of precious paintings and furniture but the rarefied 'don't touch' atmosphere means that kids can't really interact with the space as much as they would like. It's a different story, however, in the castle grounds. With a maze, an underground grotto, an aviary and lots of wide grassy spaces to run around on, the grounds provide a wonderful opportunity for kids to let off steam. What's more, family entertainments are put on in the grounds throughout the year. These include Easter celebrations with face-painting, Punch and Judy shows, circus workshops, and, of course, the famous Balloon Festival in September, when the sky around the castle become filled with weird and wonderfully shaped hot air balloons.

Stately homes & palaces
Hatfield House

Hatfield **t** (01707) 262823
Getting there Hatfield is 15 miles north of London, 7 miles from the M25 (J23), 2 miles from the A1 (J4) and is signposted from the A414 and A1000. Hatfield train station is immediately opposite. There are regular services from King's Cross which take approximately 25 min
Open Late March–late Sept House Tues–Thurs guided tours only 12 noon–4pm, Sat–Sun and Bank Hol Mon 1pm–4.30pm; Park Sat–Thur 10.30am–8pm, Fri 11am–6pm
Adm House and Park adults £4.20, children £3.10; Park only adults £1.80, children 90p
Restaurant, picnic areas, shop, mother and baby room, guided tours, disabled access, on-site parking

Come to Hatfield to see how a real princess lived. This grand red-brick Jacobean mansion was built in the early 17th century on the site of the Tudor Palace where Queen Elizabeth I spent her childhood days. A wing of the original palace still survives adjoining the main house. The vast 4,000-acre grounds will probably be of most interest to children with their formal gardens full of hedges, paths, ponds and fountains and wilderness areas to explore. Horse and carriage rides are offered in summer and there are 5 miles of marked walks. On your travels see if you can spot the oak tree under which the young Princess Elizabeth supposedly learned of her succession following the death of her sister Mary in 1558.

The house itself is very grand inside with its imposing rows of paintings (look for the portrait of Elizabeth) and vast oak staircase (appropriately named the Grand Staircase) decorated with carved figures. Kids will like the National Collection of Model Soldiers which has over 3,000 miniature figures arranged in positions of mass combat.

Knebworth House

Knebworth **t** (01438) 811908
www.knebworthhouse.com
Getting there Knebworth House is 2 miles from Stevenage; the entrance is directly off J7 of the A1
Open School hols House: 12 noon–5; park and gardens 11–5.30
Adm Adults and children £5.50, under-4s **free**, family £19
On-site parking, café–restaurant, picnic areas, gift shop, guided tours

Built in the 16th century, Knebworth was originally a simple Tudor mansion, but was covered in over-the-top gothic adornments in the 1800s at the behest of the Victorian author Edward Bulwer-Lytton who wanted the house to resemble one of the romantic locations from his books – look out for the rearing heraldic dragons and crenellations. The interior will be of only passing interest to children, with its collections of paintings and armour (quiz sheets available), it's the grounds which are the real draw. As you head south away from the house you'll encounter a sunken garden surrounded by trees, followed by an exquisite rose garden (just to the right is a pet cemetery), a wild-flower meadow and a small maze. Beyond this is a wilderness area and a huge 250-acre park where herds of red deer roam freely.

The biggest attraction for children, however, will inevitably be the Fort Knebworth adventure playground, one of the biggest and best around with lots of derring-do climbing equipment and a great selection of slides, including a suspension slide (you travel down clutching on to a rope), the four-lane Astroglide, where you travel on a helter-skelter-type rush mat down a bumpy plastic chute, a twisting corkscrew slide and a vertical-drop slide. There is also a bouncy castle and a miniature railway, which provides looping 15-minute tours of the grounds.

Buckets and spades

Eastbourne

Getting there Eastbourne is on the south coast 21 miles east of Brighton, 18 miles west of Hastings on the A259, just south of the A27. There are regular train services from London (Victoria) and Brighton.
Tourist information 3 Cornfield Road, Eastbourne **t** (01323) 411400 **www**.eastbourne.org

Part owned by the Duke of Devonshire, Eastbourne has a cultured, almost dignified air to it. Indeed for a popular British tourist resort, there's a distinct lack of the normal tourist tat. There are no souvenir shops or candyfloss sellers along the seafront, just elegant Victorian homes and a few hotels and restaurants. Nothing is allowed to disturb the resorts' relaxed and (some might say)

slightly stuffy atmosphere. Perhaps unsurprisingly, this haven of south coast tranquillity has become a popular retirement home with all the benefits (peace and quiet) and problems (too much peace and quiet) that this implies. Nonetheless, the authorities haven't managed to stamp out all the fun just yet. Despite its polished veneer, Eastbourne actually has a good deal to offer in terms of family entertainment. There's the pier, one of the best and most visited in the country; an adventure playground 'Treasure Island'; a children's adventure funpark 'Fort Fun'; a leisure complex 'The Sovereign Centre' and, of course, the beach, a long stretch of sand and shingle with numerous rock-pools (lifeguards patrol in summer). The seafront is framed by two old towers: the Redoubt Fortress, where classical concerts and firework displays are held in summer, and the Wish Tower, which holds a collection of puppets.

Southend-on-Sea

Getting there Southend lies at the southernmost tip of East Anglia, at the mouth of the Thames estuary, 40 miles east of London (reached by the A127). Trains depart from London Fenchurch Street to Southend Central station regularly (1hr), and National Express run a frequent service from London Victoria (2.5hrs)
Tourist office 19 High Street **t** (01702) 215120 **www**.southend.gov.uk

Southend, situated on the north bank of the River Thames estuary, is within easy reach of the East End of London; indeed, for decades it seemed as if the two were linked by some sort of vacation umbilical cord. Every Bank Holiday, coachloads of East End families would descend on the Essex town looking to enjoy their annual day in the sun – only to discover that they were once again about to enjoy their annual day in the pub waiting for the rain to clear. The lure of cheap Spanish package holidays may have weakened the bond slightly, but the resort is still going strong and has plenty to offer families looking for that archetypal British seaside experience. There's a seven-mile-long stretch of sandy beach where you'll find facilities for sailing, water-skiing and windsurfing; a promenade lined with typically seasidey things: crazy golf courses, arcades, children's playgrounds, beach showers etc. (there's a seafront shuttle train in summer) while jutting out from the front is the town's most famous feature, revered since its cockney heyday, Southend Pier, which at over 1.3 miles is the longest pier in the world – it's quite a walk to the tip although you can hop aboard the pier train if you don't feel quite up to it.

Nature lovers

Ashdown Forest

Getting there It's just to the southeast of East Grinstead off the A22
Tourist information East Grinstead Tourism Initiative, The Library, West Street, East Grinstead **t** (01342) 410121

Children who have grown up knowing only the Disney version of Winnie-the-Pooh and his chums may be surprised to learn that the forgetful bear is an English creation. This great swathe of West Sussex forest and heathland provided the inspiration for AA Milne's tales of the famous bear, Christopher Robin and their various furry friends. The village of Hartfield is the centre of Pooh country from where you can visit the 'Hundred-Acre' Wood where most of the Pooh stories were set and even have a game of Poohsticks off the real Poohsticks bridge. Other places which have became familiar through AA Milne's stories such as the Enchanted Place, North Pole and Roo's Sandypit are all within easy reach of Gill's Lap car park which can be found just off the B2026. Otherwise, Ashdown is serious walkers' territory with lots of nature trails and sandy tracks.

Pooh Corner

High Street, Hartfield **t** (01892) 770453
www.poohcorner.co.uk

Whipsnade Wild Animal Park

Whipsnade, Dunstable **t** 0990 200123
www.whipsnade.co.uk
Getting there It's signposted from the M25 (J21) and the M1 (J9 and J12). Green Line buses run from London Victoria **t** (020) 8668 7261. The nearest train stations are Luton (served by King's Cross Thameslink) and Hemel Hempstead (served by Euston)
Open Easter–Sept Mon–Sat 10–6, Sun and Bank Hol Mon 10–7; Oct–Easter please call in advance

Adm Adults £10.70, children £8, under-3s **free**, car entry £8
Café, picnic areas, shop, disabled access, mother and baby room, disabled access, on-site parking

It's always much more rewarding looking at animals living in large enclosures that closely resemble their natural environments, rather than in small, cramped cages. And no wildlife park in Britain gives its animals as much space to roam about in as Whipsnade which, at the last count, boasted no less than 6,000 acres of paddocks, providing a home to over 2,500 animals.

There are four ways to tour Whipsnade: on foot, which can be tiring (especially for little legs) although you will get to wander among free-roaming wallabies, peacocks and deer; in the safety of your car, for which you have to pay extra; aboard the Whipsnade narrow-gauge steam railway, for which you also have to pay extra but which takes you on a tour through herds of elephants and rhinos; or, perhaps the best option, aboard the free open-top sightseeing bus which not only offers elevated views of the animals but can deposit you at all the best walking spots.

There's a vast range of animals to see including Asian elephants, who get to enjoy Europe's largest elephant paddock; white rhinos, who also have plenty of space to run about in (a rhino in motion is a pretty fearsome sight, they can shift a lot faster than their huge bulk would seem to allow); hippos, permanently submerged in muddy water; tigers (come at feeding time when you can see these magnificent beasts on the prowl, a tiger that's not eating tends to be a tiger that's not moving around that much); giraffes, iguanas, flamingoes, penguins, wolves and chimps.

Many of the animals (thanks to the park's successful captive breeding programme) come with babies in tow. In particular, look out for the white rhino calf, the two baby tigers, Kira and Kharia, and the baby crocodiles basking on their mother's back or being carried tenderly in her mighty jaws.

Wildwood Wildlife Centre

t (01227) 712111 **www**.wildwood-centre.co.uk
Getting there Wildwood is on the A291 between Canterbury and Herne Bay
Open Daily 10–5
Adm Adult £5.25, children £3.75

Over 30 acres of ancient woodland are the setting for this wildlife discovery park which provides children with the opportunity to see a variety of rare and endangered native species from owls and otters to wild boars to beavers (the new wolf cubs, born at the centre, are proving a big hit). Behind the scenes, Wildwood carries out serious conservation work, although this is not allowed to intrude on the fun to be had from getting close to the animals.

Theme parks

Chessington World of Adventure

Chessington **t** 0870 444 7777
www.chessington.co.uk
Getting there Chessington is a couple of miles north of Epsom, just off the A243, 2 miles from the A3 and M25 (J9 from the north, J10 from the south). There are regular train services to Chessington South Station from London (Clapham Junction)
Open Mar–Nov 10–5.15 (last adm 3); later closing for Family Fright Nights
Adm Adults £19.95, children £16, under-4s **free**, family £63
Fast food outlets, on-site parking, some disabled access (safety restrictions apply on some rides – call for detailed leaflet – a limited number of wheelchairs available on request)
Note Height restriction: varies but is usually 1.2m.

Chessington has rides for all ages from top of the range rollercoasters to gentle carousels and roundabouts. The park's most intense rides are the 'Samurai', which spins people round on an enormous rotor blade, 'Ramases Revenge', which looks a bit like a great big bread tin and flips its passengers over several times before squirting them in the face with jets of water (what fun!?) and the 'Vampire', which is a more traditional rollercoaster-style ride over the park's rooftops. In summer, on 'Family Fright Nights', you have the opportunity to sample all these rides in the dark.

Younger children are well catered for at Toytown, the Dragon River log flume, Professor Burp's Bubble Works, the physically challenging 'Action Man' assault course and the new Beanoland where you can enjoy a range of rides themed on Beano char-

acters (such as Billy Whizz's Waveslinger and the Bash Street bus) and watch costumed characters acting outing out 'comic' scenes. There's also a small circus with regular performances by trapeze artists and clowns.

It's easy to forget that, in amongst all the hi-tech gadgetry, there is also a zoo. You can take a quick, theme-park style look at the resident lions, gorillas and meerkats aboard the Safari Skyrail, a monorail that trundles over the animal enclosures. There are also daily displays by sealions, penguins and hawks and, at the recently opened 'Creepy Cave', you and your kids can go 'urgh!' at the collection of spiders, insects and other crawling horrors.

Legoland

Windsor **t** 08705 040404 **www**.legoland.co.uk
Getting there Legoland is 2 miles from Windsor on the Windsor to Ascot Road, signposted from J6 of the M4. The bus service from Windsor town centre to Legoland departs from Thames Street every 15-min during opening times
Open Daily 10–6, park closes 7 mid July–Aug
Adm Adults £18.50, children £15.50
Seven restaurants/cafés and 11 catering stalls, picnic areas, mother and baby facilities, wheelchair access, wheelchair hire available, adapted toilets, on-site parking

The most imaginative of Britain's current breed of theme parks, Legoland is now firmly established as one of the country's top family attractions. The theme is Lego, the Danish multi-coloured plastic building bricks that have become a national institution (27 million of which were used during the construction of the park). Lego kits have always been a good way of getting kids to use and develop their imagination and the park is equally inspirational. It's perhaps best described as a cross between a theme park and an activity centre. It has some good thrill rides, including a dragon-themed rollercoaster that jets its way through a mock-up medieval castle and a log flume, Pirate Falls. Older children (over-10s), however, may find them a little tame compared with what's on offer at places like Alton Towers and Chessington. Legoland is geared very much towards younger children.

The most popular attractions, which often have massive queues, are the interactive zones such as Lego Traffic, where children drive electrically powered Lego cars through a model town, negotiating traffic lights, pedestrian crossings and roundabouts on the way. The most skilful drivers are awarded their own special Legoland Driving Licence. In the Imagination Centre kids are encouraged to erect and destroy model buildings on a special 'Earthquake' Table. Older children can create robotic models, whilst their younger siblings play about with the Duplo Gardens' water cannon and enjoy some gentle boat rides.

There's plenty of stimulation for body as well as mind. Many of the park's rides, including the Sky Rider and the Bone Shaker, are peddle-powered, while the Space Tower and Muscle Maker are arm-powered. These are not only a good source of exercise but, because they give children the sensation of being in control, they often prove more popular than the automatically powered rides.

Gulliver's Land

**Livingstone Drive, Newlands, Milton Keynes
t** (01908) 609001 **www.gullivers-themeparks.com
Getting there** The theme park is signposted from J14 of the M1
Open Mid April–mid Sept 10.30–5; Oct half-term 10.30–5. For special Christmas events call in advance
Adm £8.80, children under 90cm **free**
Café–restaurant, fast food, shop, picnic areas, mother and baby room, on-site parking

Small theme park where all the rides, attractions, shows and food are aimed at 3–13 year olds and which boasts a suitably child-size entrance fee (just £8.80), around half of what you'd pay at one of the bigger name parks. There are several gentle-ish rollercoasters, including a log coaster and the 'Wild Mouse'; a log flume plus a number of themed areas such as Adventureland, where you can take a Jeep Safari through a mock jungle; Discovery Bay, which has pump carts; Toyland, which boasts a soft play area for toddlers; and, the centrepiece of the park, the Lilliput Land Castle. For a full day out, combine your visit with a trip to the new Xscape shopping complex (*see* p.248) in the town centre.

Thorpe Park

Staines Road, Chertsey t 0870 444 4466
www.thorpepark.co.uk
Getting there Thorpe Park is on the A320 between Chertsey and Staines (J11 or 13 from the M25). There's a regular train service from London (Waterloo) to Staines and Chertsey, from where you can catch a bus

Open Mar–Oct, times vary but it usually opens at 9.30–10 and closes between 5 and 7.30
Adm Adults £19.95, children £15.95, under 1m **free**
Fast food outlets, gift shop, baby changing facilities, first aid centre, some wheelchair access, adapted toilets, on-site parking

All theme parks need a show-piece ride; a glittering piece of terror-inducing hardware to set against the competition. Thorpe Park's champion is the bizarrely titled 'X:/No Way Out', which, although not the first rollercoaster to operate in pitch darkness, is certainly the first to force its passengers to travel at speeds of around 65mph in the dark...backwards.

This concession to modern super-thrill-seeking trends aside, most of the attractions at Thorpe Park have clearly been designed to cater for families rather than adrenaline junkies. Children are particularly well provided for with various themed areas such as Mrs Hippo's Jungle Safari and the Mr Monkey's banana ride, as well as Model World, which features miniature versions of the Eiffel Tower, the Pyramids and Stonehenge. They can also take a boat ride to Thorpe Farm to bond with the resident goats, sheep and rabbits. Swimwear (or a change of clothes) is a must, however, unless you want to return home with a car full of bedraggled children; there are more water-themed attractions here than at most parks, including the tallest log flume in the country 'Tidal Wave', an ersatz white-water rafting adventure 'Thunder River', as well as several pools and water chutes. In the last week of October, the park holds a number of firework displays.

The village of Chertsey is worth a visit in its own right for the costume collection, steam railway and hands-on gallery in its local museum.

NEED TO KNOW

SURVIVAL

Being away from home can have its frustrations, mainly because you don't necessarily know where everything is, like where to go in an emergency or who to call for advice. London is a big city it's true, but the following list of essentials should help to put parents' minds at rest and make families feel much more at home.

24-hour chemist
Zafash Chemist
233–235 Old Brompton Road, SW5
t (020) 7373 3506

24-hour dentist
Dental Emergency Care Service
t (020) 7937 3951

Accident and Emergency
University College, London Hospital
Gower Street, WC1
t (020) 7387 9300

Babysitting
Childminders Babysitting Service
t UK (020) 7935 2049

Emergency
Police, Fire Brigade, Ambulance
t 999 or 112

Getting around
London Transport Travel
t (020) 7222 1234

Lost property
London Transport Lost Property Office
t (020) 7486 2496
Black Cab Lost Property Office
t (020) 7833 0996

Taxi
Dial-A-Black-Cab
t (020) 7253 5000

Useful websites

NHS Direct
www.nhsdirect.nhs.uk
Either log on or call 0845 4647 to obtain advice from trained hospital staff. This is a vital and reliable service that helps to cut down on unnecessary doctors' appointments and hospital visits, not to mention dragging unwell children out of their beds in the dead of night. Please use it.

Boots The Chemists
www.wellbeing.com
Boots' own website offering an online delivery service for toiletries, baby food, nappies etc, plus advice and details of local Boots' stores and other practitioners.

Maps
www.upmystreet.com
If you're staying in one area for a while you can key in your postcode and find out about all kinds of local services from dry cleaners to estate agents.
www.multimap.com
Map service that allows you to home in on a particular area and find out about local restaurants, hotels and services.

Kids in

Rain, rain, go away, come again another day! London is famous for many things, one of which is the terrible weather. It rains here – a lot. Thankfully, there is so such much to do when the rain comes that it hardly matters.

Adventure playgrounds

Indoor play areas are a very good option if you want to give the kids a chance to let off steam. Parents are usually expected to stay on the premises while their children play. Below is a selection of venues in the London area. Alternatively, you could try your nearest shopping centre or leisure complex.

Bramley's Big Adventure

136 Bramley Road, W10
t (020) 8960 1515
www.bramleysbig.co.uk
⊖ Ladbroke Grove
Bus 7, 23, 52, 74, C1
Open 10-6.30 daily
Adm under-4s £3, over-4s £3.50 term-time, £3.50, £4.50 school and bank holidays
Ages up to 11

There are slides, inflatables, monkey ropes and ball pools galore for ages 5-11. There's also a separate area for under-5s and a café for flagging parents. A popular venue for parties with play session, meal, goody bags and balloons thrown in.

Discovery Planet

Surrey Quays Shopping Centre, Redriff Road, SE16
t (020) 7237 2388
⊖ Surrey Quays
Bus 118
Open Mon-Sat 10-6, Sun 11-5
Adm Mon-Fri 10-12 £1.99 (parent & toddlers only), 12-4 creche £3.50 per child for 2 hrs, 4-6 £1.99 for 2 hrs plus free burger & fries from Burger King.
Ages Maximum age 10, under 9-months free

The main area has two slides, two ball pits, lots of soft play equipment, ropes, ladders and swings. There's also a separate baby section, toilets, and a Burger King counter on the premises. Birthday parties are avalable Mon-Fri at 4 and 5 daily and any time during opening hours at weekends.

The Discovery Zone

First Floor, The Junction Shopping Centre, SW1
t (020) 7223 1717
⇌ Clapham Junction
Bus 37, 39, 77, 77A, 219, 319, G1
Open Mon–Fri 10–6, Sat–Sun & School Hols 10–7, parent and toddler groups daily from 10am–1pm and 1pm–3pm
Adm Mon–Fri £3.99, Sat–Sun £4.99. There's also a 4 o'clock club in term-time when kids can play and eat for £1.99 Mon–Wed and £2.99 Thu–Fri
Ages 2–12

Basically, this is just a big room full of coloured soft things for kids to jump about on with enough space for over 500 leaping, bouncing tots. There is also a branch of Burger King and, best of all, a TV room for parents.

Monkey Business

222 Green Lanes, N13
t (020) 8886 7520
⊖ Manor House
⇌ Palmers Green
Bus 121, 329, W6
Open 10–7 daily
Adm Child £2.75, accompanying adult free
Ages 2–14
Height restriction is 4ft11in

Monkey-themed adventure playground aimed at very young children and toddlers. There's a tree house, a ball pond, lots of tube slides, biff-bash bags and a maze.

The Playhouse

The Old Gymnasium, Highbury Grove School, corner Highbury Grove/Highbury New park
t (020) 7704 9424
⊖ Highbury & Islington
Bus 4, 30, 19, 236
Open Mon-Thu 10-6, Fri-Sun 10-7
Adm Over-2s £3, under-2s £2.50, babies that are crawling £1.50
Ages Maximum age 10

Superior play area with a three-level climbing frame, 30ft slide, rope swings, ladders and ball pools. There's a separate section for babies and a café, plus toilets with changing facilities.

Pirates Playhouse

Sobell Leisure Centre, Hornsey Road, N7
t (020) 7609 2166
⊖ Finsbury Park, Holloway Road

Bus 43, 271
Open Mon–Fri 9–6, Sat & Sun 9.30–7
Adm Over 1 metre £3, under 1 metre £2.20

This is a great place for kids to come and play at being pirates with three levels of ropes, slides and punch bags for them to clamber over. There's also a separate soft play area for under-5s.

Rascals
Waterfront Leisure Centre, High Street, Woolwich, SE18
t (020) 8317 5000
⇌ Woolwich Arsenal, Woolwich Dockyard
Bus 51, 53, 96, 122, 177, 272, 161
Open Mon–Fri 9.30am–5pm, Sat & Sun 9.30am–2pm
Adm Non-member £3.30, member £2.30, each additioinal child £1.10, happy hour is from 4pm–5pm Mon–Fri when its £1 per child
Ages up to 9

Indoor fun for under-9s with a special soft play area for under-4s. There are supervised arts and crafts sessions every Tuesday from 10am–12 noon and 1pm–3pm during term time.

Snakes & Ladders
Syon Park, Brentford, Middlesex
t (020) 8847 0946
⇌ Gunnersbury
⊖ Kew Bridge
Bus 116, 117, 237, 267
Open 10–6 daily (last admission 5.15pm)
Adm Weekdays/term time: over-5s £3.95, under-5s £2.85; weekends/holidays: over-5s £4.65, under-5s £3.50; after 4.30pm every day: over-5s £3.25, under-5s £2.25
Ages 2–12
Maximum height 4ft8in
Socks must be worn

In the grounds of Syon Park, this is the place to come after a hard day's butterfly hunting or go-karting. It's the usual fare – slides, ropes, ball ponds, climbing frames – but still very good.

Can you spot?
The pavement surrounding Leicester Square's garden is adorned with the handprints of famous actors and directors. See who can be the first to spot them all.

Spike's Madhouse
Crystal Palace National Sports Centre, SE19
t (020) 8778 9876
⇌ Crystal Palace
Bus 157, 358, 361
Open Sat & Sun 10am–6pm
Adm Members £2, non-members £2.5
Ages 2–13

Four floors filled with slides, climbing frames and soft play equipment.

Cinemas

London is a great place to go and see a film. It may not have as many screens as it used to – the days when every high street had its own Odeon are now, sadly, long gone – but the cinemas that remain are bigger and better equipped than ever. The biggest and best of all can be found in Leicester Square, London's cinematic heart, where star-studded premières take place and where all the major blockbusters have their first runs. For a full and up-to-date list of what's on where and when check the weekly listings magazine *Time Out* or the *Evening Standard*'s *Hot Tickets* giveaway magazine which accompanies its Thursday edition.

Leicester Square
Empire
t (08700) 102030
www.uci-cinemas.co.uk
Odeon Leicester Square & Odeon West End
t (0870) 505 0007
www.odeon.co.uk
Warner Village West End
t (020) 7437 4347
www.warnervillage.co.uk

Both The Odeon and Warner Village Cinemas run special offers for kids at any of their branches apart from Leicester Square, call for details.

Cinema clubs

If you consider Leicester Square's cinematic big boys a bit brash and commercial, and find yourself longing for the halcyon days of Saturday matinees, you could be in for a very pleasant surprise. There are several smaller picture houses in London running Saturday morning film clubs for kids. The films are usually a mix of Disney cartoons and family favourites. To add to the fun, additional entertainments, such as workshops, competitions and seasonal events, are often laid on.

Barbican Centre

Silk Street, EC2
t (020) 7382 7000
www.barbican.org.uk
⊖ Barbican, Moorgate
Bus 8, 22B, 56
Times Club meeting time varies, call ahead
Adm Annual membership £5, films £3 non-members, £2.50 members.
Ages 5–11

Also organizes art and animation workshops, storytelling sessions and puppet shows.

Clapham Picture House

76 Venn Street, SW4
t (020) 7498 3323
www.picturehouse-cinemas.co.uk
⊖ Clapham Common
Bus 88, 137, 155, 345, 355
Times Club meets Sat 11.15am, film starts at 11.45am
Adm Members £2, non members £3, accompanying adult £4; annual membership £3, £5 for 2 siblings, under-5s must be accompanied by an adult
Ages to 12

At the weekly pre-screening craft workshops, kids can get in the mood for the upcoming celluloid adventures by designing their own space ship, making a cartoon picture book or moulding plasticine. Six times a year the cinema screens doggie-themed movies and invites the residents of nearby Battersea Dogs' Home over for a mutual appreciation session.

Electric Cinema

191 Portobello Road, W11
t (020) 7229 8688
infoline (020) 7727 9958
www.the-electric.co.uk
⊖ Notting Hill Gate
Times Sat, 1pm
Adm £3 members, £4 non-members, accompanying adults
Ages 4-12

Games and activities inspired by the screenings, plus birthday party specials.

Everyman Cinema

5 Holly Bush Vale, Hampstead, NW3

t (020) 7435 1600
www.everymancinema.com
⊖ Hampstead Heath
Times Films start at 12 noon
Adm £5
Ages 8-12

A more sophisticated club for older kids run by Eve McGregor in association with Film Education and supported by husband Ewan's film company, Natural Nylon. Besides the films, they run fortnightly educational workshops, held in six-week blocks, on film theory, storyboards and production techniques. The occasional movie celeb turns up to lend a hand where appropriate.

Junior NFT

National Film Theatre 2, BFI, South Bank, SE1
t (020) 7928 3232
www.bfi.org.uk/moviemagic
⊖ /⇌ Waterloo
Bus 1, 4, 26, 68, 76, 168, 171, 176, 188, 341, 501, 505, 521, X68
Times Sat afternoon, workshop time varies, call ahead, Sunday afternoon screening only
Adm £3.50 film, plus kids only workshop
Ages 6–12

A mixture of b&w classics and blockbusters, interspersed with with foreign language and animation films. Workshops are either hands-on sessions or feature talks from industry professionals.

Phoenix Cinema

52 High Road, East Finchley, N2
t (020) 8444 6789
⊖ East Finchley
Bus 102, 143, 263
Times Club meets bi-weekly Sat 11am, film starts at 12 noon
Adm Film and activity session: non-members £3.50 members £1.50; film only: non-members £2; accompanying adults £3
Ages 6–12

Art & craft activities based on the featured film.

Ritzy Cinema

Brixton Oval, Coldharbour Lane, SW2
t (020) 7733 2229
www.ritzycinema.co.uk
⊖ Brixton
Bus 35, 37, 118, 196, 250, P4, P5
Times All films start Sat 10.30am

Adm Child £1, accompanying adult £2
Ages to 12

Shows two separate programmes: one for 7s and under and the other for 8s and over. In truth this is done more for reasons of social bonding than anything else and either age group may attend either programme. There are special kids' club events organised and free tea, coffee and newspapers provided for parents.

IMAX 3-D Cinema

1 Charlie Chaplin Walk, SE1
t (020) 7902 1234
www.bfi.org.uk/imax
⊖ Waterloo, Westminster
Bus 12, 53, 76, 77, 109, 211, 507, D1, P11
Open Call ahead
Adm For one film: adult £6.95, child (under 16) £4.95, under-5s **free**, concs £5.95
Wheelchair access, lifts, adapted cinema seats and toilets
Suitable for all ages
Shows last approximately one hour each

Britain's largest cinema screen is housed in a seven-storey glass cylinder in the middle of the Waterloo bullring. The screen itself is the height of five double-decker buses, the sound system transmits 11,000 watts and the films are recorded and projected using the most up-to-date 3-D format available – it's a pretty all-encompassing experience. The programme changes regularly but you can usually be confident of seeing some kind of outer space/bottom of the ocean type spectacular or some high-tec animation, for which this is a particularly good format. Try, if you can, to check out the mind-blowing animation feature *Cyberworld* featuring a cameo from Homer Simpson or, latest to hit the big, big screen, a 3-D version of the Oscar-winning Disney animation classic *Beauty and the Beast*.

Internet cafés

If your kids are clamouring to email their mates back home or you fancy sending a cyber postcard, there are plenty of web cafés to choose from, most of which serve coffee and a limited range of snacks.

Café Internet

22-4 Buckingham Palace Road, SW1
t (020) 7233 5786
⊖/ ⇌ Victoria
Open Mon–Fri 9–9, Sat 10-8, Sun 10–6
Cost £1 per 15 mins, £2 per hour

Cyberia Cyber Café

39 Whitfield Street **t** (020) 7681 4200
⊖ Goodge Street
Open Mon–Fri 9–9, Sat 11–7, Sun 11–6
Cost £1 per half-hour

easyEverything

12–14 Wilton Road, SW1 **t** (020) 7233 8456
www.easyEverything.com
⊖/ ⇌ Victoria
Open Daily 24-hours
Cost £1 per hour

Global Café

15 Golden Square, W1 **t** (020) 7287 2242
www.globalcafe.net
⊖ Piccadilly Circus
Open Mon–Fri 9–11, Sat 10-11
Cost Membership £5, access free

Webshack

15 Dean Street, W1 **t** (020) 7287 2242
www.webshack-cafe.com
⊖ Tottenham Court Road
Open Mon–Sat 10–11, Sun 1-9
Cost £1 per 40 mins.

Museums & galleries

Outer London

London is a huge, sprawling city and can prove quite daunting for visitors. You might think you've got more than enough to cope with visiting the attractions in the centre of town, never mind the outskirts. However, it's well worth giving the suburbs some consideration. Not only can they offer smaller crowds, less congestion and better air quality, they are also home to some great local museums. There follows a selection of places that are, in general, a lot less touristy than their central London counterparts and will provide you with a much calmer day out. Most are extremely family-orientated and, best of all, free.

Bethnal Green Museum of Childhood

Cambridge Heath Road, E2
t (020) 8983 5200
Infoline **t** (020) 8980 2415
www.museumofchildhood.org.uk
⊖ Bethnal Green
Bus 8, 106, 253, 309, D6
Open Mon–Thurs, Sat & Sun 10–6
Free (donations welcome)
Suitable for all ages
Allow at least an hour

This east London branch of the Victoria & Albert Museum contains a wonderful collection of historic childhood artefacts including clothes, toys (lots and lots of toys), nursery furniture and baby equipment. Pride of place, however, goes to the two Dolls' House Streets – three centuries' worth of miniature homes lined up in chronological order. There's also a chronological display of dolls – from 17th-century porcelain beauties to pink plastic modern Barbies. The museum organizes lots of events year-round for children including quiz trails, storytelling and art workshops where children can have a go at decorating their own T-shirts, constructing finger puppets and designing jewellery. In summer the museum also stages its own theatrical productions.

Bruce Castle Museum

Church Lane, off Lordship Lane, N17
t (020) 8808 8772
www.brucecastlemuseum.org.uk
⊖ Wood Green
Bus 243
Open Wed–Sun 1pm–5pm
Free

This lively local history museum is housed in a listed Tudor building and has, in addition to its art, history and postal history exhibitions, a special 'Inventor Centre' filled with interactive experiments for kids to play with and is surrounded by 20 acres of parkland. Free activities for children are laid on at weekends between 2–4pm.

Dulwich Picture Gallery

College Road, SE21
t (020) 8693 5254
www.dulwichpicturegallery.org.uk
⇌ North Dulwich
Bus P4, P15
Open Tues–Fri 10–5, Sat , Sun and Bank Hol Mon 11–5
Adm Adults £4, children **free**, senior citizens £3, **free** to all on Fridays
Suitable for ages 10 and over
Allow at least an hour

Newly reopened following an extensive period of refurbishment, this is one of the finest galleries to be found anywhere in the country outside central London. Formerly owned by Dulwich College, a private boys' school, but now owned by an independent charitable trust, the collection includes Rembrandt's *Girl at a Window* and Gainsborough's *Linley Sisters*, as well as works by Rubens, Poussin, Canaletto and Raphael. Once your children have tired of looking at pictures, head into the adjacent park. Art workshops are held during the summer holidays when children can take part in a range of activities including collage design, T-shirt decoration and badge-making.

Firepower Museum

Royal Arsenal, SE18
t (020) 8855 7755
www.firepower.org.uk
⇌ Woolwich Arsenal
Open 10–5 daily
Adm adult £6.50, child (5-16) £5.50, under-5s **free**, family £18.
Suitable for all ages, some images may distress
Allow at least half a day

Housed in a former arsenal, the newly opened Firepower Museum aims to show what wartime life was like for artillery gunners in the 20th century. It's a noisy affair with battlefield re-enactments, ping-pong target practice and hands-on computerized simulators. Would-be cadets can stock up on their combat gear, toys and ammo in the shop.

Geffrye Museum

Kingsland Road, E2
t (020) 7739 9893
www.geffrye-museum
⊖ Old Street (south exit 8)
⇌ Dalston Kingsland

Bus 67, 149, 242, 243
Open Tues–Sat 10–5, Sun 12 noon–5pm
Free
Suitable for all ages, under-8s must be accompanied by an adult
Allow at least an hour

This charming little museum, housed in a row of 18th-century almshouses, is dedicated to the evolution of Britain's living rooms. It contains dozens of reconstructed interiors from Tudor times to the present day. Kids love wandering through the rooms, looking at all the strange archaic furniture and nosing out interesting nuggets of domestic history. The museum holds imaginative workshops on such diverse topics as wig-making, enamelling and block printing.

Horniman Museum

100 London Road, SE23
t (020) 8699 1872
www.horniman.ac.uk
➤ Forest Hill
Bus 94, 122, 176, 185
Open Mon–Sat 10.30–5.30, Sun 2–5.30
Free
Suitable for all ages
Allow at least a couple of hours

A day spent here is easily as rewarding as a day spent in one of the great Kensington collections. It was founded in the early 19th century by the tea magnate Frederick Horniman and defies classification. It's not really an anthropology museum, although it does contain a vast ethnographic collection including South American tribal masks, African head dresses and Egyptian mummies. Equally, it's not really a natural history museum but still boasts a fantastic array of animal exhibits including a collection of stuffed creatures – look out for the Goliath beetle, the largest insect in the world – as well as a huge aquarium. Neither is it a museum of music but it nonetheless holds one of the country's most important collections of musical instruments. It also has a wonderful interactive music display where, using touch-screen computers and headphones, kids can find out about (and listen to) some of the world's more obscure instruments. In fact, considering its many wonders, it's perhaps best to describe the museum simply as South London's premier treasure trove.

The museum gardens are equally wonderful and contain nature trails, an exhibition on caring for

the environment and a small animal enclosure, home to goats, rabbits and turkeys. In addition, the Horniman runs musical workshops for children. At these, kids take part in a variety of activities (at all levels) and can even get their hands on some of the museum's collection of instruments.

Free Although open, parts of the museum may be forced to close temporarily to accomodate building work currently taking place. An education centre is due to open in late spring 2002.

Keats' House

10 Keats' Grove, NW3
t (020) 7435 6166
Open April–Oct Thur–Sat 12 noon–5pm, Nov–Mid Dec & Mar Sat only 12 noon–5pm, closed Mid Dec–Feb
Free

A little museum where the young Romantic poet once lived and where he is said to have composed 'Ode to a Nightingale'.

Kenwood House

Hampstead Lane, NW3
t (020) 8348 1286
www.english-heritage.org
Open Summer 10–6 daily, winter 10–4 daily
Free

Houses a wonderful collection of art including works by Rembrandt, Gainsborough and Vermeer, and has a rather nice tearoom. In summer, the grounds play host to a series of spectacular classical music concerts which usually climax with a firework display.

Kew Bridge Steam Museum

Green Dragon Lane, Brentford, Middlesex, TW8
t (020) 8568 4757
➤ Kew Bridge Station
⊖ Gunnersbury, Kew Gardens
Bus 237, 267, 391 (Sun only)
Open 11am–5pm daily
Adm Mon–Fri adult £3, child £1, concs £2.50, family ticket (2+3) £7; Sat & Sun adult £4, child £2, concs £2.50, family £10.50
Wheelchair access to most of the museum – no access to viewing platform above beam engines
Suitable for all ages

Just across the river from the gardens (*see* p.178), Kew Bridge Steam Museum offers a nice down-to-earth contrast to all those flower beds and neatly sculpted lawns. It focuses on the development of London's water supply and sewage system from Roman times to the present day and houses a wonderful collection of Victorian water-pumping machinery, including the two largest beam engines in the world. In their prime, these noisy behemoths would have pumped six and a half million gallons of water every day into London's reservoirs. You can get some idea of the power involved when the great beasts are switched on for a short time in the afternoon at weekends. Providing water is one thing, but it's the means of taking the waste away that brings the best out of the museum. Kids love the replica London sewage system; spying through peep holes at sewer rats and mice and finding out about 'flushers' and 'toshers' – 19th-century sewer workers who made their living in quite the most smelly way imaginable. The museum's Water of Life exhibition has plenty of levers and buttons to push and pull to keep children amused. Kids can even have a go at controlling a robot as it makes its way down a pipe to find hidden messages.

London International Gallery of Children's Art

O² Centre, Finchley Road, NW3
t (020) 7435 0903
www.ligca.org
⊖ Finchley Road
Bus 13, 46, 82, 113
Open Tues–Thurs 4–6, Fri–Sun 12 noon–6pm
Free
Suitable for all ages
Allow at least half an hour

London's only gallery devoted to works of art by children. The collection contains paintings from all over the world and organises drama, dance, music and art workshops for children of all ages.

National Army Museum and Royal Hospital

Royal Hospital Road, Chelsea, SW3
t (020) 7730 0717
www.national-army-museum.ac.uk
⊖ Sloane Square
Bus 11, 19, 22, 137, 239
Open 10–5.30 daily

Free
Suitable for ages 10 and over
Allow at least an hour

Telling the story of British army life from the 16th century to the present day, the museum is well laid out and thoughtful, but perhaps a little dry for younger children. It sits next to the Christopher Wren-designed Royal Hospital, founded by Charles II in the 17th century as a home for army veterans and still home to 400 red-coated Chelsea pensioners today. In May each year the grounds play host to the Chelsea Flower Show, the country's premier gardening event.

Puppet Centre Trust

Battersea Arts Centre, Lavender Hill, SW11
t (020) 7228 5335
www.puppetcentre.com
⇌ Clapham Junction
Bus 37, 39, 77, 77A, 219, 319, G1
Open Mon–Fri 2–6
Free
Suitable for all ages
Allow at least an hour

This is the puppet world's equivalent of Oxbridge. The centre was set up as a charity in 1974 to promote the art of puppeteering and to enable would-be puppeteers to study their craft. Covering all aspects of puppetry, it holds regular training workshops where you can learn how to handle a marionette without getting the strings all tangled up, how to sit a dummy on your knee and, most importantly, how to talk like Mr Punch. There's also an excellent exhibition of puppets from around the world as well as a café and a bookshop.

Ragged School Museum

46–50 Copperfield Road, E3
t (020) 8980 6405
www.raggedschoolmuseum.org.uk
⊖ Mile End
Bus 25, 277, 309, D6, D7
Open Wed & Thurs 10–5 and first Sun of each month 2–5
Free
Suitable for all ages
Allow at least a couple of hours

In the late 19th century, thousands and thousands of children in London were living in abject poverty. There was no free education system or health care as there is today and many children had to work for a living, often in dangerous cond tions. It was an appalling state of affairs and one that Dr Barnardo, a young missionary, decided to do something about. During his life he founded over 90 homes for London's destitute children. He also ran this 'Ragged School' which provided free education for the poorest children of London's East End. Today it is a museum. Kids can walk through the classrooms, sit at the old desks and write on the slates. The museum also organizes a range of period activities including parlour games and sweet-making sessions.

Royal Air Force Museum

Grahame Park Way, NW9
t (020) 8205 2266
www.rafmuseum.org.uk
⊖ Colindale
≈ Mill Hill, Broadway
Bus 204, 303
Open 10–6 daily
Adm Adult £7.50, accompanied child **free**, concs £4.90
Suitable for ages five and over
Allow at least a couple of hours

On the site of the former Hendon Aerodrome, the museum is made up of two huge hangars stuffed full of aeronautical hardware. In Bomber Command Hall you'll find fighter planes from throughout the 20th century – from bi-planes and Battle of Britain Spitfires to the awesome vertical take-off Harrier jump jet. Once you've finished marvelling at these fearsome machines, try some of the interactive exhibits, guaranteed to get your and your kids' combative juices flowing. You can clamber inside the cockpit of a Lockheed Tristar, take the controls in a Jet Provost and find out whether you've got the reactions needed to be the 'best of the best' at the Pilot Skills test. You can even line up the sights to send a bouncing bomb crashing through a dam at a special display on the life of the inventor of the bouncing bomb, Barnes-Wallis. The highlight, however, is undoubtedly the flight simulator in which you get to take the controls of a Tornado – be warned, it's pretty intense and certainly isn't recommended if you've had a heavy lunch.

Wandsworth Museum

11 Garratt Lane, SW18
t (020) 8871 7075
www.wandsworth.gov.uk
⊖ East Putney
≈ Wandsworth Town
Bus 28, 37, 39, 44, 77a, 156, 170 220, 270, 337
Open Tue-Sat 10-5, Sun 2-5, closed bh
Free
Suitable for all ages, disabled access toilets
Allow at least one hour

Organises regular hands-on sessions for kids inspired by its permanent displays of local history.

Central London

Please see the main sightseeing chapters for details of these establishments.

Bank of England Museum

Threadneedle Street, EC2
t (020) 7601 5545. (*see* p.122)

Bramah Tea & Coffee Museum

1 Maguire Street, Butler's Wharf, SE1
t (020) 7378 0222. (*see* p.112)

Britain at War Experience

Tooley Street, SE1
t (020) 7403 3171. (*see* p.108)

British Museum

Great Russell Street, WC1
t (020) 7636 1555. (*see* p.44)

Cabinet War Rooms

King Charles Street, SW1
t (020) 7930 6961. (*see* p.89)

Clink Museum

1 Clink Street, SE1
t (020) 7403 6515. (*see* p.111)

HMS Belfast

Morgan's Lane, off Tooley Street, SE1
t (020) 7940 6328
⊖ London Bridge. (*see* p.110)

Imperial War Museum

Lambeth Road, SE1
t (020) 7416 5320. (*see* p.101)

London Canal Museum

12–13 New Wharf Road, N1
t (020) 7713 0836. (*see* p.38)

London Dungeon
Tooley Street, SE1
t (020) 7403 7221. (see p.106)

London Planetarium
Marylebone Road, NW1
t (0870 400 3000). (see p.35)

London's Transport Museum
Covent Garden, WC2
t (020) 7565 7299. (see p.68)

Madame Tussaud's
Marylebone Road, NW1
t (020) 7935 6861. (see p.34)

Museum of London
London Wall, EC2
t (020) 7600 3699. (see p.121)

National Gallery
Trafalgar Square, WC2
t (020) 7747 2885. (see p.57)

National Portrait Gallery
St Martin's Place, WC2
t (020) 7306 0055. (see p.59)

Natural History Museum
Cromwell Road, SW7
t (020) 7942 5000. (see p.128)

Old Operating Theatre
9a St Thomas Street, SE1
t (020) 7955 4791. (see p.109)

Pollock's Toy Museum
41 Whitfield Street, W1
t (020) 7636 3452. (see p.47)

Royal Academy
Burlington House, Piccadilly, W1
t (020) 7439 7438. (see p.60)

Science Museum
Exhibition Road, SW7
t (020) 7942 4455. (see p.129)

Globe Theatre
Bear Gardens, Bankside, New Globe Wall,
Southwark, SE1
t (020) 7401 9919. (see p.109)

Sherlock Holmes Museum
221b Baker Street, NW1
t (020) 7935 8866. (see p.36)

Tate Britain
Millbank, SW1
t (020) 7887 8008. (see p.90)

Tate Modern
Bankside, SE1
t (020) 7887 8000. (see p.107)

Tower of London
Tower Hill, EC3
t (020) 7709 0765. (see p.118)

Wallace Collection
Hertford House, Manchester Square, W1
t (020) 7935 0687. (see p.37)

Victoria & Albert Museum
Cromwell Road, SW7
t (020) 7942 2000. (see p.130)

Music

Listening to music

Pop is obviously a week by week phenomenon with no fixed calender of events. For details of upcoming pop concerts, consult the listing sections of the *Evening Standard*, London's principal daily newspaper, or the weekly entertainment magazine, *Time Out*. The **London Arena t** (020) 7538 1212, www.londonarena.co.uk, is a key venue for popular shows like *The Tweenies* and *Toy Story on Ice*, as well as pop concerts, as is **Wembley Arena t** (020) 8902 0902. www.ticketmaster.co.uk Classical music, on the other hand, does adhere to a calendar (admittedly a rather fluid one) and you might like to keep an eye out for the following.

Arthur Davidson Family Concerts
Fairfield Halls, Croydon
t (020) 8688 9291
⇌ East Croydon, West Croydon
Bus 109, 197, 250, 264, 468
Adm £6 each or £20 season ticket
Six concerts between Oct–May

A highly respected season of orchestral concerts for children featuring such child-friendly works as *Peter and the Wolf* and the *Flight of the Bumblebee*

Ernest Read Concerts for Children
Royal Festival Hall, South Bank, SE1
t (020) 7336 0777

www.sbc.org.uk
⊖/ ≋ Waterloo
Bus 1, 4, 26, 68, 76, 168, 171, 176, 188, 341, 501, 505, 521, X68
Adm £5–12
Six concerts between Oct–May

The Ernest Read Concerts have been going for over 50 years now. Everything is geared towards capturing and keeping children's attention. The pieces are kept short with special 'fidget times' in between and there are quizzes, cartoons and activities to stop kids from getting overwhelmed by the influx of culture.

London Symphony Orchestra Family Discovery Concerts
Barbican, Silk Street, EC2
t (020) 7638 8891
www.barbican.org.uk
⊖ Barbican
Bus 4, 56
Adm Adult £7, child (under 16) £3.50
One or two a season, call in advance

A popular annual event designed to get children aged 7–12 interested in classical music. The concert programmes are mainly made up of short pieces and there is lots of audience participation. Orchestra musicians mingle with the crowds during the interval and will provide any child who brings along an instrument with an impromptu music lesson.

Kenwood House Lakeside Concerts
Hampstead Lane, NW3
t (020) 7413 1443 (English Heritage Box Office); info **t** (020) 8233 7435
www.english-heritage.org
⊖ Hampstead, Archway, Highgate, Golders Green
Bus 210
When *July–August*
Adm Adult £16.50–30, child £2–4, under-5s **free**

Kids can play in Kenwood's grassy grounds during the concert and then rejoin their parents for the fireworks at the end. There are deckchairs and grass seating. Many families take along a hamper full of goodies to chomp through during the concert.

London Coliseum
St Martin's Lane, WC2
t (020) 7632 8300
www.eno.org.uk

⊖ Leicester Square, Charing Cross
Bus 14, 19, 24, 29, 38, 176

Operatic workshops and short performances for ages 7 and up. Children and accompanying adults can take part in plot summaries, improvisation sessions and listen to a sung excerpt from the opera in question.

Stilgoe Saturday Concerts
Royal Festival Hall, South Bank, SE1
t (020) 7336 0777
www.sbc.org.uk
⊖/ ≋ Waterloo
Bus 1, 4, 26, 68, 76, 168, 171, 176, 188, 341, 501, 505, 521, X68
Adm £4.50–12
Four concerts between Oct–April, Sats at 3.30

Wordsmith and composer Richard Stilgoe leads these family and school concerts, accompanied by the National Children's Orchestra and youth orchestras from around the country. Each concert is preceded by music in the foyer and wandering minstrels, plus children have an opportunity to learn a song in advance that Richard Stilgoe has written especially for the performance. Call **t** (020) 8870 9624 or **email** ssc@mfy.org.uk for details. www.mfy.org.uk/ssc

Wigmore Hall
36 Wigmore Street
t (020) 7935 2141
www.wigmore-hall.org.uk
⊖ Bond Street
Bus 6, 7, 10, 12, 13, 15, 23, 73, 94, 98, 113, 135, 137, 139, 159, 189

Organises Chamber Tots sound workshops for under-5s, hands-on music-making sessions for over-5s (which culminate in a concert) and school holiday music groups for over-11s.

Making Music
Whether it's pop, classical or 'world' music, your kids will always have much more fun making a racket than listening to one.

National Festival of Music for Youth
Royal Festival Hall, South Bank, SE1
t (020) 8878 9624
www.mfy.org.uk
⊖/ ≋ Waterloo
Bus 1, 4, 26, 68, 76, 168, 171, 176, 188, 341, 501, 505, 521, X68

Music workshops and classes for both adults and children are held during this annual event in July.

A vast collection of school orchestras and youth bands gather at the Royal Festival Hall for a huge musical jamboree. In November, the festival's best musicians also play three concerts at the Royal Albert Hall.

Carousel

Brompton Oratory, Brompton Road, SW6
t (020) 7938 8500
⊖ South Kensington
Bus 14, 49, 70, 345, C1

Various music-related activities are offered during the school holidays to children aged between 3 and 10 under Brompton's beautiful Oratory dome. Also drama and art workshops.

Guildhall School of Music

Silk Street, Barbican, EC2
t (020) 7638 1770
www.gsmd.ac.uk
⊖ Barbican
Bus 4, 56

This prestigious school runs weekly music courses for all abilities during term time. Children can learn an instrument or have vocal coaching and, if they reach a sufficient standard, join one of two youth orchestras.

Horniman Music Room Workshops

100 London Road, SE23
t (020) 8699 1872
www.horniman.ac.uk
⇌ Forest Hill
Bus 94, 122, 176, 185
No fixed calender, call in advance
Free

The Horniman houses one of the country's largest and most important collections of musical instruments. Children can explore their various sounds at one of the museum's regular workshops. *See* Museums & galleries, above.

Pottery Cafés

Unleash the budding Wedgewood in your family with a spot of ceramic painting. Many cafés prove great venues for parties and as well as throwing or painting pots, you can sculpt, tie-dye or style your own jewellery. Go create!

Art 4 Fun

Branches in Chiswick, Notting Hill, Muswell Hill, Mill Hill and West Hampstead
t (020) 8994 4800
www.art4fun.com
Open Sat, Sun & after school
Adm £20 half-day, £30 full
Suitable for all ages

Children can get well and truly stuck in using a variety of media ranging from ceramics and glass to wood and clay. While older kids get to grips with silk screen printing the little ones can mould some salt dough or play with papier maché.

Ceramics Café

215 King Street, W6
t (020) 8741 4140
www.ceramicscafe.com
⊖ Ravenscourt Park
Bus 9, 10, 27, 94
Open 10–10 daily
Adm £2 studio fee, £3-£12 for materials
Suitable for all ages

Personalise plates, mugs and other tableware. Party packages available.

Colour Me Mine

168-70 Randolph Avenue, W9
t (020) 8205 2266
www.colourmemine.com
⊖ Maida Vale
Bus 139
Open Mon-Thurs 9–9, Fri, Sat 9-7, Sun 10-7
Adm Adult £6.50, under-12s £4.50
Suitable for all ages, after school club ages 6 and up

Immortalize your baby's chubby wee toes by making your own special footprint plate. Older kids can busy themselves by making a mosaic or indulging a spot of wood, glass or pottery painting. Parties and classes available.

Pottery Café

735 Fulham Road, SW6
t (020) 7736 2157
www.bridgewater-pottery.co.uk
⊖ Parsons Green, Putney Bridge
Bus 14, 74, 220
Open 10–5.30 daily
Adm £17 holiday workshops
Suitable for all ages

The whole family can have fun decorating items of tableware from the Bridgewater Pottery range. Wednesdays are baby days when toddlers are let loose on ceramic plates to produce hand and foot prints or just daub away. During the summer holidays ages 5–11 can take part in 2-hour creative workshops to learn painting and glazing techniques. There's also a shop selling pottery gifts.

Theatre

On any given night, there will be well over 60 plays, shows and revues showing in the West End. Obviously not everything that gets put on is suitable for children, but there are many theatres specializing in the type of big, glossy all-singing all-dancing shows that appeal to a family audience. For further details check the daily newspapers and weekly listings magazines such as *Time Out* .

Performances are typically at 7.30pm Mon–Sat with a couple of additional matinee performances on Tue or Wed and Sat.

Cats
New London Theatre, Drury Lane, WC2
Box office **t** (020) 7405 0072
www.catsthemusical.com
⊖ Covent Garden
Bus 1, 68, 91, 168, 171, 188, 501, 505, 521, X68
Prices £10–£35

If it's not the most famous musical in the world, then it's certainly the longest-running. Andrew Lloyd Webber's spectacular adaptation of T.S. Eliot's feline poetry has been occupying the London and New York stage for over 18 years now. It's most famous song, *Memory*, has been recorded over 100 times and has been played over two million times on US radio.

The King & I
London Palladium, Argyll Street, W1
Box office **t** (020) 7494 5020
⊖ Oxford Circus
Bus 6, 7, 8, 10, 12, 13, 15, 23, 25, 55, 73, 94, 98, 113, 135, 137, 139, 159, 176, 189
Prices £15–£37.50

Bouncy and flouncy spectacle with the King of Siam falling for his childrens' tutor. The young cast are most endearing and the palace sets dazzling.

Les Misérables
Palace Theatre, Shaftesbury Avenue, W1
Box office **t** (020) 7434 0909
www.lesmis.com
⊖ Leicester Square
Bus 14, 19, 38
Prices £7–£37.50

This tale of the Parisian underworld is officially the world's most popular musical. It's been running in London since 1985, so they must be doing something right.

The Lion King
Lyceum Theatre, Wellington Street, WC2
⊖ Covent Garden, Charing Cross
Box office **t** (0870) 243 9000
Bus 1, 6, 9, 11, 13, 15, 23, 68, 77A, 91, 168, 171, 176, 188, 501, 505, 521, X68
Prices £15–£35.50

An all-singing, all-dancing extravaganza set in the heart of Africa with a plot and songs that most of the audience will already know by heart. Book well in advance.

Mamma Mia!
Prince Edward Theatre, Old Compton Street, W1
Box office **t** (020) 7447 5400
www.mamma-mia.com
⊖ Leicester Square
Bus 3, 6, 9, 11, 12, 13, 15, 23, 24, 29, 53, 88, 91, 109, 139, 159, 176, 184, 196
Performances Mon–Sat 7.30, matinees Wed & Sat 2.30. Duration 2hr40min
Prices £15–35

Theatrical karaoke – all your favourite Abba songs shoe-horned into a rather convoluted story.

The Mousetrap
St Martin's Theatre, West Street, WC2
Box office **t** (020) 7836 1443
⊖ Leicester Square
Bus 14, 19, 24, 29, 38, 176
Performances Mon–Sat 8pm, matinees Tues 2.45, Sat 5pm. Duration 2h51min
Prices £11–28

The big daddy of them all – it's the longest-running show in the world, having played continuously for the last 49 years. This gentle Agatha Christie mystery is a good way to introduce kids to the joys of the stage.

My Fair Lady
Drury Lane Theatre Royal, Catherine Street, WC2

t (020) 7494 5000
⊖ Covent Garden
Bus 6, 9, 11, 13, 15, 23, 77A, 91, 176
Performances Mon–Sat 8pm, matinees Tues 2.45,
Sat 5pm. Duration 2h51min
Prices £11–28
The adorable Cockney barrow girl is turned into a
lady by the haughty professor.

Notre Dame de Paris
Dominion Theatre, Tottenham Court Road, W1
Box office **t** (020) 7836 1443
⊖ Leicester Square
Bus 3, 6, 9, 11, 12, 13, 15, 23, 24, 29, 53, 88, 91, 109, 139,
159, 176, 184, 196
Prices £10–37.50
The story of the hunch-backed Quasimodo and
his desperate, doomed love for Esmerelda set to a
toe-tapping beat.

Behind the scenes
London is, and has always been since the days
before Shakespeare, a theatrical city, and there are
plenty of opportunities to sample the smell of the
greasepaint and the roar of the crowd. The
following theatres offer backstage tours where you
can explore dressing rooms, wardrobes and
costume departments and find out about the elaborate machinery used to get the scenery on and off
the stage.

London Palladium
Argyll Street, W1
t (020) 7494 5091
www.rutheatres.com
⊖ Oxford Circus
Bus 3, 6, 7, 8, 10, 12, 13, 15, 23, 25, 53, 55, 73, 88, 94, 98,
139, 159, 176, X53
Tour Usually 2–3 times a day, call in advance
Adm £4 per person, regardless of age

Royal National Theatre
South Bank, SE1
t (020) 7452 3400
www.nt-online.org
⊖ /≈ Waterloo
Bus 1, 4, 26, 68, 76, 168, 171, 176, 188, 341, 501, 505,
521, X68
Tour Mon–Sat 10.15, 12.45 & 5.30
Adm Adult £3.50, child £3

Theatre Royal
Drury Lane, WC2

t (020) 7494 5091
www.rutheatres.com
⊖ Covent Garden
Bus 1, 68, 91, 168, 171, 188, 501, 505, 521, X68
Tour Daily, call in advance
Adm Adult £7.50, child £5.50

Children's theatre
Going to see a big West End production is all very
well, but it's liable to get kids hankering for a life on
the stage. Thankfully, London is home to several
theatre companies which not only put on their
own child-friendly performances but offer training
and advice (often for free) to aspiring young thes-
pians. Here are some of the best.

Battersea Arts Centre
Old Town Hall, Lavender Hill, SW11
t (020) 7223 2223
www.bac.org.uk
≈ Clapham Junction
Bus 77, 77A, 345
Open 10–9 daily, until 6pm Mon
Adm Prices vary but drama workshops usually £4
per session
Organizes activity and drama workshops for all
ages and is home to the Puppet Centre Trust.
See p.168.

Half-Moon Young People's Theatre
43 White Horse Road, E1
t (020) 7265 8138
www.halfmoon.org.uk
⊖ Stepney Green
≈ Limehouse
Bus 5, 15, 15b, 25, 40, 106, 253
Open 10-6 (performance times vary)
Adm Performance: adult £4.50, child £3.25
This very serious-minded theatre group runs a
series of Saturday workshops on a range of theme
from street dance to mask-making and stages a
programme of high-quality children's theatre.

Little Angel Theatre
14 Dagmar Passage, Cross Street, N1
t (020) 7226 1787
www.littleangeltheatre.com
⊖ Angel, Highbury & Islington
Bus 4, 19, 30, 38, 43, 56, 73, 341

Open Performances are on Sat at 11am & 3pm
Adm Adult £6, child £5.50

A wonderful puppet theatre which holds regular weekend performances (two shows a day at 11am and 3pm) and holiday features. Children must be aged three or over.

London Bubble

t (020) 7237 4434
Times and prices vary, call in advance

This popular roving theatre company moves its mobile show tents around the parks of London during the summer, staying on average one week in each. The plays are aimed squarely at 11s and under. It also holds workshops for ages 3–6.

Polka Theatre

240 The Broadway, SW19
t (020) 8543 4888
www.polkatheatre.com
↔ /≷ Wimbledon, ↔ South Wimbledon
Bus 57, 93, 155
Open Tues–Fri 9.30–4.30, Sat 11–5.30
Adm Tickets for performances range from £4.50–£10.50; a one-day workshop is £25

The capital's top children's theatre; in fact it's the only purpose-built children's theatre in the country. Four shows a day are put on during the school holidays and two during term time. It also runs a series of drama workshops and after-school clubs for all ages. The shows are usually of a very high standard and are a mixture of children's classics and innovative new work.

Puppet Theatre Barge

78 Middleton Road, E8
t (020) 7249 6876
www.puppetbarge.com
Bus 6, 18, 46
Open Vary, phone ahead
Adm Adult £6.50, child £6

Moored on Regent's Canal, in the leafy surrounds of Little Venice, this old working barge provides a delightful setting in which to introduce your children to the wonders of puppetry. The Moving Stage Marionettes Company, which operates the barge, puts on a wide range of high-quality puppet shows for both children and adults throughout the year. It's easy to find: look out for the bright red and yellow awnings. The barge is moored in winter but in summer sails up and down the Thames putting on shows.

South Bank Centre

Belvedere Road, South Bank, SE1
General Information **t** (020) 7960 4242
www.sbc.org.uk
↔ /≷ Waterloo, ↔ Embankment
Bus 1, 4, 26, 68, 76, 77, 168, 171, 176, 188, 341, 501, 505, 521, D1, P11, X68

Organises a variety of programmes throughout the year and runs a 'Big Night Out Club' for young adults (ages 14–21).

Shakespeare's Globe

Bear Gardens, Bankside, New Globe Wall, Southwark, SE1
t (020) 7902 1500
www.shakespeares-globe.org
↔ London Bridge
Open Oct–April 10–5; May–Sept 9–4, for performance times call in advance
Adm (Exhibition) adults £7.50, children £5, under 5s **free**, concs £6, family £23
Workshops £8
Limited wheelchair access

Children aged between 8 and 11 can take part in Saturday afternoon Shakespeare workshops at the Globe's education centre, which involve storytelling, drama and art.

Tricycle Theatre

269 Kilburn High Road, NW6
t (020) 7328 1000
↔ Kilburn
Bus 16, 31, 32, 98, 189, 206, 316, 328
Open Performances take place on Sat at 11.30 and 2pm
Adm Performances: adults £4, children £3.50 or £3 in advance; workshops are £20 for a 10-week term

The Tricycle holds around 300 workshops a year for all ages. Disciplines taught include acting, singing, dancing, music, mime, puppetry and circus skills. Its own shows are both highly innovative and hugely popular and take place every Saturday of the academic year (Sep-June) at 11.30am and 2pm. The theatre also shows Saturday matinee films for all the family, call for details.

Unicorn Theatre

Pleasance Theatre, Carpenters Mews, North Rd, N7
t (020) 7700 0702
www.unicorntheatre.com
↔ Caledonian Road
Bus 10, 274

Adm Around £5–£10

After several years in Great Newport Street, just off Leicester Square, London's oldest professional children's theatre company recently decamped to new premises in Islington. Its productions, although child-size in terms of scope, length and price, are always of a very high standard. The theatre runs workshops for wannabe actors at weekends and during the school holidays.

www.carlton.com
Channel 4
t (020) 7396 4444
www.channel4.com
Channel 5
t (020) 7550 5555
www.channel5.co.uk

Pantomime season

The original interactive entertainment. Come December and a motley collection of retired sportsmen, soap stars and TV magicians will join forces with a host of professional vaudevillians to produce this most British of institutions. Girls dressed as boys, middle-aged men dressed as women and lots of call and response shouting are the essential ingredients. Throughout London you'll find various versions of *Aladdin*, *Cinderella* and *Jack and the Beanstalk* in production. Even if you're not a fan of pantomime yourself, you should still consider taking along the kids, who will love all the singalongs and 'Behind you!' stuff. For details of performances in your area check out the listings in the *Evening Standard* and *Time Out*.

TV and radio

Being a member of a studio audience for a TV or radio show can be quite a giggle for children. Recitals, concerts, game shows, comedy programmes, gardening debates – whatever takes your fancy, it can be almost guaranteed that there will be a show to please both you and them and, what's more, almost all are free. But, take note, tickets for the most popular shows are snapped up well in advance and many shows operate age restrictions. Listed below are details of the main terrestrial TV channels.

BBC TV and Radio
t (020) 8743 8000
www.bbc.co.uk/tickets
ITV
t (020) 7843 8000
www.itv.co.uk

Kids out

There is plenty of outdoor fun to be had in London. The city is dotted with parks – from great swathes of manicured greenery such as Hyde Park and Green Park to tiny patches of unspoilt wilderness – and there are several urban farms where kids can get close to animals and take part in a variety of art activities. At Kew Gardens and the purpose-built Wetlands Centre in Barnes, it's quite possible to while away a whole day contemplating the wonders of the natural world.

Kew Gardens

Kew, Richmond, Surrey, TW9
t (020) 8332 5622
Infoline **t** (020) 8940 1171
www.rbgkew.org.uk
⇌ Kew Bridge, Kew Gardens
⊖ Kew Gardens
Bus 65, 391, 267, R68 (Sun only)
Open 9.30–dusk
Adm Adult £5, child £2.50, under-5s **free**, concs £3.50, family ticket £13, blind, partially sighted and wheelchair users **free**
Baby changing facilities, 2 gift shops, 2 self-service restaurants, coffee bar, bakery, snack shop
Wheelchair access, adapted toilets
Suitable for all ages

When the rain pours down and there's a chill in the air it's best to head indoors and hide under a blanket. Alternatively, you could pay a visit to the one part of London where tropical weather is guaranteed 365 days a year. And, after 10 minutes spent in the sweltering heat of the Palm House, a huge Victorian conservatory where the conditions are designed to mimic those of a rainforest, you'll never complain about the British weather again.

The Royal Botanic Gardens, to give Kew its proper name, is spread over a 300-acre site on the south bank of the Thames and has grown, over the course of its 200-year history, into the largest and most comprehensive collection of living plants in the world, containing representatives of more than one in eight of all flowering plants. All year round, these beautifully manicured parks provide a dazzling display of blooms, from crocuses and bluebells in spring to strawberry trees and witch hazel in winter. There are three enormous conservatories: the above-mentioned Palm House, full of

banana, cocoa, papaya and other such tropical exotica, the late Victorian Temperate House, and the Princess of Wales Conservatory, built in the 1980s and home to both the giant Amazonian water-lilly and Titan Arum, the largest, and quite possibly the smelliest, flower in the world. There is also a 10-storey, 50m high 18th-century pagoda as well as a very good restaurant although, in summer, there's no finer place to have a picnic.

WWT Wetlands Centre

Queen Elizabeth Walk, SW13
t (020) 8409 4400
www.wetlandcentre.org.uk
⇌ Barnes
Bus rail then 33, 72
⊖ Hammersmith
Bus tube then 283
Open 9.30–dusk
Adm Adult £6.75, child (4-16) £4, under-4s **free**, concs £5.50, family ticket £17.50
Baby changing facilities, shop, self-service restaurant. Suitable for all ages

This innovative site is split into 14 simulated habitats, including arctic tundra and tropical swamp, each inhabited by an array of appropriate wildfowl. Picture boards will help you to identify what's what and give you a few quiz questions to help pass the time. Though this is obviously a trip best undertaken in good weather, the centre does boast numerous huts and hides where you can shelter from any impromptu showers and still observe the wildlife. There's also a visitors' centre with a good, spacious ground floor café (it serves up wholesome soups, salads and tasty cakes and has a special kids' menu; seating both inside and out) and, upstairs, in the observatory, an interactive area where kids can discover life through the eyes of a duck, drangonfly or bird. They can follow migratory patterns across the globe, make some bird sounds, build puzzles or just gaze out over the grounds to see which birds are one the move. There's also a small film theatre where visitors can learn more about the centre and the work of the World Wildlife Trust. Seasonal wildlife-themed activities are organised on weekends and, during the school holidays, kids can take part in bat walks, dragonfly hunts and the very popular pond safaris when, armed with nets, they go hunting by the water's edge for tiny creatures to investigate.

Open spaces

Alexandra Palace Park
Muswell Hill, N22
t (020) 8444 7696
www.alexandrapalace.com
⊖ Wood Green
≋ Alexandra Palace
Bus 184, W3
Open 24-hrs a day
Free

'Ally Pally', as it is affectionately known, has had a rather illustrious history. It was built in 1862 for the second Great Exhibition and, in 1936, was the site of Britain's first ever television broadcast. Today, the park is one of the best equipped for sports in the capital. Among its many attractions are a dry-ski slope, several football and cricket pitches, a pitch and putt golf course, an ice rink and a boating lake. There are also a couple of children's playgrounds, complete with sandpits and swings. Both adults and children will enjoy the spectacular views the park affords over London. Regular funfairs take place during the school holidays and on bank holidays with rides, side shows, kiddies rides and refreshments. The house also hosts a variety of craft and leisure activity shows, concerts and displays.

Battersea Park
Prince of Wales Drive, SW11
t (020) 8871 7530
⊖ Sloane Square
≋ Battersea Park, Queenstown Road
Bus 44, 137, 319, 344, 345
Open Dawn till dusk
Free

Battersea is one of London's best parks for children. There's a small zoo, home to deer, peacocks and wallabies, a breezy boating lake, a Victorian Pump House and, best of all, London's largest adventure playground – ropes, gangways, climbing frames, nets etc – if it can be clambered over, you'll find it here. In summer there are kids' theatre shows and pony rides. For sports fans, there are over 20 tennis courts. The park organizes lots of summer events for children including a teddy bears' picnic. In November there's usually an impressive firework display and bonfire. The Zoo, **t** (020) 8871 7540, is open April–Sept 10–5 daily, Oct–Mar Sat & Sun only 11–3, and costs adult £1.20, child & concs 60p.

Brockwell Park
Herne Hill, SE24
t (020) 8678 5918
≋ Herne Hill
Bus 2, 3, 37, 196
Open Dawn till dusk daily

Though its main draw is its famous lido (see Evian Lido p.192), especially in summer, the park has much to offer all year round. There are tennis courts, duck ponds, a bowling green, a basketball court, a football pitch and a BMX track as well as lots of open space to run around in. The First Come First Served Café, at the top of the hill, cooks up all-day breakfast and Sunday lunches, as well as sandwiches and snacks. The park is also home to the Whippersnappers Workshop Room which holds daily drop-in music workshops and a free disco on Saturdays, call (020) 7738 6633 for details.

Crystal Palace Park
Anerley Road, Crystal Palace, SE20
≋ Crystal Palace
Bus 3, 157, 176, 450
Open Dawn till dusk daily

In some respects, Crystal Palace rivals Battersea for the title of best park south of the river. The highlight is the monster trail, which is made up of 29 model dinosaurs, dotted around the park, peering menacingly out of the undergrowth and looming over trees. They were erected in the middle of the 19th century and are still amazing kids to this day. The park also contains a children's farm, a model car racetrack, a small maze and a model railway and in summer classical concerts are held at the famous concert bowl accompanied by firework displays. Other than the dinosaurs, the park's most celebrated inhabitant is a great granite statue of former London Zoo favourite, Guy the Gorilla, which stands at the northern end of the park. Children love to try and climb him and have a picture taken sitting on his back. The site of the Crystal Palace itself, a huge iron and glass structure built for the Great Exhibition of 1851 and which burned down in the 1930s, is now occupied by an enormous TV transmitter that looks a bit like a mini-version of the Eiffel Tower.

Dulwich Park

College Road, SE21
t (020) 8693 5737
⇌ North Dulwich
Bus P4, P15
Open Summer 8–9 daily, winter 8–4.30 daily
Free

A great place to come after spending the morning gawping at paintings in Dulwich Art Gallery (*see* p166), this beautiful park has a well-equipped children's playground, a boating lake, tennis courts, horse-riding tracks and a pleasant café. The London Recumbents (020) 8299 6636, have their base here, where you can hire or buy bikes, trikes and tandem cycles. They also run cycle safety courses on a one-to-one basis while the resident rangers organise a range of activities from seed hunts to bat walks.

Epping Forest

Epping Forest Field Centre, High Beech Road, Loughton, Essex
t (020) 8508 7714
⊖ Loughton
Bus 20, 167, 210, 214, 215, 219, 220, 240, 250, 301, 531, 532, 549
Open Field Centre: Mon–Sat 10–5, Sun 11–5
Free

A little piece of ancient Britain on the outskirts of modern London. Once part of a huge swathe of woodland that stretched from the River Lea to the sea, Epping Forest came into existence some 8,000 years ago, or just after the last Ice Age. Six thousand years later, Queen Boudicca supposedly fought her last battle here against the Roman Army. Today, this 10-mile crescent is a wonderful mixture of thick dense woodland, grassland, heathland and ponds inhabited by a wide range of wildlife including deer, woodpeckers, foxes and badgers. In autumn, the brambles are thick with sticky, messy blackberries – kids can colour themselves purple from head to toe in a little under half an hour. Close to the station, is the excellent field centre which provides maps of the forest and organizes various activities for children, including mini-safaris, nature trails and pond dippings, and can provide details of walks. Epping is a great place to come and escape the rigours of city life with its miles of winding paths; the farther you go into deep, dark forest, the farther away the modern world seems.

Green Park

Piccadilly W1 & The Mall, SW1
t (020) 7930 1793
See p.83.

Greenwich Park

Charlton Way, SE3
t (020) 8858 2608
See p.143.

Hampstead Heath

Hampstead, NW3
t (020) 7485 4491
⊖ Belsize Park, Hampstead
⇌ Hampstead Heath, Gospel Oak
Bus 210, 268, H3
Open 24 hrs a day
Free

After the royal parks, this is London's most famous open space. It's also Central London's most countrified area, one of the few places in the city that actually feels a little bit wild. Once the stamping ground of the poets Keats and Shelley and the highwayman Dick Turpin, these 800 acres provide a wonderfully romantic setting for a family walk. Kids will enjoy the well-equipped playground by Gospel Oak Station, complete with swings, slides and climbing frame, as well as the funfairs which are regularly set up in summer. It's wide open spaces are ideal for kite-flying and, even if you're not an active flier, it can still be a lot of fun watching others sending their colourful structures into battle against the raging winds. The park provides some wonderful views of the city, particularly from Parliament Hill (site of the famous lido), and is also home to Kenwood House where, in summer, concerts are held with firework finales.

Highgate Wood

Muswell Hill Road, N6
t (020) 8444 6129
⊖ Highgate
Bus 144, W7
Open 7.30–dusk
Free

There's a playground, a sports ground, an excellent vegetarian restaurant (*see* p.231) and a small patch of ancient woodland that is inhabited by a staggering number of flora and fauna. The wood i home to over 70 species of birds, 12 species of butterfly, 180 species of bats, 80 species of spiders, plus foxes, squirrels and all manner of under-growth-hugging beetles, slugs and worms. Pick up a nature trail from the woodland centre and head off into the trees.

Holland Park

Kensington High Street, W8
t (020) 8602 2226
⊖ Holland Park, High Street Kensington
Bus 9, 10, 27, 28, 49
Open Dawn till dusk daily
Free

Just off Kensington High Street, this is a lovely manicured park with an orangery, a Japanese Water Garden and free-roaming peacocks and pheasants. Your kids, of course, will ignore all of them, as they head to the park's groovy, multi-level adventure playground. Sticky Fingers restaurant (which on weekends is very child-friendly) is just around the corner, (see p.231).

Hyde Park/Kensington Gardens

t (020) 7298 2100
See p.132.

Regent's Park

t (020) 7486 7905
See p.36.

Richmond Park

Richmond, Surrey
t (020) 88948 3209
www.open.gov.uk/rp
⊖ /≋ Richmond
Bus 65, 371
Open Dawn till dusk daily
Free

This great swathe of west London parkland has long been closely associated with the monarchy. In the 15th century Henry VII had a viewing mound created in the park allowing him to look out over his kingdom – the mound still stands today and the views are still magnificent, stretching from Windsor Castle in the west to St Paul's Cathedral in the east. Two centuries later, both Charles I and Charles II used the park as a hunting ground. Today, although the hunting has stopped, the park is still home to the Queen's own herds of red and fallow deer which roam the park pretty much as the fancy takes them. A huge variety of other species of wildlife, among them foxes, weasels and badgers,

have also made the park their home. There are two public golf courses, some great walking trails and a good park café.

St James's Park

The Mall, SW1
t (020) 7930 1793
See p.83.

Syon Park

London Road, Brentford, Middlesex
t (020) 8560 0883
www.syonpark.co.uk
≋ Brentford, Syon Lane
Bus 235, 237, 267
Open Garden: 10–dusk daily; Butterfly House April–Sep Sat & Sun & bank holidays 11–5
Adm House: adult £2.50, child £2, house & garden: adult £5.50, child £4

Syon Park is a great place to come and get up-close-and-personal with animals. Head for the Butterfly House where you'll find clouds of beautiful free-flying butterflies who will come and settle on your head and arms as you walk around. The House also gives a home to scorpions, tarantulas and leaf-cutter ants. Afterwards, pop along to the Aquatic House in the great conservatory and say hello to the resident piranhas, crocodiles and turtles before taking a stroll in the park's gorgeous rose garden. On a different plane altogether, Syon Park also has a great indoor adventure playground, Snakes and Ladders (see p.163), a model railway and a go-kart track.

Victoria Park

Old Ford Road, E3
t (020) 8533 2057
⊖ Mile End
≋ Cambridge Heath, Hackney Wick
Bus 8, 26, 30, 55, 253, 277
Open 6am-dusk, daily

Once upon a time, this 218 acre East End park's primary source of entertainment was provided by heretics burning at the stake. Thankfully, today's leisure facilities are a good deal less grisly and include the ornamental gardens, an animal enclosure with goats and fallow deer, tennis courts, a bowling green, an adventure playground, plenty of green open spaces and 2 lakes, one housing a model boat club, the other a thriving fishing trade.

City farms and zoos

If children won't come to the countryside, then the countryside must come to the children, or so they thought back in the early 1970s. At that time, there were growing concerns about the development of London's youngsters. It was felt that they were becoming 'nature deprived'; that, because of the city's size, they had little concept of what the countryside was actually like. So the idea of the city farm was born; the aim being to bring a little bit of country life back into the inner city. Here's a selection of some of the best.

Battersea Park Children's Zoo

Albert Bridge Road, SW11
t (020) 8871 7540
⊖ Sloane Square
⇌ Battersea Park, Queenstown Road
Bus 44, 137, 319, 344, 345
Open April–Sep 10–5, Oct–Mar Sat & Sun only 11–3
Adm Adult £1.80, child 90p

Battersea really seems to know what it's doing when it comes to entertaining the children. Housed in one of London's best parks and next to one of its best outdoor adventure playgrounds, this is one of the city's best small zoos. You'll find a small reptile house as well as meerkats, flamingos, emus and wallabies. Children can, if they like, stroke and pet the long-suffering goats and sheep to their heart's content in a special contact area.

College Farm

45 Fitzalan Road, N3
t (020) 8349 0690
⊖ Finchley Central
Bus 13, 26, 82, 143, 260
Open 10–6 daily
Adm Adult £1.50, child 75p, under-3s **free** except on open days when adult £2, child £1, under-3s **free**

This large dairy farm, which in the late 19th and early 20th century produced milk for the Express Dairies, was the first farm in Britain to come up with the idea of turning itself into a tourist attraction. It's still packing them in today and is home to donkeys, pigs, sheep, shire horses, rabbits and, of course, cattle (the cuddly, long-haired Highland variety). The best time for children to visit is on the first Sunday of each month when the farm holds an open day with a craft fair, donkey rides and puppet shows among the many attractions.

Coram's Fields

93 Guilford Street, WC1
t (020) 7837 6138
⊖ Russell Square
Bus 17, 45, 46
Open Summer 9–8 daily, winter 9–dusk
Free

Adults can only visit this farm (home to goats, sheep, pigs, chickens, geese, rabbits and guinea pigs) aviary and park only if accompanied by a child. There's also a playground, paddling pool and nursery.

Deen City Farm

39 Windsor Avenue, Merton Abbey, SW19
t (020) 8543 5300
⇌ Mitcham
Bus 200
Open Tue-Sun 8.30-4.30
Free

A real hands-on experience where children can muck in with the mucking out of goats, pigs, rabbits and ponies, meet chickens, guinea fowl and geese (as well as a few more exotic wild beasts such as snakes, ferrets, chinchillas and terrapins) and go for pony rides. In summer, the farm holds special 'Farmer Days' with tractor rides and barn-dances.

Freightliners Farm

Paradise Park, Sheringham Road, off Liverpool Road, N7
t (020) 7609 0467
⊖ Holloway, Highbury & islington
Bus 43, 153, 271, 279
Open Tue-Sun 9-1, 2-5
Free

Summer playschemes allow visiting kids to get to know the farm's various breeds of sheep, pigs, goats, cattle and poultry. Children are made to feel very welcome and you can purchase free range eggs and bulk meats.

Hackney City Farm

1 Goldsmiths Row, E2
t (020) 7729 6381
⇌ Cambridge Heath
Bus 26, 48, 55
Open Tues-Sun 10-4.30
Free

In the east end of London, this converted brewe houses a collection of sheep, pigs, goats, cows, geese, turkeys etc, and runs some very popular craft workshops and activity days; when kids can have a go at pottery and weaving and find out the proper way to feed animals and shear sheep. There's also a shop selling eggs, wool, animal hair, meat and pet rabbits.

Kentish Town City Farm

1 Cressfield Close, NW5
t 020 7916 5421
⊖ Kentish Town, Chalk Farm
Bus 24, 46, C11
Open Tues-Sun 9–5
Free

Kentish Town City Farm was established in 1973, making it one of the first genuine city (as opposed to working) farms. Children can see and interact with cow, pigs and goats and there's a children's garden. Pony rides are available for £1 on weekends (the farm's horse riding club is, unfortunately, only available to Camden residents).

Mudchute Farm

Pier Street, Isle of Dogs, E14
t 020 7515 0749
DLR Mudchute
Bus D7. D8, P14
Open 9–5 daily
Free

London's largest urban farm (13 acres) was actually founded as a working farm at the end of the 19th century on the site of a dump and is home to cow, pigs, sheep and even a llama (called Larry). The site also boasts riding stables (with pony-riding available for the under 7s), a wildlife area and swathes of wood and parkland.

Surrey Docks Farm

Rotherhithe Street, SE16
t (020) 7231 1010
DLR Surrey Quays, Canada Water
Bus 225
Open 9am-1pm and 2-5pm daily, closed Mon & Fri during school holidays
Adm Free, playscheme: child £2, accompanying adult 50p

A tiny farm overlooking the River Thames where you'll find goats, sheep and ducks, as well as a working forge. In summer the farm hosts various craft demonstrations, including metal work and felt-making. The farm runs a playscheme on Tuesday, Wednesday and Thursday mornings.

Vauxhall City Farm

Tyers Street, SE11
t (020) 7582 4204
⊖ Vauxhall
Bus 2, 36, 77a, 88, 185
Open Tues–Thurs and Sat & Sun 10–5
Free

Next to the MI6 building, Vauxhall City Farm is home to all the usual suspects including pigs, rabbits, sheep, ducks and hens, as well as donkeys and ponies which give rides in summer.

Curious caves

Chislehurst Caves

Old Hill, Chislehurst **t** (020) 8467 3264
Getting there It's off the A222 on the B264 near Chislehurst railway station
Open Daily during school hols, otherwise Wed–Sun, tours hourly from 10–4
Adm Adults £3, children £1.50
Café, gift shop, on-site parking

These tunnels and caves have played host to Druids, Romans and Londoners trying to escape from the Blitz. Today experienced guides take you on 45 minute tours down into this winding 4,000 year old network of stoney tunnels and passageways stretching deep beneath the Old Hill.

Sports and activities

Whether you want to take part or just watch, you'll find London a hive of sporting activity with everything from athletics to windsurfing catered for. The capital's major clubs and sports centres are listed below along with details of any specific children's schemes or courses that they run. Remember, you can find facilities for tennis, football, basketball and softball in many of London's parks. *See* p.178 for details.

Athletics

Crystal Palace
National Sports Centre, Ledrington Road, Crystal Palace, SE19
t (020) 8778 0131
www.crystalpalace.co.uk
⇌ Crystal Palace
Bus 157, 358, 361

Crystal Palace is the spiritual home of British athletics. Every year it hosts at least one star-studded athletics Grand Prix. Would-be athletes can apply to attend one of their yearly summer sports camps. Alternatively, contact the Amateur Athletics Association on **t** (0121) 440 5000. **www**.british-athletics.co.uk

Badminton & squash

Both of these sports are great for promoting dexterity and hand-eye co-ordination. For details of child-friendly clubs contact the **Badminton Association of England t** (01908) 268400, **www**.baofe.co.uk; or the **Squash Rackets Association t** (020) 8746 1616, **www**.squash.uk.com

Baseball & softball

Du to an increase in popularity these two American sports have clubbed together to form the **BaseballSoftballUK** agency. Little Leaguers in search of some action should call **t** (020) 7453 7000. **www**.baseballsoftballuk.com.

Basketball

The **English Basketball Association** can help you find anything from a local court to have a knock-about in to a junior level club to join. Call **t** (0113) 2361166 for details. **www**.basketballengland.org.uk.

Cricket

England's most popular summer game. London's two premier grounds for watching this most tactical of sports are Lord's and the Oval. The county championship season runs from April to September with 4-day matches usually taking place between Thursday and Monday, often with a 1-day match sandwiched in between on the Sunday. Both grounds also hold a 1-day international match and a 5-day international Test Match between England and one of the other eight cricket-playing nations each year – the other nations being Australia, New Zealand, India, Pakistan, Sri Lanka, South Africa, Zimbabwe and the West Indies. Tickets are in the region of £7–£25 – slightly more expensive for international matches. Both Lord's and the Oval run cricket courses for children aged eight and over and are enthusiastic supporters of 'Kwik Cricket', an easier, quicker version of the game for younger children.

Marylebone Cricket Club (MCC) and Middlesex County Cricket Club
Lord's Cricket Ground, St John's Wood Road, NW8
t (020) 7432 1033
www.lords.org
⊖ St John's Wood
Bus 3, 82, 113, 139, 189

Surrey County Cricket Club
The Oval, Kennington, SW8
t (020) 7582 6660
www.surreyccc.co.uk
⊖ Oval, Vauxhall
Bus 36, 185

Useful contacts

The following bodies can provide information on sport and venues in and around London.

Sportsline
t (020) 7222 8000

British Sports Association for the Disabled
t (020) 7490 4919

Sport England
t (020) 7273 1500
www.sportengland.com

Fishing

A bit of string and a bent nail may be all your kids need in order to get the angling habit. Alternatively, you could decide to invest in some fancy equipment from one of the capital's many tackle shops (try The Reel Thing, 17 Opera Arcade, SW1, t (020) 7976 1830, www.reelthing.co.uk). Either way you will need a licence. Contact the **National Rivers Authority** on t (01734) 535 000, www.wheretofish.com. They will also provide you with a list of fishing sites. Fishing in the Thames (home, would you believe, to over 100 types of fish) is free, contact **The Environment Agency** on t (01189) 535651, www.visitthames.co.uk

London Anglers Association

Forest Road Hall, Hervey Park Road, E17
t (020) 8520 7477
www.londonanglers.net

Football

It has always been the nation's favourite sport, but over the past decade football has reached unprecedented levels of popularity. It now pervades all aspects of popular culture – millions of books, magazines, videos and even records are sold on the back of the game. The most successful players have become pop star-marrying superstars commanding seven-figure salaries, while the top clubs are now stock market listed businesses with massive annual turnovers. Nonetheless, for all this growth, the game itself has remained as simple as ever. It requires the minimum amount of equipment (a ball, basically; goalposts can be fashioned with whatever comes to hand) and can be played practically anywhere. No wonder more British children play football than any other sport.

London is home to over a dozen professional football clubs, the biggest of which – Arsenal, Charlton, Chelsea, Fulham, Tottenham and West Ham – play in the Premier League, the nation's most prestigious competition. League matches are played at weekends (usually kicking off at 3pm on Saturday) while cup and European matches are played midweek with the big clubs regularly attracting crowds of over 30,000. The games can be passionately exciting and the removal of the hooligan element in the late '80s has led to more families coming to matches. Most grounds have family enclosures and the facilities, especially at Premier League grounds, are usually excellent. Tickets should be booked as far in advance as possible, a seat at a Premiership match can cost between £30-£25 per adult, children half-price. League matches are cheaper at between £25-£15 with child reductions. England's international matches will be played at a variety of venues around the country until the renovation of the national stadium at Wembley is complete (and this may take anything up to 5 years).

One note of warning, however; if you've never been to a football match before, your children will hear some pretty fruity language. Chanting, singing (often obscene songs about the opposition) and swearing are all an essential part of the experience.

At their best, football clubs can be a focal, unifying point for the local community. Most London clubs now belong to the **Football in the Community** scheme whereby trained coaches organize holiday schools and after-school training for local children (both boys and girls) of all abilities.

Arsenal Football Club

Arsenal Stadium, Avenell Road, Highbury, N5
t (020) 7704 4040
www.arsenal.com
⊖ Arsenal
Bus 4, 19, 29, 43, 153, 236, 253, 271
Tickets £21–50
102 spaces for wheelchair users

There is a six-year waiting list to become one of the club's 21,000 season ticket holders.

Charlton Athletic

The Valley, Floyd Road, Charlton, SE7
t (020) 8333 4010
www.cafc.co.uk
⇌ Charlton
Tickets £15–35

Chelsea Football Club

Stamford Bridge, Fulham Road, SW10
t (020) 7385 0710
www.chelseafc.co.uk
⊖ Fulham Broadway
Bus 14, 211
Tickets £25–33. 57 seats for wheelchair users
For Disabled Supporters Association call **t** (020) 7385 5545
Club shop, match day crèche for up to 20 children aged 1–5, from two hours before kick-off

Fulham

Craven Cottage, Stevenage Road, SW6
t (020) 7384 4710
www.fulhamfc.co.uk
⊖ Putney Bridge
Bus 14, 74, 220
Tickets £16–20

Tottenham Hotspur Football Club

White Hart Lane, Bill Nicholson Way, 748 High Road, Tottenham, N17
t (0870) 011 2222
www.spurs.co.uk
⊖ Tottenham Hale, Seven Sisters
Bus 149, 259, 279, W3
Tickets £24–46
For disabled access **t** (020) 8365 5050
Club shop

West Ham United

Boleyn Ground, Green Street, Upton Park, E13
t (020) 73548 2700
www.whufc.co.uk
⊖ Putney Bridge
Bus 14, 74, 220
Tickets £27–45

Go-karting

Kids love to pull on their overalls, gloves and helmets, put their foot to the floor and race around a tyre-lined circuit. Apart from the raw thrill of speed (the karts reach a top speed of 30mph), they like the idea of doing something 'grown-up', like driving, in a decidedly 'non-grown-up, go-as-fast-as-you-can' sort of way. London's indoor circuits offer training and racing for mini racing drivers aged between 8 and 16. Everything is done with the utmost care and attention to safety. The centres provide helmets and overalls and rigorous safety advice. Children should go along wearing long sleeves and trousers.

Prices vary but expect to pay around £30 for an hour-long session.

Daytona Raceway

Atlas Road, Acton, NW10
t (020) 8961 3616
www.daytona.co.uk
⊖ North Acton
Bus 95, 260, 266

Docklands F1 City

Gate 119, Connaught Bridge, Royal Victoria Dock, E16
t (020) 7476 5678
DLR Royal Albert

Streatham Playscape Kart Raceway

390 Streatham High Road, SW16
t (020) 8677 8677
www.playscape.co.uk
⇌ Streatham
Bus 57, 109, 118, 133, 201, 250, 255

Ice-skating

London has half a dozen ice-skating rinks, many of which have popular disco nights. Most will not let children aged under three on the ice. Boots can usually be hired at the door. The average price, including skate hire is adult: £5–7, child £3–5.

Alexandra Palace Ice Rink

Alexandra Palace Way, N22
t (020) 8365 4386
⇌ Alexandra Palace

Bus 184, W3

Broadgate Ice Rink
Eldon Street, EC2
t (020) 7505 4068
⊖ /≉ Liverpool Street
Bus 133, 141, 172, 214, 271
London's only outdoor rink. It's flooded and frozen between November and March.

Lee Valley Ice Centre
Lee Bridge Road, E10
t (020) 8533 3154
⊖ Walthamstow Central
Bus 158
Don't let the distance put you off, this large, well-equipped rink has disco sessions from 8.30-11 and is open for general skating from 12 noon-4 daily.

Leisurebox
Queensway, W2
t (020) 7229 0172
⊖ Bayswater, Queensway
Bus 70
London's most famous rink. Come early and watch the pros in action.

Sobell Ice Rink
Hornsey Road, Holloway, N7
t (020) 7609 2166
www.aquaterra.org.uk
⊖ Finsbury Park, Holloway Road
Bus 91

Streatham Ice Arena
386 Streatham High Road
t (020) 8769 7771
www.streathamicearena.co.uk
≉ Streatham Common
Bus 57, 109, 118, 133, 201, 250, 255

Somerset House
The Strand, WC2
t (020) 7845 4600
www.somerset-house.org.uk
⊖ Temple, Charing Cross, Embankment, Covent Garde
A New York-style open-air ice rink is set up in this grand mansion's courtyard for a few weeks during Christmas and New Year.

Play gyms & gymnastics

Play gyms are a great way to get kids moving and develop co-ordination and motor skills. Gymnastics is also fun for kids both to watch and/or participate in, contact the **British Gymnastics Association** on **t** (01952) 820330, **www**.baga.co.uk.

Crèchendo
Various locations across London
t (020) 8675 6611
Using toys and soft climbing equipment, younger kids are encouraged to fling themselves around in the name of social development. There are four age groupings from 4 months to 5 years. Kids must be accompanied by a parent or carer. There are 17 Crèchendo centres in London.

Tumbletots & Gymbobs
Various venues across London
t (0121) 585 7003
www.tumbletots.com
Kids from crawling to pre-school can climb, jump and hang on specially designed equipment, thereby improving their balance, coordination and general physical ability. Older children from 5-7 can explore equipment designed for adults in a supervised and safe environment.

Riding

There are dozens of stables and horseriding schools in London, some offering lessons to children as young as two and a half (who presumably have only just got the hang of walking).

Barnfield Riding School
Parkfields Road (off Park Road), Kingston-upon-Thames
t (020) 8546 3616
www.barnfieldriding.co.uk
≉ Kingston
Bus 65, 371
Adm £20 for half-hour lesson
The age limit is discretionary. On the Tiny Tots course children as young as two are even allowed to ride.

Dulwich Riding School
Dulwich Common, SE21
t (020) 8693 2944
⇌ West Dulwich
Bus 63, P4, P13
Adm Groups £15 per hour; private lesson £25 per hour
Age limit 10 and over

Ealing Riding School
Gunnersby Avenue, W5
t (020) 8992 3808
⊖ Ealing Common
Bus 207, 607
Adm £17 per lesson
Age limit Five and over

Hyde Park Riding Stables
63 Bathurst Mews, W2
t (020) 7723 2813
www.hydeparkstables.com
⊖ Lancaster Gate
Bus 7, 15, 23, 27, 36

Adm £30 per hour
Age limit Five and over

London Equestrian Centre
Lullingworth Garth, Finchley, N12
t (020) 8349 1345
⊖ Mill Hill East
Bus 13, 82, 112, 143, 260
Adm from 15 per lesson
Age limit Four and over

Roehampton Gate Riding Stables
Priory Lane, SW15
t (020) 8876 7089
⊖ Richmond
Bus 33, 72, 74, 170, 265, 337
Adm Mon–Fri £15 per half hour, Sat & Sun £18 per half hour
Age limit Six and over

Ross Nye's Riding Stables
8 Bathurst Mews, W2
t (020) 7262 3791
www.ridingstable.co.uk

Sporting bodies
All England Netball Association
t (01462) 442 344
www.england-netball.co.uk
Amateur Athletics Association
t (0121) 440 5000
www.british-athletics.co.uk
Amateur Rowing Association
t (020) 8237 6700
www.ara-rowing.org
Amateur Swimming Association
t (0150) 961 8700
www.british-swimming.org
Badminton Association
t (01908) 568 822
www.baofe.co.uk
British Baseball Federation
t (020) 7453 7055
www.baseballsoftballuk.com
British Canoe Federation
t (0115) 982 1100
British Snowboarding Association
t (01494) 462 225
British Sub-Aqua Club
(0151) 350 6200
www.bsac.com
Croquet Association

t (020) 7736 3148
www.croquet.org.uk
Cyclist Touring Club
t (01483) 417 217
www.ctc.org.uk
English Basketball Association
t (0113) 2326 1166
www.basketballengland.co.uk
English Ice Hockey Association
t (01202) 303 946
www.eiha.co.uk
English Ski Council
t (0121) 501 2314
www.englishski.org
English Volleyball Association
t (0115) 981 6324
www.volleyballengland.org
Golf Foundation
t (01920) 484 044
Lawn Tennis Association
t (020) 7385 2366
www.lta.org.uk
London Anglers Association
t (020) 8520 7477
www.londonanglers.net
London Gymnastics Federation
t (020) 8529 1142

⊖ Paddington
Bus 7, 15, 23, 27, 36
Adm £30 per hour
Age limit Seven and over

Wimbledon Village Stables

24a High Street, Wimbledon, SW19
t (020) 8946 8579
www.wvstables.com
⊖ /⇌ Wimbledon
Bus 93, 200
Adm £30 per hour
Age limit Three and over

Rugby

London has several professional rugby union clubs, many of whom offer coaching for children (both boys and girls) and run mini-teams. Club matches are usually played on Saturday afternoons.

Harlequins

Stoop Memorial Ground, Langhorn Drive, Twickenham, Middlesex
t (0870) 887 0230
www.quins.co.uk
⇌ Twickenham
Bus 281
Tickets £12–£20, wheelchair users **free**
Specific entrance for wheelchair users, adapted toilets

London Wasps

Rangers Stadium, South Africa Road, W12
t (020) 8740 2545
www.wasps.co.uk
⊖ White City
Bus 72, 95, 220
Tickets £15, under-16s £7

Saracens RFC

Vicarage Road Stadium, Watford
t (01923) 475222
www.saracens.com
⇌ Watford High Street
Bus 298, 299, 307
Tickets £10–30, under-16s £5
Has an entrance for wheelchair users and a reserved section for disabled spectators.

London Irish RFC

The Avenue, Sunbury-on-Thames, Middlesex, TW16
t (01932) 783 034
www.london-irish-rugby.com
⇌ Sunbury
Bus 216, 235, 555, 557
Tickets £10–£25
Wheelchair access, adapted toilets
Welcomes kids; girls can play up to the age of 12.

London Welsh

Old Deer Park, Kew Road, Richmond, Surrey TW9
t (020) 8940 2368
www.london-welsh.co.uk
⊖ Richmond
Bus 65
Tickets £4–£11, under-16s **free**
Limited facilities for the disabled
Holiday and half-term courses; boys' and girls' teams from under-7s to under-12s.

Roller skating

Most dedicated roller skaters practise their craft on London's streets and parks – particularly Hyde Park (*see* p.132) where you can often see games of roller-hockey taking place on weekends. There are, however, a couple of centres where the less able and less extrovert can practise.

Road Runner

Unit 2, Lancaster Road, W11
t (020) 7792 0584
⊖ Ladbroke Grove
Bus 7, 23 52
Open 10–6 daily

Roehampton Recreation Centre

Laverstoke Gardens, SW15
t (020) 8785 0535
⊖ Putney
Bus 72, 74, 85, 170, 265
Open Sat 6–8.30

Skiing & snowboarding

You don't expect to come to London and go skiing, but you can if you want to. There are a surprising number of dry ski slopes in London. All have nursery slopes for beginners. Prices work out at somewhere in the region of £10–£12 for adults (for a two-hour session) and £5–£6 for children. For more facilities contact the **Ski Club of Great Britain** on **t** (020) 8410 2000, **www**.ski-club.co.uk

Beckton Alps Ski Slope
Alpine Way, E6
t (020) 7511 0351
⊖ East Ham
Bus 101, 173, 262, 276, 300
Open Sep–April 10–11 daily, Sat 9.30–11.30 children only

After a period of refurbishment the Alps will reopen for business in late 2002 with real snow.

Bromley Ski Centre
Sandy Lane, St Paul's Cray, Orpington, Kent
t (01689) 876 812
www.c-v-s.co.uk/bromleyski
⮆ St Mary Kray
Bus 61, 208, R7
Open Tues–Fri 12 noon–10pm, Sat 9–6, Sun 10–6

Crystal Palace Ski Slope
Ledrington Road, Norwood, SE19
t (020) 8778 0131
www.crystalpalace.co.uk
⮆ Crystal Palace
Bus 157, 358, 361
Open Mon–Sat 9am–10pm, Sun 9–6

Hillingdon Ski Centre
Park Road, Uxbridge, Middlesex
t (01895) 255 183
⊖ Uxbridge
Bus U1, U10
Open Mon–Fri 10–10, Sat 10–6

Sandown Sports Club
More Lane, Esher, Surrey
(01372) 467132
www.sandownsports.co.uk
⮆ Esher
Open Mon–Fri & Sun 10-10, Sat 1-8

Sports centres

There are nigh on 200 sports centres in London, offering a huge range of activities from badminton to martial arts. Many have swimming pools and most have special facilities for young children. Some of the best are listed below.

Britannia Leisure Centre
40 Hyde Road, Islington, N1
t (020) 7729 4485
⊖ Old Street
Bus 67, 76, 141, 149, 242, 243, 243A, 271

Badminton, football, gym, judo, netball, swimming – as well as canoeing and diving.

Brixton Recreation Centre
Brixton Station Road, SW9
t (020) 7926 9780
⊖ Brixton
Bus 118, 196, 250, P4

Activities catered for include badminton, gymnastics, swimming, tennis, trampolining.

Crystal Palace
National Sports Centre, Ledrington Road, Upper Norwood, SE19
t (020) 8778 0131
www.crystalpalace.co.uk
⮆ Crystal Palace
Bus 157, 358, 361

The home of British athletics, this internationally renowned sports centre boasts an athletics stadium, an Olympic-sized swimming pool and high diving board as well as excellent facilities for badminton, basketball, gymnastics, hockey and martial arts. It stages numerous international sporting competitions and offers teaching and coaching to a high standard. Would-be-athletes can apply to attend one of the centre's annual summer camps.

Michael Sobell Leisure Centre
Hornsey Road, Holloway, N7
t (020) 7609 2166
⮆ Finsbury Park, Holloway Road
Bus 91

A multi-purpose centre offering badminton, basketball, cricket, football, martial arts, squash, table tennis, trampolining and ice-skating.

SURVIVAL | KIDS IN | KIDS OUT | SPORTS AND ACTIVITIES | TRAVEL | PRACTICALITIES A-Z | SLEEP | EAT | SHOP

Oasis Sports Centre

32 Endell Street, WC2
t (020) 7831 1804
⊖ Holborn, Covent Garden
Bus 1, 14, 19, 24, 29, 38, 176

Offering facilities for badminton, football, martial arts, swimming, table tennis and trampolining, Oasis also boasts London's only heated outdoor pool as well as a paddling pool for toddlers.

Queen Mother's Sports Centre

223 Vauxhall Bridge Road, SW1
t (020) 7630 5522
⊖ /⇌ Victoria, ⊖ Pimlico
Bus 2, 36, 185

Badminton, football, martial arts, netball, rounders, swimming.

Swimming

Kids just love mucking about in water – it's the law. Whether it's in tropically heated under-5s pools or all-weather lidos, there's something deeply appealing about a good old splish-splash. Most indoor pools run mother and toddler sessions. Expect to pay around £3.50 for an adult, £2 for a child.

Indoor pools

The Arches

Trafalgar Road, SE10
t (020) 8317 5000
⇌ Greenwich
Bus 177, 180, 188, 286, 386
Open 10.30–7 daily

Various water chutes and slides.

Britannia Leisure Centre

40 Hyde Road, N1
t (020) 7729 4485
⊖ Old Street
Bus 67, 76, 141, 149, 242, 243, 243A, 271
Open Mon–Fri 9–9, Sat & Sun 9–6

Water slides, wave machine and pool inflatables.

Crystal Palace Pool

National Sports Centre, Ledrington Road, Norwood, SE19
t (020) 8778 0131
⇌ Crystal Palace

Bus 157, 358, 361
Open Mon–Fri 9–9, Sat & Sun 9–6

Olympic-size pool and high diving boards.

Fulham Pools

Normand Park, Lillie Road, SW6
t (020) 7385 7628
⊖ West Brompton
Bus 74, 190
Open Mon–Fri 9–9, Sat & Sun 9–6

Water slide, water toys, wave machine.

Latchmere Leisure Centre

Latchmere Road, SW11
t (020) 7207 8004
⊖ Clapham Junction
Bus 35, 156, 170, 219, 295, C3
Open Mon–Thurs 7–9.30pm, Fri and Sat 7–7, Sun 7–6

Extremely child-friendly and indoor pool which includes a seashore slope, wave machine and toddler's pool.

Outdoor pools

On bright summer days, and even late into the evenings, London's outdoor pools can be delightful. Parents can escape the bustle, lazing by the poolside as their children go berserk in the water while the sun beats down overhead. Prices are roughly the same as for indoor pools.

Evian Lido

Brockwell Park, Dulwich Road, SE24
t (020) 7274 3088
www.thelido.com
⊖ Brixton
⇌ Herne Hill
Bus 3, 37, 196
Open June–Sep 10–7 daily

Finchley Lido

Great North Leisure Park, High Road, N12
t (020) 8343 9830
⊖ Finchley Central
Bus 263
Open May–Sep 10–7 daily

Oasis Sports Centre

Endell Street, WC2
t (020) 7931 1804
⊖ Covent Garden
Bus 1, 14, 19, 24, 29, 38, 176
Open Mon–Fri 7.30am–8pm, Sat & Sun 9.30–5

Heated outdoor pool in the heart of London. Also has a toddlers' paddling pool.

Parliament Hill Lido

Parliament Hill, Hampstead Heath (off Gordon House Road), NW5
t (020) 7485 3873
≥ Gospel Oak
Bus 214, C2, C11
Open May–Sep 7–7 daily

Tooting Bec Lido

Tooting Bec Road, SW16
t (020) 8871 7198
⊖ Tooting Bec
Bus 249, 319
Open June–Sep 10–8pm daily

Tennis

If you and your children don't fancy overcoming the obstacles inherent to the Wimbledon experience (*see* box, above), but just want to see some grass court tennis and spot a few famous players (so long as they're male), you might like to visit the Queen's Club Tournament which takes place a couple of weeks beforehand. The atmosphere here is much more relaxed and tickets are easier to come by (and much cheaper, £10-15). If your family fancies a game, many public parks have a couple of concrete courts and there are a few tennis clubs in London offering training for children from the age of 7 upwards. You should expect to pay around £5–6 per hour for an outdoor court, £12–15 indoors.

Wimbledon (All England Lawn Tennis and Croquet Club)

Church Road, Wimbledon, SW19
t (020) 8946 2244
www.wimbledon.org
⊖ Southfields, Wimbledon Park
≥ Wimbledon
Bus 39, 93

Queen's Club

Palliser Road, W14
t (020) 7385 3421
www.queensclub.co.uk
⊖ Barons Court
Bus 28, 74, 190, 211, 220, 295, 391

New balls please

Despite playing host to Wimbledon, the game's premier tournament, Britain's attitude towards tennis is, in truth, rather ambivalent. It has significantly fewer public courts than most other countries and, as a result, significantly fewer top-class players. The last home-grown winner of Wimbledon was Fred Perry (he of the sports shirts) in the late 1930s. Only recently, has Britain managed to find itself a couple of players capable of challenging for top honours and one of those, Greg Rusedski, had to be pinched from Canada. For most of the year, the British public couldn't care less about tennis. During the last two weeks of June, however, it suddenly becomes everyone's favourite sport. Demand for Wimbledon tickets is huge, to put it mildly. In order to buy Centre Court or No.1 Court tickets, where all the big-name matches take place, you have to enter a ballot the previous September, and even then your chances of success are pretty remote. Alternatively, you could try turning up on a matchday and queuing. The queue usually starts several days prior to the championship and can stretch for over a mile. Getting tickets for Wimbledon is not impossible, but it is very difficult – and even if you do get lucky, they're not cheap. A pair of Centre Court tickets will set you back over £100. Outside court tickets are much better value at around £20 each and give you the chance to buy resale tickets for the show courts which go on sale daily at 2pm.

Islington Indoor Tennis Centre

Market Road, N7
t (020) 7700 1370
⊖Caledonian Road
Bus 73, 274

Regent's Park Tennis Centre

York Bridge Road, NW1
t (020) 7486 4216
www.rptc.co.uk
⊖ Regent's Park
Bus 274

Westway Indoor Tennis Centre

1 Crowthorne Road, W10
t (020) 8969 0992
⊖ Latimer Road
Bus 295

Watersports

Most of the centres listed below run courses in sailing, windsurfing, canoeing and rowing – children must be able to swim, usually at least 50m. For sailing activities on the Thames try the **Thames Barge Sailing Club** on **t** (020) 7642 8795. **www**.bargeclub.org.uk or the **Thames Sailing Club** on **t** (01932) 228689, **www**.thamessailingclub.org.uk

Capital Rowing Centre

Kingston Rowing Club, Lower Ham Road, Kingston-upon-Thames, Surrey
t (07973) 314199
⇌ Kingston

A rowing school giving kids and adults alike a grounding in rowing technique.

Docklands Sailing and Watersports Centre

Millwall Dock, West Ferry Road, E14
t (020) 7537 2626
www.docklandwatersports.co.uk
⊖ Mile End
Bus D1, D5, D8, P14

Canoeing, windsurfing and sailing sessions are available for ages 8 and up. Kids can also try their hand at dragonboat racing and imagine themselves as Viking marauders off to plunder new worlds.

Islington Boat Club

16–34 Graham Street, N1
t (020) 7253 0778
⊖ Angel
Bus 43, 214

London Corinthian Sailing Club

Upper Mall, W6
t (020) 8748 3280
⊖ Hammersmith
Bus 9, 10, 27

Royal Victoria Dock Watersports Centre

Gate 5, Tidal Basin Road, off Silvertown Way, E16
t (020) 7511 2326
DLR Royal Victoria

Surrey Docks Watersports Centre

Greenland Dock, Rope Street, SE16
t (020) 7237 4009
⊖ Surrey Quays

Westminster Boating Base

Dinorvic Wharf, 136 Grosvenor Road, SW1
t (020) 7821 7389
⊖ Pimlico
Bus 24, C10

Travel

London is one of the busiest gateway cities in the world, welcoming thousands of flights every day. Competition between airlines on the major routes is fierce and, wherever you're flying from, you should be able to pick up a cheap deal. Of course, when travelling with children, you may decide to forgo potential savings in return for extra comfort and some in-flight care and entertainment.

> ### Flight times to London
> **New York** 6–7 hours
> **Miami** 4–5 hours
> **Los Angeles** 9–10 hours
> **Hawaii** 18 hours
> **Montreal** 6 hours
> **Toronto** 7 hours

Flights

Many of the larger airlines, including British Airways, Air Canada and Cathay Pacific, provide on-board services for families. These can include such life-savers as designated flight attendants, play packs, seat-back computer games and children's TV channels. Charter flights may be cheap but they can be particularly hellish for children, who will not necessarily tolerate sitting in a cramped seat with nothing to do for eight hours or more. An international air ticket for a child aged 2 or under should cost just 10 percent of the adult fare. (Remember, only one reduced fare is allowed per adult.) Between the ages of 3 and 11, your child will be charged anything between 50 and 85 percent of the full adult fare but once over 12 your child is, in the eyes of the airline, officially an adult and no longer entitled to any form of discount.

Pushchairs are usually carried free on airlines and can often be taken right up to the point of boarding. Carrycots, however, are not supposed to be brought on board, although some airlines allow the collapsible kind. It can make more sense to pre-book a sky cot or bassinet.

Transatlantic flights

Transatlantic flights touch down at London's two major airports: Heathrow, **t** (0870) 000 0123, **www**.baa.co.uk/heathrow, situated 15 miles west of Central London, one of the world's largest airports with four terminals (plans for a fifth are under discussion) and Gatwick, **t** (01293) 535 353, **www**.baa.co.uk/gatwick, some 25 miles to the south, with two terminals. Concorde, the world's only supersonic passenger aircraft, arrives at Heathrow's Terminal Four.

Of London's other three airports, Stansted, **t** (0870) 000 0303, **www**.baa.co.uk/stansted, is the furthest from central London – some 35 miles

northeast. It's also the largest, the busiest (specialising in budget flights and cut-price deals) and has a pleasant, open-plan terminal designed by architect du jour Norman Foster. London City, **t** (020) 7646 0000, **www**.londoncityairport.com, is the closest, 9 miles east – it welcomes just a handful of flights each day from Britain and Europe – while Luton, **t** (01582) 405 100, **www**.londonluton.co.uk, which like Stansted mainly handles budget flights from Europe, is 31 miles to the north.

From North America

The cheapest tickets offered by the major airlines are Apex and Super Apex, which must be booked 21 days before departure and involve a stay of at least seven nights. Also, check out online discounts and consolidators – companies which buy blocks of unsold tickets to sell on at a discount. Because of the restrictions on flight times, high cancellation fees and the potential for delays, charter flights are not recommended when travelling with children.

Major Airlines
Air Canada
t US (800) 776 3000
t Canada (800) 555 1212
www.aircanada.com
American Airlines
t US (800) 433 7300
www.americanair.com
British Airways
t US (800) 247 9297
www.britishairways.com
Canadian Airlines
t US (800) 665 1177
t Canada (800) 663 0290
www.cdnair.ca
Continental Airlines
t US (800) 231 0856
www.flycontinental.com
Delta Airlines
t US (800) 221 1212
www.delta.com

TWA
t US (800) 221 2000
www.twa.com
United Airlines
t US (800) 538 2929
www.ual.com
Virgin Atlantic Airways
t US (800) 862 8621
www.virgin-atlantic.com

Consolidators in North America
Air Brokers Travel
t US (800) 883 3273
www.airbrokers.com
Jetset
t US (800) 638 3273
www.jetset.com
Travac Tours and Charters
t US (800) 872 8800
www.thetravelsite.com
UniTravel
t US (800) 325 2222
www.unitravel.com

Australia and New Zealand
Air New Zealand
t Australia (13) 2476
t New Zealand (09) 357 3000
www.airnz.co.nz
British Airways
t Australia (02) 9258 3300
t New Zealand (09) 356 8690
www.british-airways.com/regional/australia
Cathay Pacific
t Australia (13) 1747
t New Zealand (09) 379 0861
www.cathaypacific.com
Qantas
t Australia (13) 1211
t New Zealand (09) 357 8900
www.qantas.com.au

Arriving by plane

Arriving at an airport after a long-haul flight can be a fraught experience. Thankfully Heathrow and Gatwick have good facilities to help ease the strain. Both have plentiful supplies of trollies (baggage carts), which can be used free of charge, baby-changing facilities, nursing rooms and children's

Cheap flight websites
www.cheapflights.com
www.cheaptickets.com
www.farebase.net
www.lastminute.com
www.moments-notice.com
www.thetrip.com
www.travelocity.com

play rooms (Heathrow even has a crèche) as well as a plethora of shops and cafés where you can stock up on last minute essentials or take a few minutes to relax with a coffee.

Heathrow
Train – the Heathrow Express
t (0845) 600 1515
www.heathrowexpress.co.uk
Every 15 minutes between 5.10am–11.40pm
Fares Adult single First Class £20, Express Class £12, under-15s **free** if accompanied by an adult

The Heathrow Express, a direct train link between the airport and Paddington mainline station, is by far the quickest route into town. The journey costs £12 each way but takes just 15 minutes – tickets can be bought at Heathrow, on the train or in advance online which entitles you to a £1 discount (allow at least three days for delivery within the UK, five days for abroad). Paddington is connected to the Bakerloo, Hammersmith and City, Circle and District tube lines. There is a black cab rank outside.

Tube
5.30am–12midnight daily
Fares Adult single £3.40, child £1.40

One-Day Travelcards, which allow you unlimited travel on London's buses, trains and tubes, are available from 9.30am onwards on weekdays and at any time on weekends. *See* **Top tips**, p.8.

Heathrow is the first stop on the eastbound Piccadilly Line, which means you should be able to get a seat and find somewhere to put your luggage. On the downside, it can take up to an hour to reach central London and, unless your eventual destination is on the Piccadilly Line (Knightsbridge, Green Park Piccadilly Circus, Leicester Square, etc), you will have to face the prospect of negotiating corridors and escalators whilst laden with luggage and children as you change to another line. Alternatively, you may prefer to get off at ⊖ Earl's Court or South Kensington and take a taxi the rest of the way.

Airbus

t (08705) 808 080
www.gobycoach.com
Every 20–30 mins from 5.30am–6pm, then every hour till 9.45pm
Fares Adult single £7, child £3.50
Equipped for disabled passengers

There are 30 Airbus departures a day from Heathrow bound for London King's Cross station by way of Notting Hill, Marble Arch and Russell Square. The journey takes 1hr 40 mins.

Taxi

Easily the most convenient option – unfortunately it's also the most expensive. Make sure you take a licensed black cab from the official rank. Not only are black cabs metered, so you can see exactly what you have to pay, but the drivers are guaranteed to take you to your destination by the quickest route. The cab fare from Heathrow to central London should be around £30–35.

Gatwick

Train – the Gatwick Express

t 0845 748 4950 for timetable information
www.gatwickexpress.co.uk
Every 15 mins between 5.50am and 0.50am, then every hour after that at 35mins past the hour
Fares Adult single First Class £17, Express Class £10.50, under-16s pay 50% of the adult fare

By far the most practical way to get into town. The trains are not quite as speedy as their Heathrow counterparts but make good time – 30 mins platform to platform from Gatwick to Victoria – and they run through the night. There is also a stopping service during the day for passengers requiring East Croydon (20 mins) or Clapham Junction (35 mins), which takes 50 mins to reach Victoria. Tickets can be bought at Gatwick, on the train (Express service only) or pre-booked online (allow at least three days for delivery within the UK, five days for abroad).

Airbus

t (08705) 8808 080
www.gobycoach.com
Hourly from 4.15am–9.15pm
Fares Adult single £12.50, child single £6.20

The Airbus is cheaper than the train but is very slow and can take over two hours to reach Victoria, calling at Coulsdon, Wallington, Mitcham, Streatham and Pimlico on the way.

Taxi

Taking a taxi is only an option for the seriously wealthy or the seriously tired out. The journey will take over an hour and cost upwards of £60. There is a black cab rank outside the arrivals hall.

And the rest

The Stansted Express, **t** (08457) 444 422, **www**.stanstedexpress.co.uk, which links Stansted Airport with ⊖ Tottenham Hale on the Victoria line and Liverpool Street station (east of the city centre), runs every half hour from 5am–8am, then every 15mins till 4pm, then every half hour till 11pm and costs adult single £13, child single £6.50 – you can pre-book your tickets online. The journey takes 42 mins. Alternatively, you could catch the Airbus, **t** (08705) 8808 080, **www**.gobycoach.com, which runs roughly every half hour 24hrs a day and takes around an hour longer than the train, stopping enroute at Finchley Road and Marble Arch before ending up at Victoria station. It costs adult single £8, child single £4.

A taxi from London City Airport should take around half an hour to reach the centre of town and cost a little over £10. There is also a shuttle bus service to Liverpool Street. It departs every 20 minutes between 6.50am–9.10pm and tickets cost adult £5, child £2.50 under-5s free. The Docklands Light Railway (DLR) runs a service connecting Canning Town (reached from the airport via shuttle bus) with Tower Gateway or Bank stations on the east side of the city. Trains run seven days a week to 12.30am Mon-Sat, 11.30pm Sun. *See* **Top tip** p.8 for DLR savings. At Luton a free shuttle bus service connects the airport to Luton Parkway station. Thameslink provide a service from Luton to King's Cross, with trains departing every 15 mins and tickets cost adult £9.50, child £4.75.

Arriving by rail, road or ferry

By rail

Eurostar

t (0870) 6000 782
t (0870) 167 6767 for a brochure
www.eurostar.com
Twenty times a day from Paris and Brussels
Fares Vary. A standard class Apex return,which must be booked 14 days in advance, is adult £79 (under 26 £75) child £60, under-4s **free**
Check-in time 20 minutes.
No baggage weight limit.
Wheelchair users need to inform Eurostar staff of their requirements when booking

It takes just three hours to reach London from Paris or Brussels aboard a Eurostar train. Time spent under the sea is just 25 minutes. At present the trains arrive at Waterloo, although there are plans to build a new international terminus at St Pancras. Waterloo International leads into Waterloo mainline station, which, in turn, is connected to ⊖ Waterloo. Once through Customs, you're just a few minutes away from central London. Trains run from here to other mainline stations such as Victoria and Charing Cross; the Underground station is on the Northern and Bakerloo lines. A taxi to the centre of town should cost in the region of £5–10. There's a cab rank outside the station.

By ferry

The completion of the tunnel in the early 1990s transformed the cross–channel travel industry. The much–hyped advantages of ferry travel: duty free shops, restaurants and bars, fabulously bad cabaret *et al*, have paled in comparison to a 20–35 minute seasick-free jaunt under the channel. And now that duty-free shopping has finally been abolished, ferry companies are really beginning to feel the strain.

Nonetheless, for all its problems, ferry travel is still well worth considering. The main ferry links land you at Dover, Newhaven or Portsmouth from where you can continue your journey to one of London's eight mainline stations: Charing Cross, Euston, King's Cross, Liverpool Street, Paddington, St Pancras, Victoria or Waterloo. All have connections to the Underground network.

Prices are highly competitive with companies offering a range of deals in the hope of drawing some custom away from the Channel Tunnel (under-4s usually travel free and there are discounts for under-14s) and most lines can boast good family facilities—restaurants, baby-changing rooms, children's play areas and video rooms.

Calais–Dover is the quickest and most popular ferry route. P&O Stena Line **t** (0870) 600 9009 (**www**.posl.com) operate 35 sailings a day in the high season; the journey takes 1 hour 15 minutes. Fares vary hugely and it's best to shop around for the best current deal. A family of four travelling in a medium-sized car should expect to pay anything between £120–150 for a flexible return depending on the time of year.

Driving via the Channel Tunnel

Eurotunnel – Calais to Folkestone

t (08705) 353 535
www.eurotunnel.com
Four departures an hour during peak times
Fares Flexible return tickets start at around £130 if you travel before 7am. The fare is for car space only regardless of the number of passengers
Check in time At least 25 minutes but no more than two hours before departure.
No baggage weight limit. Wheelchair users need to inform staff of their requirements when booking

Eurotunnel transports cars on purpose-built carriers through the Channel Tunnel between Calais and Folkestone. The French terminal is situated off junction 13 of the A16 motorway while the British equivalent can be reached via junction 11a of the M20. The journey time is a mere 35 minutes. Most people choose to stay in their car although you can get out and wander down the corridor to stretch your legs. Toilets and a buffet service are provided. It is advisable to book in advance, although it is possible just to turn up and wait. Space is given on a first come, first served basis.

The carless alternative

You may want to consider arriving in Britain without your car and renting one once you get here. Airlines and many travel agents can arrange 'fly-drive' packages for you on request. *See* **Getting around**, p.201, for rental companies in London.

If you're arriving from the continent, remember to adjust the dip of your headlights for driving on the left. Wearing seatbelts is compulsory in Britain, front seats and back.

By bus

National Express/Eurolines

52 Grosvenor Gardens, London SW1
t (08705) 808 080
www.gobycoach.com

Operates coach routes to all the major cities in Britain and Europe. London's main coach station is at Victoria, 10 minutes' walk from the train/tube station along Buckingham Palace Road.

Coach trips are invariably a balancing act, being both the cheapest and the least pleasant way to travel long distances. National Express do not charge for under-5s and under-16s travel half-price but savings are generally far outweighed by the misery of sitting in a tiny cramped seat for hours on end.

Passports and visas

From Europe

Although a member of the European Union – which technically gives all union citizens the right to move freely in and between member states – Britain has yet to to institute a proper open border policy and it is still necessary for EU citizens to present their passports or identity cards upon entering the country.

From elsewhere

Nationals from the US, Canada, Australia, New Zealand, South Africa, Japan, Mexico and Switzerland do not need a visa in order to visit Britain for a holiday of up to three months, but must present their passport upon arrival and should expect to answer a few routine questions relating to the nature of their visit. Other nationals should check out their particular entry requirements with their respective embassies.

Customs

EU nationals over the age of 17 are no longer required to make a declaration to customs upon entry into another EU country and so can now import a limitless amount of goods for personal use. For non-EU nationals the limits are 200 cigarettes, one litre of spirits, two litres of wine, 60ml of perfume, two cameras, one movie camera and one TV.

Retail Export Scheme

Visitors from non-EU countries can make savings on purchases made in London via the Retail Export Scheme. Pick up a form from participating shops.

Pet's Passports

Until recently, no pet could be brought into the country unless it had first spent six months in quarantine to make sure it wasn't carrying any infectious diseases (particularly rabies). The rules have now relaxed slightly allowing visitors from Western Europe (and certain island states such as Cyprus and Malta) to bring in pets so long as they fulfill the following strict criteria: the pet to be brought in must not have been outside the qualifying area at any time; each pet must be fitted with an identification microchip and have been innoculated against rabies; the owner must carry with them a document (known as the Pet's Passport) proving this. 30 days after entry, the animal must undergo a further blood test.

Making your way around the maze of London's streets can be tricky. They have neither the block-by-block clarity of New York nor the accessibility of Paris. The most convenient option, if you are new to the city, is to take the Underground. This in itself can be exciting for children, especially if they have never travelled on an underground system before. When you, and they, are a little more at home in London, you'll find that buses make a welcome change, allowing you to see the sights as you travel around, albeit at a more leisurely pace. Other forms of transport, such as London's famous black cabs, can also be fun, though these are rather expensive.

By tube

Travelcards

If you're travelling after 9.30am on a weekday or at anytime on a weekend, your best bet is to get a One-Day Travelcard which lets you make unlimited journeys on London's tubes, buses (except night buses) and trains until 3am the following morning. See **Top tips** p.8.

There are 12 interconnecting lines (colour-coded) which criss-cross London from Heathrow way out to the west to Upminster in the east and from Barnet in the north to Morden in the south. In central London you're never more than five minutes from a tube station, though the system is more sparse the further from the centre you get. Tube trains run from 5.30am to 12midnight (7am on Sundays) every day apart from Christmas. Try to avoid travelling at peak times (Mon–Fri 7.30am–9.30am and 5pm–7.30pm). This is especially important if you are using a stroller or buggy.

The Docklands area in east London is served by the DLR (Docklands Light Railway), an overground monorail which links up with ⊖ Bank and ⊖ Tower Gateway. For information, call the DLR customer services **t** (020) 7363 9700. **www**.dlr.co.uk. Trains run to 12.30am Mon-Sat, 11.30pm Sun.

ollow procedure

You must buy your Underground ticket in advance. At most Underground stations you will find an 'Assistance and Tickets' window, where you can pay by card or cash, plus a bank of electronic ticket machines which accept coins and notes (not £20 notes). You can buy a carnet of 10 tickets for £10 or a weekly pass from some machines.

Some stations have ticket inspectors; most, however, have automated barriers. Place your ticket

Question 18
In Paris it's le métro, in New York it's the subway, so what is it called in London?
answer on p.249

with the black magnetic strip face down into the slot at the front of the machine. The ticket will reappear from a slot at the top of the machine. Take your ticket and the barrier will open.

Few tube stops have lifts, which means taking the stairs or (if you're sensible) the escalator. Strollers must be folded up and held on the escalator. It is the custom to stand on the right hand side and walk on the left and people may get very sniffy with you if you get this wrong. On crowded trains, young fit passengers are supposed to give up their seats for senior citizens, pregnant women and parents with babies or toddlers. Sometimes this even happens.

By bus

Despite the presence of the odd bus lane, London's ongoing traffic congestion problems make the bus an impractical choice for anyone in a hurry. If you're not working to a deadline, however, it can make a very pleasant alternative to subterranean travel. Looking out of the window on the top deck of a slow-moving double decker is a great way of getting to know the city. The standard single fare is adult £1, child 40p.

There are two main types of bus in use in London today. In the suburbs and outskirts of town, you will mostly encounter the new pay-as-you-enter buses with concertina-style doors. In the centre of town, however, you'll also find the old 1950s Routemasters – these have open backs allowing passengers to get on and sit down as quickly as possible. Tickets are then bought from a conductor once the bus is underway.

There are also two types of bus stop: white, at which buses must stop, and red, which are request stops. To hail a bus at a red stop stick your arm out. To alight at a request stop, ring the bell.

Night buses

Standard buses stop operating around midnight, at which point N-prefixed night buses take over until 5am the following morning. There are far fewer night bus routes, and fares are more expensive – you can pick up a night route map from any Underground station and most newsagents. One-Day Travelcards are not valid on night buses.

By train

For nipping around central London, stick to the tube. For longer journeys out into the suburbs, however, you may wish to switch to the train. The rail network links up with the tube at various points and, unlike the tube, there are certain services (particularly the airport routes) that run all night. To find out how trains are running throughout Britain call **t** (08457) 48 49 50. All train and tube stations have a map, known as a Journey Planner, showing London's combined tube and train network. If you buy a Travelcard (*See* p 8 **Top tips**) you can chop and change your mode of transport throughout the day, using as many trains, tubes and buses as you like.

Tickets and passes

Fares in London are based on a zonal system. The capital is divided into six concentric rings or 'zones'. Zone 1 is the centre, Zone 6 the outskirts. Your fare is worked out according to your journey within and between these zones. For instance, a single tube fare within Zone 1 is adult £1.50, child 60p, whereas a single fare between Zone 1 and Zone 2 rises to adult £1.90, child 80p. Children's fares apply between the ages of five and 15; after the age of 12 children need to show an age identification photocard (available from any tube or train station) when they purchase their ticket, under-5s go free.

Taxis

London is justifiably proud of its black cabs. Though undeniably expensive, they make up one of the most efficient and reliable taxi services in the world. Cabbies must train for two years and pass a strict test before qualifying for their taxi licenses. During this time they must learn every street and major building in the capital as well as 468 separate routes – a mean feat of learning known simply as 'The Knowledge'.

London cabs are easily recognizable. Most are black although, in this consumer age, some now sport the coloured livery of advertisers. All have orange 'For Hire' signs on their roofs which light up when the cab is available. Carseats are fitted as standard in all TX1 black cabs. The seats are built into the central arm rest in the rear of the cab and

can accommodate children between 22-36kg. You may hail a cab on the street (by sticking out your arm and shouting 'Taxi!') or, if staying at a hotel, you can ask the doorman to do it for you. There are taxi ranks outside all major railway stations. Alternatively, call Dial-A-Black-Cab, **t** (020) 7253 5000. To track down that mislaid umbrella or teddy bear, call Black Cab Lost Property on **t** (020) 7833 0996. Black cabs are licensed to carry four people at a time (sometimes five) with space next to the driver for luggage. Most black cabs can accommodate wheelchairs and some even have carseats. Minicabs are cheaper but less reliable and largely unregulated. A driving licence is pretty much all that's required to qualify as a minicab driver. Hiring a minicab can therefore be rather a risky business. There are some reputable firms:
Atlas Cars
t (020) 7602 1234
Greater London Hire
t (020) 8340 2450
Town and Country Cabs
t (020) 7622 6222
Lady Cabs
t (020) 7254 3501
A specialist service run by women (all the drivers are female) for women.

By car

If you're coming to London to see the sights, you would be better off using public transport. Otherwise you'll have to cope with congestion, unfathomable one-way systems and strict parking regulations. Going over your allotted time at a parking meter can have dire consequences. You may return to find that your vehicle now sports a bright yellow wheel clamp or, if you're particularly unlucky, that it has been towed away altogether. find out which pound to go to in order to reclaim your car call **t** (020) 7747 4747 – the main ones are at Marble Arch, Earl's Court and Camden. The fine will be a staggering £135. Using the car for trips outside London, however, does make a little more sense. Before setting off, buy a copy of the British Highway Code (available from Post Offices) in order to familiarize yourself with the British way of motoring. You don't need to carry your papers with you but, if stopped, you will usually be asked to present them at a police station within five days. If you are hiring a car, you need to be at least 21 years of age (more usually 25) and have a year's driving experience. Most airlines will be able to arrange fly-drive packages on request.

Car rental companies

Alamo
UK **t** (020) 7376 7766
US **t** (800) 522 9696
www.alamo.com
Avis
UK **t** (0990) 900 500
US **t** (800) 331 1212
www.avis.com
Eurodollar
UK **t** (01895) 233 300
Hertz
UK **t** (0990) 996 699
US **t** (800) 654 3131
www.hertz.com
Thrifty
UK **t** (0990) 168 238
US **t** (800) 367 2277
www.thrifty.com

By bike

London is not terribly cycle-friendly – certainly not when compared with somewhere like Amsterdam. Extreme congestion, rising pollution and a limited number of cycle lanes are just some of the hazards awaiting you. Cycling as part of a large tour-guided group (*see* below) is a much safer option. Here are some rental companies which provide bikes and helmets for families. Hire rates are approx adult £2 per hour, child £1.50 per hour.

On Your Bike
52–4 Tooley Street
t (020) 7378 6669
⊖ London Bridge

Dial-a-Bike
t (020) 7828 4040
Delivers to major hotels in London.

Practicalities A–Z

Climate

If you've never been to Britain before, you're probably expecting to be consumed in clouds of fog and drizzle the moment you step off the plane. Britain has a reputation for dismal weather – it's the home of the 'pea-souper' after all – and the state of the skies has long been the nation's favourite topic of conversation; which is strange as there isn't really that much to discuss, the weather is nothing if not predictable. The summers are rarely too hot, the winters seldom too cold. You may get a brief heatwave in July or the occasional week of snow cover in January (plus a small hurricane every 70 years or so) but these hardly warrant special precautions. In fact, wherever you're from, your home town probably enjoys more extreme weather conditions than London. It isn't even particularly foggy anymore – to tell the truth, it never was, the mist you see swirling down the streets in old films is smog, now largely eradicated thanks to stricter pollution laws.

In London, the average temperature is 22°C (75°F) in July and August, dropping to 7°C (44°F) in December and January. Rainfall is generally at its heaviest in November. The best time to visit is probably late spring or early autumn when you can look forward to mild temperatures, not too much rain, the odd sunny day and slightly less dense queues at the capital's major tourist attractions.

Electricity

When bringing an electrical appliance from abroad fitted with a two-prong plug, you'll need to purchase an adaptor and probably a transformer as well. Britain's electrical supply is 240 volts AC. Its appliances use a type of three prong, square pin plug that will be unfamiliar to visitors from Europe and North America. All UK plugs have fuses of 3, 5 or 13 amps.

Embassies and consulates

US Embassy
24 Grosvenor Square, W1
t (020) 7499 9000
www.usembassy.org.uk
Open Mon–Fri 8.30–5.30
*There is a 24-hour helpline for US citizens, **t** (09068) 200 290*

Australian High Commission
Australia House, The Strand, WC2
t (020) 7379 4334
www.australia.org.uk
Open Mon–Fri 9–5

Canadian High Commission
38 Grosvenor St, W1
t (020) 7258 6600
www.canada.org.uk
Open Mon–Fri 8am–11am
*There is a 24-hour telephone helpline, **t** (09068) 616 644 (60p a minute)*

Dutch Embassy
38 Hyde Park Gate, SW7
t (020) 7590 3200
www.netherlands-embassy.org.uk
Open Mon–Fri 9–5.30

High Commission of India
India House, Aldwych, WC2
t (020) 7836 8484
www.hcilondon.org
Open Mon–Fri 9.30–5.30

Irish Embassy
17 Grosvenor Place, SW1
t (020) 7235 2171
Open Mon–Fri 9.30–5

New Zealand High Commission
New Zealand House, 80 The Haymarket, SW1
t (020) 7930 8422
www.mft.govt.nz
Open Mon–Fri 10–12 noon & 2–4

South African Embassy
South Africa House, Trafalgar Square, WC2
t (020) 7930 4488
Open Mon–Fri 9.30–5

Families with special needs

Wheelchair access to London's public places – its theatres, cinemas, sports grounds etc. – is relatively good. The London Tourist Board, t (020) 7932 2000, produces a leaflet, 'Information for Wheelchair Users Visiting London', which gives access details for all London's principal attractions. Country-wide information is available from the English Tourism Council who have produced an 'Accessible Britain' guide in conjunction with the Holiday Care Service, available for £5.99, t (0870) 606 7204.

Unfortunately, public transport is something of a nightmare for disabled travellers, with access to London's tubes, trains and buses still extremely limited, although Transport for London has started to introduce special low-floor buses with 'kneeling suspension' on some routes. Transport for London's own guide, 'Access to the Underground', has information on what little lift access there is to the city's tube stations. It's available free from any tube station or by post from Transport for London Access and Mobility Unit, Windsor House, 42–50 Victoria Street SW1, t (020) 7941 4600. More comprehensive transport information can be found in the 'Access in London' guide produced by the Access Project, 39 Bradley Gardens, London W13 8HE (a donation of £7.50 for printing costs is requested). Wheelchair users and blind and partially sighted people are entitled to a 30–50 percent discount on rail fares and can apply for a Disabled Person's Railcard (£14 a year) at major rail stations. At the present time there are no discounts on London's buses.

Britain has a growing number of specialist tour operators which specifically cater for the needs of physically disabled travellers such as Can Be Done, t (020) 8907 2400. The Association of Independent Tour Operators, t (020) 8607 9080, can provide a list, as can RADAR (the Royal Association for Disability and Rehabilitation, see below) which also publishes its own guides to holidays and travel. The following organizations will provide information and advice.

Artsline
54 Charlton Street, NW1
t (020) 7388 2227

www.artsline.org.uk
Free information on access to arts venues around the capital.

Council for Disabled Children
t (020) 7843 1900
www.ncb.org.uk/cdc
Good source of information on travel health and further resources.

Disability Now
6 Markets Road, N7
t (020) 7619 7323
www.disabilitynow.org.uk
Produces a monthly newspaper with holiday ideas written by people with disabilities.

Greater London Association for Disabled People
336 Brixton Road, SW9
t (020) 7346 5800
www.glad.org.uk
Publishes a free London Disability Guide. Drop a line to the above address.

Holiday Care Service
2nd Floor, Imperial Buildings, Victoria Road, Horley, Surrey RH6 9HW
t (01293) 774 535
www.holidaycare.org.uk
Provides information sheets for families on sites that have been assessed by reps and also runs an accessible accommodation research service.

RADAR (Royal Association for Disability and Rehabilitation)
250 City Road, London EC1
t (020) 7250 3222
www.radar.org.uk
Produces excellent guide books and information packs for disabled travellers.

Royal National Institute for the Blind
224 Great Portland Street, London W1
t (08457) 669 999 (UK helpline)
t (020) 7388 1266 (for callers from outside the UK)
www.rnib.org.uk
Advises blind people on travel matters and publishes a hotel guide book for £4.99.

Tripscope
t (08457) 585 641
Telephone helpline for disabled people touring in London.

In the US
American Foundation for the Blind
11 Penn Plaza, Suite 300, New York, NY 10011
t (212) 502 7600; toll free **t** 800 232 5463
www.afb.org

Federation of the Handicapped
211 West 14th Street, New York, NY 10011
t (212) 747 4262
   Organizes summer tours for members; there is a nominal annual fee.

Mobility International
PO Box 10767, Eugene, Oregon 97440
t (541) 343 1284
www.miusa.org

SATH (Society for the Advancement of Travel for the Handicapped)
347 Fifth Avenue, Suite 610, New York 10016
t (212) 447 7284
www.sath.org

In Australia
ACROD (Australian Council for the Rehabilitation of the Disabled)
24 Cabarita Road, Cabarita, New South Wales
t (02) 9743 2699
www.acrod.org.au

Infant matters

Babysitters
   Finding a reliable and trustworthy childminder in a strange city can be a worrisome task. Large hotels usually offer a babysitting service. Small ones may be able to arrange something on request. London also has several reputable agencies offering a network of qualified babysitters, nurses and infant teachers.

Childminders
6 Nottingham St, W1
t (020) 7487 5040
www.babysitter.co.uk

Hopes and Dreams
339–341 City Road, EC1
t (020) 833 9388
www.hopesanddreams.co.uk

Babysitting from 3 months–5 years. Hotel for over-2s to 11 years old.

Pippa Pop-Ins
430 Fulham Rd, SW6
t (020) 7385 2458
   Award-winning hotel for 2–12 year olds provides a crèche, nursery school and babysitting services.

Universal Aunts
t (020) 7738 8937
   Provides babysitters, entertainers, people to meet children off trains, and even guides to take children round London.

Breastfeeding
   Public breastfeeding is not exactly taboo in London but you are best off enquiring at individual restaurants as to where you might sit and feed in relative comfort. London's principal airports and train stations and some of its department stores have mother-and-baby rooms. If in doubt, head for the nearest branch of Boots, though be aware that you may well have to feed your baby while other people change theirs. The main branch of Gap on Oxford Street, close to Bond Street station, has a dedicated nursing mothers' room.

Nappies
   You can pick up bumper packs of disposable nappies such as Pampers or Huggies or an own-name brand at any London supermarket or major chemist. Some supermarket chains stock Nature Boy & Girl nappies from Sweden which are 70% biodegradable. If you are worried about the cost (which can be formidable) or damage to the environment, London has plenty of sources of traditional re-usable nappies, although you should only consider using them if you have the time and space to wash and dry them properly.

Green Baby
345 Upper Street, Islington, N1 (020) 7359 7037
www.greenbabyco.com
   Washable nappies and disposables, plus toiletries, buggies and organic clothing available in-store or by mail order.

The Real Nappy Association
PO Box 3704, London SE26 4RX
www.realnappy.com

Send a stamped addressed envelope with two stamps for information and a listing of environment-friendly baby product suppliers.

Sam-I-Am
t (020) 8995 9204
www.nappies.net
Mail-order cotton nappies.

Snuggle Naps
t (0115) 910 7220
www.snugglenaps.co.uk
Mail-order washable, designer nappies.

Insurance

It's vital that you take out travel insurance before your trip. This should cover, at a bare minimum, cancellation due to illness, travel delays, accidents, lost luggage, lost passports, lost or stolen belongings, personal liability, legal expenses, emergency flights and medical cover. Remember, you are not obliged to buy insurance from the same travel company that sold you your holiday and it's worth shopping around to see who offers the most best cover at the most competitive rates. The majority of insurance companies offer free insurance to children under the age of two as part of the parent's policy. Also bear in mind annual insurance policies, which can be especially cost effective for families with two or more older children. Always keep the company's 24-hour emergency number close to hand – if you have a mobile, store it in the memory.

The most important aspect of any travel insurance policy is its medical cover. You should look for cover of around £5 million. If you're a resident of the European Union, Iceland, Liechtenstein or Norway, you are entitled to free or reduced-cost medical treatment as long as you carry with you the appropriate validated form. In the EU this is the E111 form, which covers families with dependent children up to the age of 16 (or 19, if in full-time education). Even so, you may have to pay for your medical treatment and then claim your expenses back at a later date, so hang on to your receipts.

In the US and Canada, you may find that your existing insurance policies give sufficient medical cover and you should always check them thoroughly before taking out a new one. Canadians, in particular, are usually covered by their provincial

health plans. Few American or Canadian insurance companies will issue on-the-spot payments following a reported theft or loss. You will usually have to wait several weeks and engage in a hefty amount of correspondence before any money is forthcoming. Here is a list of useful insurance contacts.

In the UK
Association of British Insurers
t (020) 7600 3333
www.abi.org.uk

The Financial Ombudsman Service
t (0845) 080 1800
www.financial-ombudsman.org.uk
The government-appointed regulator of the insurance industry.

ABC Holiday Extras Travel Insurance
t (0870) 844 4020
www.holidayextras.co.uk

Columbus Travel Insurance
t (020) 7375 0011
www.columbusdirect.net

Endsleigh Insurance
t (020) 7436 4451
www.endsleigh.co.uk

Medicover
t (0870) 735 3600
www.medi-cover.co.uk

World Cover Direct
t (0800) 365 121

In the US
Access America
t US (800) 284 8300
t Canada (800) 654 1908
www.accessamerica.com

Carefree Travel Insurance
t US/Canada (1-800) 727 4874
www.carefreetravel.com

Travel Assistance International
t US/Canada (800) 821 2828
www.travelassistance.com

MEDEX Assistance Corporation
t US (410) 453 6300
www.medexassist.com

Lost property

If you lose anything while out and about in London then the chances are it's gone for good. However, you never can tell, and it is always worth checking to see whether some honest citizen has handed your valuable lost item in. If you lose something while on the plane go to the nearest information desk in the airport and fill out the relevant form as soon as possible.

London Transport Lost Property Office
200 Baker Street, NW1
t (020) 7486 2496
Open Weekday mornings

Black Cab Property Offices
15 Penton Street, Islington, N1
t (020) 7833 0996
Open Mon–Fri 9–4

Maps

There's little rhyme or reason to the layout of London's streets. Minimal urban planning is a great British tradition – to a Londoner's eyes, nicely arranged grids and blocks are foreign affectations to be resisted at all costs. Your first purchase upon arriving in London should therefore be a good street map. The London Tourist Board, Victoria Station, **t** (020) 7932 2000, produces an excellent one of central London. If you're hoping to stick around for some time, or have plans to visit attractions on the outskirts of town, you should consider getting hold of a copy of the London A–Z Street Atlas, a must for all disoriented Londoners – almost every household in the capital owns one. It contains street maps of every area in Greater London and is available in a range of formats from a huge, glossy, colour, hardback version to a black and white pocket edition (£19.99 and £2.75 respectively). You will find them stocked at bookstores, newsagents and petrol stations across London.

If you are brave enought to drive in London, you might like to pick up a 'London Parking Map', published by the Clever Map Company or, for out of London, one of the Ordnance Survey's excellent series of annually updated road atlases.

Train, tube and bus maps are available from main underground and train stations. The most useful is the hybrid Journey Planner which shows both tube and rail links. You'll find all your cartographic requirements catered for at:

Stanfords
12–14 Long Acre, WC2
t (020) 7836 1321
www.stanfords.co.uk
London's largest map shop.

The Travel Bookshop
13 Blenheim Crescent, W11
t (020) 7229 5260
www.thetravelbookshop.co.uk

The London tube map (*see* inside back cover) has become an icon of the city as familiar as Big Ben or a double-decker bus. The first tube maps, which were drawn up over 100 years ago, were done to scale with spaghetti-like intertwining lines and were practically unreadable. In the 1930s, a young draughtsman called Harry Beck came up with the idea of a new map based on an electrical circuit diagram. On this new map the distances between the stations in central London were extended while those between outer London stations were shortened. The result is one of the clearest and most copied diagrams in the world.

Medical matters

Visitors from the EU, Iceland, Liechtenstein and Norway can claim free or reduced cost medical treatment under Britain's National Health Service, so long as they carry with them the appropriate form. In the EU, this is the E111 which covers families with dependent children up to the age of 16 (or 19, if in full-time education). The only things you will be expected to pay for are medical prescriptions (currently £6.10) and visits to the optician or dentist (these are free to children and senior citizens). Visitors from other countries should take out medical insurance.

In an emergency

If you require urgent medical treatment, you should call an ambulance by calling **t** 999 or 112, or drive to the nearest hospital with an Accident and Emergency Department.

Charing Cross Hospital
Fulham Palace Road, W6
t (020) 8846 1234
⊖ Barons Court, Hammersmith

Chelsea & Westminster Hospital
369 Fulham Road, SW10
t (020) 8746 8000
⊖ Fulham Broadway

Guy's Hospital
St Thomas Street, SE1
t (020) 7955 5000
⊖ London Bridge

Royal Free Hospital
Pond Street, NW3
t (020) 7794 0500
⊖ Belsize Park

Royal London Hospital
Whitechapel Road, E1
t (020) 7377 7000
⊖ Whitechapel

St Mary's Hospital
Praed Street, W2
t (020) 7886 6666
⊖ Paddington

St Thomas's Hospital
Lambeth Palace Road, SE1
t (020) 7928 9292
⊖ Waterloo, Westminster

University College London Hospital
Gower Street, WC1
t (020) 7387 9300
⊖ Euston Square, Warren Street, Goodge Street

Whittington Hospital
Highgate Hill, N19
t (020) 7272 3070
⊖ Archway

Chemists/Pharmacies

Most high streets have a dispensing chemist where you must go to buy any medicine prescribed to you by a doctor. In Britain, only a limited range of drugs can be dispensed without a doctor's prescription. Chemists will also often stock a selection of basic medical and cosmetic products such as cough mixture, plasters (band-aids), bandages, nappies, vitamins and hairspray. Your local police station can provide a list of late-opening chemists. Otherwise, try:

Bliss Chemist
5 Marble Arch, W1
t (020) 7723 6116
Open Until midnight seven days a week

Zafash Chemist
233–235 Old Brompton Road, SW5
t (020) 7373 2798
Open 24 hours a day, 365 days a year

Superstores often have chemists which are open late and on Sundays. **Boots**, www.wellbeing.com, is the UK's largest chemist chain. Its branches also usually contain a photographic service. There are branches at 198 Baker Street, W1 **t** (020) 7935 1441; 173–5 Camden High Street, NW1 **t** (020) 7485 5216; Counter Street, Hay's Galleria, SE1 **t** (020) 7407 4276; 4 James Street, Covent Garden, WC2 **t** (020) 7379 8442; 127a Kensington High Street, W8 **t** (020) 7937 9533; 439–441 Oxford St, W1 **t** (020) 7409 2857.

Other useful contacts

Action for Sick Children
300 Kingston Road, SW20
t (0800) 0744 519
www.actionforsickchildren.org

Provides advice to help parents get the best possible health care for their children.

All About Allergies
37 Soho Square, W1V 5DG
Write for a free booklet.

Dental Emergency Care Service
t (020) 7937 3951

Eye Care Information Bureau
t (020) 7928 9435

The Health Education Authority Hotline
t (0800) 555 777
Freephone advisory number.

Medical Advisory Service for Travellers Abroad
t (09068) 224 100
www.masta.org

NHS Direct
t (0845) 4647
www.nhsdirect.nhs.uk

Nurse-led 24hr helpline offering confidential health advice. You can also get information and advice online.

St John's Ambulance Supplies

t (020) 7278 7888
www.stjohnsupplies.co.uk

Money and banks

The currency in Britain is the pound sterling (written £) which is divided into 100 pence (written p). There are eight coin denominations: 1p, 2p, 5p, 10p, 20p, 50p, £1 and £2 (all issued by the Royal Mint) and four note denominations: £5, £10, £20 and £50 – the last is the most often forged and you'll find that a number of shops and restaurants refuse to accept £50 notes in any circumstances. All notes are printed by the Bank of England (apart from the forgeries, that is).

Most shops and restaurants accept the big name credit and debit cards: Visa, Delta, Mastercard, American Express, Barclaycard, Diners Club, Switch.

The biggest high street banks in London are Barclays, NatWest, HSBC and Lloyds TSB. Most have automatic cash dispensers (also known as 'holes in the wall') which can be used 24-hours a day and will often dispense money on foreign bank cards. Your bank's international banking department should be able to advise you on this. All banks are open 9.30-3.30, although many are open later (till around 5pm). Some also open on Saturday mornings. The easiest and safest way to carry large sums of money is by using travellers' cheques. These can be changed, for a small commission, at any bank or bureau de change. Try:

American Express

www.americanexpress.com
30–31 Haymarket, SW1 t (020) 7484 9610;
84 Kensington High Street, WC1 t (020) 7795 6703;
London House, Regent Street, W1 t (020) 7499 6182;
445 Oxford Street, W1 t (020) 7495 8891, 7 Wilton Road SW1, t (020) 7630 6365

Thomas Cook

www.thomascook.com
Victoria Station, SW1 t (020) 7828 4442;
90 Baker Street, W1 t (020) 7935 4015;
3/5 Coventry Street, W1 t (020) 7437 7167;

1 Marble Arch, W1 t (020) 7723 1668;
237 Oxford Street, W1 t (020) 7437 2689;
196a Piccadilly, W1 t (020) 7437 0289;
133 Regent Street, W1 t (020) 7287 3911.

Carrying money around with you

Use a money belt fastened around your waist under a tucked-in shirt or T-shirt. Pickpocketing is rife in certain parts of London, especially busy shopping areas like Oxford Street. The most recent scams to watch out for are people copying your pin number at cashpoints and then stealing your credit card, and gangs of youths jostling you or swiping something from out of your back pocket. In short, do not put your purse or any other valuables in a back pocket or the rear zipper pocket of your backpack if you wish to see them again. Always keep wallets in your front trouser pockets and hold purses and bags tightly.

National holidays

Britain's national holidays are always arranged to fall on a Monday – Christmas, New Year's Day and Good Friday excepted. This not only allows people to enjoy a 'long weekend' but stops the nation from being cheated out of a holiday that would otherwise fall on a Saturday or Sunday. Shops and services tend to operate according to their Sunday template and banks are always closed – which is why Britain's national holidays are sometimes also known as bank holidays.

School holidays

State schools

Half-term Autumn, end of October
Christmas two weeks
Half-term mid-February
Easter two weeks
Half-term Spring bank holiday, late May/June
Summer six weeks July-August

Private schools

Same half-terms
Christmas 3–4 weeks
Easter 3–4 weeks
Summer 8–9 weeks

Holidays for One-Parent Families
t (0161) 370 0337

One-Parent Family Holidays
t (01465) 821 288

Women's Travel Advisory Bureau
t (01386) 701 082

Necessities

Wherever you're travelling with kids it is always worth taking a packet of wet wipes, a full change of clothing, toys to fiddle with, drinks and snacks, plus some empty, disposable bags for unforeseen eventualities. Other items you might like to consider which could be picked up in London include:

- a torch/flashlight
- matches/lighter
- a night light
- safety pins
- an extension cord
- needle and thread
- a roll of sticky tape
- a net shopping bag
- moisturizing cream
- travel socket converters
- mild soap and baby shampoo
- playing cards, paper & crayons
- a forehead thermometer

One-parent families

There are various organizations in London offering advice and support for single parents travelling with children.

The National Council for One-Parent Families

255 Kentish Town Road, NW5
t (020) 7428 5400
www.oneparentfamilies.org.uk
Runs a lone parent helpline, **t** (0800) 018 5026

Gingerbread

16–17 Clerkenwell Close, EC1R
t (020) 7336 8183

Opening hours

The traditional opening times for shops and offices in London are 9 in the morning until 5.30 at night although these days, especially in central London, many shops observe a more continental-style day of 10–7. Most shops have one nominated day, usually Wednesday or Thursday, on which they stay open late, until 8 or 9pm. Sunday opening, most commonly between 12 noon and 5pm, has become the norm in recent years. Some of the capital's corner shops and supermarkets stay open 24-hours a day. Britain's pubs and restaurants, however, observe very strict licensing laws – no alcohol can be served outside the period between 11am–11pm – although there are increasing calls for Britain to adopt more open-ended, Euro-style opening hours.

Post offices

You can buy stamps, post parcels and pay bills in London's post offices Mon–Fri 9–5.50 and Sat 9–12 noon, although there's no need to go to one just to send a postcard. Most of the capital's newsagents sell stamps – the cost of sending a letter (under 60g) first class to anywhere in the UK or second class to anywhere in Europe is 27p while a postcard costs 37p to Europe, 40p to anywhere else and post boxes, painted the same distinctive red as the capital's buses and older phone boxes, are common. You'll find post offices at 24-28 William I Street, Trafalgar Square, WC2, **t** (020) 7484 9304 (this is the main London branch and stays open from 8am-8pm daily); 105 Abbey Street, SE1 **t** (020) 7237 8629; 43–44 Albemarle Street, W1 **t** (020) 7493 5620; 81–89 Farringdon Road, EC1 **t** (020) 7242 7262; 54–56 Great Portland Street, W1 t (020) 7636 2205; 24–27 Thayer Street W1 t (020) 7935 0239.

To find out more about Royal Mail services, log on to **www**.royalmail.com or, if you have a complaint, write to Royal Mail Customer Service, Freepost, 3rd Floor, 5 Almeida Street, N1, t (0345) 740 740.

Safety

In an emergency you can call the police, fire brigade or ambulance services on t 999 or 112. London is still a relatively law-abiding place where few policemen carry guns; as a tourist, the crimes you are most likely to fall victim to are pickpocketry and petty thievery. London's busiest shopping districts – Oxford Street, Covent Garden, King's Road, Kensington High Street – are often targeted by organized gangs of pickpockets but, as long as you remain vigilant and take sensible precautions with your valuables, you should be able to enjoy a trouble-free holiday.

Of course, when travelling with children, you need to be extra vigilant. When on the streets or in a crowded place make sure you never let them out of your sight. Always keep your children in front of you and continually take a head count. Under-2s can be kept safe on a wrist-rein. In the event that you do get separated, encourage your children to remain in one place and wait for you to find them. It is a good idea to supply youngsters with a whistle to blow in case they lose sight of you in busy areas. A bright cap or jacket makes them much easier to spot. If you have more than one child, colour match their clothes so that you only have one thing to watch out for. Older children may be trusted enough to explore by themselves within bounds. Even so, always establish a central, easy-to-find meeting place. Ensure your children carry identification at all times and make sure you have an up-to-date photograph of them too.

The golden rules
► Don't leave valuables in your hotel room.
► Keep most of your money in travellers' cheques.
► Keep all your valuables in a money belt fastened around your waist under a tucked shirt or t-shirt.
► Only keep small amounts of money in your wallet or purse. Keep your wallet in your trouser pocket and hold purses and bags close to your body with the flap facing inwards and the strap over your shoulder.
► Steer clear of unfamiliar areas of the city late at night.
► Try to avoid travelling alone on the Underground late at night.
► Do not leave bags hanging over chairs.
► Take care on busy shopping streets.

Telephones

There are still some red phone boxes left in London, although not nearly as many as the post-card industry would have you believe. British Telecom began removing these cast iron monoliths in the early 1990s with the intention of replacing them with lighter, cheaper, plastic booths. The public raised such a fuss, however, that BT was forced to leave a significant number standing. They are still quite common in parts of the West End but have almost completely disappeared from the suburbs, apart from in sleepy hamlets and villages.

Although British Telecom lost its monopoly for supplying the nation with telephones in 1984 when it was privatised, it's still by far the most popular phone company in the country. The majority of the capital's public phone booths are BT-owned, although there are now several other companies, including Mercury and AT&T, operating networks of payphones. In fact, these days, there are very few streets in central London which don't have at least one public phone. In particular, look out for the orange, European-looking Interphones. For some reason, these have proved to be London's least popular public phone booths and, as such, are the kind you are most likely to find unoccupied. All London's main tube and train stations have ranks of public phones.

Most modern pay phones accept coins (any denomination from 10p up, the minimum call charge is 20p) and phone cards (available in denominations of £1, £2, £5, £10 and £20 from newsagents or post offices) although some only accept one or the other. Some booths let you pay by swiping a credit card. If possible, avoid using the phone in your hotel room as it is quite normal for the hotel to treble or even quadruple the call rate.

Britain's domestic phones employ an unusual wide type of phone jack and, if you need to plug in a phone brought from abroad or a modem, you may have to buy an adaptor.

International calls are cheapest in the evening after 6pm and on weekends. The international dialling code is oo followed by the country code:

United States and Canada **1**
Ireland **353**
France **33**
Italy **39**
Germany **49**
Australia **61**
New Zealand **64**

The telephone code for London itself is 020 (which you needn't dial for calls made within the city) followed by either a 7 (for central London) or an 8 (for outer London). If dialling from outside the UK, remember to omit the initial 0.

The phone numbers of businesses and shops are listed the Yellow Pages, available for £5 from BT. Also, check out their website at **www**.yell.co.uk.

Time

London is the official home of time. The prime meridian, the line of 0° longitude, runs through the quiet southeast London borough of Greenwich and, since 1884, Greenwich Mean Time (GMT) has been the standard against which all other times are set. GMT is generally one hour ahead of western Europe. In summer, however, Britain switches to British Summer Time (BST) which is one hour ahead of GMT. Britain is five hours ahead of New York, eight hours ahead of San Francisco and ten hours behind Tokyo and Sydney. In everyday conversation, the majority of Londoners will use the 12-hour clock – 9am, 3pm etc. – but timetables are more often given using the 24-hour clock.

Tipping

Ten to fifteen percent is the usual rate in restaurants, taxis, hairdressers etc. You are not obliged to tip, however, especially if the service was unsatisfactory. You would not normally tip a bartender in a pub. Restaurants sometimes add a service charge of 10–15 percent which should be shown on the menu. Tipping staff such as chambermaids and porters is discretionary.

Toilets

The whereabouts of the nearest toilet is perhaps the single most important piece of information a parent can know. Most mainline stations have public toilets (20p per visit) as do London's principal department stores and some fast food outlets (notably McDonald's and Burger King). Pubs and restaurants, however, will sometimes only let you use their facilities (even in an emergency) if you're going to buy something. Public toilets on the streets of London are few and far between. The old-fashioned underground toilets have largely been phased out (there is still one in Leicester Square) but have yet to be replaced with an adequate number of street-level loos. You will come across the odd, free-standing automatic toilet known as a 'super loo' but, be warned, your 20p entitles you to a maximum 15 minutes' use of the facilities, after which the door will swoosh open revealing you (in whatever stage of undress) to the street. If in Covent Garden check out the loos in St Paul's Churchyard, which have won awards for cleanliness and 'ambience'.

Tourist information

www.londontouristboard.co.uk
t (020) 7932 2000
t (090) 6866 3344, recorded information (charged at the not inconsiderable sum of £1 per minute).

Useful Parenting Websites
www.allkids.co.uk
www.babycentre.co.uk
www.babydirectory.com
www.babiesonline
www.babyworld.com
www.familiesonline.co.uk
www.familycorner.com
www.gobabies.com
www.kidsevents.co.uk
www.kidsinmind.co.uk
www.kinderstart.com
www.motherandbaby.co.uk
www.mumsnet.com
www.parents-news.co.uk
www.allkids.co.uk
www.ukchildrensdirectory.com
www.ukparents.co.uk

Further Information

The most up-to-date information on the city's attractions and cultural life is provided by the nation's main daily newspapers – the *Daily Telegraph*, *The Times*, the *Daily Mail*, the *Independent* et al – and, in particular, by the London daily *Evening Standard* which produces a listings magazine *Hot Tickets* every Thursday (with a special Kids' Section), and the *Guardian*, whose own listings magazine The Guide accompanies its Saturday edition. You should also check out *Time Out*, the capital's best selling weekly listings magazine, available in all major newsagents.

London Tourist Offices

Main Office, Victoria Station
Open Easter–Oct 8–7 daily, Nov–Easter Mon–Sat 8–6, Sun 8.30–4

Heathrow Underground station concourse
Open 8–6 daily

Heathrow Arrivals concourse (Terminal Three)
Open 6–11 daily

Waterloo International Terminal
Open 8.30–10.30

Accommodation booking service
t (020) 7932 2020

British Visitor Centre
1 Regent Street, Piccadilly Circus, SW1
Open Mon–Fri 9–6.30, Sat & Sun 10–4

Sleep

The perfect family-friendly hotel should have all the facilities parents expect (large well-equipped bedrooms; comfortable public rooms where they can relax in peace and quiet, sometimes away from the children; a babysitting/baby listening or crêche service and a decent restaurant with a menu that extends beyond pizza and chips) as well as all the things kids need (cots, high chairs, reasonable meal times, a supervised activity area, a swimming pool or garden) but should above all display a welcoming attitude to all members of the family, whatever their age or status.

A good place to begin your search for family-friendly accommodation is the London Tourist Board's booklet 'Where to Stay in London', which lists family-friendly hotels, B&Bs and flat-hunting agents. The guide, priced £4.99, is available from tourist information centres and bookshops, or you can order one by calling **t** (020) 7604 2890. The tourist board also operates an accommodation booking service on **t** (020) 7932 2020, open Mon–Fri 9am–5.30pm, Sat 10am–2pm. You can also **email** a request on book@londontouristboard.co.uk

Hotels

If money is no object, you could, of course, go the five star route: The Ritz, the Savoy, Claridges, the Dorcheser, these are some of the most famous and and well respected names in the hotel world. They're all centrally located with family suites and excellent facilities and all offer a guaranteed supply of petting and pampering – and all will charge £400 plus a night for a family of 4; and even then there's no guarantee that your boisterous kids will be welcome in the restaurants and public rooms. At the other end of the scale are the budget hotels. A good one in the centre of town should set you back around £100 a night, for which you should get a TV, shower or bath, phone and breakfast. It can be even cheaper if you're willing to share a bathroom with other guests (not at the same time of course).

The big chains

The well-known international hotel chains are virtually guaranteed to be a safe bet. True, this type of hotel can be rather impersonal – their principal clients are, after all, businessmen, not families – but you can, at least, be sure that the rooms will be clean and well-equipped and the service reliable. Furthermore, many hotels offer a range of competitive packages and deals for families, as well as activity programmes and children's menus in their restaurants, and some provide babysitting, baby-listening, cots and high chairs as standard. **Novotel**, the French-owned chain, offer Summer Fun Breaks which include family entry to a nearby attraction while the Forte Group (who own the **Travelodge** chain among others) have, in the past, offered discounts of up to 50 per cent on some of their London hotels, a deal which includes reduced entry for kids to a West End show.

Best Western
www.bestwesternhotels.com
Doubles from £75 (prices do vary enormously, depending on the size and facilities of the hotel, this is by no means the minimum in all Best Western hotels)

Choice Hotels
t 0800 444444
www.choicehotelseurope.com
Doubles from around £100

Two children under 14 stay free in their parents' room (subject to availability), plus kids' menus available.

Corus
t 0845 300 2000
www.corushotels.com
Doubles from £60

Under-16s stay free in their parents' room (1 adult per child) or at 50 per cent in their own room. Under-6s eat free of charge, while children aged 6–15 pay a daily fixed price of £5 for breakfast and £10 for breakfast and dinner.

Novotel
t (020) 8283 4500
www.novotel.com
Doubles from £115

Queens Moat Houses
t 0646 213214
www.moathousehotels.com
Doubles from £120

Thistle
t (0800) 332244
www.thistlehotels.com
Doubles from £115

Travel Inn
t 0870 242 8000
www.travelinn.co.uk
All rooms £40.95

Travelodge
t 0800 850950
All rooms from £45.95

Recommended hotels

The following are hotels which go out of their way to welcome and provide facillities for families.

22 Jermyn Street
22 Jermyn Street, SW1
t (020) 7734 2353
www.22jermyn.com
⊖ Piccadilly Circus
Doubles from £250
Small luxury hotel tucked behind Piccadilly Circus which welcomes children with their own newsletter 'Kids' Talk' and a supply of games, children's videos, a list of local child-friendly restaurants, and even teddy bear dressing-gowns. 24hr room service; extra beds and cots available.

Ashley Hotel
15–17 Norfolk Square, W2
t (020) 7723 3375
⊖/≢ Paddington
Doubles from £34.50
Cheap and cheerful family-run hotel (50 rooms) in three warren-like houses on a quiet square near Paddington Station. The family rooms are quite cramped (with tiny ensuite shower rooms) but from £34.50 per night, they are still relatively good value. There are special rates for children sharing with parents and no charge for babies.

The Athenaem
116 Piccadilly, W1
t (020) 7499 3466
www.athenaeumhotel.com
⊖ Green Park
Doubles from £285, **apartments** from £415
The Athenaeum is an upmarket hotel-apartment complex set in a row of elegant Piccadilly townhouses that prides itself on its family-friendliness. Upon arrival, children are given a Kiddies' Pack containing colouring books, crayons, a rubber duck for the bath, a teddy bear (rather tortuously named Arthurneum) and, best of all, a gift voucher for Hamleys. The Windsor Café offers a children's

menu and you can request milk and cookies from room service. All the hotel rooms are sumptuously appointed – if a bit chintzy – and each apartment comes complete with sofas, TV, video, hi-fi, washing machine and kitchen allowing you to live a totally self-contained existence (but with the hotel's facilities on call 24-hours a day). Guests are entitled to free use of the Athenaeum spa and gym.

Blooms Hotel
7 Montague Street, WC1
t (020) 7323 1717
email blooms@mermaid.co.uk
⊖ Russell Square
Doubles from £230
Lovely small hotel near the British Museum. There are no specific children's facilities but it's happy to welcome families and the staff are friendly and helpful. There's a pretty, paved, walled garden, 24hr room service and extra cots are available. Under-10s stay for free in their parent's room.

Concorde Hotel
50 Great Cumberland Place, W1
t (020) 7402 6169
⊖ Marble Arch
Doubles from £80
Same owners (Best Western) as the equally family-friendly Bryanston Court next door, this is a small, friendly hotel with a large, comfortable lounge and well-appointed bedrooms. Triple rooms can cost as little as £95 and there are cots, high chairs and a babysitting service available. They also have furnished apartments in an adjacent building that are very popular with families.

County Hall Travel Inn Capital
Belvedere Road, SE1
t (020) 7902 1600
www.travelinn.co.uk
⊖/≢ Waterloo
Doubles £59.95
Centrally-located, excellent value hotel above the London Aquarium, next to the new London Eye and just across the Thames from the Houses of Parliament. Part of the Travel Inn chain, this hotel provides reliable, no-frills accommodation with rooms at just £59.95 per night (including family rooms); extra cots and children's menu available.

Crescent
49–50 Cartwright Gardens, WC1
t (020) 7387 1515

⊖/⇌ Euston

Doubles from £90

Family-run hotel in a quiet crescent near Euston Station offering a warm welcome to children. No charge for children under 2; cots and high chairs available and babysitting by arrangement.

Durrants Hotel

George Street, W1

t (020) 7935 8131

⊖ Bond Street

Doubles from £175

Smart, very traditional family-run hotel (90 rooms), housed in an 18th-century building behind the Wallace Collection and within easy reach of Bond Street. It has a comfortable lounge – lots of pine and mahogany panelling – a good restaurant (dinner from 6pm) and can arrange a babysitting service. Extra cots and high chairs available.

Family-friendly hotel checklist

Here is a list of things to look out for when hotel-hunting.

▶ special family packages or discounts? Do remember that British hotels tend to charge per person rather than a room rate, so cramming everyone into the same room doesn't always make sound economic sense. However, many hotels do allow children sharing their parents' room to stay free of charge.

▶ a choice of family rooms with three or more beds

▶ rooms with interconnecting doors

▶ a constantly monitored baby-listening service

▶ access to whatever leisure facilities there might be? Nothing is guaranteed to put a damper on a child's spirits more than being told they can't use the swimming-pool

▶ cots and high chairs

▶ children's meals? Are they healthy, served at a conveniently early time, in a family-friendly location, and if not, are children welcome in the restaurant

▶ designated play areas for children? If there's an outdoor play area, is it safe and supervised

▶ supplies of toys, books and, even better, computer games

▶ a babysitting service

▶ a crèche

▶ organized activities for children

▶ qualified child-care staff

Edward Lear

28–30 Seymour Street, W1

t (020) 7402 5401

www.edlear.com

⊖ Marble Arch

Doubles from £79.50

Extremely friendly hotel, just 50 yards from Oxford Street, housed in two 18th-century town-houses that were once the home of the famous nonsense verse writer (and composer of *The Owl and the Pussycat*) Edward Lear. His illustrated limericks adorn the public rooms. The bedrooms are quite spacious but not necessarily ensuite and there's no charge for under-2s or for children under 13 sharing their parents' room at weekends. Extra cots available.

Goring

Beeston Place, Grosvenor Gardens, SW1

t (020) 7396 9000

www.goringhotel.co.uk

⊖/⇌ Victoria

Doubles from £195

Right in the heart of Royal London, a stone's throw from Buckingham Palace and the great parks, this is a very grand, upright, traditionally British sort of establishment that nonetheless does its best to accommodate the needs of families. In fact, it has made a point of pampering its guests ever since it opened in 1910 when it was the first hotel in the world to have central heating and a private bathroom in each room. Today, the public rooms are furnished in country house-style with open fires in winter, the bedrooms are sumptuous with all mod cons and there's a large private garden. Guests are entitled to free use of the local health club and there's a babysitting service available.

Hart House Hotel

51 Gloucester Place, W1

t (020) 7935 2288

www.harthouse.co.uk

⊖ Baker Street, ⊖/⇌ Marylebone

Doubles from £115

Very grand B&B housed in a West End Georgian mansion. The rooms vary in size – those near the top tend to be the largest and brightest – and are decorated in a variety of styles ranging from antique to modern. Toys are provided for the kids and there are extra cots and a babysitting service is available.

Hopes and Dreams

339–341 City Road, EC1
t (020) 7833 9388
www.hopesanddreams.co.uk
⊖ Angel
  Babysitting from 3 months–5 years. Hotel for
2–11-year-olds.

Parkwood

4 Stanhope Place, W2
t (020) 7402 2241
⊖ Marble Arch
Doubles from £100
  Small hotel with several large, bright family
rooms. Extra beds, cots and high chairs available
plus babysitting by arrangement.

Pippa Pop Ins

430 Fulham Road, SW6
t (020) 7385 5706
⊖ Fulham Broadway
  This friendly establishment is something of a
novelty; a hotel just for children. Up to 12 kids can
stay here for between a night and a week –
perhaps while their parents visit friends or house
hunt in another part of the country. Activities are
organised on weekends and during the school holidays. 2–5 year olds can attend the day nursery and
there's also an after school service where children
can be picked up from school and given tea and
homework supervision until they are collected
by their parents. A second hotel 'Pippa Pop-Ins on
the Green' has recently opened at 165 New King's
Road.

Hotel La Place

17 Nottingham Place, W1
t (020) 7486 2323
email reservations@hotellaplace.com
www.hotellaplace.com
⊖ Baker Street
Price from £140
  Small, family-owned hotel on a quiet street near
Madame Tussaud's, with a good restaurant (supper
served 6–8.30, high chairs available), pleasantly
furnished rooms and a welcoming atmosphere.
babysitting can be arranged.

Apart'hotels

  A relatively new concept for the UK, these self-
catering apartments have all the facilities you'd
expect at home, plus hotel services on call 24-

hours a day. There are two sizes of room, a studio
(sleeps 4) or apartment (sleeps 6) and prices range
from £94 upwards per night, though some are
even cheaper if you stay for over a month. The
French company **Citadines t** (0800) 376 3898 has
complexes in Covent Garden, South Kensington,
Traflagar Square and Barbican.

Bed and breakfast

  A British institution, these are small guest
houses or private houses (usually located in residential areas outside the city centre) which hire
out rooms at a reasonable price. Although you may
have to share a bathroom, it is possible to get
accommodation for as little as £10–20 per person
per night. To find out how welcoming a potential
B&B is to families, try asking the following questions.
▶ Are there cots and high chairs available?
▶ Is it possible to have separate children's meals at
a time that suits them?
▶ Are the children expected to eat with the adults
or at separate tables?
▶ Is there running-around space for children?
▶ Is there a comfortable lounge for the adults to
relax in once the children have gone to bed?
  The following agencies all have extensive lists of
B&Bs throughout London.

Host and Guest Service

103 Dawes Road, SW6
t (020) 7385 9922
  Throughout London. From £15 per person per
night.

London Bed and Breakfast Agency

71 Fellows Road, NW3
t (020) 7586 2768
www.londonbb.com
  Throughout London. Double rooms from £19–41
per person per night.

Uptown Reservations

50 Christchurch Street, SW3
t (020) 7351 3445
  Mostly Kensington, Knightsbridge and Chelsea.
Family rooms £110; double rooms £85.

Renting a flat

For a stay of several weeks, or even months, it is probably worth thinking about renting a flat. Not only does this make sound economic sense, it will also give you the chance to become familiar with the local community – meeting the neighbours, shopping in the local grocery stores, etc. Self-catering also allows you to do what you like when you like. You can get up when it suits you, nurse your colicky newborn at 3am and scramble eggs whenever your toddler gets peckish. Again, there are some important questions that are worth asking.

► How far is your accommodation from the nearest shops, supermarket, launderette, restaurants, transport and park?

► How many bedrooms does the flat have? The phrase 'sleeps 6' does not necessarily mean that there will be three bedrooms; often a sofa in the living room converts into a bed, and you may even need to rearrange the room in order to create enough sleeping space.

► Are cots supplied and, if so, is there an additional charge for them?

► Are the children's rooms fitted with bunk beds and, if so, do these have safety rails?

► Is the garden or pool fenced off and are there any nearby ponds, streams or other potential hazards?

► Is it safe for children to play unsupervised in the garden?

► Can babysitting be arranged locally?

Holiday Serviced Apartments
273 Old Brompton Road, SW5
t (020) 7373 4477
www.holidayapartments.co.uk
Can supply serviced and unserviced apartments all over London; two-bed flats from £900 per week.

AE
1 Princess Mews, Belsize Crescent, NW3
t (020) 7794 1186
Apartments in northwest London; two-bed flats from £700 per week.

ourtfield Apartments
25 Courtfield Road, SW7
t (020) 7373 2455

Near ⊖ Gloucester Road; one double room plus double sofa-bed £525 per week.

Euracom
90–92 Great Portland Street, W1
t (020) 7436 3201
www.euracom.co.uk
Two-bed flats from £550 per week plus booking fee.

Globe Apartments
36 James Street, W1
t (020) 7935 9512
www.globeapt.demon.co.uk
Two-bed flats from £600 per week.

Home exchange

This can sometimes be the cheapest option of all. The principle could not be easier: you hand your home over to another family, while they take on yours. The process involves you supplying details of your home and family to an agency who lists you in their directory. You can exchange photographs and letters with as many members as you like before coming to a final decision. References may be checked and a holiday agreement exchanged for added security.

Of course, this low-cost arrangement depends very much on you living in a place that people want to visit and on you having a clean, safe and well-furnished home that meets the agency's standards. Once you are happy that you meet the criteria, the advantages of home exchange become obvious. You automatically have someone to care

Think ahead
► Be clear about your smoking policy
► Pack away anything you would prefer to remain untouched, especially if it is valuable or fragile
► Agree what food, toiletries or other items can be used without being replaced
► Be clear about what linens and towels can be used
► Consider buying each other bulky items such as nappies, to avoid having to transport them
► Check how your home contents, travel and car insurance is affected if you undertake a home exchange

for your home, and even your pets, while you are away. Most importantly, exchanging homes with a family with children the same age as yours means their home is certain to be child-proofed and ready-supplied with all the baby gear, cots, high chairs, car-seats and toys you need to make your holiday fun and hassle-free. The savings can also be huge. Your only real expenses are signing up with an agency, transport to your destination and the usual holiday expenses.

Before you take the plunge, be specific about what you require from a visiting family and the sort of daily or weekly upkeep you expect, such as feeding the cat, watering the plants, tidying the house and taking telephone messages.

To organize a home exchange contact one of the following; or try on the Internet at **www**.home-free.com.

In the UK

NCT House-Swap Register
t (01454) 311 426
Membership fee £20.

Intervac Home Exchange
t (01225) 892 208

Homelink International
t (01344) 842 642
www.homelink.org.uk
Membership fee £89.

Latitudes Home Exchange
t (01273) 581 793

In the US

Homelink USA
t (800) 638 3841
www.homelink.org

Trading Homes International
t (310) 798 3864

International Home Exchange
t (415) 435 3497

Youth Hostels

Forget the dowdy image of cheesecloth, mung beans and compulsory acoustic guitar sessions, youth hostels have now smartened up their act and are offering family rooms with no chore rotas attached. Apart from being cheap and easy-going, youth hostels can also more easily accommodate larger family groups or families travelling together. There are a few YHA hostels in London, the best for families are listed below, for reservations call **t** (020) 7373 3400, **www**.yha.org.uk

City of London Youth Hostel
36 Carter Lane, EC4
t (020) 7236 4965
⊖ St Paul's
Double room from £51 including breakfast

Hampstead Heath Youth Hostel
4 Wellgarth Road, NW11
t (020) 8458 9054
⊖ Golders Green
Double room from £46

Rotherhithe Youth Hostel
Salter Road, SE16
t (020) 7232 2114
⊖ Rotherhithe, Canada Water
Double room from £41

Eat

Kids tend to get hungry all of a sudden. One minute everything's fine, the whole family's having a great day out, and the next, absolute starvation has set in – the little ones must be fed, and fed quickly, or there will be trouble. Happily, the number of restaurants prepared to cater for the often fickle fancy of children is growing all the time. Sunday lunchtime, in particular, is often designated 'family time' in many eateries with some even going so far as to lay on entertainment in the form of magic shows and face-painting.

Cheap Eats

Café in the Crypt
St Martin-in-the-Fields, WC2
t (020) 7839 4342
Open Mon–Sat 10–8, Sun 12 noon–8pm (hot food 12 noon–3.15 & 5–7.30)
⊖ Charing Cross

Atmospheric subterranean café whose semi-dungeonesque appearance should greatly appeal to youngsters. With a wide selection of hot dishes, snacks and vegetarian choices available, this is a good place to come and warm up with a bowl of hot soup after a hard morning's sightseeing. Half portions are (rather logically) half price.

Chelsea Kitchen
98 King's Road, SW3
t (020) 7589 1330
Open Mon–Sat 8am–11.30pm, Sun 9am–11.30pm
⊖ Sloane Square

Sells a wide range of sandwiches, salads and pasta dishes.

Ed's Easy Diner
Branches open Sun–Thu 11.30am–12 midnight, Fri & Sat 11.30am–1am
362 King's Road, SW3
t (020) 7352 1956
⊖ Sloane Square
12 Moor Street W1
t (020) 7439 1955
⊖ Tottenham Court Road
O2 Centre, 255 Finchley Road, NW3
t (020)7431 1958
⊖ Finchley Road

It's a bit noisy and in your face but the burgers and chips in this mock 1950s diner are good and they have a very reasonably priced kids' menu. High chairs available.

How much?
Unless otherwise indicated you should be able to get a meal for one adult and one child, at whatever time, for less than £25.
When?
London restaurants tend to serve lunch between 12.30 and 3pm and dinner between 7 and 10pm.

Giraffe
Branches open 8am–11.30pm daily
6–8 Blandford Street, W1, **t** (020) 7935 2333;
⊖ Baker Street
46 Rosslyn Hill, NW3, **t** (020) 7435 0343;
⊖ Hampstead
29-31 Essex Road, N1 **t** (020 7359 5999;
⊖ Old Street, ⇌ Essex Road

With its bright, colourful decor and piped world music, Giraffe has a rather groovy, youthful ambience. Both adults and children are well catered for – adults with a selection of inventive breakfast, lunch and dinner menus; children with a Kids' Pac filled with games and puzzles and a children's menu (just £2.25) of simple dishes (veggie noodle sausages, burgers etc) and large fruity shakes served with a giraffe-shaped stirrer. Non-smoking throughout. High chairs available.

Manze's
87 Tower Bridge Road, SE1
t (020) 2407 2985
www.manze.co.uk
Open 10.30am–9pm daily
⊖ London Bridge, Tower Hill

Manze's is the oldest pie and mash shop in London (it first opened in 1862) and, despite the capital's many competing eateries, still one of the most popular with queues that regularly stretch right down the street at lunchtime. The food is traditional and determinedly unglamorous – minced beef pies, jellied eels and big dollops of mash all topped with bright green parsley sauce known as liquor – not to mention very cheap. Where else can you feed a family of 4 for under £

Pollo
20 Old Compton Street, W1
t (020) 7734 5917
⊖ Leicester Square, Tottenham Court Road
Open Daily noon–midnight

Long-established budget diner selling a range of reasonable pasta dishes. A little dingy but plenty of atmosphere.

American
Big Easy
332–4 King's Road, SW3
t (020) 7352 4071
⊖ Sloane Square
Open Mon–Sat 12 noon–11.30pm, Sun 12 noon–11pm

If your kids like seafood, then you've come to the right place. This excellent Louisiana-style diner specializes in huge plates of prawns, crabs and lobster (they also do burgers and ribs). Children under eight can eat for free if accompanied by an adult (1 adult per child; the menu for the second child costs £3.95). Crayons and high chairs available on request.

Chicago Rib Shack
1 Raphael Street, SW7
t (020) 7581 5595
Open Mon–Sat 12 noon–12midnight, Sun 12 noon–11pm
⊖ Knightsbridge

On Sunday lunchtimes, kids can look forward to balloons, activity menus, colouring books, competitions and some delicious barbecue-style food. The portions (even on the kids' menu) are huge and kids are entitled to a free soft drink.

Maxwell's
Branches open 11am–12midnight daily
8/9 James Street, WC2 **t** (020) 7836 0303, ⊖ Covent Garden, Embankment, Leicester Square;
76 Heath Street, Hampstead, NW3 **t** (020) 7794 5450, ⊖ Hampstead

The children's menu is full of games and puzzles; there are join-the-dots, pictures to colour in and word searches. Each week a prize is given for the menu which has been completed in the most imaginative way. It serves lots of kids' favourites including waffles, burgers, ribs and hot dogs, as well as a few tasty surprises of its own such as deep-fried ice cream.

RK Stanley's
6 Little Portland Street, W1
t (020) 7462 0099
Open Mon–Sat 12 noon–11pm
www.rkstanleys.co.uk

⊖ Oxford Circus

With its old-style 1950s décor and sausage-heavy menu, this is a good, fun choice. Kids eat for free on Saturdays; otherwise the children's menu is £4.50. Baby-changing facilities and high chairs available.

Texas Embassy Cantina
1 Cockspur Street, SW1
t (020) 7925 0077
www.texasembassy.com
Open Mon–Thur 12 noon–11pm, Fri–Sat 12 noon–12 midnight, Sun 12 noon–10.30pm
⊖ Charing Cross

Popular Tex-Mex diner just a stone's throw from Trafalgar Square housed in the former headquarters of the White Star Shipping Line (which owned the ill-fated Titanic). Its name is a reference to the brief period between 1836–45 when Texas was an independent country and opened an embassy in London near this spot. Children are catered for with a dedicated menu (which entitles them to unlimited drinks refills) of Tex-Mex-lite cuisine plus games, puzzles and balloons. High chairs available.

Fish and Chips
Geale's Fish Restaurant
2 Farmer Street, W8
t (020) 7727 7969
⊖ Notting Hill Gate
Bus 27, 28, 31, 52, 70, 94
Open Tues–Sat 12 noon–3pm & 6–11

Fish and chips, of course, is more than just food to the British; it's a tradition, part of the national way of life and, as you would expect, the capital is packed with hundreds of fish and chip restaurants of widely varying quality. This one, just off Notting Hill Gate, is one of the very best, with freshly delivered fish cooked in crisp batter.

Rock and Sole Plaice
47 Endell Street, WC2
t (020) 7836 3785
Open 11.30am–10.30pm daily
⊖ Covent Garden

The oldest fish and chip shop in the capital (it opened way back in 1871) and still one of the best serving large portions of battered fish and big fat chunky chips.

Seashell
49–51 Lisson Grove, NW1 **t** (020) 7224 9000
⊖ Marylebone

Open Mon–Fri 12 noon–2.30, 5–10.30pm, Sat noon–10.30pm

Two floors serving crisp fish and crunchy chips. Long-time favourite of Londoners.

Hot and Spicy

Blue Elephant

3–6 Fulham Broadway, SW6
t (020) 7385 6595
⊖ Fulham Broadway
Bus 11, 14. 28, 211, 295, C4
Open Mon–Fri 12 noon–3pm & 7pm–12midnight, Sat 7pm–11pm, Sun 12 noon–3.30pm

Famous Thai restaurant offering great value super-spicy Sunday lunchtime meals. Adults pay a fixed price, however much they eat, while children are split into three descending price bands: 10–15 years, 6–10 years and under-6s. There are plans to introduce a dedicated children's menu (featuring less spicy dishes) in the near future. In the meanwhile, kids will love the restaurant's jungle-like décor.

Chutney Mary

535 King's Road, SW10
t (020) 7351 3113
www.realindianfood.com
Open Mon–Sat 12 noon–2.30pm & 5.30pm–11.30pm, Sun 12.30–3pm
⊖ Fulham Broadway

The twin sister of the Veerswamy, this pleasant, modern Indian restaurant is very popular with familes, particularly on Sundays when they offer a children's menu for £7 consisting of a mixture of mild curry dishes and reliable standbys for fussy eaters – fish fingers, burgers etc. There is a very pleasant conservatory. High chairs available.

Masala Zone

9 Marshall Street, W1
t (020) 7287 9966
www.realindianfood.com
Open Mon–Sat 12 noon–2.30pm & 5.30pm–11.30pm, Sun 12.30–3pm
⊖ Oxford Circus

This brightly-coloured, subtly-lit diner is the latest venture by the excellent Chutney Mary Group and offers a menu mainly comprised of inexpensive street food dishes, which are piquant and sweet rather than overly spicy. There's also a Children's Thali (£3) available on request. The chicken burger comes highly recommended.

Weekday lunchtimes are pretty busy and there's no booking, but the no smoking policy throughout and roomy upstairs level are plus points for those with pushchairs in tow.

Veeraswamy

99–101 Regent Street, W1
t (020) 7734 1401
www.realindianfood.com
Open Mon–Sat 12 noon–2.30pm & 5.30pm–11.30pm, Sun 12.30–3pm
⊖ Piccadilly Circus

A great child-friendly Indian restaurant (it claims to be the UK's oldest) where you can sit and watch the world go by while your kids demolish mountains of popadoms. Sunday is the restaurant's designated family day when they offer a special children's menu for £7 (made up of lightly spiced Indian dishes plus a few bland children's favourites – fish fingers, burgers, chips etc), and there are crayons, colouring books and goodie bags for the kids to enjoy while they wait for their food. High chairs available.

Italian

Café Med

22–25 Dean Street, W1
t (020) 7287 9007
Open 12 noon–10.30pm daily
⊖ Tottenham Court Road

Bustling café-restaurant in the heart of trendy Soho, this is usually filled with movers and shakers at lunchtime and after work. The menu is mainly mediterranean based and there's a kids' version for £5, comprising two courses and a drink. High chairs available.

La Lanterna

6–8 Mill Street, SE1
t (020) 7252 2420
Open 12 noon–11pm
⊖ Tower Hill

Small, homely traditional Italian restaurant serving good reasonably priced fare. Half portions and high chairs available. It can get quite crowded especially in the evenings when live music is staged at the next door café (which is owned by the same people).

Monza

6 Yeoman's Row, SW3
t (020) 7591 0210

Dinner Daily 7–11.30pm, lunch Tues–Sun
12 noon–2.30pm
⊖ South Kensington, Knightsbridge

A small, quaint Italian restaurant offering a range of pizza, pasta and risotto dishes to suit all tastes. Family-orientated with excellent service, its walls are decorated with motor-racing memorabilia (Monza being the venue for the Italian Formula 1 Grand Prix).

Rez's

17–21 Tavistock Street, WC2
t (020) 7379 9991
⊖ Covent Garden
Open Daily 12 noon–4 and 5–11.45 (till 10.45 Sun)

Fantastic pizza and pasta dishes. Under-10s eat for free if accompanied by an adult (1 adult per child). You can sit outside in the summer.

Oriental

Benihana

Branches open Wed–Fri 12 noon–3pm, Mon–Fri 6–11, Sat & Sun 12 noon–11
37–43 Sackville Street, W1 **t** (020) 7494 2525,
⊖ Green Park;
77 King's Road, SW3 **t** (020) 7376 7799, ⊖ Sloane Square;
100 Avenue Road, NW3 **t** (020) 7586 9508, ⊖ Swiss Cottage
www.benihana.co.uk

Fun Japanese noodle chain for families looking to experiment. Several dishes are specifically designed for children's tastes and kids, for their part, enjoy watching the skilful chefs preparing the food at their tables – Ninja style.

China, China

3 Gerrard Street, W1
t (020) 7439 7502
⊖ Leicester Square

A good place to grab a quick bowl of noodles in between bouts of sightseeing.

Chuen Cheng Ku

17 Wardour Street, W1
t 020 7437 1398
⊖ Leicester Square

Has the longest menu in Chinatown, which can prove a little daunting – just ask for the day's specials, you're unlikely to be disappointed. If you're hoping to impress the waiters with your grasp of Cantonese, try asking for the following: Tsun Guen (mini spring rolls), Pai Gwat (steamed tiny spare

ribs) or Har Gau (rice dumplings stuffed with shrimps). It's extremely child-friendly with booster seats, high chairs and baskets of goodies for good little kiddies.

Mr Kong

21 Lisle Street, WC2
t (020) 7437 7341
⊖ Leicester Square

Good, solid Cantonese fare at a price that will not break the budget.

New World

1 Gerrard Place, W1
t (020) 7734 0396
⊖ Leicester Square

One of the best places to introduce your children to the joys of Chinese food. On Sundays it's packed with families tucking into bowls of dim sum – (Chinese dumplings, the restaurant's speciality). Try the special child-size mini dim sum.

Royal China

40 Baker Street, W1
t (020) 7487 4688
Open Mon-Sat 12 noon–11pm, Sun 11am–10pm
⊖ Baker Street

One of the capital's best Chinese restaurants outside of Chinatown itself. Children are warmly welcomed and the dim sum is superb. Children's menu and high chairs available.

Tiger Lil's

www.tigerlils.com
Branches open Mon–Fri 6pm–11.30pm, Sun 12 noon–11pm
500 King's Road, SW10, **t** (020) 7376 5003;
⊖ Fulham Broadway
15a Clapham Common, SW4, **t** (020) 7720 5433;
⊖ Clapham Common
270 Upper Street, N1, **t** (020) 7226 1118; ⊖ Highbury & Islington

Tiger Lil's offers a unique interactive dining experience which children of all ages will happily enjoy. Rather than order items from a menu, you are invited to collect together a plateful of fresh ingredients (from a selection of pre-prepared meat, fish and vegetatbles slivers) – which you then take to one of three chefs who will cook it while you wait – this in itself is very impressive with flames leaping spectacularly from super-heated woks. It's certainly not the place to go for a quiet meal, but it is lots of fun. Children's portions, high chairs and crayons are available.

Wok Wok

www.wokwok.co.uk
Branches open 12 noon–11pm
7 Kensington High Street, W8, **t** (020) 7938 1221;
⊖ High Street Kensington
51–53 Northcote Road, SW11, **t** (020) 7978 7181;
⇌ Claphan Junction
10 Frith Street, W1, **t** (020) 7437 7080; ⊖ Leicester Square
67 Upper Street, N1, **t** (020) 7288 0333; ⊖ Angel

Can't decide between Chinese, Japanese or Thai food? Well at Wok Wok you don't have to as this infectiously enthusiastic chain has taken the rather brave decision to specialise in all type of Asian cuisine including Vietnamese and Indonesian. The children's menu (a very reasonable £3.95) offers a choice between spring rolls, chicken satay or, for the unadventurous, omelette (all with chips) followed by ice cream and there are entertainment packs with crayons and activity sheets. Sunday is the restaurant's designated family day when entertainments such as magic shows and face-painting may be laid on.

Pizzas

Gourmet Pizza Company

www.gourmetpizzacompany.co.uk
Branches open 12 noon–10.30pm
7–9 Swallow Street, W1, **t** (020) 7734 5182;
⊖ Piccadilly Circus
Gabriel's Wharf, 56 Upper Ground, SE1, **t** (020) 7928 3188; ⊖ Waterloo

Small, rather upmarket chain serving reliably excellent pizzas including a few rather unusual combinations – sauteed leak and pecorino cheese, salami and artichoke etc. Thankfully, the kids menu is a little more conservative. High chairs available.

Pizza Piazza

www.pizzapiazza.co.uk
Branches open 11.30am–12midnight daily
39 Charing Cross Road, WC2 **t** (020) 7437 1686,
⊖ Leicester Square;
75 Gloucester Road, SW7 **t** (020) 7370 6575,
⊖ Gloucester Road;
This is a firm favourite with the kids. The menu doubles as a board game and children are given an activity pack when they arrive, full of animal cards, badges and colouring books. The kids' menu,

featuring mini pizza and simple pasta dishes, is imaginative and fun – kids can choose their own pizza toppings.

Pizza Organic

20 Old Brompton Road SW7
t (020) 7589 9613,
www.pizzapiazza.co.uk
Open 11.30am–12midnight daily
⊖ South Kensington

An avowedly environmentally-conscious restaurant, Pizza Organic, which is run by the same people as Pizza Piazza, offers stone-baked pizzas and a children's menu featuring the 'O-People'; five cartoon characters designed to teach children all about the exciting world of organic produce (good) and GM foods (bad). The restaurant's organic menu was designed by Jamie Oliver.

Posh Nosh

Brown's

Branches open 12 noon–10pm
47 Maddox Street, W1 **t** (020) 7491 4565, ⊖ Oxford Circus, Bond Street;
82–84 St Martin's Lane, WC2 **t** (020) 7497 5050,
⊖ Leicester Square;
114 Draycott Avenue, SW3 **t** (020) 7584 5359,
⊖ South Kensington.

Well-to-do but ever family-friendly brasserie chain. Children get their own menu and crayons can be requested. The restaurants occasionaly run deals whereby under-12s get to eat for free if accompanied by an adult. Be warned, it can be a bit pricey.

Oxo Tower Restaurant

Oxo Tower, Barge House Street, South Bank, SE1
t (020) 7803 3888
Open Mon–Sat 12 noon–3pm & 6pm–11.30pm, Sun 12 noon–3.30pm & 6.30pm–10.30pm
⊖ Waterloo

Serves great food and can offer some of the most stunning river views to be found anywhere in the capital (it's particularly magical at night). They offer a special brasserie kids' menu at weekends.

The People's Palace

Royal Festival Hall, South Bank Centre, SE1
t (020) 7928 9999
Open 12 noon–3pm & 5.30pm–11pm
⊖ Waterloo

A very grand eaterie offering superb river views and a refined contemporary European menu.

Searcy's

Level I, Barbican Centre, EC2

t (020) 7588 3008

Open Mon–Fri 12 noon–2.30pm & 6pm–10.30pm, Sat & Sun 12 noon–3pm, 5pm–6.30pm

⊖ Barbican

Recently refurbished, this bright, airy modern-looking diner overlooks the Barbican's central courtyard and fountains. It's a bit hi-falutin' (not to say a touch pricey) but does its best to accommodate families.

Spanish

La Rueda

Branches open Mon–Fri 12 noon–3pm & 6.30pm–11.30pm, Sat 12 noon–11.30pm, Sun 12 noon–10.30pm

102 Wigmore Street, W1, **t** (020) 7486 1718; ⊖ Bond Street

642 King's Road, SW6, **t** (020) 7384 2684; ⊖ Fulham Broadway

Tired of pizzas and burgers? Then try your kids on the mini-portions of paella and patatas bravas served at this lively tapas chain. There's live music and dancing here on Friday and Saturday evenings. High chairs available.

Tea Time

Coffee Gallery

23 Museum Street, WC1

t (020) 7436 0455

Open Mon–Fri 8am–5.30pm, Sat 12–5.30pm, Sun 12–5.30pm

⊖ Tottenham Court Road

With its bright, cheerful interior, the Coffee Gallery makes the perfect setting for a light snack and provides a welcome retreat from the bustling West End crowds. It serves wide range of sandwiches including filled foccacias.

Fortnum & Mason Fountain Room

181 Piccadilly, W1

t (020) 7734 8040

www.fortnumandmason.co.uk

Open Mon–Sat 7.30am–11pm

⊖ Piccadilly Circus

A wonderfully elegant tea room set in the basement of the Queen's grocers. They sell a wide and delicious range of specially made ice creams,

sorbets, sundaes and sodas. It's a haven of old-fashioned style and charm, suitable for older children. Once you've finished your ice cream, pop outside to watch the workings of the famous Fortnum & Mason clock.

Gloriette Patisserie

128 Brompton Road, SW3

t (020) 7589 4750

Open Mon-Sat 7am–7pm, Sun 9am–6pm

⊖ Knightsbridge

This is a great place for anyone with a sweet tooth. Boasting a fantastic selection of tempting cakes, from creamy chocolate gateaux to glazed fruit tarts, it also sells a wide variety of snacks, ranging from salads to assorted tasty sandwiches.

Patisserie Valerie

105 Marylebone High Street, W1

t (020) 7935 6240

⊖ Baker Street, Bond Street

43 Old Compton Street, W1

t (020) 7935 6240

⊖ Leicester Square

8 Russell Street, Covent Garden, WC2

t (020) 7240 0064

⊖ Covent Garden, Leicester Square

First established in the 1920s by Belgian born baker Madame Valerie, each branch of this patisserie-cum-café chain has a pleasant continental-esque ambience and stocks a wonderful array of sticky treats as well as savoury snacks and salads.

Richoux

Branches open 8.30am–5.30pm

172 Piccadilly, W1

t (020) 7493 2204

⊖ Green Park

41a South Audley Street, W1

t (020) 7629 5228

⊖ Green Park

Old-fashioned upmarket French coffee shop/tearoom/patisserie serving a variety of cakes, snacks and sandwiches.

Ritz Hotel

150 Piccadilly, W1 **t** (020) 7493 8181

www.theritzhotel.co.uk

Tube Green Park

Tea Daily 2–6

Afternoon tea at the Ritz is rather steep £27 a head but the grandeur of the venue and the sight of the cakes, sandwiches and scones piled high on silver platters make it an experience few children are likely to forget. Book well in advance (at least three months for a weekend) and dress smartly.

Treat Eats

Babe Ruth's

www.baberuths.com
Branches open Mon–Thurs noon–11, Fri–Sat noon-midnight, Sun noon–10.30
172–76 The Highway, E1
t (020) 7481 8181
⊖ Wapping
O2 Centre, 255 Finchley Road, NW3
t (020) 7433 3388
⊖ Finchley Road

Hugely popular sports restaurant that offers children various alternatives to actually eating, including table football, arcade games and even a mini-basketball court. Once you've got the youngsters to sit down (which may take some time) they can tuck in to some decent American fare – hot dogs, burgers, pizzas etc – and try the puzzles and games that come with the children's menu.

Deal's

Branches open Mon–Thur 12 noon–3.30pm & 5.30pm–10.30pm, Fri & Sat 12 noon–10.30pm, Sun 12 noon–6pm
14–16 Foubert's Place, W1 **t** (020) 7287 1001, ⊖ Oxford Circus;
Chelsea Harbour, SW3 **t** (020) 7795 1001, ⊖ Sloane Square;
Broadway Centre, Hammersmith, W6 **t** (020) 8563 1001, ⊖ Hammersmith

Popular restaurant offering high-class family entertainment and food on Sunday afternoons. Expect face-painting, magic shows and a simple American-style menu.

Hard Rock Café

150 Old Park Lane, W1 **t** (020) 7629 0382
www.hardrock.com
Tube Hyde Park Corner
Open Daily 11.30am-12.30am

Fries, burgers and gloopy shakes to the persistent beat of rock and roll. Kids will love it but bring a set of ear plugs if you're feeling delicate. Junior diners also get their own colour-in menus, and entertainment at weekends as well as some seasonally themed events.

Planet Hollywood

13 Coventry Street, W1 **t** (020) 7734 6220
www.planethollywood.com
Tube Piccadilly Circus, Leicester Square
Open Daily 12 noon–1.30am, except Sun noon–12.30am

Kids love this temple to Hollywood kitsch with its garish posters and cabinets full of memorabilia, highlights include the cyborg from *Terminator II*, Harrison Ford's whip from *Indiana Jones and the Last Crusade* and Charlie Chaplin's hat and cane.

Rainforest Café

20 Shaftesbury Avenue, W1
t (020) 7434 3111
www.therainforestcafe.co.uk
⊖ Piccadilly Circus, Leicester Square
Bus 3, 12, 14, 19, 22, 38
Open 12 noon–11pm daily, Fri & Sat 12 noon–12midnight
Wheelchair access and adapted toilet. Suitable for all ages

A wonderful theme restaurant, particularly popular with young children. As the name suggests, the tables and chairs have been placed in among the trees and foliage of an artificial rainforest. Inhabiting the dense undergrowth are various mechanical animals, including chimps, monkeys, alligators, birds and snakes, who come alive every 15 minutes to whoop and chatter following a rather loud artificial thunderstorm. Games and face-painting are laid on at weekends. The grill-style menu is tasty, albeit rather expensive. The 'Wild Bunch' children's menu is a rather hefty £7.95. There's also a great shop upstairs.

Smollensky's

105 The Strand, WC2 **t** (020) 7497 2101
Branches: Smollensky's NW3, O2 Centre, 255 Finchley Road, NW3 **t** (020) 7431 5007; Smollensky's Bar & Grill, Bradmore House, Queen Caroline Street, Hammersmith, W6 **t** (020) 8741 8124.
www.smollenskys.co.uk
Tube Embankment, Charing Cross
Open Mon–Wed 12 noon–11pm, Thurs–Sat noon–12.30am, Sun 12 noon–10.30pm

Weekend lunch times are dedicated to entertaining (and feeding) the children. There are Punch and Judy shows, magic demonstrations and lots of balloons and colouring books. Book in advance.

Sports Café

80 Haymarket, SW1
t (020) 7839 8300
www.thesportscafé.com
Open Mon–Wed 12 noon–1am, Thurs–Sat 12
noon–3am, Sun 12 noon–10.30pm
⊖ Piccadilly Circus, Charing Cross

Basketball hoops, pool tables, large-screen TVs
relaying sporting classics...oh and food as well. A
total sporting/food experience for hungry sports-
mad kids. The menu is reasonably priced, if a little
basic, but you come for the décor and ambience.
It's a good deal less family-friendly in the evenings
when it attracts large crowds of high-spirited (to
put it euphemistically) revellers.

Sticky Fingers

1a Phillimore Gardens, W8
t (020) 7938 5338.
www.stickyfingers.co.uk
⊖ High Street Kensington, Holland Park
Bus 9, 10, 27, 28, 31, 49, 94
Open 12 noon–12midnight daily
⊖ High Street Kensington, Holland Park

The owner, Bill Wyman, used to play bass guitar
for the Rolling Stones and the restaurant is filled
with rock and roll memorabilia – all of which will
probably be lost on the restaurant's younger visitors. Nonetheless, they will enjoy the burgers and
fries and the magic shows, activities and face
painting that are laid on on Sunday afternoons.
High chairs available.

TGI Friday's

www.tgifridays.co.uk
Branches open 12 noon–12midnight daily
6 Bedford Street, WC2, **t** (020) 7379 0585; ⊖ Covent
Garden, Leicester Square
29 Coventry Street, W1, **t** (020) 7379 6262;
⊖ Piccadilly Circus

An ever-popular choice, this lively Tex-Mex diner
can offer high chairs, booster seats, a special kids'
menu, free balloons, colouring books and pointy
red and white hats – which children wear with an
absurd level of pride.

Vegetarian

Food For Thought

31 Neal Street, WC2 **t** (020) 7836 0239
Tube Covent Garden
Open Mon–Sat 12 noon–8.30, Sun 12 noon–5

Cheap and friendly serving quiches, salads, soups
etc. It can get a little crowded so turn up for an
early lunch to be sure of a seat.

Manna

4 Erskine Road, NW1
t (020) 7722 8028

Spacious, popular and highly regarded veggie
restaurant.

Mildred's

58 Greek Street, W1 **t** (020) 7494 1634
Tube Leicester Square, Tottenham Court Road
Open Mon–Sat noon–11

A Soho institution, this offers tasty stir-frys, bean
burgers and falafels in pitta bread with salad at
reasonable prices. Limited outside seating.

Oshobasho

Highgate Wood, Muswell Hill, N10
t (020) 8444 1505
⊖ Highgate
Open 8.30am–7.30 daily, the park gates close at
8.30pm

Extremely popular vegetarian restaurant in the
idyllic setting of Highgate Wood. Familes flock to
its large outdoor seating area at the weekends.
There's also a children's play area. If you're feeling
adventurous after your meal, pick up a nature trail
from the next door woodland centre and head off
into the trees. *See* p.180.

The Food Chain

Ask Pizza

www.askcentral.co.uk
Branches open 11.30am–12midnight
48 Grafton Way, W1
t (020) 7388 8108
⊖ Warren Street
222 Kensington High Street, W8
t (020) 7937 5540
⊖ High Street Kensington
103 St John Street, EC1
t (020) 7253 0323
⊖ Farringdon
160–162 Victoria Street, SW1
t (020) 7630 8228
⊖ Victoria

Pizza Express' main rival for the title of 'best pizza
chain', Ask also specialises in thin-crust Italian-style
pizzas and has a similar continental ambience.
There's no special children's menu but families are

made to feel very welcome with children's portions and high chairs readily available.

Belgo

www.belgo-restaurants.com
Branches open Mon–Sat 12 noon–12midnight, Sun 12 noon–10.30
Belgo Centraal, 50 Earlham Street, WC2 **t** (020) 7813 2233, ⊖ Covent Garden;
Belgo Noord, 72 Chalk Farm Road, NW1 **t** (020) 7267 0718, ⊖ Chalk Farm;
Belgo Zuid, 124 Ladbroke Grove, W10 **t** (020) 8982 8400, ⊖ Ladbroke Grove, Holland Park
also see branches of **Bierodrome** their gastropub counterparts, **open**: 12 noon- 12midnight daily
173-4 Upper Street, N1 **t** (020) 7226 5835, ⊖ Angel
44-48 ClaphamHigh Street, SW4 **t** (020) 7720 1118, ⊖ Clapham Junction
678-680 Fulham Road, SW6 **t** (020) 7751 0789, ⊖ Parsons Green
67 Kingsway, Holborn, WC2 **t** (020) 7242 7469, ⊖ Holborn

Belgo Nord, Belgo Centraal and Belgo Zuid are the three branches of this very fashionable restaurant. All welcome children with open arms and free food (under-12s eat free, 1 adult per 2 kids). While adults try the Belgian specialities such as Moules Marinières (mussels with celery and onion) and Wild Boar sandwiches (they'll put hairs on your chest) kids can tuck into some of the restaurant's more kiddy-friendly fare (fish fingers, chicken nuggets etc) from the colour-in 'Mini-Belgo' menu. On weekdays the restaurant operates an innovative pricing policy known as 'beat the clock'. Between 5pm and 6.30pm the price you pay is the time on the clock when you order. Be warned, these restaurants are very trendy and, as a result can get crowded, especially at weekends.

Additional charges

Cover charge
A fixed charge sometimes imposed by the restaurant to cover the cost of table linen, etc.

Service charge
A percentage of the bill (usually 10–15 percent) added for waiter/waitress service. There is no need to tip if a service charge has been added.

Tips
If there is no service charge a 10–15 percent tip should be left behind at the table (unless the service was awful).

Café Rouge

www.caferouge.co.uk
Branches open 10am–11pm daily
29–31 Basil Street, SW3 **t** (020) 7584 2345, ⊖ Knightsbridge;
18 Chalk Farm Road, NW1, **t** (020) 7428 0998, ⊖ Chalk Farm
15 Frith Street, W1, **t** (020) 7437 4307, ⊖ Leicester Square, Tottenham Court Road
Hay's Galleria, SE1, **t** (020) 7378 0097, ⊖ London Bridge
Hillgate House, Limeburner Lane, EC4, **t** (020) 7329 1234,⊖ Blackfriars
Ibis Hotel, Stockwell Street, SE3, **t** (020) 8293 6660 **DLR** Greenwich, Cutty Sark
390 King's Road, SW3, **t** (020) 7352 2226,⊖ Sloane Square
120 St John's Wood High Street, NW8 **t** (020) 7722 8366, ⊖ Swiss Cottage;
Tooley Street, SE1 **t** (020) 7378 0097, ⊖/⇌ London Bridge;
Victoria Place, 115 Buckingham Palace Road, SW1 **t** (020) 7931 9300, ⊖ Victoria;
34 Wellington Street, WC2 **t** (020) 7836 0998, ⊖ Covent Garden

Extremely child-conscious French café chain. There are two children's menus – one aimed at toddlers, offering gloopy favourites like mashed potato and omelette, while the other features mini-portions from the adult menu. The chain also produces a very grand activity pack with stickers, puzzles, crayons and Kinder-style construction toys.

Café Pasta

www.pizzaexpress.co.uk/cpasta.htm
Branches open 11.30am–12midnight
2–4 Garrick Street, WC2, **t** (020)7497 2779; ⊖ Leicester Square
15 Greek Street, W1, **t** (020) 7434 2545; ⊖ Leicester Square, Tottenham Court Road
182–184 Shaftesbury Avenue, WC2, **t** (020) 7379 0198, ⊖ Leicester Square
229–231 Kensington High Street, W8, **t** (020) 7937 6314; ⊖ High Street Kensington
373 Kensington High Street, W8, **t** (020) 7610 5552; ⊖ High Street Kensington

Pizza Express' pasta-mad sibling, this displays many of the same qualities: attractive decor, good food and a genuinely family-friendly atmosphere achieved without recourse to games or gimmicks. High chairs available.

Caffè Uno

www.caffeuno.co.uk

5 Argyll Street, W1, **t** (020) 7437 2503, ✆ Oxford Circus

100 Baker Street, W1, **t** (020) 7486 8606, ✆ Baker Street

28 Binney Street, W1, **t** (020) 7499 9312, ✆ Charing Cross, Leicester Square

24 Charing Cross Road, WC2, **t** (020) 7240 2524, ✆ Charing Cross, Leicester Square

9 Kensington High Street, W8, **t** (020) 7937 8961, ✆ High Street Kensington

40–42 Parkway, NW1, **t** (020) 7428 9124, ✆ Camden Town

37 St Martin's Lane, WC2, **t** (020) 7836 5837, ✆ Leicester Square

64 Tottenham Court Road, **t** (020) 7636 3587, ✆ Goodge Street

Good for a quick pizza or bowl of pasta, Caffè Uno is a very reasonably priced Italian chain. Kids get a 'Secret Squirrel' menu offering a choice of main meal (penne bolognese, sausage and fries or mini pizza),2 scoops of ice cream and a free drink – all for £3.95 – and are also given games and balloons to play with. High chairs available.

Fish!

www.fishdiner.co.uk

Open Mon–Sat 11.30am–11pm, Sun 12 noon–10.30pm

Cathedral Street, SE1

t (020) 7836 3236

✆ London Bridge, Borough

County Hall, 3b Belvedere Road, SE1, t (020) 7234 3333, ✆ Waterloo

1 Lawn Terrace, 1 Lawn Terrace, Blackheath SE10, **t** (020) 7234 3333, DLR Greenwich

The bright, airy Fish! is about as far from the traditional British chippy as it's possible to get. Its greatest strength is the sheer amount of quality food and choice it offers. Not only do you get to choose the sort of fish you want – every day there are about 12 different varieties available ranging from cod, haddock and plaice to whitebait, swordfish and tuna – but also the manner in which it is cooked (steamed, grilled or fried) and the accompanying sauce (salsa, tartar, hollandaise etc). Although children may baulk at some of the choices – grilled squid in garlic butter anyone? – they're bound to find something they like on the children's menu which entitles them to two

courses, a drink and dessert (they do a very good sticky toffee pudding) for £6.95. They are also given a Kids' Pack of games and puzzles. High chairs available.

Pizza Express

www.pizzaexpress.co.uk

Branches Open 12 noon–11.30pm daily

125 Alban Gate, London Wall, EC2, **t** (020) 7600 8880, ✆ Barbican, St Paul's

133 Baker Street, W1 **t** (020) 7486 0888, ✆ Baker Street;

21–22 Barret Street, W1 **t** (020) 7629 1001, ✆ Bond Street;

9–12 Bow Street, WC2 **t** (020) 7240 3443, ✆ Covent Garden;

7 Beauchamp Place, Knightsbridge, SW3 **t** (020) 7589 2355, ✆ Knightsbridge;

Cardomom Building, Shad Thames, SE1, **t** (020) 7403 8484, ✆ Tower Hill, London Bridge

7 Charlotte Street, W1 **t** (020) 7580 1110; ✆ Goodge Street

4 Church Street, Greenwich, SE10, **t** (020) 8853 2770; **DLR** Greenwich

30 Coptic Street, Bloomsbury, WC1 **t** (020) 4636 3232, ✆ Holborn, Tottenham Court Road;

26 Cowcross Street, EC1, **t** (020) 7490 8025, ✆ Farringdon

49 Curtain Road, EC2, **t** (020) 7613 5426, ✆ Liverpool Street, Old Street

10 Dean Street, W1 **t** (020) 7439 8722, ✆ Tottenham Court Road

20 Greek Street, W1, **t** (020) 7734 7430, ✆ Leicester Square

152 King's Road, SW3, **t** (020) 7351 5031; ✆ Sloane Square

80–81 St Martins Lane, WC2, **t** (020) 7836 8001, ✆ Covent Garden

2 Salisbury House, London Wall, EC2, **t** (020) 7588 7262, ✆ Barbican, St Paul's, Bank, Liverpool Street

13–14 Thayer Street, London, W1 **t** (020) 7935 2167; ✆ Oxford Circus

154 Victoria Street, SW1, **t** (020) 7828 1477, ✆ Victoria

The White House, 9c Belvedere Road, SE1, W1 **t** (020) 7928 4091; ✆ Waterloo

Serving tasty thin-crust Italian style pizzas (plus a few pasta dishes such as lasagne and canneloni), this is by far the best pizza chain in London. Whichever one you choose, you won't go far wrong. Some of the more popular branches offer crayons and colouring books..

Tootsies

Branches open 11.30am–12midnight

35 James Street, **t** (020) 7486 1611; ⊖ Bond Street

177 New King's Road, **t** (020) 7736 4023; ⊖ Parsons Green

107 Old Brompton Road, SW7, **t** (020) 7581 8942; ⊖ South Kensington

120 Holland Park Avenue, **t** (020) 7229 8567; ⊖ Holland Park

198 Haverstock Hill, NW3, **t** (020) 7431 7609; ⊖ Belsize Park

Upmarket, brightly-coloured, rather trendy burger chain serving American-style food in American-sized portions (at, unfortunately, English prices). Children are given colouring books and crayons to help them pass the time while they wait for their food. High chairs available.

Wagamama

www.wagamama.com

Branches open Mon-Sat 12 noon-11pm, Sun 12.30pm–10pm

11 Jamestown Road, NW1, **t** (020) 7487 4688, ⊖ Camden Town

26 Kensington High Street, W8, **t** (020) 7376 1717, ⊖ High Street Kensington

10a Lexington Street, W1, **t** (020) 7292 0990, ⊖ Bond Street

4a Streatham Street, WC1, **t** (020) 7323 9223, ⊖ Tottenham Court Road

101 Wigmore Street, W1, **t** (020) 7409 0111, ⊖ Oxford Circus

Though rather canteen-like with its long refectory tables, this fast-growing noodle house chain is surprisingly family-friendly, although the (inevitable) hustle and bustle may appeal more to older children. High chairs available.

Yo! Sushi

www.yosushi.co.uk

Branches open 12 noon–12 midnight daily

52 Poland Street, **t** (020) 7287 0443; ⊖ Oxford Circus, Tottenham Court Road

County Hall, Belvedere Road, SE1, **t** (020) 7928 8871; ⊖ Waterloo

A dining experience unlike any other – you pick sushi dishes from an enormous conveyor belt whilst your drinks are prepared by a special drinks-mixing robot. Kids get a games bag and their own

menu which offers such authentic Japanese delicacies as fish fingers and chicken nuggets and comes with a pair of special child-friendly chopsticks. During the week under-12s eat for free. High chairs and clip-on baby seats available.

Shop

As far as families are concerned there are two types of shop: those that children visit under duress – clothes shops are a good example – and those that parents visit under duress – Hamleys, for instance. Inevitably, after a shopping trip, one half of the family will be left feeling pretty grumpy and upset, either because they've been made to try on a particularly nasty sweater, or because they've been dragged through a seething mass of teddy bears. We've done our best to cover both types from the most granny-friendly knitwear shops to the most overwhelming toy stores.

Arts, crafts and hobbies

The Bead Shop
21a Tower Street
t (020) 7240 0931
www.beadworks.co.uk
⊖ Covent Garden
Bus 6, 9, 11, 13, 15, 23, 77A, 91, 176
Open Mon 1–6, Tues–Fri 10.30–6.30, Sat 11.30–5

Getting kids to make their own necklaces and jewellery is a great way of filling a spare afternoon. The Bead Shop, tucked away behind Cambridge Circus, near Covent Garden, will provide the essentials. Its shelves are stocked with thousands and thousands of coloured baubles and beads. You can also pick up the strings and fasteners needed to complete your creations.

Beatties
202 High Holborn, WC1
t (020) 7405 6285
⊖ Holborn
Bus 8, 25, 242, 501, 521
Open Mon–Sat 9.30–6

Beatties is a haven of hobbydom. Train sets are its mainstay and it stocks all the principal brands including Lima, Marklin and, of course, Hornby. It also sells die-cast toy soldiers, radio-controlled cars and, that other great childhood staple, Scalextrix.

Comet Miniatures
44–48 Lavender Hill, SW11
t (020) 7228 3702
www.cometminiatures.co.uk
⇌ Clapham Junction

Bus 77, 77A, 345
Open Mon–Sat 9.30–5.30

Another store harking back to a bygone age; it stocks plastic aircraft assembly kits by the hundred. Airfix predominates, as you might expect, but you can also find some lesser-known models.

Covent Garden Candle Store
30 The Market
t (020) 7439 4220
www.candlesonthenet.co.uk
Bus 6, 9, 11, 13, 15, 23, 77A, 91, 176
Open Mon–Fri 10am–7pm, Sat 10am–8pm, Sun 10am–7.30pm

If anyone in your family is interested in candle-making, this is the place to come. It stocks a variety of colourful kits and holds regular candle-making demonstrations.

Kite Store
48 Neal Street
t (020) 7836 1666
⊖ Covent Garden
Bus 6, 9, 11, 13, 15, 23, 77A, 91, 176
Open Mon–Wed, Fri & Sat 10–6, Thurs 10–7

The Kite Store sells just about every size, shape and colour of kite imaginable, from super-speedy stunt numbers to novelty kites in the shape of butterflies and sharks. It also stocks a range of aerobatic toys including elastic-band powered aeroplanes, boomerangs, yo-yos and water-powered rockets. Pride of place in the shop, however, goes to the new cutting-edge 'flexifoil' kites, which are capable of lifting a grown man clear of the ground.

London Dolls House Company
29 The Market, Covent Garden, WC2
t (020) 7240 8681
www.london-dolls-house.sagenet.co.uk
⊖ Covent Garden
Bus 6, 9, 11, 13, 15, 23, 77A, 91, 176

Open Mon–Sat 10–7, Sun 12 noon–5pm

On Covent Garden's lower level, this shop houses a wonderful collection of miniature homes, each of which is a perfect recreation of period style – from Georgian and Victorian to Art Deco and the ultra-modern – each with appropriate stacks of beautifully crafted furniture and accessories for the serious enthusiast.

Potterycraft

8–10 Ingate Place, SW8
t (020) 7720 0050
⊖ Vauxhall
⇌ Battersea Park
Bus 44, 137, 344
Open Mon–Sat 9–5

For children ready to make the step up from plasticine and play dough – come here to pick up your clay, potting wheels, glazes and kilns.

Stanley Gibbons

399 The Strand, WC2
t (020) 7836 8444
www.stanleygibbons.com
⊖ Charing Cross
Bus 6, 9, 11, 13, 15, 23, 77A, 91, 17
Open Mon–Fri 8.30–6, Sat 9.30–5.30

The biggest name in the world of stamps, the Stanley Gibbons stamp emporium on the Strand has become a Mecca for collectors from all over the world. As well as a vast collection, it also has a museum, a show room and even an auction house. It's very grand and attracts some seriously wealthy enthusiasts but, nonetheless, is still a great place for kids to come and start a collection by picking up a £1 bag of assorted stamps.

Wheatsheaf

56 Baker Street, W1
t (020) 7935 5284
⊖ Baker Street
Bus 2, 13, 30, 74, 82, 113, 139, 159, 189, 274
Open Mon–Sat 9.30–5.30, Sun 12 noon–5pm

Stocks all the art equipment a budding Van Gogh could possibly need: brushes, paints, crayons, canvases – the potential for creating mess is almost unlimited.

Baby & Nursery Gear

Dragons of Walton Street

23 Walton Street, SW3
t (020) 7589 3795
www.dragonswaltonstreet.com
⊖ South Kensington
Open Mon–Fri 9.30am–5.30pm, Sat 10am–5pm

This is where society mothers come to furnish their nurseries in the latest designer fittings. The hand made, hand painted furniture is undeniably beautiful but also exhorbitantly expensive.

Nursery Window

83 Walton Street, SW3
t (020) 7581 3358
www.nursery window.co.uk
⊖ South Kensington
Open Mon–Sat 10–6

Not nearly as grand as the nearby Dragons, Nursery Window is still rather well to do. It sells a cheery range of fabrics, toys and accessories.

Green Baby

345 Upper Street, N1
t (020) 7359 7037
www.greenbaby.com
⊖ Angel
Bus 4, 19, 30, 38, 43, X43, 56, 73, 171a, 214
Open Mon–Sat 10–5

Baby goods for the environmentally-conscious, such as washable nappies and organic toiletries. Also stocks a range of strollers and Baby Trekkers.

Books and comics

In recent years, the London book market has been dominated by two big names Books Etc and Waterstone's. Both operate a chain of huge bookstores throughout the capital (the recently opened Waterstone's, Piccadilly, is in fact the largest book

Remember

Visitors from non-EU countries can claim back some or all of the VAT (value added tax, which currently stands at 17.5%) paid on goods to be taken out of the country via the Retail Export Scheme. Pick up a form from participating shops.

shop in Europe) with good, well stocked children's sections and comfortable interiors. Pleasant as they are, however, most of the branches are, in truth, pretty much interchangeable. For something a little different try Borders on Oxford Street. It's just as well stocked and salubrious as its competitors but tries just that little bit harder to attract a family audience providing weekend storytellings and craft demonstrations.

There are a few other stores worth considering: Foyle's on Charing Cross Road, is not so much a bookshop as a London institution. You can find almost anything on its huge floors, apart that is from the book your looking for. It's famously eclectic layout and cataloguing system, however, are part of its charm and the children's section (should you ever locate it) is fantastic.

The Children's Book Centre is the only bookshop in London aimed solely at children, so it's full of Enid Blyton, Roald Dahl and J.K Rowling favourites as well as colouring books, pop-up books and, for the modern up-to-date child, CD-Roms.

If your kids are big Spider Man comic fans, try Gosh! on Great Russell Street where you can pick up *Marvel* and *DC* back copies (as well as compilations of newspaper strip cartoons like Peanuts and The Far Side) or Comic Showcase at 63 Charing Cross Road. For science fiction, head for Forbidden Planet on New Oxford Street, which has a huge collection of SF comics, books and models.

Books Etc

www.booksetc.co.uk
Branches open 9.30am–8pm, Sunday 12 noon–6pm
30 Broadgate Circle, EC2 **t** (020) 7628 8944;
70 Cheapside, EC2 **t** (020) 7236 0398;
9–13 Cowcross Street, EC1 **t** (020) 7608 2426;
60 Fenchurch Street, EC3 **t** (020) 7481 4425;
176 Fleet Street, EC4A **t** (020) 7353 5939;
263 High Holborn, WC1 **t** (020) 404 0261;
26 James Street, WC2 **t** (020) 7379 6947;
54 London Wall, EC2 **t** (020) 7628 9708;
23 Piccadilly, W1 **t** (020) 7437 7399

Borders

www.bordersstores.amazon.com
Branches open Mon–Sat 8am–11pm, Sun 12 noon–6pm
120 Charing Cross Road, WC2, **t** (020) 7379 6838;
203–207 Oxford Street, W1, **t** (020) 7292 1600

Children's Book Centre

237 Kensington High Street, W8
t (020) 7937 7497
www.childrensbookcentre.co.uk
⊖ High Street Kensington
Bus 9, 10, 27, 28
Open Mon, Wed, Fri & Sat 9.30–6.30, Tues 9.30–6, Thurs 9.30–7, Sun 12 noon–6pm

Comic Showcase

63 Charing Cross Road, WC2
t (020) 7434 4349
⊖ Covent Garden
Bus 6, 9, 11, 13, 15, 23, 77A, 91, 176
Open Mon–Wed 10–6, Thurs–Sat 10–7

Forbidden Planet

71 New Oxford Street, WC1
t (020) 7836 4179
⊖ Tottenham Court Road
Bus 8, 25
Open Mon–Sat 10–6; Thurs & Fri till 7pm

Foyle's

113–19 Charing Cross Road, WC2
t (020) 7437 5660
www.foyles.co.uk
⊖ Tottenham Court Road
Bus 14, 19, 24, 29, 38, 176
Open Mon–Sat 9–6, Thurs till 7pm

Gosh! Comics

39 Great Russell Street, WC1
t (020) 7636 1011
⊖ Tottenham Court Road
Bus 7
Open 10–6, Thurs & Fri till 7pm

Waterstone's

www.waterstones.com
Branches open Mon–Sat 9.30am–8pm, Sun 12 noon–6pm
203–206 Piccadilly, W1 **t** (020) 7851 2400;
82 Gower Street, WC1 **t** (020) 7636 1577;
99–101 Old Brompton Road, SW7 **t** (020) 7581 8522;
128 Camden High Street, NW1 **t** (020) 7284 4948;
121–5 Charing Cross Road, WC2 **t** (020) 7973 8432;
145–147 Cheapside, EC2 **t** (020) 7726 6077;
266 Earl's Court Road, SW5 **t** (020) 7370 1616;
9/13 Garrick Street, WC2 **t** (020) 7836 6757;
11 Islington Green, N1 **t** (020) 7704 2280; 193 Kensington High Street, W8 **t** (020) 7937 8432;
39–41 Notting Hill Gate, W11 **t** (020) 7229 9444

Clothes and shoes

Anthea Moore Ede
16 Victoria Grove, W8
t (020) 7584 8826
⊖ Gloucester Road
Bus 49
Open Mon–Sat 9.30–5
Made-to-measure classic party dresses for parents who like their little girls to look just so. There's also a baby clothes section.

Barney's
6 Church Road, Wimbledon, SW19
t (020) 8944 2915
⊖ Wimbledon Park
⇌ Wimbledon
Bus 93
Open Mon–Sat 10–6, Sun 12 noon–5pm
Near the All England Tennis Club, this is the perfect place to pick up an outfit on your way to Centre Court. It stocks all the big names in children's design – Catamini, Roobarb & Custard, Paul Smith and Elle. Prices, as you might expect, are not exactly giveaway. Also stocks a sumptuous selection of gift baskets, cards and books.

o–12 Benetton
www.benetton.com
Branches open Mon–Sat 10–7, Thurs & Sat till 8pm
255–259 Regent Street, W1 **t** (020) 7647 4200, open Mon–Wed & Fri 10–7, Thurs & Sat 10–8;
131 Kensington High Street, W8 **t** (020) 7937 2960
Junior version of the publicity-seeking Italian chain store turning out strangely traditional (but still nice) jumpers and sweatshirts, which appeal to children and adults alike.

Brora
344 Kings Road, SW3
t (020) 7352 3697
www.brora.co.uk
⊖ Sloane Square
Bus 19, 22, 137, C1
Open Mon–Sat 10–6
Cashmere galore, all the way from a mill in Scotland. Makes for the most luxurious babygros and booties around.

Buckle My Shoe
18-19 St Christopher's Place, W1
t (020) 7935 5589

www.bucklemyshoe.co.uk
⊖ Bond Street
Bus 6, 7, 10, 12, 13, 15, 23, 73, 94, 98, 113, 135, 137, 139, 159, 189
Open Mon–Sat 10–6, Thurs till 7pm
Snazzy, modern footwear for snazzy modern kids with the emphasis on soft leather and classic Italian designs.

Catamini
52a South Molton Street, W1
t (020) 7629 8099
www.catamini.com
Open Mon–Sat 10–6, Thurs till 7pm
Funky printed romper suits, dresses and coordinating accessories. Catamini is one of the top names in contemporary children's wear. Mail order available.

La Cicogna Roma
6a Sloane Street, SW1
t (020) 7235 3845
⊖ Knightsbridge
Bus 19, 22, 137, C1
Open Mon–Sat 10–6, Wed till 7pm
On super-trendy Sloane Street, this is a chic children's outfitters. Italian labels dominate: Armani, Versace *et al.* The clothes are undeniably gorgeous and very expensive.

The Clark's Shop
Branches open Mon–Sat 10–6.30 (Thurs till 8pm), Sun 12 noon–6pm
260 Oxford Street, W1 **t** (020) 7499 0305;
476 Oxford Street, W1 **t** (020) 7629 9609;
203 Regent Street, W1 **t** (020) 7734 1339;
98 Kensington High Street, W8 **t** (020) 7937 4135;
99 Cheapside, EC2 **t** (020) 7606 6754
Having your feet measured here is one of the rituals of British childhood. The shoes and the designs are classic, affordable, comfortable and utterly dependable.

Clementine
73 Ledbury Road, W11
t (020) 7243 6331
⊖ Notting Hill Gate
Bus 7, 23, 27, 28, 31, 52, 70, 302
Open Mon–Sat 10–6.30
Adorn your kids and their bedrooms with the clothes and furniture range from this charming shop. Simplicity is the key, from light, cotton clothing to attractive bed linen.

The Cross

141 Portland Road, W11
t (020) 7727 6760
⊖ Notting Hill Gate
Bus 7, 23, 27, 28, 31, 52, 70, 302
Open 10.30–6 Mon–Sat

Super cool shop filled with trendy labels such as Little Punk for budding style divas as well as the more practical OshKosh range.

Gap Kids

www.gapkids.com
Branches open Mon–Sat 10–8, Sun 12 noon– 6pm
145 Brompton Street, SW3 **t** (020) 7225 1112;
208 Regent Street, W1 **t** (020) 7287 5095;
121–123 Long Acre, WC2 **t** (020) 7836 0646;
122 King's Road, SW3 **t** (020) 7823 7272;
223–225 Oxford Circus, W1 **t** (020) 7734 3312
376–384 Oxford Street, W1 **t** (020) 7408 4500
473–475 Oxford Street, W1 **t** (020) 7409 7517

Sweatshirts, T-shirts, denims etc. which are renowned for their durability. Some branches also contain a subsidiary, Baby Gap, which sells a colourful range of practical babywear and toddler clothes.

Gotham Angels

23 Islington Green, N1
t (020) 7359 8090
⊖ Angel
Bus 4, 19, 30, 38, 43, X43, 56, 73, 171a, 214
Open Mon–Wed & Fri 10.30–7, Thurs 10.30–8, Sat 10–6, Sun 12 noon–6

Fab coordinated outfits for designer mothers and daughters, plus trendy torso hugging T-shirts and baby vests for wannabe überbabies.

Gymboree

198 Regent Street, W1
t (020) 7494 1110
www.gymboree.com
⊖ Oxford Circus
Bus 3, 6, 12, 13, 15, 23, 53, 88, 94, 139, 159, X53
Open Mon–Sat 10–7 (Thur till 8pm), Sun 11.30–5.30pm

For funky little kids wanting groovy, brightly coloured attire.

H&M Hennes

www.hm.com
Branches open Mon–Sat 10–6.30 (Thurs till 8pm), Sun 12 noon–6pm

174–6 Oxford Street, W1 **t** (020) 7612 1820;
123 Kensington High Street, W8 **t** (020) 7937 3329;
261 Regent Street, W1 **t** (020) 7493 4004

Inexpensive children's clothes made from natural fibres in trendy but tasteful colours and designs. Some branches have computer terminals where kids can play games on the Hennes website.

Humla Children's Shop

23 St Christopher's Place, W1
t (020) 7224 1773
⊖ Bond Street
Bus 6, 7, 10, 12, 13, 15, 23, 73, 94, 98, 113, 135, 137, 139, 159, 189
Open Mon–Sat 10.30–6.30

One of the best children's shops around, Humla sells some wonderfully earthy original design clothes as well as traditional wooden toys and mobiles.

Instep

45 St John's Wood High Street, NW8
t (020) 7722 7634
⊖ St John's Wood
Bus 6, 13, 16, 82, 98, 113
Open Mon–Sat 9.30–5.30

A sort of halfway house between Clark's and Buckle My Shoe, this is an excellent place to pick up everything from school shoes and sandals to ballet pumps. Also stocks some continental designs.

Jigsaw Junior

www.jigsaw-junior.com
Branches open Mon–Sat 10.30–6
126–127 New Bond Street, W1, **t** (020) 7491 4484;
65 Kensington High Street, W8, **t** (020) 7937 3572;
124 King's Road, SW3, **t** (020) 7589 5083;
57 Regent Street, W1, **t** (020) 7734 7604

Stocks a good range of colourful children's clothes – flower print jerseys, apple-green shorts and the like. Prices are fairly reasonable.

Joanna's Tent

289b King's Road, SW3
t (020) 7352 1151
⊖ Sloane Square
Bus 11, 19, 22, 211, 319
Open Mon–Sat 10–6, Sun 1pm–5pm

Top of the range designer kids' clothes – Junior Armani, Paul Smith for Kids etc – all at designer prices.

Laura Ashley

Branches open Mon–Wed 10–6.30, Thurs 10–8, Fri & Sat 10–7, Sun 12 noon–6pm
35 Bow Street, WC2 **t** (020) 7240 1997;
47 Brompton Road, SW3 **t** (020) 7823 9700;
449 Oxford Street, W1 **t** (020) 7355 1363;
256–8 Regent Street, W1 **t** (020) 7437 9760

Despite its recent attempt to liven up its image, this is still the shop that puts the girly in girly with racks of frilly, puffy, frou frou, flowery dresses

Marks & Spencer

www.marksandspencer.co.uk
Branches open Mon–Sat 10–6.30 (Thurs till 8pm), Sun 12 noon–6pm
458 Oxford St., W1 (Marble Arch) **t** (020) 7935 7954;
173 Oxford St., W1 (Oxford Circus) **t** (020) 7437 7722;
143 Camden High Street, NW1 **t** (020) 7267 6055;
113 Kensington High Street, W8 **t** (020) 7938 3711

The high temple of British underwear, Marks has been going through a difficult time recently. Even so, it still sells an excellent range of sturdy, classic children's designs. Best of all, if you have second thoughts, you can take your purchases back for a full refund, no questions asked.

Miki House

107 Walton Street, SW3
t (020) 7838 0006
www. Mikihouse.co.uk
⊖ Knightsbridge
Bus 10, 19, 52, 74, 137
Open Mon–Sat 10–6

Nice, bright cheerful clothes; lots of red and yellow T-shirts and shirts, corduroy dresses etc – all bearing the smiling Miki bear motif.

Minors

11 New Cavendish Street, W1
t (020) 7486 8299
⊖ Baker Street
Open Mon–Sat 10–6.30

For youngsters with expensive tastes. Drop in here to browse their range of top Italian and French designer clobber for the under-16s.

Mothercare

www.mothercare.com
Branches open Mon–Wed & Sat 10–7, Thurs & Fri 10–8, Sun 12 noon–6pm
461 Oxford Street, W1 **t** (020) 7629 6621 ;
145 Brompton Road, SW3 **t** (020) 7584 1397;
129 Victoria Street, SW1 **t** (020) 7828 0499

This is perhaps the country's most famous and reliable children's chainstore. It's been around for years and is still selling well-made, reliable clothes, toys, nursery equipment and maternity wear at reasonable prices. Also has a nappy delivery room and a mother-and-baby room.

Next

www.next.co.uk
Branches open Mon–Fri 10–6.30, Thurs till 8pm, Sun 12 noon–6pm
38 Brompton Road, SW3 **t** (020) 7584 0619;
44 Cheapside, EC2 **t** (020) 7248 1737;
54/60 Kensington High St., W8 **t** (020) 7938 4211;
72 King's Road, SW3 **t** (020) 7584 1308;
526 Oxford Street, W1 **t** (020) 7355 4929;
203 Oxford Street, W1 **t** (020) 7434 0477;
11 Strand, WC2 **t** (020) 7930 0416

High street staple selling good kidswear.

O'Neill

9–15 Neal Street, WC2
t (020) 7836 7686
www.oneilleurope.com
⊖ Covent Garden
Bus 6, 9, 11, 13, 15, 23, 77A, 91, 176
Open Mon–Sat 10–7, Thurs till 8, Sun 12 noon–6

For the cool street surfer look that older kids and teens are after.

OshKosh B'gosh

17 King's Road, SW3
t (020) 7730 1341
⊖ Sloane Square
Bus 11, 19, 22, 211, 319
Open Mon–Sat 9.30–6, Wed till 7pm

Good name, good shop – colourful, practical clothes of which both parents and children will approve. Its patterned collection is for kids ages 0–6. Children aged seven and over must make do with the simpler designs of the 'basic' collection – jeans, plain colour shirts and sweaters. The indestructible dungarees, however, are perhaps the cutest to be found on the market.

Paul Smith for Children

40–44 Floral Street, WC2
t (020) 7379 7133
www.paulsmith.co.uk
⊖ Covent Garden
Bus 6, 9, 11, 13, 15, 23, 77A, 91, 176
Open Mon–Wed & Fri 10.30–6.30, Thurs 10.30–7, Sat 10–6.30, Sun 1–5

Expensive and innovative designer clothes for parents who really want to go to town. Swimsuits and separates for eye-catching occasions.

Please Mum

Branches open Mon–Sat 10–6.30, Thurs till 7.30
69 New Bond Street, W1 **t** (020) 7493 5880;
85 Knightsbridge, SW1 **t** (020) 7486 1380

Lovely bright, colourful clothes and special occasion outfits for children aged between 0 and 15 and parents with healthy bank balances.

Rainbow

249 Archway Road, N6
t (020) 8340 8003
⊖ Highgate
Bus 43, 134, 263
Open Mon–Sat 10–6

Good for older children, Rainbow sells a range of rugged boys' wear – hooded sweatshirts, cargo pants etc. It also stocks OshKosh clothes, baby equipment and toys.

Semmalina

225 Ebury Street, SW1
t (020) 7730 9333
⊖ Sloane Square
Bus 19, 22, 137, C1
Open Mon–Sat 9.30–5.30

A real fairytale shop with dolls' houses, jewels and a drawbridge play area. It sells a good range of funky labels as well as its own clothing line. A good place to off-load some pocket money.

Slam City Skates

16 Neal's Yard, WC2
t (020) 7240 0928
www.slamcity.com
⊖ Covent Garden
Bus 6, 9, 11, 13, 15, 23, 77A, 91, 176
Open Mon–Sat 10–6.30, Sun 1–5

All you need for the baggy, laid-back skater look. Decks and accessories are also available if you want to do more than just look the part.

Tartine et Chocolat

66 South Molton Street, W1
t (020) 7629 7233
⊖ Bond Street
Bus 7, 23, 27, 28, 31, 52, 70, 302
Open Mon–Sat 10–6

Adorable babywear from Paris.

Trotters

www.trotters.co.uk
Branches open Mon–Sat 9–6.30, Wed till 7pm, Sun 10–6
127 Kensington High Street, W8 **t** (020) 7937 9373;
34 King's Road, SW3 **t** (020) 7259 9620

The clothes are good but designery – Paul Smith and Ralph Lauren are prominent labels – and there's a wide selection of toys and books to keep the kids amused while parents browse and make their purchases.

What Katy Did

49 Kensington Church Street, W8
t (020) 7229 2201
⊖ Notting Hill Gate
Bus 7, 23, 27, 28, 31, 52, 70, 302
Open Mon–Fri 10.30–6, Sat 10–6.30

Cute little boutique full of unusual labels.

Young England

47 Elizabeth Street, SW1
t (020) 7259 9003
⊖ Sloane Square, Victoria
Bus C1
Open Mon–Fri 9.30–5.30

A rather patriotic establishment. All the clothes are made in England using home-grown materials and are based on traditional designs.

Department stores

London is home to some of the shopping world's most famous department stores. There's Harrods, of course (see below and p.134), and Harvey Nichols in Knightsbridge; Peter Jones in Sloane Square, and Selfridges and John Lewis on Oxford Street. All have good children's clothes and/or toy departments. There's one department store in London, however, devoted solely to children. Daisy & Tom, is a Harrods for the under-15s. Founded by bookshop mogul Tim Waterstone (and named after two of his children), it's got pretty much everything a child could want. It's even got a hairdressing salon where kids can pick up a First Haircut certificate.

Dickins & Jones

224–244 Regent Street, W1
t (020) 7734 7070
www.houseoffraser.co.uk

⊖ Oxford Circus, Piccadilly Circus
Open Mon & Tue 10–6.30, Wed, Fri & Sat 10–7, Thurs 10–8, Sun 11–5

DH Evans
318 Oxford Street, W1
t (020) 7629 8800
www.houseoffraser.co.uk
⊖ Oxford Circus
Open Mon–Wed & Fri 10–7, Thurs 10–8, Sat 9.30-7, Sun 12 noon–6pm

Fenwick of Bond Street
63 New Bond Street, W1
t (020) 7629 9161
www.fenwick.co.uk
⊖ Bond Street
Open Mon–Wed, Fri & Sat 10–6.30, Thurs till 8pm

Harrods
87–135 Brompton Road, SW1
t (020) 7730 1234
www.harrods.com
⊖ Knightsbridge
Bus 10, 19, 52, 74, 137
Open Mon–Sat 10–7

Harvey Nichols
109–125 Knightsbridge, SW1
t (020) 7235 5000
www.harveynichols.com
⊖ Knightsbridge
Bus 10, 19, 52, 74, 137
Open Mon–Fri 10–6, Sat 10–5

John Lewis
278–306 Oxford Street, W1
t (020) 7629 7711
www.johnlewis.co.uk
⊖ Oxford Circus
Bus 6, 7, 10, 12, 13, 15, 23, 73 94, 98, 113, 135, 137, 139, 159, 189
Open Mon–Sat 9.30–6, Thurs till 8pm

Liberty
Regent Street, W1
t (020) 7734 1234
www.liberty.co.uk
⊖ Oxford Circus
Open Mon–Wed 10–6.30, Thurs till 8pm, Fri & Sat till 7pm

Peter Jones
Sloane Square, SW1

t (020) 7730 3434
www.peterjones.co.uk
⊖ Sloane Square
Bus 19, 22, 137, C1
Open Mon–Sat 9.30–6, Wed till 7pm

Selfridges
400 Oxford Street
t (020) 7629 1234
www.selfridge.co.uk
⊖ Oxford Circus
Bus 6, 7, 10, 12, 13, 15, 23, 73 94, 98, 113, 135, 137, 139, 159, 189
Open Mon–Sat 9.30–6, Thurs till 8pm

Daisy & Tom
181–3 King's Road
t (020) 7352 5000
⊖ Sloane Square
Bus 11, 19, 22, 211, 319
Open Mon–Sat 10–6 (Wed until 7), Sun 12 noon–6pm

Markets

For antique toys head towards Notting Hill for Portobello, (the world's largest antiques market) or Camden Passage in Islington. For bric-a-brac and the odd discovery, Brick Lane on Sunday mornings is well worth a visit – be sure to turn up early if you want to get the best bargains. Going to Brick Lane market also gives you a chance to see a fascinating but less well-known part of London. For trendy clothes, music and what-nots, Camden is worth a look, while Greenwich on Saturdays and Sundays has a good range of market fodder, from CDs and clothes to antique furniture, bric-a-brac and toys.

Brick Lane
Brick Lane, E1 and surrounds
⊖ Aldgate East, Shoreditch, Bethnal Green, Liverpool Street
≈ Liverpool Street
Open Sun 6am–1pm

Camden Lock
Camden Lock Place, off Chalk Farm Road, NW1
t (020) 7284 2084
www.camdenlock.net
⊖ Camden Town, Chalk Farm
≈ Camden Road

Bus 24, 27, 29, 31, 134, 135, 168, 214, 253, 274, C2
Open Sat & Sun 10–6

Camden Passage
Camden Passage, off Islington High Street, N1
⊖ Angel
Bus 4, 19, 30, 38, 43, X43, 56, 73, 171a, 214
Open Wed 7–2

Greenwich
Stockwell Street, SE10 and surrounds
⇌ Greenwich
Bus 53, X53, 177, 180, 188, 199, 286, 386
Open Sat & Sun 9–5

Portobello
Portobello Road. W11 and surrounds
⊖ Notting Hill Gate, Ladbroke Grove, Westbourne Park
Bus 7, 23, 27, 28, 31, 52, 70, 302
Open Sat 5.30am–3pm

Music

London is home to several vast record emporia, each with floors filled with copious amounts of CDs, tapes, videos, DVDs and computer games. The Virgin Megastore on Oxford Street is supposedly the largest, but they are all pretty big.

HMV
150 Oxford Street, W1
t (020) 7631 3423
www.hmv.com
⊖ Oxford Circus
Bus 6, 7, 10, 12, 13, 15, 23, 73 94, 98, 113, 135, 137, 139, 159, 189
Open Mon–Sat 9.30–8, Sun 12 noon–6pm

Tower Records
1 Piccadilly Circus
t (020) 7439 2500
www.towerrecords.co.uk
⊖ Piccadilly Circus, W1
Bus 3, 6, 9, 12, 13, 14, 15, 19, 22, 23, 38, 53, 88, 94, 139, 159
Open Mon–Sat 9am–12midnight, Sun 12 noon–6pm
Bus 3, 6, 9, 12, 13, 14, 15, 19, 22, 23, 38, 53, 88, 94, 139, 159

Virgin Megastore
14–16 Oxford Street, W1
t (020) 7631 1234
www.virgin.com
⊖ Tottenham Court Road, Oxford Circus
Bus 3, 6, 9, 12, 13, 14, 15, 19, 22, 23, 38, 53, 88, 94, 139, 159
Open Mon–Sat 9.30am–9pm, Sun 12 noon–6pm
Bus 3, 6, 9, 12, 13, 14, 15, 19, 22, 23, 38, 53, 88, 94, 139, 159

Sports shops

Niketown
236 Oxford Street, W1
t (020) 7612 0800
www.nike.com
⊖ Oxford Circus
Bus 6, 7, 8, 10, 12, 13, 15, 23, 25, 55, 73, 94, 98, 113, 135, 137, 139, 159, 176, 189
Open Mon–Wed 10–7, Thurs–Sat 10–8, Sun 12 noon–6pm

In the early 1980s Nike reinvented the whole sports clothing and footwear business from the ground up. It turned trainers from functional pieces of athletic equipment into desirable and overpriced fashion accessories, and sweatshirts into style statements. In the process the Nike swoosh became one of the world's most recognizable logos. It's now hoping to pull off a similar trick with the sports shop. The £50 million Niketown store is destined, so its creators hope, to become something more than a mere shop. It is meant to be an attraction in its own right, somewhere for people to explore and experience as well as just buy things. *See* p.50 for more details.

Lillywhites
24–36 Regent's Street, W1
t (020) 7409 2619
⊖ Piccadilly Circus
Bus 3, 6, 12, 13, 15, 23, 53, 88, 94, 139, 159, X53
Open Mon–Sat 10–7, Thurs till 8, Sun 12–6

This is a well-established sports equipment store catering for everyone from footballers and cricketers to abseilers, skateboarders and canoeists.

First Sport
Whiteley's Shopping Centre, Queensway, W2
t (020) 7792 1139

www.firstsport.co.uk
⊖ Queensway
Open Mon–Sat 10–9, Sun 12 noon–6
Flagship store of a large sportswear chain. Good range of trainers, with sizes small enough for toddlers' feet.

Hamleys
188–196 Regent Street, W1
t (020) 7494 2000
www.hamleys.com
⊖ Oxford Circus
Open Mon–Fri 10–8, Sat 9.30–8, Sun 12 noon–6pm
This is one of the most famous toy shops in the world. The fifth floor of the giant toy store is dedicated to sports equipment and clothing and also houses a branch of the Manchester United Club Shop. *See* p.49.

JD Sport
267 Oxford Street, W1
t (020) 7491 7677
www.jdsports.co.uk

⊖ Oxford Circus
Bus 6, 7, 10, 12, 13, 15, 23, 73 94, 98, 113, 135, 137, 139, 159, 189
Open Mon, Tues, Sat 9am–8pm, Wed–Fri 9am–9pm
Well-stocked sportswear chain, particularly in the trainer department.

JJB Sports
301–9 Oxford Street, W1
t (020) 7409 2619
www.jjb.co.uk
Bus 3, 6, 12, 13, 15, 23, 53, 88, 94, 139, 159, X53
⊖ Oxford Circus
Bus 6, 7, 10, 12, 13, 15, 23, 73 94, 98, 113, 135, 137, 139, 159, 189
Open Mon–Sat 10–7, Thurs till 8, Sun 12 noon–6
Very busy and chaotic sportswear shop with good range of reduced-price clothing and footwear.

Soccerscene
56–7 Carnaby Street, W1
t (020) 7439 0778
⊖ Oxford Circus
Bus 6, 7, 10, 12, 13, 15, 23, 73 94, 98, 113, 135, 137, 139, 159, 189
Open Mon–Sat 9.30–7
Easily the best football shop in London. You can pick up the kit of almost any team in the world here as well as any amount of balls, boots and shin pads, not to mention books, magazines and videos galore.

Strange shops

Not all of London's shops are classifiable into neat categories and some shops even revel in their acute specialization on a single theme. Here are a couple of the best.

Anything Left Handed
57 Brewer Street, W1
t (020) 7437 3910
⊖ Piccadilly
Open Mon–Fri 9.30–5, Sat 10–5
Bus 3, 6, 12, 13, 14, 15, 23, 38, 53, 88, 94, 139
Shop for left-handers selling everything from corkscrews to boomerangs.

The Back Shop

14 New Cavendish Street, W1
t (020) 7371 5232
www.thebackshop.co.uk
⊖ Bond Street
Bus 135, C2
Open Mon–Fri 10–5.45, Sat 10–2

If your children suffer from bad posture, this is the place to come for chairs and desks designed to help them sit up straight.

Theme stores

The Disney Store

www.disneystores.com
Branches open Mon–Sat 10–8, Sun 12 noon–6
140 Regent Street, W1, **t** (020) 7287 6558;
10 Russell Street, WC2, **t** (020) 7497 3001

Shamelessly commercial, yet also rather heart-warming, the store is full of tacky bits of plastic and fur covered in logos and trademarks that are, at the same time, lovable characters as familiar as friends. As you'd expect, there's a vast array of cartoon-related merchandise on offer: videos, play figures, mugs and costumes, clothes, games and every conceivable Disney what-not. The video screen belting out singalong classics never fails to attract a gaggle of painfully warbling children.

Warner Brothers Studio Store

178–82 Regent Street, W1
t (020) 7434 3334
⊖ Oxford Circus, Piccadilly Circus
Bus 3, 6, 12, 13, 15, 23, 53, 88, 94, 139, 159, X53
Open Mon–Wed and Fri 10–7, Thurs and Sat 10–8, Sun 12 noon–6pm

Bugs and Daffy were always Mickey and Donald's more streetwise cousins and the Warner shops, though based on much the same format, are a touch more funky than their Disney counterparts. You can get every type of Warner-related gear from key rings to tea towels.

Toys and games

Cheeky Monkeys

202 Kensington Park Road, W11
t (020) 7792 9022
⊖ Notting Hill Gate
Bus 7, 23, 27, 28, 31, 52, 70, 302
Open Mon–Fri 9.30–5.30, Sat 10–5.30

Nice selection of wooden toys and imaginative fancy dress outfits. There are 4 other branches across town.

Early Learning Centre

www.elc.co.uk
Branches open Mon–Sat 9–6, Wed till 7, Sun 11–5
225 Kensington High Street, W8, **t** (020) 7937 0419;
36 King's Road, SW3, **t** (020) 7581 5764

A toy shop with an agenda, the Early Learning Centre is concerned about the impact toys can have on a child's development. Anything remotely sexist or violent is out. Clean, uncontroversial, wholesome fun is the name of the game. Nonetheless, the toys, which are aimed mainly at the pre-school age group, are uniformly excellent. The shop has several special play areas where kids can try out the toys.

Hamleys

188–196 Regent Street, W1
t (020) 7734 3161
www.hamleys.com
⊖ Oxford Circus
Bus 3, 6, 12, 13, 15, 23, 53, 88, 94, 139, 159, X53
Open Mon–Fri 10–8, Sat 9.30–8, Sun 12 noon–6pm

London's premier toy store, Hamleys has six floors of the latest must-have playthings. *See* p.49 for more details. There's a much smaller branch of Hamleys at Covent Garden, 3 The Market, The Piazza, Covent Garden, WC2; **t** (020) 7240 4646, open Mon–Wed Fri & Sat 10–7, Thurs 10–8, Sun 12 noon–6pm.

Harlequin House

3 Kensington Mall, W8
t (020) 7221 8629
⊖ High Street Kensington
Bus 9, 10, 27, 28, 31, 49
Open Tues, Fri & Sat 11am–5.30pm

A fascinating puppet and mask shop full of bizarre and quirky playthings that will captivate children. Be prepared for a bombardment of home puppet shows after visiting.

Harrods

87–135 Brompton Road, SW1
t (020) 7730 1234
www.harrods.com
⊖ Knightsbridge
Bus 10, 19, 52, 74, 137
Open Mon–Sat 10–7

Harrods has the best toy department of any department store. The Toy Kingdom on the fourth floor even rivals Hamleys for the sheer range of toys on offer. You can find everything, from limited edition Steiff Teddies and third-size Ferraris with full leather interior (a snip at £42,000) to the latest video games. There's also a well-stocked children's bookshop and, next door, Planet Harrods, an American-style restaurant where cartoons play constantly on big screens. Throughout the year the toy department organizes various events and activities for children including such delights as Teddy Bear Days and Easter Egg hunts.

Just Games

71 Brewer Street, W1
t (020) 7437 0761
⊖ Piccadilly Circus
Bus 6, 12, 13, 14, 15, 19, 23, 38, 53, 88, 94, 139, 159, X53
Open Mon–Sat 10–6, Thurs till 7pm

Just Games stocks all the family favourites including such long-lived classics as Monopoly, Jenga, Snakes & Ladders, Cluedo and Mouse Trap alongside any number of chess sets, backgammon boards and domino sets.

Traditional toys

It's not all bleeps, bangs and crashes in London's toy shops. Parents who despair of modern trends in toy design will be pleased to know that there are several shops in London specializing in more traditional toys. These range from miniature theatre sets and handpainted wooden puppets to carved wooden animals, kaleidoscopes and paper aeroplanes. Look out for the Hill Toy Company, Benjamin Pollock's Toy Shop (where miniature theatre sets are a particular speciality; *see* p.71), mail order specialists Tridias and the self-explanatory Traditional Toys, which stocks old-fashioned toys from all round the world.

Hill Toy Company

71 Abingdon Road, W8
t (020) 7937 8797
www.hilltoy.co.uk
⊖ High Street Kensington
Bus 9, 10, 27, 28, 31, 49
Open Mon–Fri 9.30–5.30, Sat 10–5

Benjamin Pollock's Toy Shop

44 Covent Garden Market, WC2
t (020) 7379 7866
www.pollocks-coventgarden.co.uk
⊖ Covent Garden, Leicester Square
Bus 6, 9, 11, 13, 15, 23, 77A, 91, 176
Open Mon–Sat 10.30–6, Sun 12 noon–5pm

Peter Rabbit & Friends

42 The Market, Covent Garden, WC2
t (020) 7497 1777
⊖ Covent Garden
Bus 6, 9, 11, 13, 15, 23, 77A, 91, 176
Open Mon–Sat 10–8, Sun 10–6

Rainbow

253 Archway Road, N6
t (020) 8340 8003
⊖ Highgate
Bus 43, 134, 263
Open Mon–Sat 10.30–5.30

Tridias

25 Bute Street, SW7
t (020) 7584 2330
www.tridias.co.uk
⊖ South Kensington
Bus 49, C1
Open Mon–Fri 9.30–6. Sat 10–6

Traditional Toys

53 Godfrey Street, SW3
t (020) 7352 1718
⊖ South Kensington
Bus 11, 19, 22, 49, 211, 319, 345
Open Mon–Fri 10–5.30, Sat 10–6, Sun 11–4.30

Shopping Centres

Though these huge monuments to retail can be a little soulless – and certainly don't have the charm or character of some of the central London shopping areas – they do at least offer the convenience of having everything (shops, restaurants, leisure facilities etc) under one roof. They also have crêches, thereby allowing you a couple of hours tantrum-free retail therapy.

Bluewater

Greenhithe, Kent
t 08456 021021
www.bluewater.co.uk
⇌ Greenhithe
Open Mon–Fri 10am–9pm, Sat 9am–8pm, Sun 11am–5pm

Still the big daddy of shopping centres, the massive Bluewater not only offers some 320 shops, dozens of fast-food outlets and chain restaurants, a multiplex cinema and the Academy Crêche (which takes children up to the age of 12), but also has facilities for a range of activities (including a fishing lake, a Wintergarden, an outdoor play area, a boating lake and cycle paths) for when you begin to wither under the constant glare of the fluorescent shop lighting. Of particular note to health-conscious parents, however, the centre has a unique fresh-air, air-conditioning system and is non-smoking throughout.

Brent Cross Shopping Centre

Brent Cross, NW4
t (020) 8202 8095
www.brentcross-london.com
⊖ Brent Cross, Hendon Central
Open Mon–Fri 9am–8pm, Sat 9am–7pm, Sun 11am–5pm

Around 90 shops, plenty of places for food and a kids play centre called the Nipperboat.

Centre Court Shopping Centre

4 Queen's Road, Wimbledon, SW19
t (020) 8944 8323
⊖ Wimbledon
Open Mon–Fri 9.30am–7pm, Thurs till 8pm, Sat 9am–7pm, Sun 11am–5pm

Not quite in the Bluewater league, but there's a good selection of shops and Kids Club shoppers' crêche.

Lakeside Thurrock

West Thurrock, Essex
t (01708) 869933
⇌ Lakeside
Open Mon–Fri 10am–10pm, Sat 9am–7.30pm, Sun 11am–5pm

Over 300 shops and food outlets, market stalls, cinema and a Stay 'n' Play Crêche for 2–7-year-olds.

Xscape

602 Marlborough Gate, Milton Keynes
t (01908) 200020
www.xscape.co.uk
⇌ Milton Keynes
Open From 9am, closing times vary

Retail and leisure centre with shops, a cinema, a bowling alley, indoor climbing walls and a fitness club. The real treat here is the Snozone, the country's largest 'real' snow slope. You'll find none of that funny dry netting stuff here; Snozone uses snow-cannons and keeps the temperature at a constantly chilly -2°C, making it suitable for proper skiing and snowboarding. Lessons are offered.

Quiz answers

1

Mercury, Venus, Earth, Mars, Jupiter, Saturn, Uranus, Neptune, Pluto.

2

The Ashes are the burnt remains of the stumps which were presented to the English team by the Melbourne ladies following an English tour of Australia. It's also the name given to the Test Match series that takes place between the two countries every two years. The winner receives a replica urn – the original can be seen in the museum at Lord's Cricket Ground.

3

West Ham.

4

A. The second tallest is the Natwest Tower at 600ft but the tallest by far is Canary Wharf, a whopping 812ft tall, making it the tallest building in the whole country.

5

They make up the yellow set on the board of the London version of Monopoly.

6

The answer is c), a whopping 17,000, or roughly one for every 350 people living in the capital.

7

Decency Boards were wooden panels that ran along the top deck of old horse-drawn buses. They were designed to prevent unscrupulous gentlemen from getting a crafty look at ladies' ankles.

8

It is named after an aviary that James I had installed near this avenue.

9

Sir Henry Tate, of Tate & Lyle sugar fame, invented the sugar lump and so made his fortune.

10

They both have blue blood running through their veins. Of course, the Royal Family actually has red blood, like everyone else. 'Blue blood' is an expression used to denote that someone has aristocratic ancestry. Lobsters, on the other hand, do actually have blue blood.

11

A groundling was the name given in Elizabethan times to the members of the audience who watched a play standing in front of the stage.

12

Richard III. His evil scheme didn't do him much good, however. Within a couple of years he too was dead, slain at the Battle of Bosworth Field by the future Henry VII.

13

Parading through the streets of London as part of the Lord Mayor's Show (see London's Year for November, p.22).

14

The Royal Mint. The Bank of England is the government's bank and the only bank in England and Wales that can issue paper money. It's also the bank of all the High Street banks such as Natwest, Barclays and Lloyds TSB. Many, many billions of pounds are stored in its vaults.

15

a) Triceratops means '3-horned face'.

b) Deinocheirus means 'terrible hand'.

c) Baronyx means 'big claw'.

16

It took 10 years to build the Victoria and Albert Museum's current home. On its completion in 1899 it was given its royal name, having previously been nicknamed the 'Brompton Boilers'.

17

It took Sir Francis Chichester nine months and one day to sail around the world.

18

The Underground, or more commonly, the tube is the correct name for the English subterranean rail system.

take the kids series

- ► the first series of its kind for parents
- ► lots of family holiday ideas, top tips and themes
- ► expert advice on health, safety and budgets
- ► what to do in an emergency
- ► stress-busting games and stories for bored kids

titles 2003

- ► South of France
- ► Southern Spain

also available

- ► Short Breaks From London
- ► England
- ► Paris And Disneyland® Resort Paris
- ► Travelling

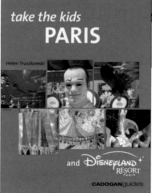

Further information

Cadogan Guides
Network House
1 Ariel Way
London
W12 7SL
t (020) 8600 3550
f (020) 8600 3599
e info@cadoganguides.com
www.cadoganguides.com

Distribution

Grantham Book Services Ltd
Isaac Newton Way
Alma Park Industial Estate
Grantham
NG31 9SD
t (01476) 541080
f (01476) 541061